Linebe

Lutheran Theological Southern Seminary    Columbia, S. C.

# SOUTHERN COOKING

Henrietta Stanley Dull.

# SOUTHERN COOKING

## MRS. S. R. DULL

*With a foreword by*

*Damon Lee Fowler*

*Illustrated by Lucina Wakefield*

THE UNIVERSITY OF GEORGIA PRESS

Athens and London

Published in 2006 by The University of Georgia Press
Athens, Georgia 30602
© 1928, 1941 by Mrs. S. R. Dull
Foreword by Damon Lee Fowler
© 2006 by the University of Georgia Press

The paper in this book meets the guidelines for
permanence and durability of the Committee on
Production Guidelines for Book Longevity of the
Council on Library Resources.

Printed in the United States of America
08  09  10  11  12  C  6  5  4  3  2

*Library of Congress Cataloging-in-Publication Data*

Dull, S. R., Mrs., 1863–1963.
Southern cooking / Mrs. S. R. Dull ;
with a foreword by Damon Lee Fowler ;
illustrated by Lucina Wakefield.
p.  cm.
Includes bibliographical references and index.
ISBN-13: 978-0-8203-2853-9 (hardcover : alk. paper)
ISBN-10: 0-8203-2853-7 (hardcover : alk. paper)
1. Cookery, American–Southern style.  2. Menus.  I. Title.
TX715.2.S68D85 2006
641.5975–dc22          2006013895

*British Library Cataloging-in-Publication Data available*

*Dedicated to*
*My Friends, the Women of Atlanta, of Georgia,*
*and of the South*

# CONTENTS

# FOREWORD

Her name is synonymous with Southern cooking, and not just because that was the simple, fitting title for her landmark book. On equal footing with such figures as Mary Randolph (*The Virginia House-wife*, 1824), Lettice Bryan (*The Kentucky Housewife*, 1839), Sarah Rutledge (*The Carolina Housewife*, 1842), and Annabella Hill (*Mrs. Hill's New Cook Book*, 1867), her work stands out among the hundreds of books that have chronicled what has been called America's first genuine regional cuisine. Yet, Henrietta Stanley Dull was not just a cookbook author, journalist, and apologist for regional cooking; she was an icon in her own right, a unique voice and force of personality who helped to shape modern food writing in the South.

She was born Henrietta ("Hennie") Celestia Stanley on December 7, 1863, in Stanley Mill, Laurens County, Georgia, to Ira Eli and Mary Mourning Elizabeth Breazeal Stanley. Before her first birthday, the world into which she was born had been swept away by General Sherman's infamous march to the sea, and the particulars of her early life are sketchy. In the aftermath of the war—sometime between 1870 and 1880—her family moved to Flowery Branch in Hall County. On June 15, 1887, in Atlanta, she married widower Samuel Rice Dull, a railroad clerk originally from Virginia. The couple raised six children, including Mr. Dull's daughter from his first marriage: Ethel, Henrietta, Samuel, Mary, Louise, and Ira.

Mrs. Dull's long career in food began when her husband's health failed scarcely a decade into their marriage, obliging her to become the breadwinner for their large family. She first made and sold baked goods from her home kitchen, predominantly to friends at First Baptist Church, Atlanta, but it was not long before she was in demand as a full-service caterer. In 1910, she was hired by the Atlanta Gas Light Company to demonstrate the safety and efficiency of cooking on the new gas-fired ranges. Her lectures and demonstrations were soon packing houses, and according to those who heard her speak, her word, when it came to cooking, was considered gospel. This authority would later make her a highly sought spokesperson, not only for the gas company but also for products based in the South, such as White Lily Flour.

ix

Mr. Dull died in 1919, and the following year, the *Atlanta Journal* named Mrs. Dull editor of the home economics page of their new Sunday magazine, for which she wrote a weekly column called "Mrs. Dull's Cooking Lessons." The column enjoyed a twenty-five-year run, during which the format did not vary: illustrated with a photograph of the author engaged in some kind of cooking or baking, it included a running dialogue between the author and her readers, sharing recipes, cooking tips, and housekeeping advice. Readers' steady requests for recipes—both previously unpublished and from past columns—inevitably led Mrs. Dull to write her landmark cookbook, first published in 1928. She was by then sixty-five years old—an age when most people were beginning to retire, but not she. The columns kept coming until 1945, when, at the age of eighty-two, she was asked to step down.

Containing some 1,300 no-nonsense recipes for everything from refined cream soups to delicate cakes to how to butcher, dress, and bake an opossum, *Southern Cooking* was almost encyclopedic in scope and would be her magnum opus, remaining continuously in print for more than five decades. First published by Ruralist Press in Atlanta, it sold 14,000 copies in thirteen years, a more than respectable run for a small regional publisher. In 1941, New York publishers Grosset and Dunlap acquired the rights, publishing a revised and expanded edition that went on to sell more than 150,000 copies in its first twelve years, a rare accomplishment for any cookbook, let alone a strictly regional one. It would also influence generations of cooks all over America and preserve a legacy of regional cooking that was, in those days, being threatened with extinction, both by the homogenizing effects of modernization and by the advent of the convenience food revolution that captured the American imagination in the boom years following World War II.

After Mrs. Dull's death on January 29, 1964, Grosset and Dunlap kept printing *Southern Cooking*, even though its tersely worded recipe style, lacking technical detail, was by then considered old-fashioned. It finally went out of print sometime after 1980, but was back on bookstore shelves before the decade was out: in 1989, Cherokee Publishing Company of Atlanta began printing a facsimile of the first (1928) edition. As a testament to Mrs. Dull's enduring influence, it remained in print for nearly fifteen years.

Though the original volume is valuable to culinary historians, the extensive additions of 1941 are equally important—Mrs. Dull herself authorized them and, by her own account, felt that they rectified the egregious omission of many traditional recipes that she had previously overlooked. For example, it is only in the 1941 edition that we find Cornmeal Lace Cakes (162–63), a lacy-edged griddle cake that was a specialty of rural Georgia for centuries, and Roast Pork and Sweet Potatoes (34). Reproduced here is the full 1941 text, which includes all of Mrs. Dull's additions and revisions to the 1928 edition. A list of the recipes that were added begins on page xv.

More than seventy-five years after its first publication, *Southern Cooking* remains important not only because of its widespread popularity, nor even because it preserves a picture of the regional cuisine as it was in the early to mid-twentieth century, but because its author provides a rare, critical link in the transition from the nineteenth century to the modern world. Born in the midst of the cataclysm of the Civil War, Mrs. Dull witnessed a literal technological revolution in the kitchen, from open hearth, to cast-iron woodstove, to gas, and finally, to electricity.

Family lore holds that Mrs. Dull cooked her first corn pone on an open hearth at the tender age of six; she cooked her last one, nearly a century later, on a modern range. Consider, too, the radical changes that she witnessed in cold storage—from springhouse, to ice box, to electric refrigerator, to deep-freezing. (A form of mechanical refrigeration was patented for railway cars in 1868, but its application remained predominantly commercial for decades and did not become commonplace in the South until well into the twentieth century.) Because Mrs. Dull lived through this revolution, embracing its changes and yet holding onto her culinary roots, her book provides an important chronicle of a cuisine and a region in transition.

Another reason that this book remains important is the author herself. While her straightforward, no-nonsense style has become legendary (Southern food historian John Egerton once said, "She didn't want to be chatty or trendy: she wanted you to pay attention because she was only going to tell you once"), in real life she was warm, lively, gregarious, and possessed a healthy sense of humor, both about herself and about the world at large.

"She had such a generous spirit," her granddaughter Mary Frances Woodside remembered. "You know, she was like a second mother to me—and, oh, just such a lot of fun!" adding that people who met her grandmother did not easily forget her. A large part of Mrs. Dull's legacy must rest on the force of that personality alone; its far-reaching influence is still being felt more than sixty years after her retirement and more than forty years after her death.

"She had a tremendous influence on the cooking of this area," said Susan Puckett, the food editor for the *Atlanta Journal-Constitution*, "and it's still strong to this day. We have a regular feature on local cooks, and when they're asked what their favorite cookbook is, Mrs. Dull's still ranks right up there. I wonder whether there's another food editor anywhere in the country that has left that kind of legacy."

Atlanta chef Scott Peacock, whose professional cooking remains steeped in Southern tradition by design, believes that part of Mrs. Dull's enduring appeal lies in the confidence that her forthright style inspires. Because she was absolutely sure of herself, the recipes, in their starkness, project a quiet, comfortably reassuring authority. He said, "With Mrs. Dull, more so than with any of the other classic Southern cookbook authors, I always had this absolute confidence that every recipe would work, a sense that she was intimate with them, that she wrote from experience."

Southern cookbook author and longtime Atlanta resident Nathalie Dupree agrees with both observations. "She was meticulous in a way that few of her contemporaries were—not only in her column but in the cookbook and its revisions. She was really in tune with what people were eating and wanted to eat at home—and she wanted to accurately present it. I've long thought that hers was one of the most important Southern cookbooks of the twentieth century."

Even in Mrs. Dull's heyday, many of the recipes in *Southern Cooking* would have been considered old-fashioned, and yet it could not be said that she was old-fashioned. She embraced each new technology and idea as it came her way. While she didn't fall victim to the craze for canned–cream soup casseroles, boxed cake mixes, and other packaged convenience foods that often adulterated many traditional dishes, she didn't shy from technological conveniences or new culinary concepts. For example, she wholly embraced the congealed salad, all the rage during the first half of the twentieth century, and included in her cookbook a collection of frozen composed salads, the popularity of which was due, no doubt, to the advent of affordable home refrigerators and freezers. Among these is a zesty savory tomato sherbet (Frozen Tomato Salad No. 1, 143), which would be considered cutting edge even in today's reinventive climate. When Fried Cornmeal Pones (162) acquired their present enigmatic name "Hush Puppies" along with enrichments such as egg, milk, and onion in the 1930s, Mrs. Dull added that recipe to her 1941 revisions (164) but kept the older recipe as well.

Journalist Jim Auchmutey, who wrote a handsome retrospective of Mrs. Dull in the *Atlanta Journal-Constitution* in 1999, calls *Southern Cooking* an autobiography in recipes. Indeed, most of the recipes seem to have a story behind them. For example, descendants of Cecilia Ann Philips Cannon, proprietress of the Blue Ridge Hotel in Clayton, Georgia, claim that a number of recipes, including My Favorite Lemon Pie (183–84), were passed on to Mrs. Dull during her many summer visits to the hotel.

In summing up Mrs. Dull's life and character, Auchmutey points to some of Mrs. Dull's speech notes that Mrs. Woodside shared with him: "It said, 'Suddenly I found I had to be the breadwinner. I knew how to make good things to eat and have them made. I mastered a gas range. I made it work for me and talk for me.' I think that just sums up her life nicely. She did it because she had to, and she did it well because she didn't know how to do anything halfway."

After Mrs. Dull's first ride in an airplane, her granddaughter recalled her joking that she'd gone from horse and buggy to flying and expected that she'd finish by going to the moon and, sighing, added, "She'd have done it, too."

*Damon Lee Fowler*
Savannah, Georgia

# USING MRS. DULL'S RECIPES TODAY

Thanks to the thoroughness that made her reputation, Mrs. Dull's recipes are as lucid and usable today as they were in 1928. By then, wet and dry measurements—the eight-ounce cup, teaspoon, and tablespoon—were standardized. Modern cooks will not, therefore, need to remember that a tumbler was eight ounces, a teacup was six ounces, a soupspoon equaled a tablespoon, a coffee spoon equaled about half a teaspoon, and a salt spoon was about one-eighth to one-quarter teaspoon. However, a few notes here may be useful.

Before attempting a recipe, read all the opening chapter notes, especially those for baking. While the recipe intent is usually clear, the notes contain necessary details that Mrs. Dull rarely repeats in the recipes. This will also ensure that the reader is not misled by a modern spin on an old direction, since the meaning of some cooking terms has changed over time. For example, in Mrs. Dull's day, *dredge* meant sprinkle or dust; today it means drag—which would result in a heavier coating than she intended. The notes also clarify changes in ingredients since Mrs. Dull's day. Her frying chickens weighed in at less than two pounds, a broiler merely half a pound. Try to find such wonders today. Without Mrs. Dull's notes, you would not know to adjust her cooking times for our larger, big-breasted birds.

Finally, before thermostatically controlled ovens, temperature settings were given not in degrees but as *slow, medium,* and *hot* (or *quick*)—a standard more reliable than we realize today. Mrs. Dull continued to use that designation in most of the recipes dating from 1928 (though, even then, she did give temperatures in degrees when she wanted something out of the ordinary). By 1941, thermostatic controls had made degree temperatures standard, and most of the added recipes followed suit. Where the old designation is used, see Mrs. Dull's explanation of slow, medium, and hot ovens on pages 5–6. A caution: oven thermostats are not always reliable and can be off by anywhere from twenty-five to one hundred degrees. Cooks who did not have such gadgets to mislead them knew what a slow, moderate, and hot oven felt like and rarely made temperature mistakes. The modern cook unaccustomed to judging temperature by feel will do well to check the thermostat with a reliable oven thermometer and adjust the settings accordingly.

# RECIPES ADDED IN 1941

*Note:* Below, listed in order of occurrence, are recipes that Mrs. Dull added to the 1941 edition. She did not cut any of the recipes from the original, 1928 edition; nor were any altered. She did rearrange some of the recipes, either to place them in a more logical order within the chapter or to move them to more appropriate sections.

# PREFACE

The interest taken in my weekly page, in the magazine section of the *Atlanta Journal,* which I edited for twenty years, convinced me of the need for an authoritative source of information on the preparation of foodstuffs "the Southern way", and as a consequence "Southern Cooking" was born in 1928.

Its immediate acceptance throughout the United States and in several foreign countries confirmed my judgment, and it is with a feeling of pride that I now present my cookbook, brought up-to-date by the addition of many more Southern recipes, in a new dress, and through the medium of a nationally known New York firm of publishers.

"Southern Cooking" is just what the title implies. It is a compilation of recipes and information gleaned from over forty years of my experience in the practical study and application of cooking in the Southern way.

"Southern Cooking" represents many years of patient study, research and experimenting which no amount of cold type can reveal in these pages. I have been careful, in my selection of recipes, to publish only those which I know to be good and can recommend, and I am sure that if care is taken in the measurements of the ingredients and the instructions for mixing them are carefully followed, even the most inexperienced housewife will be rewarded with success.

I hope my work will be the means of facilitating the duties of the bride, the matron or the chef who may have occasion to refer to the recipes and information found in the pages of "Southern Cooking."

*Henrietta Stanley Dull.*

*(Mrs. S. R. Dull)*

# AN APPRECIATION

It is a fetish in the South that the sun shines just a little brighter, the moon rays are just a little softer, the breezes blow just a little gentler, the birds sing just a little sweeter, the flowers are just a little prettier, and its climate just a little more salubrious. When going from one section to another, all of us have an idea that we know by instinct just when we cross the line out of the South or into it. Some one has said:

> "Down where the sun's most always shining,
> Where poverty clouds have a silver lining,
> Where there's chicken and cornbread with every dining,
> That's where the South begins.

> "Down where Knighthood's still in flower,
> Where they marry for love without a dower,
> Where money is useful, but not a power,
> That's where the South begins.

> "Down where the latch-string's outside the door,
> Where a friend's a friend, whether rich or poor,
> Where they trace their ancestry back to Noah,
> That's where the South begins."

Of course, the South is famed for excellent cooking. Nowhere in the world is the cuisine excelled, and not often is it equalled. It is certain that we have in every community cooks that are equal to every occasion, but now and then one arises who can, like Abou Ben Adhem, "lead all the rest." It is natural that such a person should write a book entitled:

## "SOUTHERN COOKING"

Mrs. S. R. Dull, nee Henrietta Stanley, is famed all over the Southern country for her skill in the culinary art. Reared in an atmosphere of "good livers," Mrs. Dull absorbed much that later stood her in good stead when she chose the teaching of cooking as a vocation. Naturally possessed of a very engaging personality; gifted by inheritance with a bright intellect;

endowed with the qualities of leadership and living in an environment which gave her the opportunity to put into practice her chosen profession, it is but natural that she has made a marvelous success and is known wherever good cooking is appreciated.

Not only by word of mouth has Mrs. Dull imparted her knowledge to those who desire to secure expert advice, but she edits each week the Home Economics page of the Atlanta Journal, which housekeepers read before turning to the society pages.

Although talented beyond her fellows in matters relating to palatable food, just why she should embrace the teaching of cooking, I doubt if Mrs. Dull herself could easily answer. Perhaps she gravitated naturally towards things she liked best to do, perchance it was accidental. My own opinion is that while reading "Lucile," she subconsciously absorbed the apostrophe to good cooking by Owen Meredith, the second Lord Lytton. As one remembers it, the lines run as follows:

> "We may live without poetry, music and art;
> We may live without conscience, and live without heart;
> We may live without friends; we may live without books;
> But civilized men cannot live without cooks."

Mrs. Dull was born in Laurens County, Georgia. Her father was Ira Eli Stanley, and her mother was Mary Breazeal. She is a granddaughter of Ira Stanley, son of James Stanley, who moved to Laurens County from Newbern, North Carolina. Thomas McCall, who at one time was Surveyor General of Georgia, was her great-grandfather, and Colonel James McCall, of the Revolutionary War, was her great-great-grandfather. Hugh McCall, a Brevet Major in the War of 1812, and who wrote the first history of Georgia, was a great-great uncle. On her mother's side she is a descendant of Solomon Wood who took part in exposing the Yazoo fraud. Her maternal grandfather was Henry Breazeal.

In addition to being a proficient teacher Mrs. Dull is a most estimable woman. The charm of her personality and the sweetness of her disposition endear her to every one with whom she comes in contact. Already she is greatly beloved by very many people in the South. She will be remembered in the future, not only for what she has already done, but for the very excellent recipes which this book contains. Her fame is established, but those who follow her advice will always appreciate the fact that a gentle, Southern woman has put her knowledge upon the printed page and thus benefited mankind.

*Hal M. Stanley.*

*Atlanta, Georgia.*

# SOUTHERN COOKING

# the kitchen

# CHAPTER I

## The Kitchen

### Utensils, Stove, Time Table, Measurements, Refrigerator

THE woman is the heart of the home, and the kitchen is the heart of the house.

Since the kitchen is such an important room quite a number of things should be considered to make it convenient, usable and cheery.

The size for ordinary families should be about 10 feet by 12 feet, but this will vary with the needs of the family. A kitchen medium in size is best because it is more easily kept, less steps being required to do the necessary work, thus saving the woman time which may be used for recreation.

Windows on two sides of the kitchen admit better light and give better ventilation. Nothing gets on a woman's nerves quite so much as working in a dark, poorly ventilated kitchen. For better ventilation a hood may be placed over range with a pipe connected directly into the flue. This will carry out smoke and fumes.

Artificial lighting must be placed to suit the worker. Quite a bit of time is wasted when light is back of the worker. Less light will be needed if walls and woodwork are of a light color.

Only the woman in her own kitchen can place things conveniently for herself.

The sink should be under a window. With a cabinet for small supplies, a pantry of medium size for larger utensils and supplies is necessary. A window in this pantry is very essential. A stool to sit on when preparing food is a great help and saves tired feet and nerves. It is no longer considered lazy to sit down when preparing food or washing dishes.

A table in the center of the kitchen is one of the most convenient arrangements a kitchen can have. It saves time and steps.

The height of table, sink, stool and stove will depend on the individual; a person 5 feet 4 inches requiring a 32-inch height for working surface, and increasing 2 inches for every inch of person's height.

This is the age for beauty and color in the kitchen, but if you can't have both, beauty will have to be sacrificed for convenience.

3

## UTENSILS

Utensils may be of high grade aluminum, high grade enamelware, and heavy iron pans for frying.

| | | |
|---|---|---|
| Coffee pot | Stew pan | Boilers |
| Double boiler | Frying pans | Roasting pan |
| Bread pans | Cake pans | Baking sheet |
| Muffin pans | Pie pans | Potato masher |
| Colander | Wire strainer | Flour sifter |
| Mixing bowls | Mixing spoons | Measuring spoons |
| Pint and quart measure | Scales | Bread boards |
| Rolling pin | Can opener | Corkscrew |
| Bread knife | Meat knife | Paring knives |
| Kitchen forks | Meat grinder | Chopping knife |
| Vegetable brush | Home-made pastry brush | Spice containers |
| Grater | Lemon squeezer | Scissors |
| Egg beater | Spatula | Soap shaker |
| Towel rack | Hand towels | Soap dish |
| Dish pan | Dish towels | Asbestos mats |
| Flour bin, etc. | Clock | Bread and cake boxes |
| Ice cream freezer | Dish drainer | |

If a cabinet is purchased quite a number of utensils mentioned above will be in the cabinet.

## THE REFRIGERATOR—ITS USE AND CARE

Every one is interested in health, and refrigeration is vital to health. The storage and preservation of food is of great importance from the stand-point of health as well as economics, and the present-day home-maker must have a thorough knowledge of refrigeration to be efficient in its use.

For more than a decade the home refrigeration has been given much thought and study and today the interested woman in the home desires to know how to *keep* her family well instead of how to *get* them well. We have progressed in our standards of living until it seems essential today for every home to have a refrigerator. For years ice boxes and ice refrigerators were our only way of refrigeration and often these containers were poor, but it was the only way we had for preserving food until electrical refrigeration came and then refrigeration took on new life. The ice man and the ice refrig-erator manufacturer awakened too, and improvements were rapid and wonderful.

There are today four methods of refrigeration: Ice, Oil, Gas and Electri-city, with various types and models of refrigerators. Each year brings changes and improvements in all types, and it is truly up to the individual to make her choice and select the one best suited to her needs. Each method has its distinct advantages and circumstances vary the suitability. According to Government reports based on tests, different foods require different degrees of cold and moisture for preservation, and such facts should be kept in mind to get the best results from your refrigerator.

With each type of refrigerator there are specific directions for its use and care. If a modern air conditioned ice refrigerator is used a self cleaning stationary drain should be installed which prevents stoppage. No drip pan is ever found today in any carefully conducted household. The modern ice refrigerator is efficient and economical and measures up to all requirements for good refrigeration; it needs icing not more than twice a week even in the "deep South", if properly cared for. Automatic refrigerators are available for gas and oil operation, and they are truly worthy of the praise bestowed upon them by their users. Each day the home-maker discovers new uses and advantages. This is equally true of the electric refrigerators. Any and all of these types are today extremely efficient.

Never make the mistake of purchasing a refrigerator that is too small. There must be room for the circulation of cold air even when the refrigerator is filled with food. All food should be cold, before placing in any refrigerator. If put in warm it will not only set up unpleasant odors but the cold outside driving the warmth to the center causes spoilage very quickly. It is as well to leave food out altogether as to put it in when hot.

The maintenance of any good refrigerator is small if correctly used and handled whether it be ice, oil, gas or electrical type. Manufacturers' instructions should be carefully followed, and in using mechanical refrigerators de-frosting should be done at least once a week in accordance with instructions usually in the refrigerator, when purchased. With usage comes knowledge, comfort, and the satisfaction of knowing that the health of the family is protected by the science of modern refrigeration in our daily lives.

## THE RANGE

1. SELECTION AND CARE

The size of your family is the first thing to consider.

The surface burners are usually the same number on all standard ranges but the oven may be large or small.

An enamel stove is much easier to care for because of non-rusting. A tiny little spot shows up on a light color and the range is kept clean day by day. There are valuable instructions that come with every range and these are worth keeping to pass on to the cook.

2. PLACING THE RANGE

There are right and left hand ovens in gas and electric ranges and you must first determine what you need.

It is never wise or convenient to place the surface burners in a corner, such close quarters cause steam and heat to come up into your face, which is unpleasant and injurious. If you have a side wall to place your range against you do not need to consider this point. Place it where you can see rather than where it looks well.

3. UNDERSTANDING THE RANGE

This is the day of efficiency, and the woman who admits she can never get through in the kitchen is a thing of the past. In order to be efficient she must know how to manage and get the best results both from the top of the range and the oven. She must know how long it requires to get the oven hot, whether she needs a hot, medium or slow heat, and how to turn valves and switches to maintain the required heat, and just in what position food must be placed to get the best results. Most of the cooking done for a family requires a medium heat.

In gas, electric and oil ovens the general rule is: thin things at the center and above the center of oven with a hot or quick heat. Thick things from the center down with less heat. There are a few exceptions which are usually explained in the given recipe.

A very hot oven means from 500 to 550 degrees F.

A hot or quick oven means 450 to 500 degrees F., and held at this temperature while being used.

A medium oven means 350 to 375 degrees F.

A slow oven means 275 to 300 degrees F.

A very slow oven means 250 degrees F.

To get these heats without a thermometer or oven indicator the following rules may be observed. Preheat oven until hot or very hot and continue the full heat while cooking the dishes calling for that heat. To get a medium heat reduce a hot oven by cutting down about one half. A slow oven may be obtained by reducing a medium heat one half. Of course, no heat beyond that required is necessary if one has any way of determining the heat required. This method has been used successfully in a gas range.

For general use three heats are required—hot, medium and slow, medium being the heat used most generally for the three meals a day. For unusual dishes the recipe usually specifies what temperature is required.

## PREPARING A MEAL

Making up a proper menu, serving a meal properly, even properly cooking the individual dishes avails nothing unless one knows just when each separate dish should start cooking in order that the entire meal may be ready to serve at a given time.

That is the worst problem with which the young or inexperienced housewife has to contend. It is almost too easy for those who have had practical experience, and often these older heads do not have the patience to help the young strugglers.

Cook books do not always tell very much about timing meals, or make this point as plain as it should be, and the inexperienced are often too sensitive to display their ignorance for fear of ridicule.

They may be able to take any one dish and cook it well, but to take six articles and have them all ready for lunch or dinner at a given time is something else.

Today more than half of the housewives have no cooks, at all, and are really and truly trying to have nice, well-prepared meals, and want to learn to cook.

In preparing a meal there are many dishes which can stand after being prepared and not deteriorate, while there are just as many which are ruined, unless served at the proper time.

I find one trouble is that most people do not allow enough time to do the work, so that the whole process is hurry, flurry and rush. What usually happens doesn't look well in print, and we all know that haste makes waste.

On the other hand, people should train themselves not to be too slow, for slowness is just as much a fault as the haste.

There are as many dishes to be cooked quickly as slowly, so plan and think over what is to be done, consider the time to be given to getting the meal and usually it will end well.

Two and a half hours will enable one to cook quite a big dinner and that does not mean to stay in the kitchen that length of time; it simply means to start the long cooking dishes when they should be, lower the fire and let them cook slowly and for a long time. One not only saves food and fuel, but nerves as well.

Some dishes may require two and a half hours, some one hour, others only fifteen minutes. For example, snap beans require long, slow cooking, two to three hours, while Irish potatoes, when boiled, require only about thirty minutes, and green corn on the cob not over ten minutes. Light rolls require from twenty to thirty minutes, according to the size, while biscuits need only ten minutes.

If the breakfast consists of fruit, coffee, toast, bacon and eggs, fifteen minutes is all the time required. The coffee will require the full fifteen minutes, and the other things can be prepared during that time.

In one hour, Irish potatoes, broiled steak, hot biscuit, coffee and some kind of a salad could be easily prepared, cooked and ready to serve without any great rush.

But should a prime rib roast, weighing five pounds, be on the menu, then one and a half hours must be allowed for the roast to be cooked medium done. A pot roast of the same weight would require at the very least two and a half hours. The pot roast, being a cheaper and tougher cut of meat, requires long, slow cooking.

A time table is given of a few every-day dishes which will give some idea of the time required for cooking.

Lest you forget, just boiling (simmering) is cooking as well as hard boiling. The hard boiling reduces water rapidly, tears the food to pieces and often the extreme heat toughens the food, particularly meats.

There are some styles of cooking which must be done quickly, namely, broiling and frying. Quick breads, rice, Irish potatoes and cabbage should be cooked quickly, and layer cake requires a quick oven, too.

Except for those above mentioned foods a medium and slow cooking is usually the required heat. Of course, the oven should be pre-heated and hot for most cooking. All meats should be seared first, to keep the juices in.

## COOKING TIME TABLE

### Vegetables

Turnips—30 to 40 minutes; boil rapidly, uncovered.
Cabbage—20 to 30 minutes; boil rapidly, uncovered.
Spinach—30 minutes, moderately.
Fresh Lima Beans—45 to 60 minutes.
Dried Lima Beans—1 hour to 1½ hours, slowly, after being soaked in cold water overnight.

Dried Field Peas—Same as dried beans.
String Beans—2 to 2½ hours, slowly.
Onions—40 to 50 minutes, according to size.
Carrots—30 to 50 minutes.
Irish Potatoes—Boiled 30 to 40 minutes, rather fast.
Irish and Sweet Potatoes (baked)—45 to 60 minutes, according to size; medium heat after oven is hot.
Green Corn on Cob—10 minutes.
Green Corn, Cut—20 to 30 minutes.
Rice—Boiled rapidly 20 minutes, drained and steamed 20 minutes.
Macaroni and Spaghetti—20 to 40 minutes, rapidly.
All vegetables should be started in hot water except dried ones. These should be soaked several hours in cold water, then started in cold water.

### Breads

Loaf Bread—45 to 60 minutes; according to size.
Light Rolls—20 to 30 minutes; medium heat after oven is hot.
Biscuit—8 to 12 minutes, hot oven.
Wheat Muffins—10 to 20 minutes, hot oven.
Corn Muffins—15 to 30 minutes, according to size.  Hot oven.
Pone Cornbread—30 to 40 minutes.  Medium oven.
Have oven hot for quick breads, and continue hot fire.

### Meats

Roast beef, prime rib (medium done)—20 minutes to the pound after searing.
Pork roast—25 minutes to the pound.
Lamb roast—25 minutes to the pound.
Lamb (boiled)—20 minutes to the pound.
Fish (boiled)—15 minutes per pound.
Fish (baked)—15 to 20 minutes per pound.
Hens (roasted)—25 minutes per pound or longer, according to age.
Turkeys—25 minutes per pound.
This time table means medium heat after searing, unless otherwise specified.

## MEASUREMENTS

60 drops make 1 teaspoon
2 teaspoons equal 1 soup or dessert spoon
3 teaspoons equal 1 tablespoon
16 tablespoons equal 1 cup
2 cups equal 1 pint
2 pints equal 1 quart
4 quarts equal 1 gallon
2 cups butter equal 1 pound
4 cups flour equal 1 pound
4 cups milk equal 1 quart

2 cups granulated sugar equal 1 pound
2 ⅔ cups powdered sugar equals 1 pound
2 ⅔ cups brown sugar equal 1 pound
2 cups rice equal 1 pound
3 cups corn meal equal 1 pound
2 cups chopped meat (packed) equal 1 pound
2 tablespoons butter equal 1 ounce
4 tablespoons flour equal 1 ounce

All measurements in this book are level unless otherwise stated.  All cup measurements in this book are based on the standard ½ pint measuring cup.

# cocktails

# CHAPTER II

## Cocktails

COCKTAIL, both word and mixture, is purely American—an appetizer. At one time it was made almost entirely of liquors. Today it is made of fruits, vegetables or fish. A good cocktail is usually seasoned very highly with seasoning belonging to the nature of the material used.

### Cocktail Sauce

1 cup tomato catsup
2 tablespoons Worcestershire sauce
2 tablespoons lemon juice
A few drops of tobasco, or enough cayenne to make hot
1 teaspoon salt

Mix and pour over shrimp or crab meat. If convenient the heart of celery chopped fine and added is a nice change, about half cup. Half chili and half catsup is liked by many.

### Crab Cocktail

Make cocktail sauce, using 2 cups of crab flakes, 1 cup of sauce. Let the mixture stand at least one hour on ice before serving. Serve in glasses or dishes suitable.

### Crab Meat Cocktail

In the center of a plate filled with crushed ice place a green pepper filled with cocktail sauce. On either side place a crab shell, line with small crisp lettuce leaves, and pile the crab meat high on these and serve.

A small glass or a lemon hull may take the place of the green pepper for holding the sauce.

Serve with a small fork and plain crackers.

### Fruit Cocktail

Any one fruit may be used for a cocktail, or a mixture of two or more fresh fruits: strawberries, bananas, pineapple, oranges, grapefruit and grapes.

The fruit should be cut in small sections; grapes peeled and seeded saving all the juice. There should be about as much juice as fruit. Lemon or grape juice, sweet cider, melted jelly may be added to combine many flavors—a clove sometimes adds flavor.

The mixture should be very cold and served in glasses. About one-half cup is the usual portion. Very little sugar is used, for the cocktail is usually tart and tasty.

9

### Oyster Cocktail

Select small oysters, allowing about five for each person. See that no pieces of shell cling to the oysters. For a pint of oysters about one cup of sauce will be required. Pour the sauce over the oysters at least an hour before serving so the seasoning will strike through. Place on ice until ready to put into cocktail glasses or some suitable dish; serve with a fork and crackers. A sauce ready prepared can be purchased at almost any grocery store.

### Shrimp Cocktail

Break or mince shrimps, and prepare the same as oyster or crab meat.

### Grapefruit Cocktail

Cut grapefruit in half crosswise, remove seed with a small paring or grapefruit knife, cut the pulp free from the sections of white skin. Save all juice.

Serve in cocktail glasses with a sprinkle of sugar or a spoon full of maraschino juice. Allow half a grapefruit for each serving. Have very cold when served.

### Grapefruit and Orange Cocktail

Prepare fruits as above using equal parts. Serve in cocktail glasses.

### Banana Cocktail

Peel, scrape and make the banana into balls, using a potato baller. Sprinkle with lemon juice to prevent turning dark. Cover with orange or grape juice.

### Avocado Cocktail

Ball or cut in small cubes the avocados. Mix with cocktail sauce and serve very cold.

### Tomato Cocktail

Peel and cut in small portions 3 large ripe tomatoes saving juice. Peel and mince 1 tender cucumber. Make 1 cup cocktail sauce to which has been added chopped celery.

Mix together and place on ice to season and become very cold. Serve in cocktail glasses with plain crackers.

## Cantaloupe Cocktail

Ball or cut in small cubes. Serve with cocktail sauce or lemon juice. Any fruit may be used for cocktails, seasoned with fruit juices or the regular cocktail sauce.

## Cranberry Cocktail

1 lb. of cranberries          2 cups of water
1 lb. of sugar

Place in saucepan, cover closely and cook for 20 minutes; turn into a jelly bag, or filter by lining the colander with two paper napkins, and then pouring in the cranberries.

Set the colander over a large bowl or crock, and let the mixture drip through slowly.

This cranberry cocktail will be sparkling clear, and have a pretty color.

To serve—Brush the edge of thin glass with white of egg, forming a band about one inch deep; roll in sugar and set aside to dry; fill glass about half full of finely crushed ice, then fill with prepared cranberry cocktail, garnish with spoon of whipped cream.

## Banana Pineapple Cocktail

Peel banana, scrape off the coarse threads. With a potato ball scoop out balls from bananas and sprinkle with lemon juice to prevent discoloring.

Add portions of sliced pineapple, sprinkle slightly with sugar and pour over a few spoons full of maraschino cherries. Cover top with a topping of freshly grated cocoanut. This gives a pink cocktail. For lavender or purple use grape juice.

## Grape Juice Cocktail

Pepare sections of orange and grape fruit, and save juice. Add to grape juice, cover the fruits well and serve. Have all ingredients ice cold.

## Summer Cocktails

Select small cantaloupes, 1 for each serving, and chill. Have 1 nice peach, 1 sprig of mint, 1 teaspoon sugar, and 1 teaspoon lemon juice, for each cantaloupe.

From one end of cantaloupe cut a slice, taking off about ⅓ the melon, and remove seed. Peel and dice the slice removed, dice the peach, add sugar and lemon juice and fill the cantaloupe. Sprinkle the mint, which has been minced very fine, over the top and serve. Everything must be very cold. Several fresh cherries over the top would add to the cocktail.

## Apple Cocktail

Make apple balls by using a French ball cutter, allowing 4 balls for each cocktail.  Drop into lemon water to prevent turning dark, using 2 cups water and juice of 1 lemon.

Make rings of apple, ⅓ inch thick, leaving peel on.  Make as many rings as are needed.  Drop into lemon water with balls.  Have ready 4 maraschino cherries, or peeled grapes.  Then mix 1 tablespoon maraschino cherry juice and 1 tablespoon of orange juice.

Place ring of apple on crisp lettuce leaf, put balls, apples and grapes on slice of apple, alternating in a ring or pile together.  Sprinkle with grated cocoanut and pour over all the fruit juices.  Serve on a dainty plate with fork.  Everything should be very cold.  Any fruits may be used in place of those given.

# CHAPTER III

# Soups

THE clear soups are bouillon and consomme. These are made from the juices of lean meat, seasoned. Both of these soups may have a few vegetables to add to the flavor. The clear soups have more stimulating powers than nourishment and so are served, usually, for dinner when a very heavy meal is to follow. Cream and vegetable soups are the ones most commonly used.

Cream soups are very nourishing on account of the milk used in them and so should be counted as part of the nourishment of the meal. A cream soup is usually made of one particular vegetable and milk, seasoned and thickened to suit the individual taste.

Corn, beans, peas, celery, asparagus, tomatoes, potatoes, onions, are the vegetables most commonly used for making cream soups. The vegetable is cooked very tender and put through a sieve to make it fine. Then a portion of flour is added to make it creamy when the milk is put in. Potatoes, peas and beans are usually sufficiently thick without adding any flour.

Vegetable soup is the favorite of all soups. It may be good, rich and thick or it may be a clear soup with a few vegetables.

To make good soup one must use lean meat and bone, not much fat. The bones should be broken so the substance will be released. However, do not have it chopped too much or the soup will be full of little bones.

Always start the soup bone in cold water bringing to a boil gently, allowing the juices to be drawn out into the water. Soup meat or vegetables should never be boiled hard but allowed to simmer, for best results. Hard boiling reduces the water and throws off the flavors. If you have to add fresh water every little while oftentimes the flavor is not so good. Do not add the vegetables too soon, because this too injures the flavor.

Vegetable soup is a good means of using up the odds and ends. There are nearly always left in the icebox a few pieces of celery, a spoonful of peas or maybe a carrot or two, to make the start. If you must start from the beginning vegetable soup is not cheap. By the time you buy meat and half a dozen vegetables it counts up.

Bouillon is a clear soup made of lean beef from which all bones are removed. The seasoning is added to the meat when boiled. It is then strained or cleared and ready to serve.

Consomme is made of several kinds of meat, bones and all. The seasoning is added while cooking. This, too, is clarified. Consomme is much lighter in color on account of the light meats used.

## Bouillon

| | |
|---|---|
| 2 lbs. lean beef | 1 carrot, diced |
| 2 quarts cold water | 2 stalks of celery, diced |
| 1 teaspoon salt | 1 slice of onion |
| 2 whole cloves | 2 slices of turnip |
| 6 whole pepper corns | |

Remove all fat from beef, cut into small pieces, into a hot fry pan put cubes and sear well but do not scorch. This gives color and flavor. Put into the cold water and let stand for half hour.

Add all other seasoning, bring to boil and simmer until well done and liquid is reduced to one quart. Strain, cool, remove all grease. Season to suit the taste. If necessary, strain again, heat and serve. Be sure to rinse all the brown from the fry pan, as this dark red is needed to color bouillon. Any other seasoning desired may be added. A slice of lemon, peel and all, is sometimes used in the cup.

### Consomme

| | |
|---|---|
| 2 lbs. lean beef | 3 quarts water, cold |
| 1 medium knuckle of veal | 1 tablespoon salt |
| 1 small hen | 10 whole pepper corns |
| 1 cup diced vegetables (carrot, onion, celery, turnip), or more | 6 whole cloves |
| | 6 whole spices |

Cut meat into cubes and sear well in heavy fry pan. Add to cold water, being careful to get all browned juices from the skillet.

Let stand half hour. Bring to boil slowly, add all seasoning; simmer until done and water is reduced about half. Strain, cool, remove all grease. Measure, for each pint of liquid use one egg, white and shell. Crush shell, beat white just enough to break well. Add one cup of stock to dilute. Add mixture to soup, mix well and bring to a hard boil. Boil for two minutes. Strain through several thicknesses of cheese cloth, letting it strain without pressing. This removes all sediment and soup will be clear as water, or light color. Reheat and serve. If any more seasoning is needed, add before clearing.

### Vegetable Bouillon

One bunch of soup greens, 1 three pound can of tomatoes, cook together till done but not too thick; strain through colander. To one quart stock; clear with whites and shells of 2 eggs; add salt and pepper to taste. If pretty pink is desired, add pink coloring.

### Tomato Bouillon

Two quart cans of tomatoes stewed until tender but not thick; strain, add salt and pepper. Clarify (see recipe); add coloring to make as red as wanted. Reheat; serve in bouillon cups with slice of fresh tomato.

### To Clarify Soups

After soup is done, strain through colander or strainer, let cool and remove all grease; drain carefully, leaving all sediment in the bowl, which should be added to meat if going to be used for any food. Now for every quart of stock use one egg—white and shell, being careful to wash the egg and remove the yolk. Crush shell, and mix both white and shell with ½ cup of the stock, beating it together well, then add this to the remainder of the stock, and bring to a boil and let boil for three or four minutes, or till the egg forms a scummy looking substance on the top of the stock; stir occasionally. Allow to settle, and then wet and wring dry a piece of cheese cloth (1 yd. square and fold to have three or four thicknesses);

place over colander which is resting over a bowl, pour in soup and let drain of its own accord.

## Royal Custard for Clear Soups

Yolks 2 eggs                    1 cup clear meat stock

Beat eggs and add stock; pour into a buttered pudding cup; stand in boiling water; cook about 20 minutes in moderate oven; cool; turn out; cut into fancy shapes and drop into clear soup or bouillon.

White of egg may be poached in a buttered mold, turned out, sliced and cut and dropped into soup.

## Cream of Tomato Soup

1 quart can of tomatoes              1 quart milk
1 slice of onion                    4 tablespoons butter
¾ teaspoon soda, lightly measured   4 tablespoons flour
Salt and pepper

Boil tomatoes in their own liquid until done (about 15 or 20 minutes). To this add the onion and when done, strain. Scald the milk and add thickening before putting in tomatoes to which soda has been added and it will not curdle. Keep hot, but do not allow to boil.

## Cream of Celery Soup

2 cups celery                  3 tablespoons flour
1 quart cold water             2 tablespoons butter
3 cups sweet milk              Salt and red pepper to taste

Wash and dice celery and boil very tender in the water; there should be at least two cups of the water when finished. Rub the celery through a strainer and return to the water in which it was boiled. Add the salt and pepper. Mix the flour and butter to a paste, and add to the milk, which should be warm. Mix with the celery mixture; boil gently for ten minutes and serve.

Use a double boiler for cooking.

## Cream of Chestnut Soup

1 quart of chestnuts                 2 tablespoons of butter
1 pint of chicken or veal stock      2 tablespoons flour
1 pint of milk                       Salt and pepper to taste

With a paring knife make a slit in each chestnut. Into a skillet put one tablespoon of cooking oil or grease, put in the chestnuts and heat for five minutes, stirring to get them all hot. Remove and peel nuts. This method removes the brown skin with the hull.

Boil nuts in the stock until very soft, put through a coarse strainer, mashing any nuts through.

Melt butter, add flour and cook without browning as for white sauce; add hot milk. (Use double boiler.) Keep hot until slightly thickened, add chestnut mixture, seasoning and keep steaming for about ten minutes. It should be a creamy soup, not too thick. Add stock or milk if needed. Serve in soup cups with a spoonful of whipped cream on top. Sprinkle minced parsley over this.

### Green Pea Soup

2 cups pea puree fresh or canned
1 quart full milk
3 tablespoons butter

4 tablespoons flour
Seasoning—salt and pepper

Boil peas until tender, add slice of onion if liked. Put through colander or coarse strainer. Blend butter and flour together, add hot milk, add peas, season. Serve very hot. Use white or red pepper.

A spoonful of whipped cream may be added. Sprinkle top with parsley. Serve in cream soup cups or plates.

### Split Pea Soup

Wash and soak overnight one cup of split peas. Put them to boil in one quart of water; cook until tender and the water is reduced somewhat. Put through strainer to give a puree. Heat one quart of milk, add peas, season with salt and pepper.

Usually the peas thicken the soup sufficiently. A little flour may be added. Use whole milk or add a small portion of butter. Sometimes other seasonings are added—a slice of onion, stalk of celery, a carrot. These are cooked with the peas.

### Onion Soup

Cook 1 large Bermuda onion, sliced thin, in 2 tablespoons butter for ten minutes. Add 1 quart of white stock (chicken or veal), ½ cup white bread crumbs, and simmer for 1 hour then rub through a puree sieve. Add 2 cups milk, and season with white or red pepper. Blend together 2 tablespoons flour with 2 of butter, add 1 cup of soup; mix until smooth and return to soup. Have all piping hot and serve with toast or bread sticks.

### Asparagus Soup

1 quart chicken or veal stock
3 cups diced fresh asparagus
2 cups milk

4 tablespoons butter
4 tablespoons flour
Salt and pepper to taste

Boil asparagus in stock until tender. Make a white sauce of the butter, flour and milk. Add the cooked asparagus, stock and seasoning; and serve.

Cook stock and asparagus slowly so it will not be reduced too much.

### Duchess Soup

2 cups stock
1 slice carrot
4 tablespoons butter
2 cups sweet milk

1 stalk celery
1 slice onion
2 tablespoons flour
¼ cup grated cheese

Cook seasoning with stock; strain; make thin white sauce of flour, butter and milk; add to the stock. When ready to serve, add grated cheese. Salt and pepper to taste.

### Vegetable Soup

1 soup bone (medium size)
1 can of soup mixture
1 bunch of soup greens or two cups
of celery, carrots, turnips, onions,

cabbage or leftovers
¼ cup rice or macaroni, or leftovers
Salt and pepper to taste

Wash and put soup bone into two quarts of cold water, bring to a boil gently and simmer one hour or more. Wash and add rice when meat is half done. Allow one hour for vegetables, simmering gently always. Keep pot covered and see that the right amount of water is in the pot when vegetables are added.

This is for two quarts of soup of medium thickness; more or less rice may be used.

This soup is started from fresh material. When the soup is kept just simmering the water decreases very little.

## Potato Soup

2 cups diced Irish potatoes  
2 cups hot water  
2 cupfuls milk  
Salt and pepper to taste

Cook potatoes rapidly about ten minutes, stirring to break partly. Add salt and white or red pepper. Have milk hot, add when potatoes are done, season to taste and serve with dry toast sticks or crackers. Small pieces of the potatoes are better than if put through a strainer. A bit of butter may be added if desired.

## Cabbage Soup

2 cups fine chopped cabbage  
1 small onion cut fine  
2 cups milk  
3 tablespoons butter  
3 tablespoons flour  
Salt and pepper to taste

Put cabbage and onion in one quart water, boil until very tender, melt butter, add flour and cook one minute without browning; add warm milk and cook until smooth. Pour into the cabbage mixture, heat to boiling point, sprinkle with paprika or chopped parsley. Serve with brown toast.

## Bean Soup

1 cup dry beans  
½ pound boiling meat  
2 quarts water  
1 quart full milk  
1 slice onion  
1 carrot  
2 stalks celery  
Salt and pepper to taste

Wash and soak beans overnight. Boil meat with vegetables in the water until very tender, remove; add beans and cook until all to pieces. Put through a strainer to remove skins. Cut meat into tiny pieces, add to bean pulp, put in hot milk and seasoning. Serve piping hot.

The vegetables are used for flavoring and may be used or not. Any dry beans or peas may be used. A can of tomatoes may be added.

## A New Soup

One quart of chicken stock which has been made for soup, clarify and season to taste (see recipe); heat; add ½ cup each of diced cooked carrots, white turnips, asparagus. Serve very hot with toasted bread sticks.

### Mrs. Macy's Soup

| | |
|---|---|
| ¼ lb. butter | 2 sprigs parsley |
| 1 medium size onion | 1 cup broken vermicelli |
| 1 cup diced potatoes | 2 pieces celery cut fine |
| 2 leaves cabbage, shredded | 3 tomatoes peeled and sliced thin |
| 3 quarts boiling water | Salt and pepper to taste |
| 2 carrots | |

Into a soup pot melt the butter; into this put the carrots, onion and parsley; cook slightly; add water; add all other ingredients and cook slowly 3 or 4 hours.

### Miss Cora's "Sunshine City" Chowder

| | |
|---|---|
| 1 lb. shredded fish | 1 cup Irish potatoes |
| 1 cup tomatoes | ½ cup onions |
| ½ cup celery or | ½ pint sweet milk |
| ½ teaspoon celery salt | Pepper and salt to taste |
| 2 tablespoons butter | |

Boil fish in 1 quart water; shred and add ingredients to water in which fish was boiled; cook until done; add milk and let come to boil then add 1 tablespoon tomato catsup.

### Miss Cora's Spanish Gumbo

| | |
|---|---|
| 1 cup boiling water | 1 cup okra |
| 1 cup tomatoes | 1 cup onions |
| 1 cup green peppers | Pinch of red pepper |
| ¼ teaspoon black pepper | ¼ teaspoon celery seed |
| 1 rounding tablespoon butter | Salt to taste |

Heat butter and fry sliced onions until a light brown; add tomatoes and okra sliced fine; add seasoning and cup water; cook until thick enough to be eaten with fork.

### Oyster Soup

| | |
|---|---|
| 1 quart milk | 1 pint water |
| 1 pint stew oysters | 2 tablespoons flour |
| 4 tablespoons butter | Salt and pepper to taste |
| 1 cup diced celery chopped very fine | |

Cook celery in the water until very tender; pour into colander and rub through, using water and all. Melt butter; add flour and blend together, scald milk; add and make a white sauce. Keep hot over hot water. Put oysters into a sauce pan and plump well in their own liquor; remove from fire; chop and put through colander; add oysters and celery to milk; season and serve.

### Oyster Bisque

| | |
|---|---|
| 1 pint oysters | 6 tablespoons butter |
| 1 quart milk | Salt and pepper to taste |
| 6 tablespoons flour | |

Scald oysters in their own liquor, drain and add liquor to milk. Heat milk. Melt butter, blend in the flour without browning, add hot milk and cook until a thin cream mixture; add seasoning and minced oysters and serve.

Any shellfish may be used in place of the oysters. The foundation is the same as cream soup with fish.

### Tomato Bisque

| | |
|---|---|
| 4 cups milk | 6 cloves |
| ¾ cup stale bread crumbs | 1 can tomatoes |
| 1 small onion | 2 teaspoons sugar |
| Sprig of parsley | ½ teaspoon soda |

Scald milk, pour over crumbs, and rub through sieve. Have tomatoes stewed with seasoning, and strained; reheat milk, add tomatoes in which soda has been dissolved, add butter the size of an egg. Serve at once.

### Tomato Bisque With Rice

Make tomato bisque after the usual recipe. Have ready some rice, boiled with a slice of beet in the water, which should color the rice a delicate pink, drained and each grain separate and distinct. Put the bisque in cups or soup plates and garnish each portion with a large spoonful of the pink rice.

### Cream of Chicken Soup No. 1

Make a cream soup of chicken broth using half stock and half full milk. When ready to serve drop into the soup tips of asparagus half an inch long, and tiny squares of sweet peppers which have been boiled in salt water until tender. Serve at once with crackers or croutons.

Canned pimentoes may be used.

Royal custard might be liked in place of the asparagus.

### Cream of Chicken Soup No. 2

| | |
|---|---|
| 2 cups chicken stock | 2 tablespoons rice |
| ¼ cup diced celery | |

Cook together until rice and celery are soft. Strain and rub through a strainer the rice and celery and add to stock. Add 2 cups hot milk, season with salt and cayenne pepper. Sprinkle chopped parsley over top.

This should be a medium cream soup and more or less milk may be used. Serve with toasted crackers.

### Chicken Soup for Invalids

| | |
|---|---|
| 1 well grown chicken | ½ cup rice |
| 3 quarts cold water | Seasoning |

An old fowl is best. Dress, split down the back, chop through the flesh and bones. Place in water for half an hour, bring to a boil slowly, and simmer until chicken is very tender. Take from fire, cool and remove all grease. Add rice which has been well washed and soaked in a cup of water or chicken stock for 30 minutes. Boil slowly, add seasoning, and stir often to keep rice from scorching. Cook until rice is soft and tender. There should be six or eight cups when finished.

Add more or less rice to suit the individual.

## Mutton Broth

1 mutton neck and shoulder (2 or     1 quart cold water for each pound
   3 lbs.)

Wash the mutton well, cut into small pieces and chop bones. Let stand in cold water 1 hour; bring slowly to a boil, and boil gently until meat will fall from the bones. Strain, cool and remove the grease. Measure and add 2 tablespoons of rice for each quart of stock. Boil gently until rice is very soft (about 1 hour.)

A slice of onion or a few stalks of celery may be added to the first cooking if liked. Wash and soak rice for 30 minutes before cooking.

## Fruit Soup

Boil 1 pint of fruit with 1 pint of water until juice flows freely. Strain through a cloth; add small portion of sugar to break the very tart taste, a pinch of salt, and 2 tablespoons flour (this amount of flour will thicken 1 pint of juice). A whole clove and whole spice may be dropped into juice.

Serve in bouillon cups with plenty of cracked ice.

Grape juice diluted with half water is good. Cherries, grapes, apple juice and pineapple juice make good fruit soups.

Pearl tapioca boiled until clear is nice for thickening. Use 1 to 2 tablespoons of the mixture for every cup of soup; using the pearls and liquid both in the fruit juice. Season with sugar, salt, spices or sherry jell. Arrowroot used for thickening does not change the color as flour does.

## Spinach Soup

1 lb. spinach cooked in 2 cups of     3 tablespoons butter
   water     3 tablespoons flour
2 cups milk     Salt and pepper
2 cups stock

Boil spinach until done, chop and mash through strainer the water and spinach. Add to stock. Heat milk, melt butter, add flour and blend together until it bubbles, then add milk, cook until creamy and add to spinach and stock; mix well, add seasoning and serve.

## Lettuce Soup

1 large head lettuce     1 small carrot
1 quart veal or chicken stock     1 teaspoon salt
1 slice onion     ⅛ teaspoon white pepper
1 slice green pepper

Separate leaves of lettuce. Shred the outer leaves, using half or more. Put into saucepan with stock and vegetables, simmer 30 to 40 minutes. Strain and rub through strainer the vegetables, add to stock. Add salt and pepper and the remaining lettuce, shredded very fine. Cook 30 minutes. Serve with cheese crackers.

A little thickening may be added if liked—use 2 tablespoons flour, rub to a paste, strain, add and cook a few minutes after adding.

# CHAPTER IV

## Meats

### Beef, Veal, Lamb, Pork, Fowls, Game, Fish and Shellfish

In a brief discussion of meats, I will consider those we rely upon for daily consumption, namely, beef, veal, mutton, lamb, pork and fowls. It is necessary that we know something of the different cuts. Decide first whether you want the choice or the cheaper cuts. The choice cuts are those that require a short time to cook, such as broiling or the oven cooked choice roasts. The cheaper cuts are just as nutritious but require long slow cooking to make tender and good. A meat thermometer helps greatly to determine the doneness of meats, especially roasts. It is quite an efficient instrument, easy to use.

The cooking of meats, particularly beef, has changed greatly in the last few years. There has been much experimenting, and it has been thought by many that the choicer cuts for broiling and roasting, if done slowly will lose less in the cooking, also that searing first is not essential to hold in the juices.

The loss in weight depends on the average cooking temperature. Certainly any piece of meat can be over cooked, fast or slow, until all juice is dried out. While searing was particularly done for flavor as well as to hold in the juices, it is still believed that browning well at first or during the long roasting adds to the flavor.

Slow broiling is recommended, too; however, I am leaving the old rules for meat cooking in my cook book, and adding this latest method, for I find many like the first way and others like the last method. The greatest thing to recommend the last method is that it does not have to be watched so strenuously. Everyone should try and decide for herself which method to use. No good cook, even in quick roasting or broiling, burns her meat or cooks so fast that it is not pleasing to the eye or taste.

The salting of steaks, before, after or during cooking, is another moot question, so you must experiment for yourself to decide which time suits you best.

Pork, veal and lamb usually are cooked slower, longer and done, so there is little or no change in the cooking of these meats. New methods are always welcomed; however, unless these methods result in better and more tasty food, they do not count for much. There is no more fuel used in a low, long period than the fast method of cooking.

The cooking of meat may be put in two general classes—dry heat and moist heat. The first is oven roasting, broiling in oven, or pan—this requires the choice or tender and expensive cuts. The moist heat takes care of the less choice and cheaper cuts and requires slow and long cooking, such as pot roast, stews and cuts to be boiled, all of which should be cooked at simmering on surface burner or in the oven, well covered.

## BEEF

Beef should be bright red, with fine streaks of fat through the meat, and plenty of firm fat around the outer edge.

A four pound pot roast, shoulder clod or a chuck roast will require two or three hours of slow cooking, while the prime rib, which we consider our most choice roast, will cook in an hour or an hour and a half according to whether you wish it rare or done. I allow twenty minutes per pound after searing. A prime rib roast, less than four pounds, is not apt to be very juicy because it will be so thin the juices will escape.

By searing the roast first the juices are kept in. Even the stews should be seared or browned, thus making a rich gravy both in color and flavor.

Steaks cut an inch or more thick are more satisfactory. Broiling a steak is simply searing first one side then the other until as done as desired.

The round of beef makes an excellent swiss or smothered steak, a meat loaf or individual meat balls, but I do not consider it good for roast.

In my recipes I have tried to make very plain directions for the best and most generally used cuts.

## VEAL

Veal is used more during the summer months. Many think because veal is young beef, that it is much easier to cook. This is not true. Veal must be well cooked to bring out the best flavor and nutritive value. The meat should be firm and pink. The cuts are much the same as lamb, there being the chops, cutlets, roast, and stew.

Calf liver is now considered very nutritious. Sweetbreads from veal and lamb are quite a delicacy. Brains from veal are considered more delicate than beef brains, but are not as firm. I prefer beef brains for croquettes or for using for creamed dishes.

## MUTTON AND LAMB

In large markets mutton and lamb are always to be found. Spring lamb and baby lamb is usually plentiful during the spring and summer months.

Mutton and lamb should be well scrubbed before cooking. The outside skin or membrane, known as the fell, often gives an objectionable flavor and for this reason some people do not care for this meat. Remove the skin or fell from lamb chops before broiling. Larger pieces, however, should be scrubbed and for this purpose I use a little cooking soda, wiping the meat thoroughly afterwards. The various cuts are: steaks, chops, cutlets, breast, shoulder, leg o' lamb and stews.

## PORK

Pork being rich with fat is used freely during cold weather and sparingly in warm weather. In addition to the chops, loin, ham and shoulder, it furnishes spare ribs, backbones and a choice piece of lean meat called the tenderloin, which is most delicious when broiled thoroughly and served very hot.

Pork may be roasted, boiled, broiled, fried or stewed, and should always be cooked thoroughly. During the winter season pork has always been consumed very freely throughout the South and Southerners enjoy the "hog killing" season, which, in addition to providing the cuts already mentioned, furnishes material for pork sausage, cracklin' bread, liver pudding and hoghead cheese.

## FOWL

Of course I could not write a Southern cook book without mentioning fried chicken, although under the head of fowl comes duck, geese, turkeys, pigeons, squabs, guineas and, of course, the popular domestic chicken.

The South is noted for its fried chicken, which nowhere else seems to be quite so good or quite so deliciously prepared. Chicken pie and smothered chicken are two other popular dishes calling for young chickens, weighing from 1½ lbs. to 2 lbs. However, during the season, broiled chicken seems to be a well-liked dish in the South. Broilers usually weigh from ½ lb. to 1 lb.; larger than that are not considered choice. Baked chicken, which calls for the grown hen, is used mostly during the winter, with various dressings and sauces.

## FISH

A more general use of fish would tend to decrease the cost of living. Fish, in its food composition, is very similar to beef and contains many valuable nutrititive properties.

The popular belief that fish is a good brain stimulant has been disproved by research authorities, as it has no more phosphorus than lean beef. It is however, an easily prepared and digested protein food.

The digestibility varies with the different kinds of fish. As a general rule fish of fine texture is more easily digested. Smoked and dried fish is not as digestible as the fresh fish.

Both fish and shellfish abound in our Southern waters.

## BEEF AND VEAL RECIPES

### Standing Prime Rib Roast

Select a standing prime roast which is well trimmed with ribs cut to desired length. Save trimmings for stock and gravy. A piece of fat should accompany each roast. Wipe and scrub rind to remove any bad flavor from hanging. Sprinkle well with flour, and dot each cut side with pieces of fat.

Place under blaze or in hot oven to sear well, turning and browning the cut sides. When seared reduce heat to medium (350 degrees) and cook 20 minutes to the pound for medium rare, longer for well done, and less for very rare. Do not cover. Add no water. There should be enough

grease to baste it occasionally. Roast may be turned if not cooking evenly.
When half done salt and pepper both sides, and add flour to grease to
brown for gravy. There should be no juices in pan, just grease.

If cooking is too slow or pan covered, juice will flow, otherwise juices
stay in meat. Do not stick fork in choice part as this also allows the juices
to flow.

### To Make Gravy

Bones and trimmings from a roast should be put into cold water
(covered well) and boiled to make stock. The usual roast and trimmings
will make about 2 cups of gravy.

For thickening gravy use 3 tablespoons flour to 1 cup stock.

Remove roast from pan and pour off all grease except just enough to mix
with flour. Rub smooth, and add stock from trimmings. Stir and blend
all together and strain. No grease should be evident on top of gravy. It
requires more flour to thicken when it is browned than when left white.

### Prime Roast Rolled

Have butcher bone and roll roast. Cook same as a standing roast. Make
gravy same also.

### Pot Roast

Select a roast of the cheaper cuts of meat, wipe well and remove any
objectionable part. Place in a pot or heavy sauce pan and sear well on both
sides. Sometimes it is necessary to rub a little grease over it. The heat
should be great to sear well and quickly to prevent the juices from flowing.

When searing is done reduce heat, cover and start to cooking slowly.

It is better to rest the meat on a trivet to prevent scorching, the meat
being heavy will press tightly on bottom of pan causing no juice or liquor
to be there.

It will require from 2½ to 3 hours to cook a five pound pot roast.
The secret of a good pot roast is long, slow cooking. If cooked too fast
a little water may have to be added; otherwise there will be sufficient
juice supplied for the cooking.

To make gravy, remove excess grease, thicken with white or browned
flour, add water and seasoning and cook until as thick as wanted.

### Pot Roast With Potatoes

Cook roast as directed above, add peeled Irish potatoes, about 45 minutes
before serving, or long enough to cook the potatoes (potatoes should be of
uniform size), before making the gravy.

### An Oven Pot Roast

Prepare roast by wiping with a damp cloth. Place in roaster and sear
in hot oven or under blaze until well browned on both sides. Salt, pepper
and season with anything desired. If potatoes are wished, peel and place

around roast. Place on cover, lower heat, and cook slowly until roast is done at 275°. No water is added at all. With slow cooking there will be sufficient juice or gravy. The gravy may be thickened or not.

## Beef Stew

| | |
|---|---|
| 2 lbs. short ribs of beef | 4 medium size Irish potatoes |
| 1 onion | Water for stewing |
| 1 carrot | Salt and pepper to season |
| 1 green pepper | |

Wash ribs well. Into a skillet put sufficient bacon drippings to sear ribs. Put ribs in pot or sauce pan, add vegetables cut small, and enough hot water to cover. Bring to a boil then simmer until very tender. About 20 minutes before serving add potatoes cut in large cubes. Cook long enough for potatoes to get done and add seasoning. Serve. There are many other cuts for stewing. Cook same way. Vegetables may be added or not.

## Broiled Steak

Select a choice cut and have it one inch thick or more. Wipe with damp cloth and remove any objectionable skin or gristle. Clip edge to prevent curling.

Place steak on a broiling pan and put under blaze as near as possible not to touch blaze or heat unit. Cook about 3 minutes, turn, broil the other side, turn again, repeat until as done as wanted.

Remove to a hot platter, add salt, pepper and melted butter. To make gravy add 2 or 3 tablespoons water to the pan and drippings, pour over steak.

To broil satisfactorily requires a hot pan, hot broiler and HOT fire. Leave oven door open and the steak will not catch on fire. About 12 minutes will be required to broil medium done.

The broiling pan, with rack, slides in and out. Pull out to turn steak, push back quickly to prevent getting cold. Never salt or add butter while cooking. Large or small steaks may be broiled this way.

## To Pan Broil

Use a heavy fry pan or griddle and have VERY hot.

Prepare steak as for oven broiling, place on sizzling hot pan, turn every 2 or 3 minutes until as done as desired. No grease is used. Sometimes the skillet is rubbed with a piece of steak fat to prevent sticking too much.

Never cover any meat that is being broiled as this draws out the juice, A hot skillet and frequent turning holds juices in. Add salt, pepper and butter after it is on hot platter. Broil any meat the same.

## To Plank a Steak

Have all vegetables cooked, seasoned and hot ready to dress the plank.

Mashed potatoes, carrots, beets, white turnips with plenty of parsley will give color and make the plank attractive.

Prepare steak 1 inch or more thick the same as for broiling. Place on broiling pan and broil one side thoroughly. Remove steak and place cooked side down on hot, buttered plank. Place plank on pan to handle easily. The edge of plank left exposed beyond the steak must be covered with a light coating of wet salt to prevent burning. Run pan, plank and all in oven very near the blaze and broil. No turning is necessary. When well browned remove, brush and wipe salt from plank, season with salt, pepper and butter. Pipe potatoes around the edge of plank and arrange other vegetables attractively. The plank may be placed in hot oven to reheat if necessary.

If potatoes are to be browned they must be brushed with a mixture of egg and milk before returning to the stove to brown.

Place plank on a platter or in holder and serve immediately.

Sometimes the steak is broiled entirely in the broiling pan, placed on a hot buttered plank with vegetables arranged attractively around it.

Broiled chicken, meat loaf or a thick slice of ham may be prepared and served on a plank with vegetables. A plank of vegetables only is very attractive. Cook each vegetable and then arrange on plank.

### Stuffed Flank Steak

Pound a large flank steak until it is flat, then make a stuffing of equal parts of sausage meat and bread crumbs, seasoning with minced onion. Roll up, tie into shape, roll so that when served, the steak will be cut across fibers. Sear in hot fat. Cover with stock or water and let simmer 2 hours or longer. Season gravy, pour over meat and serve.

### Spanish Steak

| | |
|---|---|
| 1 flank steak | 4 tablespoons cooking oil or drippings |
| 1 cup of sliced onions | 2 tablespoons butter |
| 1 cup of canned tomatoes | Salt and pepper to taste |

Into a fry pan put cooking oil and sear steak well. Remove, season with salt and pepper, roll up and place in a baking pan. Fry onions in the remaining grease in pan until brown. Spread over steak, pour over the cup of tomatoes, add butter, cover and cook in slow oven one hour or longer. Baste steak several times. Make gravy of drippings by adding a little flour to thicken, and a little water. Pour over steak, serve hot. Broiled mushrooms may be added.

### Smothered Steak

Select a thick, good cut of round. Wipe, remove rind and cut into sections suitable to serve. Pound with edge of a heavy plate or steak hammer until well beaten. Dip into flour, covering both sides well.

Into a skillet put a small amount of fat; have very hot, put in the pieces of steak and sear both sides well.

Cover with boiling water, cover pan, lower the heat and simmer one hour. When half done salt and pepper to taste. When finished cooking there should be plenty of gravy. If the water boils away more may be added. The cooking must be slow if you wish the meat tender. Onions may be added if liked. Add them sliced when the water is put in and cook until tender. Do not use too much grease. There will be sufficient flour on steak to thicken the gravy.

### Swiss Steak

Select a good round steak, trim and gash edges. Pound with the edge of a thick plate, or steak hammer. Sprinkle well with flour and pound again.

Place on a hot broiling pan, place near the gas blaze and sear, brush over top with butter or drippings, sear again, turn and treat other side same, turn two or three times until as done as liked.

Place on hot platter, salt and pepper, dot with bits of butter, serve at once. This will require about fifteen minutes to cook. If cooked too long it will be tough. Serve with French fried potatoes.

### A New Meat Loaf

Prepare the steak the same as for Swiss. Spread the steak with pork sausage half inch thick, season with salt and pepper, roll up the same as making a jelly roll, tie in several places to keep together, place in hot pan and cook in oven 40 to 60 minutes or until the juice is pink, not red. The time depends on the size.

Place on hot platter, remove the strings, serve hot or cold, slicing crosswise. Bread stuffing may be used in place of the sausage. The steak should be an inch thick when using this way.

### Meat Loaf

| | |
|---|---|
| 2 lbs. veal or beef ground | 1 egg |
| ½ lb. fresh pork ground | ½ cup hot water |
| 1 cup bread crumbs | Put butter into hot water, add all |
| 3 tablespoons of butter or substitute | ingredients and mix well |
| 2 teaspoons salt, pepper to taste | |

The mixture should be stiff enough to be shaped into a loaf. Place in hot baking pan, sear top quickly, then cook in moderate oven from 30 to 40 minutes, just long enough for the juice to be light pink (test with a fork). If cooked too long it will be dry. Serve hot or cold. Onion or tomato catsup is used in seasoning sometimes.

### Mrs. Singer's Beef Jardiniere

| | |
|---|---|
| 2 cups cold roast or soup meat, cut into cubes or strips | 1 cup turnips, diced |
| 1 cup celery cut crosswise | 1 cup tender snapbeans broken into pieces |
| 1 cup English peas | 2 green peppers, shredded |
| 1 cup carrots cut crosswise | |

Put into layers in casserole, cover with broth or gravy, season with salt and pepper as placed into casserole. Cover tightly and bake from 2 to 4 hours in slow oven. Vegetables are all raw when put on.

## Corned Beef and Cabbage

Soak corned beef 1 hour, drain and cover with cold water; bring to a boil quickly, skim, then simmer for 3 hours or allow 40 minutes to the pound. About three quarters of an hour before serving remove all grease from the liquor. Put a portion of the water from the beef into another kettle, and boil the cabbage until tender, from 30 to 40 minutes.

When cooking just corned beef, 1 carrot, 1 onion and 1 tablespoon vinegar to the pound gives a good flavor.

Allow the meat to remain in the liquor for 30 minutes after the cooking stops.

When ready to serve rub with a bit of butter.

Corned beef sliced and broiled is a good luncheon dish.

## Hamburg and Rice Loaf

| | |
|---|---|
| 2 cups hamburg (ground round steak) | 4 tablespoons bacon dripping or butter |
| ½ cup rice | A few spoonfuls of hot water if too stiff |
| 1 cup boiling water | |
| Salt and pepper to taste | |

Wash rice, cook in boiling water until all water is absorbed. Turn into bowl, add meat and seasoning. Add water to make as soft as can handle. Shape into loaf, place in baking pan, cook for forty-five minutes. Serve with hot tomato or creole sauce.

## Creole Stew

Put into casserole or Dutch oven a pound of lean meat. Around this put as many potatoes as the family will need, 3 carrots sliced, 1 pint of tomatoes, 1 onion, 1 green pepper with seed removed, 1 cup of butter beans, 3 ears of corn cut from the cob. Sprinkle the top with salt and pepper, fill the vessel with water, put into a slow oven and cook until the meat is tender. Add a little flour thickening, 2 tablespoons of chopped parsley, 2 tablespoons of Worcestershire sauce and one small pod of garlic.

Continue the cooking until seasoning strikes through well. Should the water cook out, replenish when the stew is half done. If added too late it will not be so good.

The gravy is rich and thick, and the entire meal can be cooked with little attention. Serve on a large platter and place the vegetables around the dish.

What is left over can be reheated the next day, and is just as good or better.

## Kidney Stew

| | |
|---|---|
| 2 kidneys | 1 slice each of onion, carrot, green pepper |
| 1 cup stock | |
| 3 tablespoons butter | 1 stalk celery |
| 4 tablespoons flour | Salt and pepper to taste |

Wash and split kidneys lengthwise. soak in cold water for 2 hours, changing water once during the time. Drop into boiling water and cook slowly until tender. When done remove any membrane, cut in thin slices or dice. Make a brown sauce. Slice and cook vegetables in butter; remove; add flour and brown. Add cup of stock, season and add kidneys and let simmer to absorb seasoning.

Serve on toast or in a dish.

## Veal Loaf No. 1

| | |
|---|---|
| 2 cups ground veal | 4 tablespoons butter |
| 1 cup stale bread crumbs | 1 egg |
| Enough hot milk to moisten the crumbs | Season with salt, pepper and parsley |

Mix together and bind with well beaten egg. Put into buttered pan, cover with buttered paper and bake in moderate oven about 1 hour. Chicken or rabbit may be used, having the meat raw.

## Veal Loaf No. 2

| | |
|---|---|
| 2 lbs. veal from the round | 1 egg |
| ¼ lb. of pork | 1 cup dry bread crumbs |
| 2 tablespoons tomato catsup | 3 tablespoons of butter or drippings |
| 2 tablespoons minced parsley | Cayenne pepper to taste (⅛ teaspoon) |
| 1 tablespoon grated onion | |
| 2 teaspoons salt | |

After wiping and removing the rind or skin, put the meat through a food chopper. Put all ingredients into meat and mix into a loaf, using a little water if it seems too stiff. Shape into a loaf and bake in moderate oven about 30 minutes, or until it is done. This loaf should be seared on the top to keep in the juices.

## Jellied Veal

| | |
|---|---|
| 4 lbs. leg of veal | Salt, pepper and any seasoning wanted |
| 1 veal knuckle | |

Boil meat until it will fall from bones. Remove bones, shred or grind meat and season. Remove all grease from liquor and reduce to about 3 cups of stock. Put meat into pan, pour over stock just to barely cover the meat. Set aside to jelly. Slice and serve cold or broil.

All seasoning must be added to meat and liquor before putting together. Green and red pepper may be boiled until tender, shredded and mixed with the meat.

## To Cook Liver

Have liver cut ¾ inch thick. Pour hot water over it and let stand 15 minutes; take membrane from edge and score well with knife. Salt, pepper and dip in flour, covering well. Into a frying pan put two or three tablespoons of bacon grease and get very hot; sear each piece of liver on both sides, thus browning the flour; when all is browned, cover with boiling water and cook gently for 15 minutes, or until done as you like. Put on a platter with the gravy; serve very hot. If cooked too long it will be tough. It only takes a few minutes to do the searing.

Beef or calf's liver is good, calf's liver being a little more delicate.

If bacon is to be served with this, first broil the bacon, remove and keep crisp. Use the grease for the liver.

### Broiled Liver

Have liver sliced about ½ inch thick. Pour hot water over and let stand 5 minutes, drain, remove the membrane around edge and any other objectionable part.

Into a fry pan place just enough bacon drippings or butter to prevent sticking. Place liver in and turn often, two or three times, until as done as desired.

Place on hot dish, add salt, pepper and melted butter. Serve immediately.

### Liver Pudding

Take one hog liver, lights, and one jowl. Boil all together until tender. Mash well or grind in food chopper. Add 1½ or 2 cups of cooked rice, 1 medium size onion chopped fine, salt and pepper to taste. Pack in a bowl.

### Philadelphia Scrapple

We use the head and feet of the hog with beef brisket equivalent to half the weight of the pork used. The head and feet well cleaned are put on to boil with the brisket in salted water, which just covers the meat. Boil slowly until the meat leaves the bone and you have a rich stock. When cool enough to handle, grind the meat in a food chopper and strain the stock for bone particles. Add the stock to the ground meat in a heavy vessel and bring to a boil, then add alternately a cup of corn meal and a cup of oatmeal until it is the consistency of mush. Stir continuously for about twenty minutes as it has a tendency to stick. Season with salt and red pepper to taste, add sweet marjoram. About one-third box of sweet marjoram will season about eighteen pounds of pork. Pour into loaf pans and when cold slice and fry in a hot frying pan. Sage may be used in place of the marjoram.

### Scrapple

Boil 1 hog liver until tender, take up, mash fine and return to stock, or part of it if there is very much. Add 1 pint sifted meal, salt, pepper and a little sage. Press, slice, cook in oven to brown or broil.

### Brains and Eggs

| | |
|---|---|
| 1 set brains | 2 tablespoons butter |
| 2 or 3 eggs | Salt and pepper to taste |

Soak brains in cold salt water until they will clean easily. Remove all membrane, drop into boiling water and boil until tender, about fifteen minutes. Drain well. Into a fry pan put butter and brains, mash well and add unbeaten eggs, cook same as scrambled eggs, add salt and pepper and they are ready to serve.

### Brains and Tomatoes

| | |
|---|---|
| 2 sets brains (calves brains preferred) | 3 tablespoons flour |
| | 1 teaspoon salt |
| 1 pint can tomatoes cooked and strained | ⅛ teaspoon cayenne pepper |
| 3 tablespoons butter | 1 teaspoon each grated onion, chopped parsley, Worcestershire sauce |

Soak brains in cold salt water for one hour, clean, boil until tender, chill. Slice and broil in the butter, remove to platter. To the butter add flour and brown. Add seasoning, cook for one minute, add tomatoes, blend together, cook for ten minutes. Pour over brains as a sauce. Serve on toast. Each slice of brains may be placed on toast and the sauce poured over all. Tomato puree may be used adding equal amount of water. The dish must be hot to be good.

### Creamed Sweetbreads

| | |
|---|---|
| 1 lb. sweetbreads | 1 teaspoon salt |
| 1 tablespoon chopped parsley | ⅛ teaspoon white pepper |
| 1 cup white sauce | |

Boil and remove the skins or membrane from the sweetbreads. Make the usual white sauce, add to sweetbreads, add seasoning. Serve in timbales or on toast.

### Broiled Sweetbreads

Wash and boil sweetbreads for 30 minutes. Cool, remove any outside membrane, slice lengthwise, sprinkle with salt and pepper. Into a fry pan put a small portion of butter, just sufficient to brown sweetbreads and prevent sticking. Cook for about 5 minutes, browning both sides; place on hot platter, pour over a portion of melted butter and serve at once.

Very small tender sweetbreads may be broiled without boiling, cooking longer to get done. They may be sliced or not. Soak in cold water before broiling. Remove any ends of membrane around edge.

### LAMB

Lamb is plain, everyday food, yet it is one which may be dressed up with frills and furbelows if you wish. There are choice, and very choice, cuts—there are plain and very plain parts which anyone may have if they only "know how" to buy.

Anyone should be able to tell lamb from mutton by two distinct ways, the size of a whole lamb weighs about twenty-five to thirty pounds and a quarter is a small portion. The other way, examine the bone where the foot has been removed, the bone is ridged like knuckles, for the foot of a lamb is broken off, not chopped.

The rind of lamb if scrubbed with a bit of cooking soda, then well rinsed or wiped off, will not have that unpleasant taste which is so often found.   Dip a damp cloth in dry soda, scrub the rind of the meat, then with cold water remove all traces of soda.   Shipped meat is hung a long time, so this outside skin must be well wiped to get rid of any taste. Always remove the outside skin from chops.

Lamb is roasted, broiled or stewed the same as beef, so if you know how to cook one you know how to cook all.

Many like a boiled leg of lamb, hot or cold.   There are many ways of using lamb while we are waiting for fried chicken to come in, so take your choice and see how well the family will like it.

Mutton is the grown lamb.   To cook, follow recipes for lamb, cooking a longer period.

### Crown Roast of Lamb

A crown roast is a very handsome dish and is made from the loin and rib chops, requiring enough ribs to make the crown.   The ribs are separated at the backbone, but left together, so when serving the knife goes down between each rib, through the cut, and the section is lifted out and served. A crown roast is prepared by the butcher.   The ribs are frenched and form the crown.   A good sized crown will weigh 8 or 10 pounds.

### To Cook a Crown Roast

Wipe, salt and pepper the roast.   Cover each end of the ribs with a cube of boiling meat or a small Irish potato, or wrap with several thicknesses of wax paper.

Place in hot oven for 15 minutes to sear; reduce heat to 300 F. and add a cup of hot water, to prevent the drippings from scorching, and baste frequently.   Cook 1½ hours or longer according to size, the same as roasting.   Do not cover, cook in an open pan.

A cup pressed down in center will keep the roast a nice shape.   Sometimes a force meat is used as a filling for the center.   However, I prefer potatoes or some other vegetable filled in, after roasting.

### Roast Leg o' Lamb

Scrub lamb well with soda and wipe the meat off with cold water.   Dry. Rub over with some kind of fat and sprinkle with flour.   Place in baking pan and sear well on both sides, having a hot oven, or under the flame of a gas range.   Reduce heat, add one cup of hot water, roast twenty minutes to the pound, basting occasionally.   When half done, salt, pepper and add any seasoning desired, catsup, onion or mustard.

Turn to brown all sides.   If water cooks away, add more, a little at a time.   Cook in open pan.   When done, serve with mint sauce or plain.

## Smothered Lamb

| | |
|---|---|
| 1 small forequarter of lamb | 4 tablespoons of bacon drippings or butter |
| 2 carrots | |
| 2 onions | 1 tablespoon Worcestershire sauce |
| 1 clove of garlic | 2 teaspoons salt |
| 1 green pepper | Cayenne pepper to taste |

Boil or steam lamb until very tender, in just enough water to cover.

Into a fry pan put bacon drippings and cut and brown slightly all the vegetables. Place lamb in baking pan, add vegetables and two cups of the water in which it was boiled.

Cook slowly until meat is browned and well seasoned, about one hour. The meat may be sprinkled with flour several times during the cooking. This helps to brown and thicken the sauce or gravy. A cupful of tomatoes, a teaspoon of prepared mustard may be added if liked.

This is good served with macaroni, rice or bread and butter.

## To Broil Lamb Chops

Prepare the chops by removing the outside skin and any extra fat. Have a very hot frying pan or skillet, place the chops in it and as soon as the side next to pan is browned, turn. Turn several times, keeping pan hot, never cover, cook about eight to ten minutes. The chops should be about one inch thick. When done remove to a hot platter, season with salt, pepper and melted butter. Serve at once.

## Lamb Cutlets

Boil breast of lamb until very tender. When half done, season with salt and pepper and slice of onion. Let stay in water until cold. Cut portions of lamb, roll in beaten egg, then crumbs, fry in deep fat until a nice brown.

## Lamb Chops With Eggplant

Have as many chops as guests. Remove the piece of backbone leaving the rib bone, and mash as flat as possible.

Broil nicely and place a chop on a thick slice of fried eggplant. Make a brown sauce of brown butter, flour and stock or milk. Season highly with Worcestershire and chili sauce; pour over all and serve.

## Lamb Chops With Grape Jelly

Broil chops—salt, pepper and spread a portion of butter over each chop. Have ½ cup of thin brown sauce ready, add to this ½ glass of grape jelly, blend together well and add a little kitchen bouquet or Worcestershire sauce. Season well with salt and pepper, and pour around the chop. Serve at once.

## Lamb Stew

| | |
|---|---|
| 2 pounds of lamb stew | 2 sweet green peppers |
| 4 tablespoons of bacon drippings | 3 whole cloves |
| 1 large onion | 1 can tomatoes, about two cups |
| 1 bunch of carrots (or two cupfuls) | Salt and pepper to taste |
| 1 cup diced celery | |

Cut lamb to pieces and sear in the bacon grease. Cut all vegetables in small pieces, add tomatoes, vegetables and seasoning, cook slowly until very tender. Add a little water if necessary.

When done, remove grease if too much, add a little flour or half cup of bread crumbs to thicken, serve over dry rice. Irish potatoes may be boiled, diced and added to take the place of the rice.

## Barbecued Lamb

Use any part of the forequarter of lamb. Cook as smothered lamb (see recipe). Add barbecue sauce in place of vegetables, continue cooking until very tender and well seasoned.

# PORK

## Pork Roast With Dressing

Select pork, have a pocket prepared by the butcher and stuff with the following:

| | |
|---|---|
| 1 cup chopped apples | 1 teaspoon salt |
| 2 cups soft bread crumbs | 1/8 teaspoon pepper |
| 1 cup of seedless raisins | 1 tablespoon butter |
| 1 teaspoon chopped onion | 3/4 cup hot water |

Mix apples, crumbs, all seasoning and raisins together. Melt butter in hot water, add to other mixtures, use for stuffing.

Goose, duck, birds, veal breast, or spare ribs may be used same as pork.

## Roast Pork and Sweet Potatoes

| | |
|---|---|
| Loin roast or shoulder of ham | Medium size sweet potatoes cut in |
| Salt | half lengthwise |
| Pepper | |

Season roast with salt and pepper, cook in open pan in moderate oven, 30 to 40 minutes per pound, basting occasionally with the drippings, turning once or more. Boil potatoes until half done, drain and place around roast 45 minutes before serving. Baste potatoes and turn several times to season. Serve potatoes around roast. Gravy may be made from drippings left in roasting pan. For different flavor crush and sprinkle four or five ginger wafers over roast while cooking.

## Pork Tenderloin

Slice tenderloin about half inch thick, broil on broiler exactly as steak, giving a little longer time and keep turning. Place on hot platter, season with salt, pepper and butter. Serve with tiny thin hoecakes.

### Backbone

Wash backbone and have chopped or cut into pieces convenient to serve. Sprinkle with salt and pepper, place in a baking pan and add two cups of boiling water. Have oven hot for 10 minutes then cook with medium heat. Baste and turn, cook about two hours. If a crusty outside is liked dredge with flour when half done and cook uncovered.

When ready to serve, remove from pan, pour off all grease from top of gravy, add sufficient browned flour to thicken. Serve with baked sweet potatoes.

### Boiled Backbone With Macaroni or Dumplings

Prepare bones for cooking, drop into boiling water and boil gently for two or more hours, add salt and pepper when half done. Cook until tender. Have ready some cooked and blanched macaroni, add to backbones and cook just long enough to season well. Dumplings may be used in place of macaroni.

### Stuffed Spareribs

Select a long strip of spareribs, wash and dry. Make the usual dressing of stale bread using a portion of corn muffin crumbs. Season with salt, pepper and any other seasoning at hand or liked, such as celery, parsley, onions. Place stuffing on half of the strip, fold over the other half, bringing the sides together forming a pocket. Fasten with stout toothpicks and a string or skewers. Sprinkle with flour, place in baking pan, roast until meat is tender and brown. Use moderate heat for roasting. No water is used, but if ribs seem tough, a very little may be used, allowing it to steam, then dry out and brown.

### Spareribs and Sauerkraut

Boil ribs until very tender, having right good quantity of water. Salt to taste. When done, remove ribs and drop in sauerkraut, boil for 20 to 30 minutes, drain and place on platter; arrange ribs around the mound. Serve with some of the raw kraut and baked sweet potatoes.

### To Boil a Ham

Scrub a ham until the rind is clean. Soak overnight in cold water if necessary. Put into large boiler and cover with cold water. Let come to the boil slowly and simmer until done, allowing twenty minutes to a pound. Let stay in the water until cold; remove and trim off the skin and any undesirable parts. If very fat, remove a portion. Into the fat and rind rub brown sugar, using about 1 cup, then cover the top with bread crumbs; stick one dozen cloves over the top and dot with spots of black pepper. Dampen the end of finger, dip into the black pepper and press onto the ham; place in oven and brown quickly and it is ready to serve either hot or cold.

To test if done, insert a sharp fork or hat pin in the thickest part on under side. If the juice is pink it is done, if red it is not and must be cooked longer.  If cooked too long the juice will be white.  It will have to be placed on a platter to test.  If boiled too hard the outer side will tear; the inside not done.  Some like ½ cup molasses and ½ cup of vinegar put into the water when boiling.

### To Bake a Ham in Dough

Select a ham which you can depend on as not being too salty.  Wash and scrub and soak overnight in cold water if necessary.  Remove and wipe dry and let the outer side dry out so it will hold the paste.  Mix flour and water to a very stiff paste—almost a dough.  Cover the ham well with this (about ¼ inch), and pat dry flour over so you can handle.  Place skin side down.  Put into a baking pan and place in a hot oven for ten minutes or more until the dough hardens a little; then reduce heat and cook in a slow oven twenty minutes for every pound.  When done, test, using a hat pin the same as when boiling.  Let get cool; remove the flour well; trim to look nice; rub with brown sugar; cover with bread crumbs, and brown in quick oven.  It is then ready to serve hot or cold.  Cloves and pepper may be added the same as when boiled.  There is no water used at all; the ham is baked in a dry pan.

There is no basting required.  If you are sure the ham is sweet, soaking overnight is not necessary.

There is a grade which does not require the soaking.  A ham cooked this way is very juicy and most delicious.  A half of one could be cooked this way nicely.  The cut end would be sealed up.

### Baked Ham

Select a ham of dependable make.  Scrub and place in a baking pan with a trivet or rack to hold it from resting on the bottom.  Put skin side on rack, place in hot oven for fifteen to twenty minutes with fire hot to sear outside, reduce heat to low (275 degrees F.) and bake twenty minutes to the pound.  No basting is necessary.  Never cover—have open pan.  When done let cool sufficiently to handle.  Remove skin and trim off any objectional outside.  First rub with a bit of mustard, dry or mixed; then rub all over with sugar as much as will soak in.  Cover skin side with bread crumbs.  Brown in quick oven.  If doubtful soak ham in cold water overnight, wipe dry and follow directions.  Sweet spiced vinegar is sometimes used with the mustard to give flavor.  For very fancy ham, over the crumbs place slices of canned pineapple with a red cherry (maraschino) in the center of each pineapple ring, and brown.

### Baked Ham With Red Apples

Arrange slices of hot baked ham on large platter, covering generously with essence of ham.  Arrange baked apples around the ham, allowing one apple for each slice of ham.  Apples should be hot.  See recipe for Chrismas Apples.

## Ham Loaf

| | |
|---|---|
| 1½ cups raw ground ham, fat and lean | 1 large onion |
| 1½ cups cold rice | 2 pimentoes |
| 1 cup bread crumbs | 2 sprigs of parsley |
| 1½ cups white sauce | 1 teaspoon salt |
| 4 stalks celery | ⅛ teaspoon pepper or more |

When ham is ground put seasoning through the food chopper.

Grease and flour a loaf bread pan well, pack meat in pan, place pan into another pan containing hot water, and bake 1 hour.

Serve hot or cold.

Tomato sauce may be used and makes a nice change.

## Sugared Ham

| | |
|---|---|
| 1 slice ham, one inch thick | 4 cloves |
| 1 cup dark brown sugar, more if needed | ½ cup water |
| | Vinegar, water for soaking |

Trim ham and place in sufficient tart vinegar and water to cover well. Let soak two hours. Drain and wipe well. Cover with sugar, rub in well, do this on both sides, place into a baking dish, pour over the half-cup water, stick in cloves, cover top with more sugar. Bake slowly for 2 hours. Remove from pan, make sauce of dripping, using flour and water with sauces to season well. Serve the sauce in separate dish. Cider in place of water is more delicious if easy to obtain.

## Baked Slice of Ham

| | |
|---|---|
| Center cut of ham about 3 inches thick | ½ cup brown sugar |
| 1 cup of boiling water | Spices (as desired, cloves, cinnamon, etc.) |
| 3 tablespoons vinegar | |

Place slice of ham in baking pan and pour 1 cup of boiling water with vinegar and half of the brown sugar over it. Bake for two hours in moderate oven—350 degrees. When half done add a sprinkle of spices and remainder of brown sugar, basting occasionally until done. To carve, cut diagonally thru slice beginning at one end. If ham is salty or very dry, it may be soaked several hours in cold water before baking.

## Delicious Ham No. 1

Soak a slice of ham in equal parts of sweet milk and water for an hour then wipe and broil as usual.

## Delicious Ham No. 2

One slice of ham 1½ inches thick; trim off the skin and rind; sprinkle with brown sugar, using two teaspoons; place in casserole or baking pan; pour over 1½ cups of sweet milk (or just cover); bake in moderate oven one hour. Serve with lye hominy.

### Sizzled Ham

Purchase boiled ham, having it sliced quite thin. In a hot skillet broil until crisp; drain free of any grease; serve with fried hominy (grits).

### To Broil Ham

Cut slices of usual thickness. Have heavy skillet hot; trim edges of slices and put into pan; turn several times until done. To make red gravy, sprinkle each good-sized slice with 1 teaspoon of sugar; broil, turning twice until the outer surface is well seared and meat done, remove to platter. Keep the fry pan hot, but not burning. Put in several tablespoons of water to make the gravy, pour over the ham. The sugar caramels and makes the red gravy. An iron skillet makes redder gravy than any other ware. To broil in a gas oven, treat in same way, placing near the flame, turn until done, make gravy in the pan and pour over the meat.

### Etowah Ham Loaf

| | |
|---|---|
| 4 cups ground lean ham | 3 pimentoes |
| 1 cup finely chopped celery | 2 green (bell) peppers |
| 1 cup crushed snowflake crackers | 1 small onion |
| ½ cup mayonnaise | 1 tablespoon lemon juice |
| 1 box of granulated gelatine dissolved in ½ cup of cold water | 3 tablespoons salad dressing |
| | 3 hard boiled eggs |

Grind and measure ham. Grind peppers and onion. Chop celery very fine. Dice eggs. Break crackers with fingers (do not roll). Then measure. Melt gelatine over boiling water. Mix all into the ham, add gelatine and mix well. Last, add the mayonnaise and mix well with forks; turn into mold to get firm. This slices nicely and will serve about fifteen. Serve on lettuce with more mayonnaise or as a cold meat.

### Ham a la King

| | |
|---|---|
| 2 cups cooked and diced lean ham | 2 green peppers, boiled, skinned and cut fine, seed removed |
| 2 cups white sauce | |
| 1 cup chopped mushrooms | ½ cup top milk or thin cream |
| ½ cup chopped almonds (blanched) | 4 egg yolks |
| 2 pimentoes, chopped | Salt and pepper to taste |

Use cold boiled lean ham. Make white sauce; mix all ingredients, using double boiler. Mix yolks of eggs into the milk, add to the mixture and cook until thick.

The cooking of the eggs thickens mixture. Serve in timbales, on toast, or from a serving dish.

### Mock Sweetbreads

| | |
|---|---|
| 1 cup of minced lean ham | 1½ cups of white sauce |
| 1 cup of diced hard-boiled eggs | Salt and pepper to season |

Into a skillet put minced ham and sear until it is partly crisp. Mix all together and fill green, sweet peppers, cover top with buttered crumbs, put peppers into a baking pan which has been slightly greased and bake in moderate oven until brown on top.

Do not bake too long or peppers will shrink too much to look pretty. Cover bottom of pan with hot water. This will keep the peppers plump. To make in baking dish, slice in rings or grind 2 green peppers to flavor. Cover top with buttered crumbs.

## Ham Mousse

| | |
|---|---|
| 2 cups boiled lean ham, ground before measuring | 1 teaspoon prepared mustard |
| 1 cup whipped cream | ⅛ teaspoon cayenne |
| 1 cup cooked mayonnaise | 2 tablespoons gelatine, dissolved in 1/3 cup cold water |
| 1 tablespoon chili sauce | |

Dissolve gelatine in cold water for five minutes, then melt over boiling water and let cool slightly. Mix with the dressing, add the seasoning, then the whipped cream. Into this mix the ham. Pour into wet mold and let stand until congealed. Serve as a cold meat, in mold or sliced.

## Ham Rolls

Cut thin, large slices of baked ham, spread lightly with mayonnaise, then minced cucumber pickles, roll up like a sweet wafer, fasten with a toothpick, stick an olive on the end of the pick, place on platter, garnish with parsley and olives, or roll each ham roll in wax paper, twist each end and it is ready to serve at the picnic. Boiled ham may be used just as well.

## FOWL

### To Dress a Turkey

The turkey is better to bleed when killed, as it gives whiter meat and the feathers are usually dry picked. Hold turkey over a gas flame or burning paper to singe off the long hair-like feathers. Turn every side, open wings so all parts may be reached.

Place in pan of water, scrub skin well, rinse and dry. Remove feet at first joint. The sinews may be pulled out with the removal of feet, but it is much easier to remove them after cooking. Place turkey on table, and with a large knife or cleaver chop off head, leaving a long neck. Push back the skin and remove neck near the shoulders, leaving the skin intact. Make a long cut at back of neck through the skin and remove crop. This leaves the breast covered with skin.

Turn turkey on its back, make a generous cut (about 2 inches) crosswise at the end of the breast bone; make the second cut just through the skin near the end of fowl, leaving a wide section of skin. Free skin under the "parson's nose"; this frees the intestines. Pull out through the opening at the end of the breast bone, drop for a moment, insert the fingers and free the gizzard and other organs joining the backbone. Remove carefully without breaking. Examine to see that every part has been removed —heart and lungs. Remove oil sac. Rinse well with cold water and dry.

Run drumstick through the cut at the breastbone under the strip of skin out through the second or lower cut, thus putting them in shape for roasting. Turkey is now ready to chill. When ready to roast, rub inside and out with salt and pepper.

When stuffing: Fill opening where crop was removed, being careful not to crowd, leaving room for swelling. Sew up cut at the back, in the skin which covered the neck, draw skin together at neck bone, leaving it loose. Gather and tie with string; this gives a beautiful, round, full breast. Skin of neck is tucked under back until roasted. Fill carcass with stuffing, not crowding, truss wings by using a coarse needle and thread—one stitch in each wing, turning to hold flat to the body. The strings in all three places should be removed before sending to the table.

### To Dress a Hen

Use directions for turkey. Hens are picked dry, or scalded.

### To Roast a Turkey

After the stuffing is made and put in the turkey, make a thin paste of melted butter and flour and rub over turkey. Place in baking pan with a trivet or something to lift bird slightly from the pan. Place in hot oven to sear the outside until it just begins to brown; if kept too long the skin might burst. When seared, lower the heat, toss over the turkey a cup of hot water and melted butter.

Now the real roasting beings. Never cover, leave open, basting often with the drippings in the pan. Should the water cook away, add half a cup more, just enough to prevent drippings from scorching. Turn turkey to brown on all sides. Allow 25 minutes to a pound and cook slowly (about 275 degrees) until done and well browned. The last half hour turn breast down so the juices will flow to the white meat.

If turkey is very large and any part should be sufficiently brown, cover with a greased cloth or paper of several thicknesses to prevent burning.

A turkey cooked in an open pan is far better and just as tender as when cooked in a roaster.

The giblets, neck, gizzard and liver are boiled in water to make the gravy. Use stock and minced giblets with drippings in the roasting pan.

Never parboil a turkey, it loses its sweetness. To test when done, pull the wing or thigh bone loose from the body. If it breaks easily and the joint shows no red meat, it is done. Never stick a fork in a turkey or choice roast, as it allows the juice to escape. Some turkeys cook much quicker than others, due to the condition of the fowl. A very large turkey will require slower cooking than one weighing 10 or 12 pounds.

### Creamed Turkey

See recipe for Creamed Chicken.

## To Broil Chickens

Use young chickens weighing from a half to three-fourths pounds each. Dress and cut in half. Bend drumstick back to thigh, and cut through the muscle to make joint limp, shape and place in pan, skin side up. Broil, adding small amount of butter, turning often to prevent burning. Season while cooking. When done, remove to platter, make gravy of the browned juices and butter, and pour over the chicken.

Toast may be arranged around the platter, or each half of chicken placed on a piece.

Very young chickens are not fat, so require quite a bit of butter.

## To Smother Broil Chickens

Prepare young chickens the same as for broiling. Place in hot broiling pan, skin side down; dot with butter and place under blaze in broiling oven. Cook until seared, turn, dot with butter and broil again, keeping pan far enough from the blaze to prevent butter catching fire. When both sides are browned, add a cup of hot water (the amount depending on the number of chickens being broiled) and let steam and cook in pan; add seasoning and plenty of butter; let cook slowly until very tender, turning and browning. More water may be required. When tender, allow all liquid to cook away and again crisp the chicken. There should be sufficient butter to do this. Place on platter, make brown gravy, pour over the chickens and serve.

A few spoons of water added to the hot pan will make gravy of the browned juices and butter. Garnish with parsley, broiled pineapple, peaches or tomatoes. Mushrooms may be added during the cooking if used. A cream or thick gravy is sometimes preferred.

## To Pan Smother Broil Chicken

Prepare chicken and broil as directed for broiling. After searing on both sides several times, add a few spoons of water, cover to steam to make very tender, repeating if necessary. When tender, remove top, broil down until chicken is crisp and serve immediately.

Make gravy by adding a little water to the juice and butter. Salt and pepper during the cooking. This way of cooking makes the chicken very tender.

## Chicken and Ham a la Georgia
### (A Company Dish)

Broil small chickens as usual, having ½ chicken for each guest. Place chicken in center of large platter. Arrange slices of hot baked ham around chicken. Over each slice of ham put a generous spoon of the ham essence. This blends with the chicken gravy and is most delicious. Serve chicken, ham and gravy to each guest.

## To Clean and Dress Chicken for Frying

Remove feathers, wash with a coarse cloth, singe to remove pin feathers and wash again. Remove drumstick and second joint together, then wings, crop and oil bag. Slip knife under the shoulder blade, which runs parallel with the backbone; cut towards the breast to free the bone. With the left hand, catch the shoulder blades near the breast, take neck and backbone with the right hand and tear the two pieces apart, thus freeing the entrails. Remove the gizzard and liver. Cut breast in half lengthwise and disjoint the drumstick. Cut the back in two pieces; this gives 6 meaty pieces and 6 bony pieces. Rinse and chill. Some like to salt chicken when setting aside to chill. Care must be taken not to break or cut too near the gall bag. Cut through the thick side of the gizzard down to the lining which holds the grit; peel off the outside and rinse until it is clear.

All fowl should be chilled thoroughly to remove the body heat.

### Fried Chicken

Select a young chicken weighing from 1½ to 2 lbs. Dress and disjoint, chill. When ready, have a deep fry pan with grease at least two inches deep.

Sift enough flour in which to roll the chicken pieces (a cup and a half or two cups). Add salt and pepper to the flour, roll each piece in flour and place in the hot grease. Put the largest pieces in first and on the hottest part of the pan. When all is in, cover for 5 minutes. Remove top and turn when the underside is well browned. Replace top for another 5 minutes, remove and cook in open pan until the bottom side is browned. About 30 minutes in all will be required for cooking chicken if it is not too large. Do not turn chicken but once; too much turning and too long cooking will destroy the fine flavor which is there when well cooked.

The fat should be deep enough to cover the pieces when it boils up.

To make cream gravy:

Pour off the grease, leaving 2 to 3 tablespoons in the pan with the browned crumbs. Add 2 tablespoons butter, 4 tablespoons flour, blend and cook until a golden brown; add 1 cup milk and 1 cup hot water. Stir until smooth and the right thickness and add salt and black pepper. Pour into a gravy boat and serve with hot biscuit or dry rice. Never pour gravy over chicken if you wish Georgia fried chicken.

### Baked Chicken

Select a nice, plump hen in good condition. Prepare for cooking. Make a stuffing and fill chicken after it has been salted and peppered. Rub over the outside with butter and sprinkle with flour. Place in a roaster and put in hot oven to sear. When seared well, cover and reduce heat to medium or slow. Roast until done. Remove top and brown again to make crisp.

Make gravy of drippings in the pan, and giblets; thicken with flour. About 2 cups of water, milk or stock will be needed for the gravy, and 2 tablespoons flour for thickening. If flour is browned more will be required than when white is used.

## Roasted Capon

Prepare and roast exactly the same as turkey. Capon will cook very easily. Stuff the same as turkey and make gravy with giblets.

## Chicken Surprise

| | |
|---|---|
| 1 cooked hen | 2 teaspoons salt |
| 1 tablespoon butter | ¼ teaspoon pepper |
| 1 cup sweet milk | |

Put hen through meat chopper and mix with other ingredients; roll out small pieces of biscuit dough, little larger than a tea cup; put in a spoonful of the meat, wet edges, draw up, make a ball; fry a nice brown in deep fat.

This will make about 2 dozen.

Use a frying basket.

It is better to have meat warm.

Cook and serve immediately.

Use more or less milk to moisten the meat.

## Dish for Sunday Night Supper

Take breast of cold chicken or any meaty pieces and with scissors cut into pieces like fingers. Have a dish of cooked cauliflower flowerettes about the size of half a dollar.

Place leaves of lettuce on platter; on each leaf put slice of tomato and on this a piece of chicken, strips of pimento, a spoonful of mayonnaise and on this the cauliflower. To be passed. Any combination desired may be used.

## Chicken Gumbo

| | |
|---|---|
| 1 young hen | 3 tablespoons of butter if the chicken |
| 1 quart okra | is not very fat (or bacon drip- |
| 6 ripe tomatoes | pings). |
| 1 large onion | Salt and pepper to taste |

Boil the chicken until very tender. Pull the meat from the bones and return to the water in which it was cooked—there should be about three cups of water.

Peel and chop the tomatoes; cut okra in small pieces, also the onion; add seasoning and cook slowly until the vegetables are done and the mixture is thick; stir often as you would a hash or Brunswick stew. Sometimes chicken and rice are cooked together this way. The latter dish I call "pilau."

## Chicken Brunswick Stew

| | |
|---|---|
| 1 fowl | 1 pint of butterbeans |
| 1 quart of corn | 2 onions |
| 1 quart of tomatoes | Salt and pepper to taste |
| 1 pint of okra | |

Boil chicken until it will leave the bones and be very tender. Pull meat from bones and cut into large cubes, return to the water in which it was cooked, add vegetables and cook down until a thick mixture. Cook slowly and stir often to prevent scorching.

All vegetables must be cut fine before adding. Bread crumbs may be added to thicken chicken if necessary; use only the crumbs.

### Creamed Chicken

One hen boiled until tender, remove meat from bones, cut in cubes as for salad. Make the usual white sauce and mix with the chicken, usually two cups of chicken will require one or one and a half of white sauce. Season with salt and pepper to taste. Use white or red pepper. Use about four tablespoons of flour for one cup of milk in making the white sauce. Canned mushrooms (or fresh ones) are often put with creamed chicken, as well as celery and pimentoes. The celery is cut small, boiled until tender, drained and added.

### Chicken a la King

| | |
|---|---|
| 1 hen | 1 cup chopped almonds (blanched) |
| 1 can mushrooms | Yolks of 4 eggs |
| 3 green peppers | 2 cups of white sauce |
| 2 pimentoes | Salt and cayenne pepper to taste |
| ½ cup cream | |

Boil hen until tender, as for salad; dice, remove all skin and veins. Make white sauce the usual way. Remove seed from green peppers, boil until tender in salt water; remove the skin and chop with red peppers, blanch and chop almonds. Put all the ingredients into the white sauce while it is hot (in a double boiler); beat yolks of eggs into cream; add to mixture and cook over hot water until the eggs are cooked and it thickens. Serve in timbales, on toast, or from a serving dish. This will serve about one dozen.

### Chicken Shortbread

Make the usual egg bread and bake as directed. (See recipe for Egg Bread.) Cut in pieces about 4 inches square. Split open. Have ready creamed chicken, place bottom piece of bread on plate, cover top with creamed chicken, place top piece of bread and cover generously with more creamed chicken. Garnish with minced parsley and serve piping hot. Chicken a la King may be used. Served with a drink this as a meal within itself.

### Chicken Croquettes

Boil a chicken (hen) until very tender, pick meat from bones, rejecting any gristle and skin. Put through food chopper.

For every cup of ground chicken use half a cup of white sauce, season with salt, pepper and finely chopped parsley. Mix and set aside to get cold so the croquettes may be shaped; then make into any desired shape, roll in fine, dry bread crumbs, beaten egg, then crumbs again. Fry in deep fat until a golden brown. Drain on paper napkin. Use the whole egg, add one tablespoon of cold water to the egg.

Have the mixture soft so the inside will be soft and creamy. Do not put raw eggs into croquettes, it makes them tough. One hen usually makes about two dozen croquettes.

## Molded Chicken

| | |
|---|---|
| 2 cups chicken broth | 2 cups finely chopped chicken |
| 4 egg yolks | 2 cups whipped cream |
| 2 tablespoons flour | Salt and pepper to taste |
| 2 tablespoons gelatine soaked in 1/2 cup of water or stock | |

Put gelatine to soak for five minutes, mix flour to smooth paste with a small quantity of broth, add balance of broth which has been heated. Cook until thick, add gelatine and thoroughly melt, add chicken and seasoning. Let get cold. Add whipped cream, turn into mold to get firm, small or large, serve on lettuce with mayonnaise.

## Hot Chicken Mold

| | |
|---|---|
| 2 cups cooked ground chicken | 3 eggs |
| 1 cup thin white sauce | Season with salt and pepper |

Boil chicken until very tender, remove from bones and put through food chopper. Mix with the white sauce, season, add eggs which have been beaten together, mix well and pour into a buttered mold. Steam about 30 to 40 minutes or until done in moderate oven. Unmold on a platter, pour over all a brown nut sauce, serve very hot. This is for a meat or an entree.

## Chicken Mousse No. 1

| | |
|---|---|
| 1 cup cooked chicken put through food chopper | 1 tablespoon spiced vinegar |
| 3 tablespoons cold white sauce | Whites 2 eggs |
| | Salt and pepper to suit taste |

Mix chicken and white sauce; season well with salt and pepper and 1 tablespoon spiced vinegar.

Beat whites of eggs stiff and fold into mixture. Place pan, uncovered, in hot water and cook like cup custard in moderate oven for 15 minutes. Unmold and serve hot with hot white sauce. Individual molds may be used. Have mold well greased.

## Chicken Mousse No. 2

| | |
|---|---|
| 1 cup cold cooked chicken put through food chopper (breast preferred) | 1 tablespoon gelatine dissolved in ¼ cup chicken broth |
| ¼ lb. fresh mushrooms broiled and put through food chopper | 1 cup hot chicken broth |
| | Season with salt and pepper very highly |

Mix well and set aside to cool. When this begins to stiffen, beat 1 cup of cream stiff and fold into mixture. Pour into mold or form to get firm. Slice and serve on lettuce leaf as a salad or as a cold meat.

## Southern Dry Stuffing
### (Using Bread Crumbs and Egg Bread)

Make a rich egg bread or corn meal muffins doubling the number of eggs used. Make the day before using for stuffing. Crumble crust and all using equal amount of dry bread crumbs and egg bread crumbs. Mix same as when using only bread crumbs. Add teaspoon baking powder when mixing. No raw eggs are used. It will require four or five cups each of the dry bread crumbs and egg bread crumbs to fill a 12 pound turkey.

### Turkey Stuffing

½ cup butter
4 cups wet bread

Onion, celery, parsley, salt and pepper

Melt butter in skillet, fry the onion and celery to get flavor, then remove. Put the wet bread into the pan, mix well, add salt and pepper and chopped parsley. Fill turkey. Use stale bread, cover with cold water until moist, squeeze dry and use. Use no eggs. This stuffing may be used for hens, fish or any meats.

### Dry Stuffing for Turkey or Chicken

4 cups stale dry bread crumbs
¼ lb. butter
1 small onion sliced

2 stalks celery cut very fine
Pepper to taste

Melt butter, cook onion in butter until a golden brown. Remove onion, pour butter over bread crumbs, add celery, pepper and more salt if necessary. Fill turkey or hen with stuffing and roast as directed.

More butter may be used.

Egg bread crumbs may be mixed with the bread crumbs.

Mushrooms or boiled chestnuts may be added to stuffing.

### Mushroom Stuffing

Peel and wash fresh mushrooms. Broil in butter and make gravy by adding a little water, chop and add to stuffing, being careful not to lose a drop of the gravy. Add to any one of the recipes for stuffing.

A small quantity of mushrooms (about ¼ lb.) will season, more will be better. Canned mushrooms may be used, but they do not have the same flavor.

### Mushroom Stuffing for Turkey

One-half pound fresh mushrooms broiled, then stewed in 2 cups water for 15 minutes. Cut stale bread in slices, then in cubes, fry brown in half cup butter. Mix mushrooms and bread together, being careful not to break the cubes of bread. Fill turkey and roast as usual.

### Chestnut Stuffing

For stuffing with chestnuts, make the usual dressing. I prefer the dry crumbs with seasoning and moistened with butter. Peel chestnuts and re-move dark skin, boil in salt water until done, which will not require very long. Drain and add to dressing. Use whole or mash. Stuff turkey and roast as usual. To peel chestnuts, see Nuts.

## Corn Meal Stuffing

Make a rich egg bread (see recipe for Egg Bread), using more eggs. Let cool, crumble and pulverize crust well. Add melted butter, season with anything desired (see Turkey Stuffing). Fill hen or turkey and roast.

## Raisin Stuffing for Poultry

| | |
|---|---|
| 1 cup chopped apples | ½ teaspoon poultry seasoning |
| 2 cups soft bread crumbs | 1 cup seedless raisins |
| 1 teaspoon chopped onions | 2 tablespoons butter |
| 1 teaspoon salt | ¾ cup hot water |
| ⅛ teaspoon pepper | |

Mix apples, crumbs, onion, salt, salt, pepper, poultry seasoning and raisins. Melt butter in hot water and add. Mix thoroughly and use for stuffing goose, duck, turkey, chicken or roast of pork, or birds.

## Drop Dumplings

| | |
|---|---|
| 2 cups flour | 1 teaspoon salt |
| 4 teaspoons baking powder | |

Sift together and mix into a dough, using a cup of milk, more or less, as necessary. With a fork and spoon drop into a stew, meat or vegetable, pieces about as large as a walnut. Let boil rapidly 10 minutes, taking care not to uncover pot until dumplings are to be removed. Keeping pot covered causes them to be light and fluffy.

## SUGGESTIONS FOR COOKING GAME

The game laws of Georgia for some years have been such that unless you did the hunting, or owned a lodge or plantation, there was no game in store for you, for the choice game is not for sale at the present time.

Our common game are ducks, birds and rabbits, and they're plentiful in many sections, while venison and wild turkey are only for the favored few.

The venison, cooked according to the following instructions, is delicious. For the roast, soak in salt water for six hours, using one tablespoon of salt to enough water to cover. Dry, rub with butter, season with salt and pepper, place in roasting pan, add a sliced onion and one carrot. Place in a hot oven, add a little hot water and roast rapidly, basting frequently with the gravy. Five pounds will require 45 minutes of cooking. Kitchen bouquet, A-1 sauce or any sauces may be added to the gravy. Make gravy as any other gravy and add to it a glass of tart jelly. Keep everything piping hot. The roast may be cooked longer if a very done meat is preferred.

Venison steak should be broiled quickly in a piping hot pan or under a very hot fire. Do not have steak more than half or three-quarters of an inch thick. Turn often and cook 5 to 7 minutes. Place on hot platter and serve very hot.

Wild turkey is prepared and roasted exactly as our domestic ones, perhaps in a little less time. Give it plenty of time, however, for there is nothing quite so bad as a tough turkey. Stuffing or dry rice, with rich brown gravy, cranberries or tart jelly with celery would complete the meal for many.

Vegetables may be added.

Ducks and wild turkeys are stronger than our chickens and turkeys, and some like this, while others dislike the wild flavor.

Ducks usually weigh from three to six pounds. The young fowls may be identified by the wind pipe which is easily broken when pressed between the fingers. The breastbone is soft and almost transparent, and the under-bill will break easily.

A duck is prepared differently from chickens owing to the short legs. Draw the thighs close to the body and hold them by inserting a skewer under the middle joint through the body and under the joint on the other side, wind a string around each end of the skewer, first one side, then the other, to hold the thighs in place and close to the body. Do the wings the same way, running the skewer through wings and body.

Draw the neck skin under the back and secure with a third skewer. Season with salt and pepper, rub inside with one tablespoon of ground ginger and sprinkle with flour. Inside, place a small onion, a medium apple, and the duck is ready to go in the roaster. Ducks are usually quite fat, so a trivet in the roaster or pan is best to hold it up out of the grease.

Ducks, like our turkey, should be carefully prepared and roasted if you want them good. They may be stuffed or not, just as one wishes. Some use the same stuffing as for turkey, and some like a mashed Irish potato stuffing, highly seasoned with onions, tomato catsup, salt and pepper. Usually no stuffing is used, rice being served in place of stuffing. Brown rice and wild rice are particularly good with any kind of game.

It is generally believed that a covered roaster is preferable to an open pan for ducks. Allow 20 minutes per pound. Roast in a very hot oven for the first half hour. Reduce heat slightly for the next half hour and continue the roasting with a fairly hot oven, about 400 degrees. The apple and onion are removed before sending to the table, and so are the skewers and strings. Pour off fat from the roasting pan, leaving only a few spoonfuls to blend with the flour, making the gravy same as for turkey or chicken, using the minced giblets.

A glass of very tart jelly with a little mustard is often added to the gravy, using sufficient water to the flour and grease to make the required amount.

Birds may be broiled, fried or roasted. Broiling is the most popular way. My experience has been that the broiling must be done quickly, not over 10 or 15 minutes if you want them tender and juicy. Use a heavy iron fry pan, slightly greased.

Place the inside of bird next to the pan first. It is necessary to press the bird flat to prevent the legs from sticking up, thus ruining its looks when served.

To keep the legs from sticking up use a flat top slightly smaller than the skillet and a weight. I use an old flat iron as a weight and press down until the bird has gotten hot enough to hold the right shape. Leave space so the steam can escape, and the broiling begins. Turn and broil other side, keeping weight on for a moment, then remove top and weight and continue cooking for the given time. Have melted butter ready, salt and pepper when half done. Place on hot platter and serve very hot. Sometimes just the breast is broiled and put on heart-shaped toast. The breast resembles a heart very much and this is quite a pretty way to serve it. The joints may later be used in a pie.

Next comes "Br'er Rabbit" and he is common game in Georgia. When young and tender, rabbit may be fried like chicken. Rabbit stew is a real standby during the cold winter days.

The opossum is a rich food and it isn't every one who likes it, but when well prepared and roasted it is good, and used freely during the winter months not only for food but furnishing fine sport in the hunting.

### Roast Goose

Select a plump bird, pick and remove the pin feathers. Singe and draw, then wash well in warm water, using a vegetable brush to scrub the skin. Plunge into cold water until chilled. Now place the goose in a preserving kettle and add 1 fagot of soup herbs, and 2 onions. Sufficient boiling water to cover. Bring to a boil and cook for three-quarters of an hour. Remove and let cool. Place ½ cup of shortening in a large frying pan and add 1½ cups of finely chopped onions. Cook until soft and add 2 cups mashed potatoes, 1 cup fine bread crumbs, ½ cup finely chopped parsley, ½ cup finely chopped celery leaves, ½ cup finely chopped pimentos, the meat picked from the neck and giblets, chopped fine, also 1 teaspoon thyme, ¾ teaspoon sweet marjoram, ¼ teaspoon sage, ½ teaspoon poultry seasoning. Cook slowly, turning frequently for one-half hour. Cool and then fill the goose. Sew the opening with darning needle and stout string. Fasten the flap and neck, then rub the bird well with plenty of shortening. Dust thickly with flour. Place in a roasting pan in hot oven for 20 minutes, then commence to baste, using boiling water. Reduce the heat to moderate, turn the goose breast down and cook for two and one-half hours. About one-half hour before removing from the oven turn the bird on its back and let the breast brown nicely. Lift to a warm plate and garnish with baked apples. To make the gravy, drain nearly all the fat from the pan, add sufficient boiling water and cook for a few minutes.

### To Roast a Duck

Prepare duck as any fowl; rub with salt and pepper. Take two tablespoons of ground ginger and rub inside and out. Place on inside one small onion which has been cut across the top; into this stick four cloves. Melt ½ cup of butter, add 1 cup hot water, pour over duck and roast, basting often. When nearly done sprinkle with flour and baste often with the gravy. If more water is needed, add. Never have a great quantity at one time.

Ducks are not usually stuffed, but if so desired use a dressing the same as for turkey. Chestnuts may be added and are delicious. Mushrooms, fresh or canned, may be used. The gravy should be highly seasoned.

Oftentimes a portion of tart jelly is added to the gravy the last part of the cooking.

## Duck Salad

Cut the meat of a cold duck into cubes and season well with a French dressing. Let stand an hour. Drain well and mix with equal quantity of minced celery. Serve with portion of mayonnaise and garnish with slices of orange with the peeling left on.

Diced artichokes will take the place of celery. Scrape and dice small. Dill pickles may be used.

## Yorkshire Ducks

| | |
|---|---|
| ½ lb. lean pork | 1 cup soft bread crumbs |
| ½ lb. beef suet | ¼ cup water |
| 1 egg | Season with salt, pepper and sage |
| ½ lb. veal | |

Grind meat and suet. Mix bread crumbs and egg with water then blend into the meat; mix well and shape into 6 small loaves. Place in a dripping pan and bake 45 minutes.

Fat pork instead of suet may be used if preferred.

## To Cook Squabs

Dress and open down the back, same as a chicken; place in deep pan and cover with boiling water, adding enough apple vinegar to make real tart, boil about an hour or till tender, drain off water, (saving 2 cups), dot squabs with butter, add salt and pepper and sprinkle generously with flour, put in broiler near fire and brown on both sides well; now add the broth, put in oven and cook another hour slowly, adding more water if necessary, letting the gravy be dark and rich, having 2 cups when done. Put on hot platter and pour gravy over. Serve with dry rice. Mushrooms may be added the last hour, which makes a nice dish.

## Broiled Birds

Dress birds, open down the back. Flatten open with hands or some heavy implement. Have skillet hot and just slightly buttered to prevent birds sticking. Salt, pepper, place bird in, inside down. With a small top and heavy weight (a sad iron), press on bird to hold flat and keep so, this requires just long enough to get it heated and "set." Turn and repeat until well seared. Turn often to prevent burning. There must be sufficient opening around the edge of pan and top to allow the steam to escape.

After the searing is done the weight is removed, a bit of butter is added. Continue cooking and turning for 8 to 15 minutes. Place on hot dish, dot with butter or use melted. Into the skillet put a tiny bit of hot water to get up all of the browned juices, pour this gravy over the bird, garnish and serve.

Points of toast may be used.

## Smothered Rabbit

Select a young rabbit. Cut up and let stand in salt water for 30 minutes. Into a heavy skillet put 4 tablespoons of cooking oil or butter and have very hot. Season rabbit with salt and pepper, sprinkle slightly with flour. Brown pieces well on all sides; when brown add ½ cup of hot water; cover and continue to cook very slowly (about 1 hour); the pan may be set into the oven. Cook until tender and the water is all gone; put on platter. Add lump of butter to pan and brown; add ½ cup of hot water to make the brown gravy; pour over the rabbit and serve. If the meat is not tender, add a little more water and cook longer.

## To Fry Rabbit

Cut up and soak in salt water for 1 hour. Put salt and pepper into portion of flour, roll rabbit in the flour and fry as you would chicken, in plenty of hot fat.

## Barbecued Rabbit

Prepare and cook same as smothered rabbit. When tender add barbecue sauce, continue cooking until well seasoned and very tender.

## Rabbit Stew

Prepare, cut, and boil rabbit until tender. When about half done add butter, salt and pepper to season. Boil and blanch ½ pound of macaroni. Add to rabbit stew long enough to thoroughly season before serving. There should not be too much gravy.

## Alma's Recipe for 'Possum

Put ½ cup lime in about 1 gallon of boiling water and scald quickly, and pull off hair while hot. Scrape well—remove feet, tail and entrails— like you would a pig. Cut off ears, remove eyes and head if desired. Pour hot water over it and clean thoroughly.

Put 1 cup salt in sufficient cold water to cover "possum," add 1 pod red pepper and let stand over night. In the morning remove salt water and pour boiling water over it. Cook in enough boiling water to boil up over "possum" but not enough to cover. Cook until skin can be pierced with a fork easily, and let stand in water until ready for baking.

When ready to bake, place "possum" in pan with skin side up. Bake in a moderate oven until crisp and brown. If fire is too hot skin will blister and burn.

Carve "possum" and surround with potatoes (sliced or quartered) which have been previously baked.

## Georgia Barbecue

This recipe for barbecue and Brunswick stew was given me by a friend, who was an expert and made barbecues for his friends and neighbors, as well as himself.

First, select first-class meat, weighing from 35 to 50 pounds. Remove head near shoulders and feet just above the first joint. Cut or saw smoothly, longitudinally through the center of backbone so the pig will open perfectly flat. Cut out the thin flanks on each side of carcass in a circular cut and throw away. Now it is ready for the pit. Run sharpened iron rods (or oak sticks) longitudinally through hams and shoulders, allowing extensions of both sides to catch the banks of the pit. This makes it convenient to hold carcass up and furnishes hand holds to turn.

These rods should be inserted near the skin and under the ribs in order that the neck, shoulders and hams may go down lower into the pit for better cooking, and the rods under the ribs prevent their falling out when tender.

Laterally insert three or four small rods (iron or oak) which must be stuck through at proper intervals at sides extending through the carcass. This prevents meat from dropping off when done. The rods are strapped in place by using hay wire.

The pit is sixteen inches deep and as long as needed. Small green oak wood is best to use for making the red coals. The heat must not be too great when the cooking is first begun. When the meat is warm, baste with a strong solution of warm salt water containing a little cayenne pepper. This is continued at intervals until meat is nearly done. The moisture from the water prevents the meat from scorching. As often as the meat becomes dry, turn meat side up and baste with this salt solution. Never salt before cooking. About one quart of salt made into strong solution will be necessary for basting a 50 pound pig.

As the meat cooks, more heat may be applied. Keep the coals bunched under the shoulders and hams, allowing the thin part of the pig to have less heat. When meat is nearly done, baste two or three times with plain warm water. This drives the salt in and washes off the outside salt. Always use warm water, never cold. Place carcass over pit, meat side down and cook this way, only turning long enough to baste the inside and allowing the skin to become hot from time to time. Meat must not burn and should be watched carefully.

When nearly done, place skin side down and begin basting with the butter sauce. When done and very tender, remove some of the coals from pit, turn skin down to brown and crisp. At this time it should be watched closely. The skin should be brown and crisp, not gummy. During this last cooking the meat side is up and the basting done frequently.

The sauce, as well as the salt water, must be kept warm. Remember the cooking is slow and takes a long time, so it will require a good deal of salt water. Again let me say during the first cooking when the salt water is used the meat side is kept turned to the coals.

When ready to serve, cut up, putting skin in one pan, meat into another. Baste meat frequently with the butter sauce. Do not put any sauce over the skin, this will make skin soft and gummy. To be good it must be crisp and brittle.

## Barbecue Points

Make pit four feet wide, sixteen or eighteen inches deep and as long as necessary.

Use young small carcasses, which will require from seven hours or longer, according to size.

Do not salt until meat is warm, then baste with strong salt solution which is kept warm.

Keep meat side next to fire. Baste as often as meat looks dry.

Use iron rods to keep meat flat and able to turn when necessary.

Never keep skin side to the fire except to baste top.

One quart of strong salt water will be sufficient to salt about fifty pounds.

Each sauce recipe given will be sufficient for about fifty pounds of meat. More or less vinegar may be used.

Make a mop of cheese cloth on the end of long stick for the basting.

When ready to serve the meat is carved and chopped into pieces suitable to handle, put into pans where sauce and juice keep meat moist.

Cold slaw, pickles, onions, tomatoes, rye bread, white bread, and coffee all seem a part of a barbecue feast.

## Barbecue Sauce

2½ lbs. of butter
2 quarts of apple vinegar
1 pint of water
1 tablespoon dry mustard
½ cup minced onion
1 bottle of Worcestershire sauce
1 pint of tomato catsup

1 pint chili sauce (medium size)
2 lemons, juice only
½ lemon, put in whole (seed removed)
3 cloves of garlic chopped fine and tied in bag
2 teaspoons of sugar

Mix all together, cook to season well. With a mop baste meat. This is used when meat is about three-fourths done. The sauce must be kept warm. This is for a large quantity. It can be reduced to the quantity desired.

## Brunswick Stew No. 1

1 pig's head, feet, liver and heart
4 quarts of peeled, diced Irish potatoes
2 quarts of peeled and diced tomatoes
1 quart of finely cut okra
18 ears of finely cut corn (or two cans)
2 large onions, cut fine
4 garlic buttons, tied in a cheese cloth

1 tablespoon dry mustard
Juice of 1 lemon
½ lemon, put in whole, seed removed
1 bottle Worcestershire sauce
1 medium bottle chili sauce
1 pint bottle tomato catsup
½ lb. butter
Salt, black and red pepper to taste.
Sweet pepper, both green and red, may be used if desired.

Thoroughly clean pig's head and feet. From the head remove the teeth and gums, upper and lower. Place head, feet, liver and heart into boiling water and cook slowly until meat falls from the bones and will come to pieces. Remove from the liquor, remove all bone and any tough part, pull to pieces and mash or chop until fine. From the liquor remove scum and replace the meat. If not much liquor, add hot water. Add vegetables and seasoning; cook slowly and for several hours. If too thick, add hot water; if thin, add light bread crumbs, one large loaf.

When ready to serve, add half pound of butter. Stir almost constantly during the cooking. If it should stick or scorch, change the vessel, as any scorch will ruin the entire stew. Fresh vegetables are always preferable, canned ones may be used. Cut fine and fry the okra in a little grease. This prevents being slick. Brunswick stew must be served hot. Chili powder and chili peppers are good to use if obtainable.

Tasting when nearly done will help to get the seasoning just right. There should be enough liquor to cover the meat and vegetables to cook. The stew must be thick enough to eat with a fork when served. If bread crumbs are needed add near the end of cooking.

A wash pot of heavy iron should be used for cooking. Chicken, rabbit, squirrel or lamb may be used.

### Brunswick Stew No. 2

| | |
|---|---|
| 1 hen | 1 tablespoon Worcestershire sauce |
| 2 lbs. veal | 1 teaspoon tobasco sauce |
| 4 hard boiled eggs | 2 tablespoons salt |
| 1 lb. veal liver or liver lights and sweetbreads from one hog | 2 teaspoons white pepper |
| 1 can English peas | 1 can corn |
| 1 large onion | 1 can mushrooms |
| 2 cans tomatoes | 1 cup butterbeans |
| 1 bottle tomato catsup | 1 cup cut okra |
| | 2 lbs. butter |

Put chicken and other meats on to boil in three pints of water, cook until meat will be very tender. Remove bones, pull to pieces and return to the liquid.

Add tomatoes, okra, onions and seasonings. Cook slowly and thoroughly, stir often.

Fifteen minutes before serving add English peas, mushrooms, butter and diced hard-boiled eggs. One cup of diced olives is liked by many, these to be added the last minute.

For a large 'cue use six times this recipe.

This is a famous Macon recipe and I do not believe a better one can be found anywhere.

### Family Brunswick Stew

| | |
|---|---|
| 1 fowl | 1 pint butterbeans |
| 1 quart of corn | 2 onions |
| 1 quart of tomatoes | Salt and pepper to taste |
| 1 pint okra | |

Boil chicken until it will leave the bones and be very tender. Pull meat from bones and cut into large cubes, return to the water in which it was cooked, add vegetables and cook down until a thick mixture. Cook slowly and stir often to prevent scorching.

Fresh vegetables are best, but the canned may be used. Any vegetables liked may be added.

## Barbecue Sauces

Also see Sauces for Meats.

### American Chop Suey

2 cups of sliced and chopped onions
2 cups chopped celery
2 cups diced pork or chicken
½ cup mushrooms (fresh preferred)

2 tablespoons soy bean sauce
4 tablespoons cooking oil
Salt and pepper to taste

Put oil into skillet and fry vegetables; add meat. Cook until meat is very tender and the whole is a thick sauce. If fresh mushrooms are used, dice and broil in butter and add when meat is added. Canned ones may be put in without any previous cooking, adding at time of meat. Cook slowly. Serve with dry rice.

### Glorified Wieners

1 cup tomato catsup
1 cup boiling water
1 tablespoon sugar
1 tablespoon vinegar
3 tablespoons diced onion

1 tablespoon prepared mustard
½ teaspoon salt
⅛ teaspoon pepper
1 teaspoon curry powder (if desired)
½ lb. (or more) weiners

Mix catsup, water and vinegar. Add sugar, mustard, salt, pepper, curry powder and diced onion. Simmer for 20 to 30 minutes. Add wieners and simmer 15 minutes longer. Remove wieners, place on platter, pour sauce over wieners, and serve with corn muffins or Irish potato cakes.

### Mexican Chili

Wash, split and remove seed from one dozen chili peppers and put through a food chopper. Add one pint thick strained tomatoes, one large onion minced fine, salt to taste, simmer for thirty minutes.

Have ready two cups of diced cold meat, chicken or beef; place in a saucepan, pour over the chili sauce, keep hot for thirty minutes to allow the seasoning to strike through. Serve with rice.

### Hot Tamales

Boil a chicken in just enough water to cover until very tender. Salt while cooking. When done pull from bones and chop fine or grind. Open one dozen chili peppers, remove seed, cover with boiling water, cook until very tender and soft. Put through sieve to remove skin.

Into a frying pan put three tablespoons of cooking oil or butter. Add two medium onions chopped fine, cook until brown, add chili pulp, add half cup of the chicken water, simmer for twenty minutes, keep covered.

Into a bowl put one quart of corn meal, pour over sufficient water in which chicken was boiled to make a stiff dough. Mix well, add salt, if necessary.

Have ready corn husks, large ones, washed and trimmed, and dipped in hot water to make soft. Mix with the chicken the chili paste.

On a broad husk place a portion of the corn meal, making a kind of layer. In the center, the entire length, put a portion of the chicken, roll up the husks, the meal should entirely cover the meat; fold over the ends of husk, tie up well.

Continue until all are made. Return the bones of chicken to the remaining chicken water; place tamales in and boil one hour. Cover while cooking; serve hot. Beef or veal may be used. Red peppers cooked and sufficient hot pepper to season may be used if the chili cannot be obtained.

## FISH AND SHELLFISH

### To Prepare Fish for Broiling

Scale, wash and open down the front to remove inside; using scissors for cutting. Remove inside and wash well. With a stiff, small knife make a half inch cut through the ribs close to the backbone on each side from head to tail. Turn head towards you and with the fingers press meat from the bones. Free the end of backbone at head and pull; the entire bone will then come out easily.

With palm of the hand mash and flatten out the thick, meaty part at center of the back.

Wipe with damp cloth to remove any blood.

With a stiff paring knife pull out the long ribs. Place point of knife about center of rib and give a good pull (in the same way as removing bastings.) Repeat until all the large bones are removed. Cut out the patch of bones which holds each fin.

To open and bone a fish requires about ten minutes.

Any fish may be boned. Shad, trout, Spanish mackerel are very easily boned.

### To Broil a Fish

Have broiler piping hot, also broiling pan to prevent fish sticking. Place fish on pan skin side down, run pan under blaze or heat element leaving just space enough to prevent the blaze (gas broiler) from touching the fish. While fish is heating prepare melted butter for basting. Draw pan out, sprinkle with salt and pepper, baste with butter, and return to broiler. Repeat the basting several times during the cooking. When sufficiently done and browned, place on hot platter. Again baste with melted butter and squeeze over it the juice of half a lemon.

It requires about 12 to 20 minutes to broil a large fish. It is never turned when broiled in the oven.

If lemon juice is used during the cooking it is apt to catch fire.

Broiling must be done with an intense heat, and quickly, if it is to be the best. Have broiler hot with burners going full during the entire broiling.

If a little dry flour is sprinkled on the skin of the fish before placing on the pan, this will also prevent sticking.

## To Plank a Shad

Prepare fish the same as broiling. Have plank very hot; also oven; butter plank; place skin side down; baste with melted butter, salt, pepper and place plank on broiling pan to gas stove; put in broiling oven very near the fire; while broiling, baste several times; when well brown, lower pan to cook thoroughly. Let the door of broiler be open while broiling. From 15 to 20 minutes are required to cook fish.

That part of the plank left uncovered by the fish cover with damp salt. This prevents the plank scorching; when done brush salt off and cover with cooked veketables—any kind you might wish. Pipe mashed hot potatoes on the edge—this gives a pretty border, and holds in place the other vegetables. Use a heavy cloth bag, and large star end pastry tube. Potatoes and other vegetables must be seasoned before using on plank.

Put lemon juice over fish after removing from fire for juice sometimes causes popping, and is apt to catch on fire.

Potatoes, green peas, yellow squash, beets, and stuffed or broiled tomatoes decorate a plank prettily. The many colors add to the looks. Every vegetable MUST be kept hot, and cooked in the usual way before putting on plank. Place plank on platter to serve. Keep broiler door open while broiling. From 15 to 20 minutes will be required to broil a fish of medium size.

## To Boil Fish

Prepare for cooking, leaving it in one whole piece. Place on a kitchen plate of porcelain, tie the plate and fish both in a piece of cheesecloth and place in a pan of boiling water which has a slice or two of lemon or a portion of vinegar, salt and slice of onion if liked. Have boiling water to cover well, cook fifteen minutes to the pound and allow an extra ten minutes for the heating of plate.

When ready, lift out, drain and serve very hot with any dressing liked—cooked mayonnaise or white sauce with lots of parsley.

## To Cream Fish

Proceed as for boiling. When done, remove skin and bones and flake it with a fork.

Use two cups of fish and one of medium white sauce and mix until creamy and smooth, using more or less sauce to suit your taste. Put into a buttered baking dish, cover top with buttered crumbs, bake until well heated and brown on top. Season with any special liking. The butter and milk goes into the making of the white sauce. Garnish with potato roses, radishes or parsley.

## Baked Fish

Select the desired size fish, dress, leaving the head on. Open down the front from head to tail, cut half inch deep on each side of backbone and remove the bone. Open the fish and season with salt and pepper. Fill with a stuffing made same as for turkey or chicken. Sew fish up with a few stitches of coarse thread leaving the string so it can be pulled out when done.

Rub over with butter or drippings and place into a baking pan, sprinkle with flour and put into a very hot oven for five or ten minutes.

Reduce the heat, add half cup of hot water to baste with. Cook fifteen minutes to the pound and have the skin well browned, basting occasionally. When done place on platter. To serve, cut entirely through the fish, giving a portion of fish and dressing.

Rich sauce or gravy may be made from the drippings and removed bone, seasoned highly with vinegar, mustard, catsup and sauces, and served over each portion.

If the fish is baked on a pyrex platter, no moving is required. A small flat tin in the baking pan aids in getting the fish on the platter without breaking.

The eyes should be removed and when done fill place with a small radish or cranberry.

When baking a whole fish the head and tail add greatly to the looks if left on. The head is filled with the stuffing, as well as the body. Take several stitches with coarse needle and thread in the fish to hold it together.

### Stuffing for Baked Fish

½ cup butter                     Onion, celery, parsley, salt and
4 cups wet bread           pepper

Melt butter in skillet, fry the onion and celery to get flavor, then remove. Put the wet bread into the pan, mix well, add salt and pepper and chopped parsley. Fill fish. Use stale bread, cover with cold water until moist, squeeze dry and use. Use no eggs.

### Fish Timbales

2 lbs. red snapper steak       1 cup white sauce
3 eggs                           1 teaspoon salt
½ teaspoon paprika          1 teaspoon grated rind of lemon

Boil fish, remove bone and skin and flake fine; add white sauce and seasoning and mix well; let cool; beat eggs and add to fish which will be a soft mixture, put into well buttered mold (or individual ones). Put several thicknesses of paper into a roasting pan and fill half full of water which is boiling; place molds in the pan of water and bake in a moderate oven 20 or 30 minutes or till firm in the center. Turn out and serve with Hollandaise sauce or a white sauce with nuts; this makes a beautiful mold.

Fish may be molded in a round ring, putting diced potatoes, carrots, turnips or green peas in the center. The mold must be buttered with soft butter (not melted), so it will turn out easily.

### Roe Timbales

2 cups roe boiled and broken fine     Salt and pepper to taste
½ cup dried bread crumbs          Enough sweet milk to make real
1 tablespoon chopped parsley       moist
2 eggs, beaten together (or 3 yolks)

Butter timbale molds; fill ¾ full with mixture, stand in pan of hot water and steam thirty minutes. Turn onto hot platter and serve with cream sauce or tomato sauce. Garnish dish with parsley.

## Fish Mold

| | |
|---|---|
| 2 cups flaked fish | 3 eggs |
| 1 cup white sauce | Salt and pepper to taste |

Tie fish in a piece of cheesecloth and boil in water in which there are several slices of lemon. When done remove skin and bones and flake fine. Make white sauce and add, stirring until smooth and well mixed. Beat eggs together until light, add to mixture. Pour into well-buttered mold, place in pan, surrounded with boiling water, put into moderate oven, cover with oiled paper and cook until firm. Serve with a tomato or shrimp sauce. There are molds in the shape of a fish which make a very effective dish.

## Salmon Fritters

| | |
|---|---|
| 2 cups flaked salmon | 1½ teaspoons baking powder |
| 1 teaspoon vinegar | 1 egg |
| 1 teaspoon mayonnaise | 1¼ teaspoons salt |
| 1 cup flour | 2/3 cup milk |

Make a batter of the beaten egg, milk and flour sifted with salt and baking powder, mixing them in the order given. Mix salmon, from which all bones have been removed, with vinegar and mayonnaise and combine with the batter. Drop by spoonful into a pan of deep hot fat and fry until a golden brown. Serve with a cream caper sauce.

## Oyster Stew No. 1

| | |
|---|---|
| 1 quart oysters | Salt and pepper to taste |
| 1 quart sweet milk | |

Remove any shell from oysters, melt butter and add to the milk and heat, never letting it boil. When hot add oysters and keep just below the boiling point until oysters are done. Add salt and papper last and serve quickly or they will be overdone. Allowance should be made for extra cooking after they are taken from the fire if a large quantity is prepared. The oyster should be steamed until the gills curl or the oyster becomes what is called plumped. Too much cooking makes them small and tough.

## Oyster Stew No. 2

| | |
|---|---|
| 1 quart milk | 3 tablespoons crushed crackers |
| 1 pint oysters | Salt and pepper to taste |
| 3 tablespoons butter | |

Put milk in double boiler to heat, add crushed crackers.
Into a sauce pan melt butter, drain oysters, and add liquor, if any, to milk. Pour oysters into butter and cook, stirring constantly until as done as desired (not over cooked). Add salt and pepper and pour the mixture into the hot milk. Allow for a little more cooking of oysters in the hot milk. Serve at once.

### Fried Oysters

Select large oysters, drain and remove any pieces of shell. Have a pan of flour seasoned with pepper and salt. Have cracker crumbs and eggs in which to roll them. To each egg add one tablespoon of cold water, using the whole egg, beat just enough to break and mix with the water. Dip oysters in flour to coat well, then into the egg, then crumbs. Keep the oysters spread out while dipping them, to allow the egg and crumbs to harden slightly, then they fry better and take up less grease. Fry in deep fat. For small quantities (a quart), I prefer a deep saucepan, and cook them like doughnuts, using a slit spoon or flat egg-beater to remove them. Do not cook too many at one time, they will chill the grease. Cracker crumbs do not absorb the grease as much as bread crumbs. Post Toasties make a nice covering. If oysters are small, lap two together after they have been rolled in the flour, then proceed just the same.

### Creamed Oysters

| | |
|---|---|
| 1 quart of oysters | Grated rind of lemon |
| 1 cup of thick white sauce | Salt and cayenne pepper to taste |

When making white sauce for creamed oysters, make it very thick by putting in more flour, about twice as much as for other things.

Plump oysters by warming them until gills are slightly curled. Pour into a colander and drain, saving the liquor. Mix with the white sauce place over hot water and steam until oysters are done, add as much of the liquor as needed if too stiff. The mixture should be thick enough to stay on a fork. The oysters in cooking usually send out more liquor to make the mixture just the right consistency.

### Scalloped Oysters

| | |
|---|---|
| 1 quart select oysters | ½ cup of buttered bread crumbs |
| 2 cups of oysterette crackers | 3 tablespoons of butter |
| 1 egg | Salt and pepper to taste |
| ½ cup sweet milk | |

Remove any pieces of shell from oysters, warm, but do not cook, drain in colander. In a baking pan, from which they are to be served, put a layer of oysters, salt, pepper and bits of butter, then a layer of crushed crackers (having them not too fine). Continue until all are used, having oysters on the top. Break egg into the milk and mix well. Pour over the dish of oysters and let it go into the mixture. Cover top with the buttered crumbs, bake in a moderate oven about 30 minutes or until the oysters and egg are cooked. Serve at once if you want them to be at their best.

### Broiled Oysters

Select large oysters, remove any shell, drain and dip in flour to which has been added salt and pepper. Into a skillet place a small quantity of butter, have hot, put oysters in, broiling quickly on one side, turn and brown other side. Have as many slices as needed of hot buttered toast, put oysters on toast and serve at once. Cook just long enough to brown the flour.

### Pickled Oysters

| | |
|---|---|
| 1 quart large oysters | 1 dozen whole allspice |
| 1 cup of apple vinegar | 1 teaspoon salt |
| 1 dozen whole cloves | 1 pinch cayenne pepper |

Put oysters on to warm. When tepid, drain well. Put oysters and seasonings and vinegar together and heat until the oysters are done. Set aside to get cold. Serve as a salad on lettuce with mayonnaise.

### Oyster Pie

| | |
|---|---|
| 1 quart large oysters | 3 cups of flour, made into a rich pas- |
| 4 hard-boiled eggs | try, the same as for chicken pie |
| 1 cup of top milk | Salt and pepper |
| 4 tablespoons butter | |

Make as you would a chicken pie, putting a layer of oysters, sliced egg, pastry, seasoning, until all is used. Put a pastry over the top, making a good cut in top to let the steam out.

Cook in a moderate oven about 30 to 40 minutes, or until the pastry is brown.

### Oysters in the Shell

Scrub shells well, place in a baking pan and put into a hot oven and let stay until they open. Remove the upper shell, season with salt and pepper on each oyster. Place shells on hot plate. Serve piping hot with piece of lemon and crackers.

### Minced Oysters No. 1

| | |
|---|---|
| 1 pint of oysters | A slice of green pepper, onion and |
| 1 cup milk | carrot |
| 2 tablespoons of butter | A stalk of celery |
| 4 tablespoons of flour | ½ cup of toasted bread crumbs |
| Salt and pepper to taste | 2 egg yolks |
| Rind of lemon grated | |

Heat oysters until they curl slightly. Drain and chop.

Melt butter in a frying pan and cook the vegetables until brown. Remove and put in the flour and brown, being careful not to burn. Add the milk which is warm and make a thick sauce. Remove from the fire and cool slightly. Add oysters, seasoning and crumbs, when well mixed, add beaten eggs; put into shells, individual dishes, or one large dish, cover top with buttered crumbs, and cook just long enough to cook the egg and get very hot.

Serve immediately. If the mixture should be too stiff after getting together use a little of the drained oyster liquor. Any kind of seasonings liked may be used in place of those mentioned. A rich brown sauce is better than a white one, thus the brown sauce is given. The white could be used if preferred. This will serve five.

### Minced Oysters No. 2

| | |
|---|---|
| 1 quart oysters | 4 tablespoons butter |
| 3 eggs | 1 cup buttered bread crumbs |
| 1 teaspoon grated onion | Salt and cayenne pepper to taste |
| 1 cup stale bread crumbs | Pinch each of allspice and nutmeg |

Warm oysters in their own liquor; drain and chop fine; add seasoning. Beat eggs together until light and add to the mixture; add crumbs; heat until hot, adding in a portion of the liquor needed. Fill ramekins, shells or baking dish; cover with buttered crumbs and bake in moderate oven just long enough to brown and cook the eggs. Serve very hot.

### Oysters With Spaghetti a la Maude

| | |
|---|---|
| 1 quart oysters | 1 cup stewed tomatoes or can of soup |
| ½ lb. spaghetti | 1 cup buttered crumbs |
| 1 cup white sauce | Salt and pepper to taste |

Cook spaghetti in boiling salt water until done. Drain and blanch. Warm oysters slightly. Into a baking dish put a layer of spaghetti, a layer of oysters, salt and pepper. Repeat until all material is used. Over all pour the cup of white sauce, then the tomato sauce. Cover the top with crumbs and bake in moderate oven just long enough to cook oysters and brown top. Serve.
A delightful luncheon dish.

### Oyster Filling for Patties and Timbales

| | |
|---|---|
| 1 quart oysters (select preferred) | ½ teaspoon grated rind of lemon |
| 1 set of beef brains | Salt and pepper to taste |
| 1 pint cream sauce | |

Clean and boil the brains and blanch them in cold water to make them firm. Cut into small pieces about as large as the end of thumb, using scissors.

Put the oysters over a gentle fire and heat until tepid in their own liquor. When warm, drain off the water which the heating causes to form.

Chop the oysters slightly, add the brains. Make a very thick white sauce using two heaping tablespoons of flour to each cup of milk, and two tablespoons of butter. Into the hot sauce put the oysters and brains.

Put the sauce pan holding the mixture over boiling water, add seasoning and cook until oysters are done.

The cooking will cause more water to be thrown out and thus thins the mixtures to the right consistency.

This will fill about a dozen good sized timbales.

### Oyster Fritters No. 1

| | |
|---|---|
| 1 pint oysters | 1 teaspoon salt |
| 1 egg | 1 tablespoon butter |
| 1½ cups flour | Pepper |
| 2 teaspoons baking powder | |

Drain and chop oysters. Add seasoning and flour, using liquor if needed.

Beat egg white stiff, add yolk, then fold into oyster mixture. Drop small portions of mixture from end of spoon into deep, hot fat. Fry until done. Drain on paper and serve hot.

### Oyster Fritters No. 2

| | |
|---|---|
| 25 oysters (or 1 cup) | 1 teaspoon paprika |
| 2 cups flour | 2 tablespoons chopped parsley |
| 2 teaspoons of baking powder | 1 tablespoon grated onion |
| 1 teaspoon salt | 1 egg |

Chop oysters; mix batter; mix all together; drop a spoonful into deep, hot fat and fry until brown; drain on paper and serve hot.

### Deviled Oysters No. 1

| | |
|---|---|
| 1 pint oysters | 1 teaspoon grated onion |
| 2 egg yolks | ½ teaspoon grated lemon rind |
| 1 cup bread crumbs | Pinch of spice |
| 1 teaspoon minced parsley | Salt and pepper to taste |

Pick over the oysters to remove any pieces of shell. Put oysters into a sauce pan and heat slightly. Drain well and chop oysters. Add crumbs, seasoning and egg yolks. If too stiff add a portion of the liquor drained off. Mix well; fill shells; cover top with buttered crumbs, and bake in hot oven until browned. Serve hot.

Oyster shells, scalloped shells or ramekins may be used.

A large baking dish may be used, covering the top with crumbs and baking until thoroughly done and brown.

### Deviled Oysters No. 2

| | |
|---|---|
| 1 cup oysters | 2 tablespoons milk |
| ½ cup cold chicken | 2 egg yolks |
| 4 medium mushrooms (fresh) broiled then chopped | Pinch of spice |
| 1 teaspoon grated onion | Salt and pepper to taste |

Chop oysters, chicken and mushrooms fine; put into a sauce pan and heat. Add milk and egg yolks beaten together; add seasoning and cook over gentle heat until quite thick. Remove from fire and let get cool and firm. When cold make into rolls as large as your finger and about two inches long. Wrap each roll in very thin slices of bacon, folding and closing ends as well as possible. Dip these in batter and fry in deep fat until brown. Drain and serve very hot.

### Oyster Salad No. 1

| | |
|---|---|
| 3 cups cold diced potatoes | 3 slices of bacon fried crisp and chipped |
| 3 cups plumped and chilled oysters | |
| 1 tablespoon onion minced fine | Salt and pepper to taste |

Get ready all ingredients and have cold, when ready to serve, mix well with 1 cup French dressing. Serve at once.

## Oyster Salad No. 2

Parboil, drain and wipe dry 1 quart oysters.

Marinate with French dressing— first the oil, then the vinegar or lemon juice, salt and pepper. Chill; mix with one-third of the bulk of finely chopped celery (or shredded cabbage). Serve on lettuce, and place small pickles, or stuffed olives, or slices of pickles around the portion of salad.

# SAUCES FOR MEATS AND VEGETABLES
## White Sauce

1 cup milk                          4 to 6 tablespoons of flour
2 to 4 tablespoons butter

Melt butter without browning, add flour and cook until it blends and bubbles well. Heat milk, remove butter and flour from fire, pour in the hot milk all at once and quickly stir well until mixed and thick. Return to fire if not thick enough, and cook until it thickens.

### A Brown Nut Sauce

2 cups stock or sweet milk          1 carrot
1 cup chopped pecans                2 slices green pepper
4 tablespoons butter                1 stalk of celery
8 tablespoons flour                 1 slice of onion.
Salt and pepper

Put butter into a sauce pan and cut the vegetables in small slices and cook, but do not let the butter burn. When done remove. Add the flour and brown well. Add the stock which should be hot, and let thicken. Add salt and pepper to taste and serve over rice croquettes.

### Tomato Sauce

2 tablespoons butter                1 tablespoon sugar
2 tablespoons flour                 ½ teaspoon allspice
1 cup canned tomatoes               A goood pinch cloves
Salt and pepper to taste

Make same as white sauce, use the cup of tomatoes for the liquid; add seasoning and serve. The tomatoes may be strained if desired. This is good over baked fish, rice or macaroni and cheese.

### Mushroom Sauce

½ pound mushrooms (or 1 can)        ½ teaspoon salt
4 tablespoons butter                1 cup sweet cream or top milk
4 tablespoons flour

Peel and slice mushrooms and broil in the butter, sift in the flour and brown slightly, add cream or milk, cook until it thickens. Pour over broiled steak or chicken.

## Horseradish Sauce

1 cup whipped cream
½ teaspoon salt
1 teaspoon paprika

2 tablespoons grated horseradish
1 tablespoon lemon juice

Mix well and serve as any dressing.

## Shrimp Sauce

1 cup chopped shrimp
1 cup of sauce made with hot water
instead of milk

2 tablespoons of lemon juice
Salt and cayenne pepper to taste

To make the sauce use either hot water or a cup of the water in which the fish was boiled. Blend butter and flour together, add the water. Cook until thick and smooth. Add seasoning and a little red coloring, serve over the fish. Garnish with parsley.

Two yolks of eggs and half a cup of thin cream or top milk may be added to sauce if a richer and yellow sauce is desired. Cook over hot water after adding to sauce until thick like custard.

## Sour Cream Dressing

1 cup sour cream
2 tablespoons vinegar
1 tablespoon sugar

1 teaspoon salt
1 teaspoon mustard (French)
1 teaspoon paprika

Whip cream about half, mix all other ingredients together, add slowly to cream and continue whipping until stiff enough to stand. Serve over sliced tomatoes.

## A Quick Hollandaise Sauce

1 cup vinegar (more or less according to acid)
1 cup water
¼ cup oil or butter
1/3 cup flour

Yolks of 4 eggs
1 teaspoon salt
1/8 teaspoon cayenne pepper
1 teaspoon mustard and slice of onion if desired.

Put vinegar, water, oil, salt, pepper and slice of onion together in a sauce pan and bring to a boil. Mix the flour to a paste and mix free of lumps. Add the unbeaten yolks, mix well. Have this mixture thin enough to strain to remove any lump.

Into the flour mixture pour a half cup of the hot mixture carefully to warm; remove the sauce pan from the fire and pour the flour mixture into it hot, stirring constantly.

It should begin to thicken at once. When all is in, return to a very gentle fire and stir constantly until thick and smooth. Never let the mixture boil (it will surely curdle). Keep below the boiling point until thick.

Remove the slice of onion before pouring in the flour mixture.

Use lemon juice if preferred, about one-fourth cup, adding water to make the required amount of liquid. The mustard should be added to the flour. Use a double boiler unless you are very careful.

## Hollandaise Sauce

½ cup butter (divide in 3 parts)   1/3 cup boiling water
2 egg yolks                        Season with salt and pepper
1 tablespoon lemon juice

Have butter soft. To first part add eggs and lemon juice and cook over hot water. When it begins to thicken, add the second part of butter and then the third, stirring constantly until thick. Cool and add cream.

When cold, add heaping tablespoon whipped cream. Some like grated horseradish, 3 tablespoons.

## Never Fail Hollandaise

2 egg yolks             ½ cup melted butter
½ teaspoon salt         1 tablespoon lemon juice
  Speck of cayenne pepper

Beat egg yolks thick, add salt, cayenne, and 3 tablespoons of melted butter, a drop at a time, beating it in. Beat in the rest of the butter and the lemon juice alternately. You can store it in the refrigerator and reheat it over warm water when it is needed, stirring constantly.

## Seasonings—Lemon Peel

When the flavor of lemon peel is wanted, peel off long strips of the rind, using just the yellow part, put into the boiling mixture. When sufficiently seasoned, remove.

Lemon peel grated, just the yellow rind, is delicious for fish and all sea foods, in sauces or stuffings.

## Vinagrette Sauce

Vinagrette sauce is only a thin French dressing with the following condiments added: Paprika, green pepper, parsley, onion, chopped pickles, putting in as much as desired.

## Butter Sauce No. 1

1 cup butter creamed until soft    ½ teaspoon paprika
2 tablespoons Worcestershire sauce  Cayenne pepper to taste
½ teaspoon salt

Add all seasonings together and beat into soft butter.

## Butter Sauce No. 2

2 tablespoons butter    1 cup boiling water
4 tablespoons flour     ½ lb. butter which has been creamed

Make butter, flour and water into a paste as white sauce. Remove from fire, let cool slightly, add soft butter slowly in small portions. If it should become oily add a tablespoon of cold water, mix and continue adding butter until all of it is in.

To be served with fish or steak.

## Butter Sauce No. 3

4 tablespoons creamed butter
1 teaspoon each chopped olives, tarragon vinegar, lemon juice

Pinch of mustard, a bit of salt and cayenne pepper
A few drops of onion juice

Mix all together, pack in small round mold until firm—slice and serve over fish or steak.

## Velvet Sauce

2 tablespoons butter
2 tablespoons flour
2 egg yolks
Juice of ½ lemon

½ cup hot water
1 tablespoon chopped parsley
Salt and pepper to taste

Blend butter and flour together, add water, lemon and seasoning: let cook slowly for 10 minutes. Remove from fire and pour over the well beaten eggs, add parsley and serve immediately over the fish or steak.

## Olive Sauce

3 tablespoons butter
3 tablespoons flour
Salt and pepper to taste

2 cups stock (or water using bouillon cubes)

Melt butter, add flour and brown slightly. Add stock and seasoning and cook until smooth. Then add:

4 tablespoons chopped olives
2 tablespoons chopped green peppers
2 tablespoons chopped pimentoes

4 tablespoons chopped celery
2 tablespoons tomato catsup
1 tablespoon Worcestershire sauce

Serve over lamb, pork or any other meat.

## Raisin Sauce

Make the same as Olive Sauce for the first part; then add

1 cup raisins
½ cup chopped nut meats

2 tablespoons sweet spiced vinegar from pickles

Serve over roast lamb or pork.

## Jelly Sauce

Melt a tumbler of tart jelly, add ½ teaspoon Worcestershire sauce and season with salt and pepper. Serve with chops.

The jelly may be added to half a cup of thin brown sauce.

## Mrs. H's Jelly Sauce

1 glass tart jelly
½ teaspoon dry mustard

½ cup cream

Melt jelly, mix and add mustard. Let cool thoroughly then add cream, more or less, to give a pink color.

Serve with baked ham or any other meat.

### Mint Sauce

| | |
|---|---|
| 1 cup mint leaves | 2 teaspoons sugar |
| ½ cup vinegar, more or less | ½ teaspoon salt |
| ½ cup hot water | ⅛ teaspoon pepper |

Strip leaves from stems of mint, chop fine, pour over them the hot water, cover until cold, add seasoning and vinegar. Serve from a bowl with lamb, hot or cold.

### Raisin Sauce for Hot Baked Ham

| | |
|---|---|
| ½ cup brown sugar | 4 tablespoons vinegar |
| 2 tablespoons sifted flour | ½ cup raisins |
| ½ teaspoon dry mustard | 1½ cups hot water |

Add all ingredients to hot water and cook over low heat until slightly thick and well blended. Serve over hot sliced baked ham. (Sweet spiced vinegar from pickles may be used, or half spiced vinegar and half plain vinegar.)

### Apple Butter Sauce

| | |
|---|---|
| ½ cup apple butter | 2 tablespoons freshly grated horse- |
| ¼ cup hot water (more or less) | radish |

Mix all together and serve with meats.

### Barbecue Sauce No. 1

| | |
|---|---|
| 1 quart vinegar | 1 bottle prepared mustard |
| 1 bottle catsup | 2 lemons |
| 1 bottle Worcestershire sauce | ¼ lb. butter |

Black and red pepper and salt to taste. Baste meat with sauce until done. This makes a large quantity, and for family use, one fourth.

This may be used over lamb, chicken or pork.

### Barbecue Sauce No. 2

| | |
|---|---|
| 1/3 cup each vinegar, catsup and Wor- | ⅛ teaspoon cayenne |
| cestershire sauce | 2 teaspoons mustard |
| 1 cup water | 1 teaspoon salt |

Mix all together and baste meat.

## CROQUETTES

Croquettes are both delicious and economical. Leftover meat and many leftover vegetables furnish material for this dainty dish.

Sometimes croquettes are shunned on account of being fried, but when properly crumbed, rolled in beaten egg and crumbed again, there is little, if any chance for them to be greasy when properly fried in deep hot grease. If they were fried in shallow grease they would probably be very greasy and indigestible, but when they are immersed in hot deep fat and entirely covered they cook on all sides and take up little grease. It is quite true a good deal of grease is required to completely cover but this is the only correct way to fry croquettes, and the grease may be used again and again for the frying of various other products.

When frying a large quantity, a kettle and a frying basket are quite essential, but for a small quantity, say one or two dozen, a small saucepan, four or five inches deep and seven or eight inches wide, may be used very successfully. A flat egg whip is used as a basket for the putting in and removing of the croquette, and by being careful, there will be no splashing of grease. Have the grease about two inches deep or sufficiently deep to entirely cover the croquettes when dropped in. The grease will rise when the croquettes are in, so there should be enough room in the pan to allow the grease to boil up without running over.

Two or three croquettes at a time will not chill the grease. It requires about one minute to brown them. Shortening or cooking oil is preferable for frying (drippings of various kinds might give some disagreeable flavor).

If not using a frying thermometer, heat grease until a cube of bread will brown in forty counts. Do not have grease smoking hot.

When finished drain grease, fry a few slices of Irish potatoes and save to use again for any frying purposes.

White sauce plays an important part in making croquettes as it is used for mixing and binding them. Eggs have a tendency to make them tough and stiff when cooked. The white sauce may be made thick or thin according to the material used. Two cups of ground meat, veal or chicken, will require one or more cups of white sauce. Make the mixture soft and creamy, let cool so the croquettes can be shaped, then crumb when ready to fry.

After shaping, roll in crumbs, then beaten egg, then crumbs again. Use the entire egg with one tablespoon of cold water to each egg. Mix together without much frothing. Too much beating will cause bubbles which break and leave holes for the grease to enter. One egg and one tablespoon of water will coat about one dozen croquettes of medium size. The white of the egg may be used with the water, without the yolk, but the yolk and water would not be good because this makes a soft coating. It is the white of the egg that seals up the outer side of the croquette. The crumbing and egging will make them even more firm if allowed to stand a half hour for the coating to dry.

After frying, drain on a paper napkin. If croquettes are fried too slowly or too long they will burst, thus allowing the inside to come out or lose the pretty shape.

Keep hot until served. To reheat put in hot oven long enough to heat. Croquettes are round, long or pear-shaped. When the latter shape put a whole clove in the small end to represent the stem of the pear.

### Brain Croquettes

| | |
|---|---|
| 2 sets of beef brains | ⅛ teaspoon cayenne pepper, or black |
| 1 cup thick white sauce (or more) | pepper |
| 1 teaspoon salt | Grated rind of lemon |

Put brains in strong salt water for one hour. This will cause the membrane to be removed easily and will also draw the blood out, leaving them white; every particle of the skin or membrane should be removed. Boil in water 15 or 20 minutes or until done. Drain well and mash, adding the white sauce and other ingredients. Place on platter to cool and get firm. When ready to fry make into balls, crumb, egg and crumb again. Fry in deep fat.

This mixture will be soft and it is better to make it into balls because they shape better and the crumbing and egg hold them so. If too soft to handle, add a few bread crumbs to stiffen, but care should be taken to keep them soft so they will be good. Parsley and Worcestershire sauce make a good seasoning as well as the lemon. Most croquettes are better when made without eggs in the mixture.

Eggs cause them to be tough and hard. Always use whole egg for covering.

### Chicken Croquettes No. 1

| | |
|---|---|
| 2 cups chicken | 1 cup white sauce |
| 1 teaspoon chopped parsley | Salt and pepper to taste |

Mix and put on ice to get firm; make into croquettes; roll in crumbs, then in egg, crumbs again; fry in oil or hot grease deep enough to cover until light brown; have fat boiling, but not smoking hot. Cook about half minute.

### Chicken Croquettes No. 2—3 Dozen

| | |
|---|---|
| 1 hen boiled until tender | 3 sets brains |
| ½ cup soft butter | 1 cup bread crumbs |
| 1 tablespoon chopped parsley | A little milk if mixture is too stiff |
| A little celery salt | Salt and pepper to taste |

Grind chicken; clean and cook brains; mash; add butter and crumbs; season; place in ice box to get firm; shape; crumb; roll in egg, then in crumbs; fry in deep fat.

Note: 1 egg with 1 teaspoon water will coat one dozen croquettes. To test fat, put in piece of bread, count forty, if brown, fat is hot enough.

### Salmon Croquettes

Two cups salmon, 1 cup thick white sauce, few grains cayenne pepper, 1 teaspoon salt, grated rind of lemon.

Flake salmon, removing any bones, add seasoning, drop on a platter portions large enough for croquette. Set aside to get firm. When ready to fry, crumb, roll in egg, crumb again, fry in deep fat.

### Ham Croquettes

| | |
|---|---|
| 2 cups mashed potatoes | 2 tablespoons butter |
| 1 cup lean ground ham | 1 cup bread crumbs |
| Salt and pepper to taste | Chopped parsley to season |
| Sufficient sweet milk to make soft enough to handle | |

Mix ham and seasoning while potatoes are hot; let get a little cool;

make into balls, roll into crumbs, egg and then crumbs again until all are fixed. Fry in deep fat until a pretty brown. One egg and 1 tablespoon of cold water will coat 1 dozen croquettes of medium size. Do not froth the egg; beat with knife to break, and mix with the water.

## Veal Croquettes

Follow recipe for chicken, using veal instead.

## Stanley Rice Croquettes

| | |
|---|---|
| 1½ cups dry rice, hot or cold | Salt and pepper to taste |
| 1 cup rich white sauce | Egg and crumbs for coating |
| 1 tablespoon minced parsley | |

Mix rice and seasoning together, having it firm enough to shape. Make in any desired shape, roll in crumbs, then egg and crumb again, fry in deep fat a golden brown, drain and serve plain or with cheese or brown nut sauce.

## Rice Croquettes No. 1

| | |
|---|---|
| ½ cup rice | 2 eggs |
| 1 cup boiling water | 1 teaspoon salt |
| 1 cup milk | 2 tablespoons butter |

Wash rice and cook in water until all is absorbed. Add milk, which must be hot—cook until rice is soft. Remove from fire, add salt, butter and yolks of eggs. Spread in pan to cool. Shape into balls as large as an egg, roll in dry cracker crumbs, shape into nests. Take whites of eggs, beat just enough to break and add 1 tablespoon of cold water. Brush each nest well with the egg and roll in dry crumbs as any croquette. Fry in deep fat until brown. Serve with broiled chicken.

Into each nest put a spoon of red jelly. Garnish with parsley.

## Rice Croquettes No. 2

First part: Cook ½ cup rice in 1 cup stock until liquid is absorbed.

Second part: 1 cup of tomato sauce which has been cooked with slice of onion, 2 cloves, 1 stalk of celery, 1 teaspoon sugar and strained. Add to rice and continue cooking until tender and stiff.

Third part: Remove from fire, add 2 tablespoons grated cheese, 2 egg yolks, season with salt and pepper. Put aside to cool, shape in croquettes, roll in crumbs and egg, fry in deep fat, drain and serve. The whites may be used for the coating, add 1 tablespoon cold water and mix.

## Sweet Potato Croquettes No. 1

Boil and put through vegetable press or mash well 2 cups potatoes, add 1 tablespoon butter, 1 teaspoon salt, ⅓ cup sweet milk or enough to make potatoes thin enough to make into round balls. Let get cold and set. Crumb, dip in egg, then crumb again, fry in deep fat. Serve as a vegetable.

Nuts and raisins may be added to this mixture and make it delicious to serve with baked chicken. Potatoes this way take the place of candied yams. A little sugar may be added if real sweet is liked.

### Sweet Potato Croquettes No. 2

2 cups mashed potatoes
½ cup seedless raisins
¼ cup chopped nut meats

2 tablespoons butter
Sufficient milk to make soft to roll into balls

Shape, roll in grated cocoanut, run into hot oven to heat and slightly brown tips of cocoanut. Serve hot. Cover raisins with warm water, let stand half hour, drain well, before adding to potatoes.

### Macaroni Croquettes

Use left over macaroni and cheese, make into balls. Crumb, dip in eggs, crumb again, fry in deep fat, drain and serve with hot tomato sauce. See how to cook croquettes.

### Sausage Croquettes

Cut cooked sausages in half if as long as finger, remove skin. Roll in mashed, seasoned potato, dip in egg, then crumbs and fry in deep fat.
Serve on slice of broiled tomato or apple.

### Cottage Cheese Croquettes

2 cups cheese
⅛ teaspoon salt
1 egg
Dash cayenne pepper

2 teaspoons chopped parsley
1 cup bread crumbs
1 tablespoon cold water

Mix cheese, parsley and seasoning together, shape into balls, roll in bread crumbs, then in egg and water mixed together, then crumbs again. Fry in deep fat until a nice brown. Serve with a salad.

### Cheese and Rice Croquettes

2 cups dry rice (leftover or fresh)
1 cup thick white sauce
½ cup diced cheese
1 tablespoon tomato catsup

1 teaspoon salt
Cayenne pepper to taste
Egg and crumbs for coating

Make the white sauce, having it quite thick, and add cheese, stirring to thoroughly melt, add all seasoning, then the rice and set aside to cool. Shape into croquettes, roll in crumbs, then the beaten egg and crumb again. (See Croquettes). Fry in deep grease, drain and serve.

### Chicken Pie

1 young chicken
1 cup milk
¼ cup butter
2½ cups flour made into pastry

Salt and pepper to season
Stock in which the chicken was cooked, ¼ cup or more

Select a young chicken, about 1½ lbs., dress and cut as for frying. Into a stew pan place pieces and barely cover with boiling water. Cook slowly until tender.

Make pastry, using recipe for plain pastry, but use only half the quantity of shortening called for. Mix and divide into two parts. Roll out one piece quite thin, line sides of pan or dish, put in layer of chicken, dot with butter, salt and pepper. Cut pastry in strips and cover chicken, then put another layer of chicken, alternating the chicken and pastry until all is used. Add the milk and any water in which the chicken was cooked—there should be enough water to almost cover the contents in the pan.

Take the second piece of pastry, roll out and dot with remaining shortening, from the pastry recipe, fold and roll until all of the shortening is used. Roll out thin, cover top of pie; press edges together, stick with fork and make a generous cross cut in center to allow steam to escape.

Bake in moderate oven, 30 to 40 minutes until contents are cooked and the crust is browned. If any pastry is left, roll thin, cut in strips, bake and arrange around pie.

Usually chicken pie is served in the pan in which it is baked.

# milk and cheese

# CHAPTER V

## Milk and Cheese

### MILK

Bread is called the "staff" of life, and milk may be called the "sustainer" of life.

Milk has ceased to be termed just a drink, but is now called a food. It is considered the most important food because it is an almost complete food, and is a protective food. It contains all elements necessary for protecting health and promoting growth.

Milk is a nourishing food for people of all ages and classes. It furnishes 16 per cent of the total food of the average American family.

Milk is a cheap food for it furnishes more food value for the money than any other food, and may be combined with every class of food in various ways. Certified—Grade A raw milk is best if it can be bought, and cheaper even though it may be more expensive.

Every adult should have at least 1 pint of milk per day, and each child 1½ pints to 1 quart per day. If children do not like milk it is usually because they were allowed to eat meat and highly seasoned foods before they were six years old. This made milk seem tasteless to them. A few children are unable to take milk raw—in this case it may be mixed with vegetables, eggs, etc., and cooked in various ways to tempt the appetite.

Milk absorbs odors, and may contain many kinds of germs so it is very important that it should be pure, clean and have the right per cent of butter fat.

Milk to be fit for children to drink should be milked in a SANITARY barn, from CLEAN cows (and free from disease), and drawn into CLEAN vessels (which have been thoroughly cleansed in live steam or boiling water and sunned or aired). Milkers should be free of disease and be scrupulously clean. All cloths should be perfectly clean and not used for anything else. After milking process is completed the milk should be kept at 50 degrees or less. If not kept cold harmful bacteria will multiply very rapidly and make milk unfit for drinking. If a person is not sure about the sanitary condition of the dairy the milk may be pasteurized (kept at 180 degrees for 30 minutes).

Recipes for the use of milk will be found in various sections of this book.

## CHEESE

It is believed that cheese is the oldest dairy product and its origin was due to the desire to use the surplus milk, and store for future use. Without a doubt, cheese is the oldest manufactured food we have.

Cheese is made from whole milk, cream and skim milk, and in the past few years, there has been great progress made in the manufacturing, packing and handling of this product. Cheese is convenient to keep and its price is within the reach of all.

American cheeses have made marvelous strides in context and flavor and compare favorably with imported brands.

Common American cheese is often found with various characteristics, such as soft, rich, creamy, pale to deep yellow, dry, firm, tough, mild and nippy. This is due to the milk used and the length of time required to ripen the cheese. American cheese is mostly copied from the English Cheddar, with variations. There are quite a number of varieties of hard and soft cheese, and we also have Philadelphia cream, Neufchatel and cottage cheese.

Cheese is a very nutritious, concentrated food and is thought by some to be hard to digest. This however, is often due to excessive indulgence along with a heavy meal. For a long time cheese was used sparingly as a condiment, to flavor dishes and as a "company" dish, and was considered a winter dish. Today, the thought uppermost in the study and knowledge of foods, is to eat properly to keep well, and this has brought out the importance of many things we eat, that was previously unknown.

Cheese is a protein food and a muscle builder and should be used as a meat substitute. America is considered a small cheese eating nation when compared to many other countries. Americans are partial to meat.

One pound of cheese is equal in food value to two pounds of beef, two dozen eggs or four pounds of fish, so the importance of cheese can readily be seen. Those who do not like milk may use more cheese.

The popular imported brands to be found in our general stores are English Cheddar, English Dairy, Swiss, Pineapple, Parmesan, Roquefort and Limberger, each one coming from a locality noted for its production. Of course, imported cheese is far more expensive than our American brands, and for that reason domestic cheese enjoys a larger sale.

# eggs, omelets, souffles and cheese dishes

# CHAPTER VI

# Eggs, Omelets, Souffles and Cheese Dishes

### Scrambled Eggs a la Stanley

Into a heavy skillet put butter or bacon drippings (1 teaspoon for each egg.) Have pan moderately hot. Break egg in dish and turn into pan. Just as soon as the white begins to cook (turn white) stir gently, allowing more white to reach the pan taking care not to break the yolks until half of the white is cooked; then gently stir white and yolk—continue until cooked sufficiently. By using gentle heat the eggs will be tender and soft but done and most delicious. Serve eggs on a warm dish.

### Hard-Boiled Eggs

Drop eggs into warm water, let come to a boil, and continue boiling for 20 minutes. Stir several times at first to prevent yolk from dropping to one side, which would give a very thin white on one side. When done drop into cold water. Crack each shell so water will enter and make the shell come off easily without breaking the white. An egg a day or two old will peel better than a very fresh one.

### Soft-Boiled Eggs

Drop egg into boiling water, boil 2 or 3 minutes until cooked as desired.

### To Cook an Egg for an Invalid

Take a small saucepan as deep as a tea cup; half fill with boiling water. Into this put a tea cup to get hot. When hot put a small piece of butter and break in the egg. Keep the water boiling and when the white begins to cook, stir from the side of the cup for more to cook; when the white is nearly all a white jelly, break the yolk and continue stirring gently until as stiff as desired; season and serve in the cup in which it is cooked. This is easily done and is good, the egg being very tender and jelly-like.

### To Soft Boil an Egg for an Invalid

Fill a quart cup with boiling water to heat, empty and refill; place on table and drop in an egg, cover top with saucer and let the egg stay in for eight minutes. Take out and you have one with a jelly-like white which is very easily digested.

### Eggs Poached in Water

Grease a skillet or fry pan and fill with water sufficient to cover eggs. Let water come to the boiling point (but not boil), break and turn each egg into water. Keep water hot, just simmering, until white is cooked and yolk as done as desired. Remove with a perforated spoon and place on toast or platter.

### Eggs Cooked in Poacher

Have poacher filled with hot water, and egg container greased. Place an egg in each cup, lower container into hot water and cook until done. Lift out and slide eggs on platter.

Some egg poachers have cups for eggs, and they are cooked entirely by steam from the boiling water below. For this utensil each cup should have a small portion of melted butter ready when eggs are dropped in. Steam until eggs are as firm as desired.

### Poached Eggs a la Lewis

#### (Sunday Night Dish)

Poach as many eggs as needed. Drain and place on a platter.

Make a thick white sauce, season with salt and pepper. Pour over eggs. Place in hot oven to brown slightly on top. Sprinkle top generously with minced parsley and paprika. Serve at once.

In a gas oven place platter under the fire to brown on top.

### To Cook Egg Yolks

#### (1 dozen yolks)

In a saucepan put one quart of hot water, add two teaspoons of salt. Have boiling. With a whip or electric beater whip the yolks until light and frothy. Pour into the water, which should be boiling hard, stirring with egg whip constantly for two or three minutes until small particles show or the mixture has a curdled look. Have ready a strainer lined with 2 layers of cheese cloth. Pour in hot mixture and drain off water. There will be a light, fluffy mixture. Turn on platter and serve as an omelet or to garnish spinach or use as a sandwich base or salad. Grated or cream cheese or mayonnaise may be mixed with the cooked eggs. This is delicious and very versatile.

### Another Way to Cook Egg Yolks

Have a sauce pan with sufficient hot water to float the yolks. As the eggs are broken and white removed drop each yolk into the water. When all are in, place pan over a medium heat and boil gently until yolks are firm. Remove and use as any egg yolk for salad, garnishing or sandwiches.

### Stuffed Eggs

6 hard boiled eggs
3 slices of crisp broiled bacon
3 cucumber pickles

1 tablespoon of prepared mustard
Salt, pepper, bacon drippings or butter to season

Place eggs in warm water to boil, shake pan several times to turn the eggs so they will boil more perfectly. Cook about 20 minutes. Crack shells and drop into cold water. Peel and cut in half and remove yolks. With a fork mash yolks to a paste, chop all ingredients into smallpieces and mix with the seasoning into the yolks until well blended.

Refill the white sections, having them very full. Arrange daintily on platter, garnish with rings of green pepper and sprigs of parsley.

## Baked Eggs

6 eggs                                        Salt and pepper to taste
⅛ lb. butter

Break eggs into muffin pans, which should be cold, with plenty of fat to prevent sticking, put butter, salt and pepper over each egg. Bake in a moderate oven to suit taste, remove with knife and serve while hot on toast.

## Eggs a la Henrietta

6 pieces of buttered toast            ⅛ teaspoon salt for whites of eggs
6 eggs                                        Salt, pepper and minced parsley

Make toast. Have a pan of very hot water sufficient to float yolks. Separate eggs, dropping yolks in water, and whites in a bowl. Add salt to whites and beat until stiff. Place toast on baking sheet, and on each piece of toast, form a nest of whites, making a depression in the center for the yolks; drop in yolks and place sheet in moderate oven and bake until whites are a delicate brown, and yolks are cooked. Sprinkle with salt, pepper and minced parsley, and serve immediately. The yolks must be lifted from hot water with a slit spoon to drain. The hot water warms and partly cooks yolks and allows them to be handled without breaking.

## Puffy Omelet

3 eggs                                        ½ teaspoon salt
3 tablespoons of water (or sweet-     1 tablespoon butter
    milk)                                     Dash of cayenne pepper

Use a heavy frying pan or omelet pan; put over a slow fire to heat; gently melt butter, but don't burn; separate egg; beat yolks light, and add water, salt and pepper. Beat whites until quite stiff and firm. Pour the yolk mixture over whites and fold together. Increase heat under pan, and pour the mixture in. Put over medium heat and cover. When risen and brown around the edge, put into a hot oven and finish cooking, and brown top.

When well browned, make a deep cut through the center; fold together and turn out onto a platter. Serve at once. Grated ham, cheese, marmalade, or jelly may be spread on top before folding, if liked.

## Spanish Omelet

### First Part

3 eggs                                        2 tablespoons of water
3 tablespoons of butter or oil        Salt and pepper to taste

Put butter into heavy fry pan, beat eggs together until light; add water, turn into hot pan, cover bottom, remove to gentle heat and cook slowly until set.

Spread on sauce, roll up, turn onto hot platter and serve at once.

### Second Part—Sauce

| | |
|---|---|
| 2 medium tomatoes | 2 tablespoons green peas |
| 1 onion | 1 pimento |
| 6 large stuffed olives | 1 green pepper, which has been par- |
| 2 tablespoons butter | boiled |

Peel, chop and drain tomatoes, put butter into pan, grate and add onion and tomatoes; cook for few minutes, add other ingredients; cook gently until ready to pour on omelet. The sauce should be rather dry.

A fluffy omelet is used same way.

## Quick Omelet

Break as many eggs as needed into a dish, beat very little, until the yolks and whites are slightly mixed. Into a fry pan put a little butter to melt (about 2 tablespoons for 4 eggs). Pour in the eggs, let cook through until the top is soft, and the part next to the pan slightly browned. Do not turn. Roll up and place on a warm platter. Serve at once.

Any filling—minced bacon, diced ham, creole sauce or jelly may be spread on before rolling and serving.

## Traveler's Omelet

Beat 2 eggs together until very light, add ¼ teaspoon salt and dash of pepper. Cook on griddle as you would batter cakes, having the heat very moderate, turn when firm enough, but slightly brown. Put on platter to cool. When cool enough to handle, spread with sardine butter and roll like a jelly roll. Roll in wax paper like kisses, place in lunch basket. A cream cheese could take the place of the sardines.

## Cheese Souffle No. 1

| | |
|---|---|
| 1 cup bread crumbs | 2 eggs |
| 1 cup grated cheese | Salt and pepper to taste |
| 1½ cups milk | |

Heat milk just tepid, pour over crumbs and mix well. Add beaten eggs and all other ingredients, pour into a buttered baking dish and bake in moderate oven until firm (about 20 to 30 minutes), the time depending on the thickness or quantity.

## Cheese Souffle No. 2

| | |
|---|---|
| 1 cup white sauce | 1 teaspoon salt |
| 1 cup grated cheese | ⅛ teaspoon cayenne pepper |
| 3 eggs | |

Make white sauce; take from fire, add grated cheese, salt and pepper. Let cool while beating whites of eggs very stiff. When well beaten mix into cheese mixture the yolks slightly beaten. This will thin the mixture enough to pour over the stiff whites and fold in. Do this carefully; pour into a greased baking dish; place dish in pan of boiling water; put into a moderate oven, bake 25 to 40 minutes. To test, insert handle of spoon through middle; if it comes out clean, it is done; if mixture sticks to handle, cook 5 to 7 minutes longer. Serve at once. Souffles, like omelets, must be eaten at once. They fall.

## Corn Meal Souffle

| | |
|---|---|
| 1 pint sweet milk | 1 teaspoon salt |
| ¾ cup sifted meal | 3 eggs |
| 2 tablespoons butter | |

Heat milk in double boiler until smoking, but do not boil. Pour in meal slowly and cook until thick like a stiff white sauce. Take from fire to cool, add salt and butter. While the mixture is cooling, separate eggs and beat whites stiff, break yolks and add to meal mixture, then pour this mixture over stiff whites, fold in (do not beat), pour into a buttered pan, cook in moderate oven 25 to 30 minutes. When done serve at once from the pan in which it is baked. See Cheese Souffle No. 2 for testing when done.

## Fish Souffle

Make same as cheese recipe, using one cup of flaked fish, cooked instead of cheese. Do not bake in water; use any seasoning liked.

## Ham Souffle

Same as fish.

## Chicken Souffle

Same as fish.

## Oyster Souffle

First steam the oysters in their own liquor until they curl slightly. Remove and drain; chop fine and use three-fourths cupful.

Make the white sauce, using half oyster liquor, half milk. Make as any souffle, using the three eggs. Season with salt, pepper, and a grated lemon rind, being careful to use only the yellow part, about one-half teaspoon. The amount of oysters used is less on account of the mixture measuring so solidly. Bake as directed until firm.

## Corn Souffle

| | |
|---|---|
| 1 cup fresh or leftover corn | 3 eggs |
| 1 cup white sauce | Salt and pepper to taste |

Make sauce as usual for medium thickness; add corn and let cool. Beat egg whites until stiff. Mix yolks into the corn mixture; add seasoning, fold in the whites.

Pour into a buttered pan and bake in a moderate oven about 25 minutes or until done. Test by inserting a spoon handle into center. If it comes out without the mixture sticking, it is done; if sticking, cook a little longer.

## Squash Souffle

Make same as corn, using one cup of cooked and mashed squash.

## Apple Souffle

3 cups stewed and strained apples    4 eggs
1 cup sugar                            Season with spices to taste

Have apples free of lumps. Add sugar and spices while hot, let cool, beat egg together light, mix into apples. Pour into baking dish.
Bake until firm. Serve with roast pork.

## Macaroni and Cheese

½ pound macaroni            ⅛ teaspoon cayenne pepper
1 cup cheese chips           ½ cup milk
3 tablespoons butter        1 egg
1 teaspoon salt               ½ cup buttered bread crumbs

Break and boil macaroni in salt water until tender (about 20 minutes). Blanch in cold water to prevent sticking. Cover bottom of baking dish with layer of macaroni, a sprinkle of cheese, bits of butter, salt and pepper.
Continue until all is used, having cheese on top.
Mix milk and egg together, pour over the dish, cover top with crumbs, bake in moderate oven long enough to brown top and cook egg and milk. Serve in the same dish.
A thin white sauce is someimes used instead of the milk and egg.
This dish, when left over, makes nice croquettes. Serve with tomato sauce.

## Convent Pudding—Colonial Tea Room Recipe

½ cup macaroni            1 tablespoon chopped green pepper
1 cup milk                  1 tablespoon onion juice
1 cup soft bread crumbs    1 tablespoon chopped parsley
¼ cup butter               3 eggs
1 cup grated cheese       1 teaspoon salt

Cook macaroni until tender. Scald milk, add all ingredients (eggs slightly beaten). Grease dish with butter, pour in mixture, place dish in boiling water with several thicknesses of paper at bottom and bake in boiling water for 30 to 40 minutes. Serve with tomato or mushroom sauce.

## Cheese Custard

Cut sufficient layers of bread needed, spread with butter, sprinkle with cheese, salt and pepper; make two layers in baking dish, cover with 2 cups milk and 2 eggs beaten together. Bake half hour. Serve from dish in which it was baked.
Pepper and mustard may be added.

## English Monkey

1 cup bread crumbs
1 cup milk
½ cup soft cheese chips
2 tablespoons of butter

1 egg
½ teaspoon salt
⅛ teaspoon cayenne pepper

Soak the bread crumbs in the milk for fifteen minutes. Melt butter and cheese over a gentle heat. When melted, add soaked crumbs, the egg slightly beaten and seasonings. Cook 2 or 3 minutes. Pour over toasted crackers or bread, which has been slightly buttered, or serve from a hot dish with hot biscuit or wheat muffins.

## "Ring Tum Ditty"

½ lb. American cheese
1 can tomato soup
2 cups rich milk
2 tablespoons butter

2 tablespoons flour
1 teaspoon sugar
Pinch soda

Grate cheese, and when all ingredients are near a boiling point add the cheese. Care should be taken in not letting it boil. An onion and a pinch of mustard may be added. Serve over crackers or toast.

## Cheese Sauce

1 cup white sauce
1 cup diced cheese

Salt and pepper to taste, using the red pepper

Make white sauce, add the cheese, and stir until well melted and blended together. Pour into a hot dish to serve. This is good over rice, hominy, or toast. Also used to serve as a sauce over rice croquettes.

## White Sauce

1 cup milk
3 tablespoons of flour

2 tablespoons of butter
Salt and pepper

Put milk into double boiler to heat. Into a saucepan place butter to melt. Add flour and blend together. When ready remove the saucepan from the fire, add the milk all at once and stir to thicken, then add cheese or serve as a sauce over any dish.

## Cheese Jelly

Use recipe for Cheese Sauce. Add 2 tablespoons of gelatine dissolved in ¼ cup cold water, and add to sauce while hot and thoroughly melt. Let cool partly. Sprinkle well a layer cake pan with grated cheese. Pour the jelly in to congeal; when cold cut in squares, roll in grated cheese.

To be served with a salad.

## Cheese and Potatoes

Boil, season and mash as many potatoes as needed, whip very light and mix one or more cups of grated cheese according to the quantity needed.

Pile on a shallow pan and bake until slightly browned and very hot, serve at once from the pan in which it is baked.

The potatoes may be baked, scooped from the skins. Season as above, refill the shells, bake just long enough to brown top and melt cheese. Serve with broiled fish.

### Cheese Aigrettes

½ cup water
¼ cup butter
½ cup dry grated cheese
½ cup flour

2 eggs and 1 yolk
¼ cup bottled Parmesan cheese
Salt and cayenne

Boil water and butter, add flour (as in making cream puffs), cook until it leaves the sides of pan. Cool slightly, add eggs one at a time and mix well. Lastly add the cheese. Drop in hot fat pieces as large as a walnut and fry a golden brown. Drain on paper and serve on a folded napkin.

### Cheese Fritters

2 cups grated cheese
3 tablespoons flour

4 egg whites (½ cup)
Red pepper and salt

Mix flour, salt, pepper and cheese. Just before frying—beat egg whites very stiff and fold in cheese mixture. Dip a tablespoon of mixture each time and fry in deep fat. Drain on brown paper.

### Cheese Balls

1 cup grated cheese
1 cup bread crumbs
2 egg whites, beaten stiff

½ teaspoon salt
Dash cayenne pepper

Mix all ingredients together, make in balls the size of walnuts, fry in deep fat, drain, serve with salad.

### Welsh Rarebit

1 lb. grated English dairy cheese
2 tablespoons butter
3 tablespoons flour
⅛ teaspoon cayenne pepper

¾ cup milk
¼ cup cream
1 teaspoon salt

Melt butter in a saucepan or chafing dish, add flour and cook, without browning, until well mixed, stirring all the time; add milk and half of cheese, still stirring; when thoroughly heated and well mixed, add balance of cheese, being careful to stir all the time; when thick pour over nicely browned hot toast and serve.

### Sweet Butter

1 lb. creamery butter
1 pint whole milk

Place butter in bowl and let soften to room temperature. Leave milk at room temperature until just cool. With a wire mixer or slitted spoon cream butter until soft and easy to stir. Add milk a little at a time, like making mayonnaise, blending milk and butter until all the milk is added, and no milk is noticeable. Make in cottage prints. This will give 2 pounds of butter that will taste like fresh dairy butter. No more salt is added. Delicious.

### Cottage Cheese

Allow the skimmed milk to clabber, over the clabbered milk pour hot water (not quite boiling), using about one quart of water to one quart of clabber. Allow it to stand until tepid.

Over a colander or strainer spread a cheese cloth, pour the mixture into this to drip, allowing it to drain until it is quite firm. Place in ice box to chill. Serve with sugar and cream, with a dash of nutmeg if liked. Served with salt, pepper and thick cream as a cheese.

Served with strawberry preserves this makes a nice dish.

### Cheese Balls

To make cheese balls use cottage cheese, Neufchatel or Philadelphia cream. Moisten with thin cream or full milk to make a medium paste, add salt and cayenne pepper to taste. If any color is desired add now.

Make into small balls, roll in chopped parsley or chopped nuts. Fill celery stalks or use to make ribbon sandwiches.

### Neufchatel Cheese Balls

Mash and make into a stiff paste two or three cakes of Neufchatel cheese using sweet cream or milk to moisten, season with plenty of salt and cayenne pepper, and make into balls the size of an English walnut. Press two halves of English walnut meats on each ball, place in ice box until very cold, serve with salad.

# CHAPTER VII

## Vegetables

### A Simple Classification of Vegetables
#### Succulent Vegetables

Those containing minerals, vitamins and those juicy in texture.

| | | |
|---|---|---|
| Turnip greens | Celery | Cucumbers |
| Mustard greens | Cabbage | Turnips |
| Spinach | Collards | Tomatoes |
| Kale | Asparagus | Eggplant |
| Chard | Brussels Sprouts | Okra |
| Watercress | Beets | Onions |
| Lettuce | Carrots | Parsnips |
| | Cauliflowers | Radishes |

#### Carbohydrate Vegetables

| | |
|---|---|
| Sweet corn | Irish potatoes |
| Squash | Sweet potatoes |

#### Protein Vegetables

| | | |
|---|---|---|
| String beans | Kidney beans | Lady peas |
| Butterbeans | English peas | Field or blackeyed peas |

---

### Asparagus—Plain

Scrape, clean and boil asparagus in salt water till tender, about 30 minutes, drain and serve with white sauce or melted butter to which has been added salt, pepper and lemon juice. Have dish hot before putting asparagus in.

### Fricasseed Asparagus

| | |
|---|---|
| 2 cups canned asparagus | 1 head lettuce |
| 1 small onion | 1 tablespoon butter |
| 2 tablespoons flour | 1 cup of stock or milk |

Make sauce of butter, flour and milk; chop asparagus in 1 inch pieces; cut lettuce rather coarse and pour both into sauce, season well with salt and pepper; add one egg and stir over a gentle fire about one minute, or until bound together and egg is cooked; serve at once.

### Fresh Asparagus With Vinagrette Sauce

| | |
|---|---|
| 3 tablespoons melted butter or oil | 1 tablespoon grated onion |
| 1 tablespoon tarragon vinegar | 1 teaspoon salt |
| 2 tablespoons cider vinegar | ½ teaspoon paprika |
| 1 tablespoon chopped parsley | Cayenne pepper to suit taste |

Melt butter; add vinegar and the seasonings; heat and pour hot over asparagus or cauliflower and serve immediately.

### Canned Asparagus With Vinagrette Sauce

Open and heat the asparagus. Make and pour the sauce over, and serve.

### French Fried Asparagus

Asparagus also lends itself to the French fry treatment. Drain the asparagus from its liquor, dip each stalk in fine crumbs, then into beaten egg, and into fine crumbs again. Drop in deep hot fat and fry to a golden brown. Dress with sweet pickled onions.

### Cabbage

Cabbage should be boiled rapidly about 30 minutes in plenty of salted water in open pot, preferably without meat. At least when cooked without meat it is more digestible. Serve with melted butter or white sauce.

### Lady Cabbage

| | |
|---|---|
| 1 cabbage (about 2 lbs.) cut in sections | 2 eggs |
| | ½ cup rich milk |
| 1 tablespoon butter | ¼ teaspoon white pepper |
| 1 teaspoon salt | |

Boil cabbage rapidly for 15 minutes, change water, have it boiling, and boil another 15 minutes, or till tender; drain and chop fine, add seasoning. Beat eggs light, add to the milk and then add to the cabbage; pour into a buttered baking dish and bake in a moderate oven from 20 to 30 minutes. If cooked too fast the eggs and milk will curdle. Cheese may be added if liked. Serve from the baking dish.

### Stuffed Cabbage

| | |
|---|---|
| 1 medium cabbage (about 2 lbs.) | 1 cup bread crumbs |
| 1 cup pork sausage | 1 egg |
| 1 cup chopped cabbage | ½ teaspoon salt |

Cut cabbage from top towards stem half way into 8 sections and drop into warm water for 10 minutes. Fold back the sections leaving each section 4 or 5 leaves thick. scoop out center leaving an opening sufficient to hold stuffing. Chop cabbage removed; make a force meat of the ingredients called for and fill the cabbage. Bring the sections back over the stuffing, tie in cheese cloth. Drop in boiling water and cook for 1 hour. When done lift out and drain well; place on platter and pour over a cup of white sauce. Sprinkle with minced parsley or grated cheese and serve.

### Hot Slaw

| | |
|---|---|
| ½ cup vinegar | ¼ cup sugar or less |
| ½ teaspoon mustard | 2 teaspoons salad oil or butter |
| ½ cup sweet cream or top milk | Salt and pepper to taste |
| 1 egg | Cabbage |

Shred 1 medium cabbage, boil in lots of water 15 minutes. Drain. Add hot dressing. Serve at once.

Bring vinegar and seasoning to boil. Beat egg and cream together, add hot vinegar, keep hot over boiling water for one minute. Pour over hot cabbage.

## Mrs. R's Coleslaw

| | |
|---|---|
| 1 white cabbage (about 1 lb.) | 1 onion |
| 1 stalk celery | 2 tablespoons prepared mustard |
| 2 green peppers | 1 cup mayonnaise |
| 2 red peppers | 1/4 cup of vinegar |

Chop all very fine, mix in bowl and add mayonnaise. Add salt and pepper to taste. Let stand for an hour. When ready to use, stir well and you have something good.

## Coleslaw

Use fresh white cabbage, cut into quarters and let stand in cold water for an hour. When ready to make, drain and shred fine. Use the following dressing:

| | |
|---|---|
| 1/2 cup water | 1 tablespoon flour |
| 1/4 cup vinegar | 1/2 teaspoon dry mustard |
| 1 tablespoon sugar | 2 hard-boiled eggs |
| 1 tablespoon oil or butter | Salt and pepper to taste |

Mix flour, sugar and mustard together. Mix vinegar, water and oil. Bring to a boil, pour over dry ingredients and cook until thick. Mash yolks of egg with a little of the dressing, add to mixture, and let cool. Chop whites with cabbage, pour the dressing on, season to taste, and serve.

## Cabbage Gumbo (South Carolina Dish)

| | |
|---|---|
| 1 small cabbage | 1 onion |
| 1 small slice ham | 2 tablespoons butter |
| 1 cup pork sausage | 3 tablespoons flour |
| 2 cups milk | Salt and cayenne pepper to taste |

Wash and chop cabbage as for slaw. Cut ham into small pieces. Into a heavy fry pan or pot put butter. Add ham, then sliced onion. Cook for a few minutes—now add cabbage, sausage and seasoning and enough water to prevent scorching, cook, stirring occasionally until cabbage is tender, about thirty minutes. When cabbage is done, mix flour into a small portion of milk, heat milk, add to the mixture, cook for a few minutes and serve with rice.

Have rice cooked as usual and dry. Put rice on platter, leaving a hole in center large enough to hold the gumbo.

## Cabbage Lily for Salad

Select a medium size firm cabbage. Strip off outside leaves and trim stalk even. From the top cut in quarters half way through; cut each quarter again, making eight sections. Turn top down and drop in tepid water to stay until limp. Remove, open up the sections and scoop out center, leaving shell five or six leaves deep on outside of each section. The opening should be large enough to hold a quart or more of salad. With scissors cut each section into still smaller strips like long slim petals or leaves as deep as the first cutting, still leaving the lower part intact. Into a large deep dishpan or lard can filled with cold or ice water sufficient to float the cabbage, drop cabbage cut side down. Let stay several hours until it opens out, curls and becomes very crisp. Drain well; place in glass bowl or on platter and fill center with salad. Garnish petals with strips of pimentoes and rings of stuffed olives. Any garnishing sprinkled over top will be pretty.

### Brussels Sprouts

Remove any withered leaves and drop into cold water to freshen. Cook and season the same as cauliflower or cabbage.

### Cauliflower

Strip off the coarse green stalks and trim neatly near the flower. Drop in cold salt water for 20 to 30 minutes; then drop into boiling salt water and cook until tender. Drain and serve with melted butter or white sauce.

The large flower may be broken into small pieces (flowerets) if preferred. Cook uncovered and rapidly.

### To Clean Spinach

Use a large vessel and have plenty of water. Do not crowd the pan. Take a large handful at a time, shake and dip up and down into the water, thus shaking off the grit which goes to the bottom of the pan. Change the water (and rinse the pan well) four or five times until clean. New Zealand spinach is usually not very gritty.

### To Cook Spinach

Pick, wash and drain the required amount of spinach. Put the spinach into a kettle or saucepan without any water, have a moderate fire. In a few minutes the spinach will wilt and send out sufficient water to cook it Boil for 20 to 30 minutes briskly so the water will be reduced, season with butter, chop fine, garnish with eggs and serve.

### Plain Spinach

Wash and cook half peck of spinach, as directed above. Drain well, chop fine or put through a coarse sieve. Fry two or three slices of bacon, remove and into the grease put spinach and season with the grease, add salt and pepper to taste, a small amount of vinegar if liked. Serve as any greens.

### To Cooked Canned Spinach

Open a can of spinach and turn into a sauce pan of cold water. Stir with a fork to loosen well; let it stand about thirty minutes.

Take out of water with a skimmer; drain well; heat in a small quantity of water or butter until done (about ten minutes). Season with salt, pepper, and serve.

## A Mold of Spinach

2 cups spinach                              Salt and pepper to taste
1 cup white sauce                         Onion, catsup, paprika, if desired
3 eggs

Cook, drain and chop the spinach or put through a coarse sieve, then measure. Make and add the white sauce. Beat eggs together until well broken, add to spinach, but do not let the mixture be hot enough to cook the eggs.

Butter a border mold generously with soft (not melted) butter, pour in the mixture until ¾ full. Place mold in pan of boiling water and steam until firm. Inside the oven or top of stove may be used. Cover top lightly to prevent browning if oven is used.

Use a baking pan for steaming, putting several thicknesses of paper on bottom to protect the bottom of mold which is the top when turned out. Have water half or three-fourths the depth of mold so it will not boil over into mold.

Individual molds may be used, standing them in hot water the same as any other. Turn out (the same as any mold or jelly) onto hot platter, serve with grated cheese, eggs or carrots. More white sauce may be poured over the mold. Small Irish potatoes with white sauce filled in the center make a very attractive dish.

## Spinach Souffle

2 cups cooked spinach                    1 cup milk
2 tablespoons butter                     4 tablespoons flour
3 eggs                                   Salt and pepper to taste

Chop spinach fine and put through coarse strainer; make milk, butter and flour into white sauce; add spinach; let cool enough not to cook yolks of eggs, which should be beaten and added. Whip whites stiff and fold into mixture. Pour into a buttered baking dish and cook in a moderate oven 25 minutes, or until firm.

## Broiled Spinach

Select crisp leaves of fresh spinach. Into a fry pan put butter or bacon drippings; then put in leaves, turn, cooking on both sides for a few minutes. Lift carefully to a plate and serve piping hot.

## Turnip Greens

Turnip greens should be thoroughly washed to be free of grit. Remove any objectionable part of tough stems. For ½ peck of greens use just enough water to cover ¼ lb. seasoning meat. Bring meat and water to a boil, add greens and bring to a hard boil, then lower heat and cook slowly for 2 hours or until tender, and water reduced to about a cup.

Young, tender greens cook in less time than older plants.

Greens should not be greasy but tasty and seasoned. More salt may be added if necessary. If too much water is used much of the food value is lost (left in the liquor).

All kinds of greens are cooked as turnip greens in this section of the South.

## Chard

Beet tops, swiss chard and spinach may be cooked as turnip greens, or put into a pot without water. Cook slowly for a few minutes until enough water has come from the leaves to do the cooking. Cook moderately about 30 minutes. Drain, chop, season with salt, pepper, melted butter or white sauce.

## Kale

Cook the same as turnip greens.

## Swiss Chard

Cook leaves as greens or spinach.

Cook stalks. Boil in salt water until tender; serve with melted butter or white sauce.

## Rape

See Kale.

## Mustard

Mustard is used mixed with other greens and cooked the same as turnip greens.

Curly mustard is used for garnishing the same as parsley.

## Collards

The blue and white stem collards are strictly a southern vegetable, and not good until the frost and cold have made them brittle and tender. The leaf is dark green with a large, thick stem running through the center about half the length of leaf.

Collards are boiled with seasoning meat or ham hock about 2 hours. They must be boiled slowly, and kept well under water.

## Collard Sprouts

After the collard has been cut and used the stalk if left standing will in the spring send out very tender sprouts. These sprouts are cooked the same as collards, not requiring as long cooking or as much water.

## Collard Stalks

Strip off the leafy part and cut stalks in 1 inch pieces. Boil until tender in salt water. Drain and serve with melted butter or white sauce.

## Snap Beans

String snap beans should be cooked with boiling meat slowly from 2 to 3 hours. Use ⅛ pound of meat for a quart of beans. Cover with water and when boiled slowly the water is not condensed too fast. There should be about one cup full when done.

If beans are boiled rapidly and water added often they are never as good. Rapid cooking tears them open and causes them to be "stringy." Start in boiling water.

## To String Beans

Break off blossom end first towards inside curve, pull string down to stem end. Break small piece from stem end and pull off string back to starting end. Break in several pieces and drop into cold water to freshen. All vegetables are improved in flavor if crisped or dropped into cold water before cooking.

Southern people prefer most vegetables being cooked with a piece of meat instead of serving with butter or cream.

Vegetables should not be too heavily salted as it destroys the flavor.

## Barbecued String Beans

| | |
|---|---|
| 3 cups beans | 1 tablespoon prepared mustard |
| 4 tablespoons butter | 1 teaspoon curry powder (optional) |
| 1 tablespoon minced onion | 1 teaspoon prepared horseradish |
| 1 tablespoon minced pepper | 1 teaspoon salt |
| ¼ cup chili sauce | ⅛ teaspoon red pepper |
| ¼ cup vinegar | 1½ cups boiling water |

Cook beans in salt water until tender and done. Melt butter in fry pan, add onions and pepper and cook until done. Add all seasoning and hot water, cook five minutes before adding beans. Simmer slowly until beans are well seasoned. Serve.

## Butterbeans

Shell and remove any faulty beans, use twice as much water (cold) as beans. Boil gently until tender and water is almost cooked away. Add salt, butter and small portion of sweet cream. Some prefer a piece of seasoning meat to cook with beans instead of butter.

## Lima Beans

Cook the same as butterbeans. As these are a larger and somewhat coarser variety, longer cooking will perhaps be required.

## Dried Lima Beans

Wash, pick out faulty beans and soak in cold water over night. When ready to cook cover with cold water and bring to a boil gradually. Drain and cover with boiling water, and cook until tender. A small piece of seasoning meat or butter may be used in cooking.

## Baked Beans a la Maumee

One quart dry beans, soaked over night in cold water. Next morning parboil until you can blow on the beans and the skin will crack. Cover bottom of the crock or pan with slices of salt pork. Sprinkle with red pepper, black pepper and salt. Slice a small onion over the meat. Now place in the beans and put cubes of pork all through them about one and a half inches square, using six to ten cubes. Add two tablespoons of molasses or syrup, then water enough to just cover the beans, using fresh water. Place in slow oven and bake all day. If they should cook too fast, more water should be added, but it is best not to have to add any. There should be no water at all when ready to serve, but dry and a dark brown. They should be served from the crock with "brown bread," and you really have something good to eat.

## Garden Peas

Garden peas should be boiled gently in water unsalted if you want them tender. Hard cooking makes them hard and so does salt. Season with butter and cream.

## Green Crowder Field Peas

Shell and remove any faulty peas, wash and drain. Boil with a piece of seasoning meat or ham hock. Start in cold water and boil gently. To a pint of peas use 1 quart of water which should reduce itself to one-third in cooking.

## Field Peas a la Georgia

Prepare and cook peas using half the amount of water. When half cooked and water almost evaporated add a can of tomatoes, 1 small onion, and half a clove of garlic. Continue cooking until about 1 cup of liquor or sauce is left.

## Dried Field Peas

Remove any faulty peas, wash and soak in cold water over night. Follow recipe for cooking green field peas.

## Green Field Peas a la Virginia

Prepare peas and boil in clear water until very tender. Drain. Fry several strips of bacon or seasoning meat in a heavy skillet. Remove meat if desired; pour in the peas, stir, mash and mix until very dry and well seasoned. Serve hot. For a pint of peas about 4 tablespoons grease or butter will be necessary.

## Lady Peas

Cook same as field peas after soaking one hour or more. Boil gently to prevent bursting. Season with meat, drippings, or butter.

### To Cook Squash

Select tender squash, scrub, remove ends and cut in slices; boil in salt water until tender. Drain. Into a fry pan put bacon drippings, butter, or butter substitute, pour in the squash, mash and cook until all water is dried out. Season with pepper, a little onion and more salt if necessary. There should be no grease evident, yet plenty to season.

A little flour sprinkled into squash while cooking is a binder and improves the dish (about 2 tablespoons to a medium dish).

If squash are old, peel and remove large seed or put through a food chopper.

Yellow squash are considered better than white, although both are grown and prepared the same way.

### Squash Cakes

1 cup leftover squash      2 tablespoons flour
1 egg

Mix together, add enough sweet milk to make the consistency of batter cakes, and cook as such or fry as a fritter in shallow grease. Serve hot.

This makes a nice luncheon dish.

### Plain Squash Souffle

2 cups squash cooked, mashed and measured      3 tablespoons bacon drippings or butter
1 cup dry bread crumbs      2 eggs
1 cup milk      Salt and pepper to taste
1 tablespoon grated onion

Melt butter in hot milk; pour over bread crumbs, mix well, add to squash. Add seasoning, beat eggs all together and add to mixture. Pour into a baking dish and bake 20 to 30 minutes in moderate oven. Serve from the dish. The top may be covered with buttered crumbs, using extra crumbs for topping.

### Squash Souffle

1 cup white sauce      1 teaspoon salt
1 cup mashed squash (left over)      White or cayenne pepper to taste
3 eggs

Make white sauce, using an extra portion of flour, one to two tablespoons, to have it quite stiff. Add squash to sauce while hot. This heats the squash and cools the sauce. Add seasoning. Separate eggs, beat whites stiff. When ready, mix the yolks into the sauce and squash mixture, then fold into the whites. Pour into a buttered pan, bake in a moderate oven 30 minutes. To test insert knife or spoon handle into the center. If it comes out clean it is done; if sticky, cook longer. Serve in the pan in which it was baked. It must be served at once.

## Squash Mold

2 cups of mashed squash
1 cup thick white sauce
3 eggs

1 teaspoon grated onion
Salt and pepper to taste

Steam or boil the squash until tender, drain well and put through a coarse sieve. Mix and fill mold. See directions for Spinach Mold.

## Stuffed Squashes

Select tender, yellow squashes of uniform size, about as large around as a tumbler. Cut a small slice from the blossom end and then cut off the neck, leaving the body of uniform size. Cut in half crosswise. This gives the cup-shaped pieces. With a spoon scoop out the inside, leaving the walls and bottom about one-fourth of an inch thick. Have the large end for the top. Put into salt water and boil until tender. Lift out and drain. Cook the part scooped out, the ends and as much more as will be needed. Steam or boil in salt water until tender; drain, mash, add any seasoning liked— onions, peppers, butter, cream or bacon drippings. Cook until dry. Sometimes a small portion of flour will hold together; fill the cups; cover the tops with buttered crumbs; put into a greased pan and bake until the crumbs are a golden brown. The squashes will retain their yellow look.
Serve on a platter or individually.

## Scalloped Squash

Follow recipe for Eggplant. Grated onion is an improvement to squash.

## To Stew Corn

6 ears corn
¾ cup water
½ cup sweet milk or cream

3 tablespoons butter or bacon
drippings

Select full tender corn. Shuck and remove silks. With a knife split each row of grains. Cut off about one-third of the grain all around. Repeat the cutting and then scrape the remaining pulp.
This gives a fine cut corn.
Add water. Put grease into a saucepan and make hot. Pour in the corn and stir constantly until hot. Lower the fire and cook slowly for 30 minutes. Heat and add milk, salt and pepper. Mix well and it is ready to serve. Sometimes there is more starch in the corn and it thickens more or less. Add more or less water to suit. Have the consistency to eat with a fork.
Corn should be cooked from twenty to forty minutes. That depends on the age and quantity. Too much and too long heat will toughen corn.
Usually the canned vegetables require very little cooking.

## To Boil Corn on Cob

Have water boiling, drop in the corn and bring to a boil, lower heat so it will boil gently for 10 or 15 minutes. Cover pot. When done lift out, drain, send to table either in a covered dish or covered with a napkin. Each person puts his own salt, pepper and butter on as eaten. If you like, split the grains when it comes from the pot before sending to table.

### Steamed Corn

Place ears of corn in a colander over boiling water, cover colander. Boil water hard to steam corn until done (about 30 minutes).

### Miss Phoebe's Corn on Cob

Prepare tender corn, amount needed, place ears in a large saucepan and cover with cold water. Place over fire; bring water just to boil; remove from fire and allow corn to stand in hot water for 10 or 15 minutes. If corn is quite large let stand a little longer.

Remove from water and serve.

A tablespoon of sugar may be added to water if liked—never any salt.

### Fried Corn

| | |
|---|---|
| 3 cups of cut corn | 2 teaspoons salt |
| 3 tablespoons butter or bacon drippings | ⅛ teaspoon pepper |

Into a heavy skillet put grease and get very hot, add corn and cook about 20 minutes. Stir often to prevent scorching. This will be thick and some parts brown.

### Corn Pudding

| | |
|---|---|
| 2 cups corn | 2 tablespoons flour |
| 1 cup sweet milk | 1 tablespoon sugar |
| 2 tablespoons butter | 3 eggs |
| 2 teaspoons salt | Red or white pepper to taste |

Cut corn as usual or use left over. Add all the seasonings. Beat eggs together until light, put into the mixture, pour into a buttered baking dish and bake in a moderate oven.

If it is cooked too fast, the custard or milk and egg will curdle. It should be firm, like a cup custard.

Place dish with pudding into a pan of boiling water and it will cook slower. Serve in the dish in which it is cooked. By warming the milk it will cook quicker.

### South Carolina Corn Pudding

| | |
|---|---|
| 4 or 5 ears of well-filled but tender corn | 2 eggs |
| 1 pint sweet milk heated until warm | 2 tablespoons butter |
| | Salt, pepper |

Grate the corn on vegetable or coconut grater. Beat eggs, add to corn, add milk and melted butter, salt, pepper; mix well. Bake in greased pan, preferably greased with cooking oil. in moderate oven, about 25 minutes, until well set, but do not let it reach boiling temperature or the eggs and milk will separate. This may sound like any other corn pudding, but the grating is what makes it "different."

The pan may be set in boiling water to prevent over-cooking.

This will serve six persons.

### Corn Pudding au Gratin

| | |
|---|---|
| 2 cups canned corn | 1 cup milk |
| 1 cup diced cheese | 1 tablespoon sugar |
| 2 tablespoons flour | 2 tablespoons butter |
| 1 teaspoon salt | 1/8 teaspoon pepper |
| 2 eggs | 1/2 cup bread crumbs (buttered) |

Add cheese, flour, sugar and other seasoning to corn and mix well. Beat eggs; add to corn. Heat milk, add to mixture; pour into greased baking dish and cover top with crumbs. Bake until firm.

Serve in pan in which it is cooked.

### Corn Souffle

| | |
|---|---|
| 1 cup fresh or leftover corn | 3 eggs |
| 1 cup white sauce | Salt and pepper to taste |

Make sauce as usual for medium thickness; add corn and let cool. Beat egg whites until stiff. Mix yolks into the corn mixture; add seasoning, fold in whites.

Pour into a buttered pan and bake in a moderate oven about 25 minutes or until done. Test by inserting a spoon handle into center. If it comes out without the mixture sticking, it is done; if sticking, cook a little longer.

### Green Corn Spoon Bread

| | |
|---|---|
| 2 cups milk | 2 teaspoons sugar |
| 1/3 cup corn meal | 1 teaspoon salt |
| 3 ears corn cut very fine | 4 tablespoons butter |
| 2 eggs, beaten separately | |

Bring to a boil 1 cup of the milk, add corn and the meal, stirring constantly and cook for five minutes. Remove from the fire and beat in butter, sugar, salt and the rest of the milk, which is cold and this cools the mixture. Add beaten yolks, then fold in stiffly beaten whites. Pour in buttered dish or pan and bake 30 minutes in moderate oven. Serve with fried chicken or lamb chops.

### Scalloped Corn and Tomatoes

Put a layer of corn into a baking pan; then a layer of bread crumbs, dot with butter, salt and pepper. Put a layer of sliced tomatoes, season as the crumbs (with butter, salt and pepper). Continue with alternate layers of corn, crumbs and tomatoes until pan is full, having crumbs on top. Bake in moderate oven 30 minutes or until crumbs are brown. Serve in dish in which it was baked.

## Corn Fritters

| | |
|---|---|
| 1 cup corn pulp | 1 tablespoon milk (if corn is very |
| 1 tablespoon butter | dry) |
| 1 egg | Salt and pepper to taste |
| Flour enough to make stiff batter | |

Cut corn quite fine from cob; add flour, egg, milk and seasoning. Cook like batter cakes, using enough fat to make them turn, or drop into deep fat and fry like doughnuts. Serve around a platter of fried chicken or other meat.

## Lucile's Corn Fritters

| | |
|---|---|
| 2 cups finely cut corn or 1 can | 1 teaspoon salt |
| 1 cup cracker crumbs | 1 teaspoon sugar |
| 2 teaspoons baking powder | 2 eggs |
| ½ teaspoon paprika | Hot pepper if liked |

Separate eggs, beat yolks well and mix with corn. Beat whites stiff, and add to mixture. Add seasoning and sufficient cracker crumbs to make stiff enough to shape. Into a heavy frying pan put enough grease for shallow frying, have hot. With a spoon put in the fritters, making about as large as a tea biscuit. When brown on one side turn and brown other side, cooking long enough to cook corn. Drain on paper. Serve with fried chicken. A little flour may be added if necessary to hold together.

## Mrs. L's Lye Hominy

Put a scant "kitchen" spoon of giant potash in a gallon of water, to which add two quarts of corn. Let stand overnight. Set on fire to boil until the husks are loosened—about 15 minutes—drain off the water, put corn in dishpan of cold water and scrub well with the hands. Then pour into a perforated pan (perforations being large as cooked rice), and hold under faucet, that the water may wash out husks. Put the corn again in fresh water to boil until tender. Water may be changed to brighten the corn, or lessen the strength of the lye.

## Mrs. F. H's Lye Hominy

Soak corn over night by pouring over the amount you wish to make, in hot water. In the morning put it into an iron kettle with warm water enough to just cover it; and for each quart of corn put in baking soda, one tablespoon, and boil till the hulls come off readily; then wash in clear water, rubbing off the hulls, soaking and washing to remove the alkali taste; then boil till very tender, salting towards the last to taste. Turn into sieve and drain thoroughly.

## Stuffed Green Peppers a la Mary
### (Mock Sweet Bread)

Take slice from side of 6 nice smooth peppers; remove seed; let stand in cold salt water until ready to use. Allow one egg for each large pepper.

### Filling

| | |
|---|---|
| 1 cup chopped eggs | ½ cup minced boiled ham |
| 1 cup white sauce | Salt and pepper to taste |

Boil eggs hard, peel and chop. For every cup of eggs, use one cup of white sauce.

Use cold boiled ham, broil crisp, mince fine; mix all together; fill peppers; cover with buttered crumbs; put peppers into pan; add hot water about ¼ inch deep; bake until peppers begin to shrink; serve hot. This is delicious.

The peppers may be parboiled for 5 minutes if desired, this makes them a little more delicate.

## A New Stuffed Pepper

Remove a slice from side of pepper, take out seed and white sections, but leave stem on. Parboil for 5 minutes and drain well. Make the following mixture:

| | |
|---|---|
| 1 cup bread crumbs | 1 small onion |
| 2 tablespoons butter | Salt, pepper and catsup |

Melt butter, mince onion and fry until brown; remove from fire, add crumbs and mix well. Into each pepper put 1 tablespoon crumbs. Place peppers in baking dish, break an egg into each pepper, cover with more of the seasoned crumbs, filling pepper full. Bake in moderate oven for 10 minutes or until egg is cooked

## Stuffed Peppers

| | |
|---|---|
| 1 cup cooked carrots | 2 tablespoons butter or drippings |
| 1 cup white turnips | 1 teaspoon grated onion |
| 1 cup bread crumbs | Enough sweet milk to moisten |
| 1 egg | |

Cook carrots and turnips in boiling salt water, add as much sugar as salt used. Mix all ingredients together, season, stuff peppers, cover top with buttered crumbs. Bake just long enough to brown on top.

## Filling for Green Peppers

| | |
|---|---|
| 1 cup cold rice | 1 teaspoon salt |
| ½ cup cold diced meat | Any kind of flavoring liked |
| 2 tablespoons butter | |

Moisten with canned or fresh tomatoes, fill peppers; cover top with buttered crumbs; cook in a moderate oven 30 minutes, or till tender or brown; serve hot.

Peppers may be parboiled if preferred.

## Green Peppers as a Relish

Wash and place on ice to crisp. Slice, remove seed and serve with salad, or as a raw vegetable.

### To Cook Okra

Wash well and trim stem end, leaving enough of the pod to keep the juices in that the mucilage does not come out. Cover with boiling water and boil gently until tender. When half done, add salt. When ready to serve, drain, pour into a hot dish and add melted butter sufficient to season. A bit of lemon juice or vinegar is liked by some over the okra when eating.

To cook okra with a piece of boiling meat in place of using butter is a favorite way with many.

### Boiled Okra

Select tender pods of okra of uniform size, about 2½ inches long. Remove stems but do not cut into pod. Boil in salted water until tender but not soft.

Serve with Hollandaise sauce.

### Fried Okra

Select small, tender pods.

Boil until tender, drain, season with salt and pepper, roll in crumbs, then in egg and crumb again. Fry in deep fat. This is crumbed and egged the same as a croquette.

### To Fry Okra

Cut into half-inch slices, crosswise; sprinkle generously with meal and fry in grease like French fried potatoes. Sprinkle with salt; serve hot.

### Georgia Gumbo

| | |
|---|---|
| ¼ cup bacon drippings | 1 quart of cup okra |
| 1 large onion | 1 cup of boiling water |
| 6 fresh tomatoes, peeled and sliced | Salt and pepper to taste |

Into a heavy fry pan put grease; slice onion quite thin and fry in grease a very light brown. Care must be taken not to burn or cook too much, for this would ruin the entire dish. Add tomatoes, okra and water; stir often; add seasoning when half done.

Cook about 1 hour. The mixture should be thick enough to be eaten with a fork. Serve with dry rice or as a vegetable with small individual corn meal hoe cakes, which should be well done and crusty.

Half a dozen fresh mushrooms broiled, chopped and added would make the dish more delicious. To rub the pan with a cut clove of garlic gives another added charm.

This mixture prepared and put into green peppers and baked would be another way of using.

## Okra Gumbo

| | |
|---|---|
| 1 quart diced okra | 1 clove of garlic |
| 3 strips breakfast bacon | 1 green pepper (seed removed) |
| 3 tomatoes | 6 stuffed olives |
| 1 onion | Salt and pepper to taste |

Wash and cut okra, cut all vegetables into rather fine pieces, peeling tomatoes before cutting. Fry bacon until crisp, remove and mince. Into fry pan put okra, onion, olives and pepper and cook until seared but not burned, add tomatoes and cook slowly until done, about 30 minutes. When served sprinkle minced bacon and parsley over top of dish. Serve with dry rice or toast points.

## Scalloped Eggplant

Slice, peel and boil in salted water until tender one medium size eggplant. Drain and chop.

Into a baking dish put a layer of eggplant, bits of butter and a sprinkle of black pepper, then a layer of crushed crackers, until all is used, having eggplant on the top.

Mix one egg with one cup of milk and pour over the dish, using just enough to peep through the top. Cover top with buttered crumbs. Bake in medium oven until crumbs are brown and milk and egg are cooked, about 30 minutes, serve from dish in which it was cooked. Use oyster or snowflake crackers. An extra egg makes the dish richer.

## Stuffed Eggplant

Select a good sized eggplant; cut a good slice from the side leaving large enough to fill and serve from. Remove the inside, leaving the rind intact. Boil the eggplant in salt water until done; drain, season with butter or bacon drippings, salt and pepper; add a little milk, one egg and a few bread crumbs. Return to the shell, cover the opening with buttered crumbs and bake until they are a good brown and long enough to cook the egg.

## Baked Eggplant

Peel, boil, mash and let cool enough eggplant to make about two cups. Season with salt, pepper to taste. Beat 2 eggs together well; add 4 tablespoons of milk, 2 tablespoons of melted butter. Mix with the eggplant, pour into a buttered baking dish; cover top with buttered crumbs.

Use a moderate oven. Bake just long enough to cook the eggs and brown the top; about 20 minutes. Sometimes the rind of the eggplant is used in place of a pan. Cut a slice from side or end, scoop out the inside, boil and when seasoned refill the shell and bake. Place on a platter and garnish the dish.

## Eggplant Janet

Remove a slice from the side of an eggplant, scoop out and boil pulp until tender, drain. Mix with 1 cup of white sauce, ¼ cup grated cheese, ½ cup cold meat, ground. Cover top with buttered crumbs, bake until brown. Serve from the shell.

### Broiled Eggplant

Peel and slice plant ¾ inch thick—let stand in cold water 15 minutes, drain and wrap in towel to dry. Broil exactly as you would a steak, turning and browning until tender. Put on hot platter, season with salt, melted butter, and a good sprinkling of lemon juice. Serve.

### Fried Eggplant

Peel and cut in ¼ inch slices crosswise. Soak slices in salt water 30 minutes; drain, and wipe dry. Dip each slice in flour, then in beaten egg and then cracker crumbs. Cook in deep fat like a croquette only a little less rapidly, giving time to cook slice thoroughly. Drain on paper and serve hot.

### Eggplant Fritters

| | |
|---|---|
| 1 egg | 1 medium (or 1 cup) eggplant |
| 2 teaspoons baking powder | 1 tablespoon butter |
| 2 tablespoons flour | |

Peel, slice and cook the eggplant in salt water until tender; drain and mash. There should be about 1 cup. Add beaten egg, butter and flour. Drop into hot grease and fry until brown, or cook like cakes, using just enough grease to turn them.

### Eggplant Souffle

| | |
|---|---|
| 1 medium eggplant boiled and mashed fine | 1 cup bread crumbs |
| | 1 onion |
| 1 tablespoon butter | 2 eggs |
| ¼ cup milk | Salt and pepper to taste |

Mix all ingredients together, cover top with the bread crumbs and bake in moderate oven 30 to 40 minutes.

### Tomatoes

It was not many years ago that no thought was given to the food value of tomatoes. Only the seasoning put in them counted, and all tomatoes were small in size. But the cultivation and improvements by Luthter Burbank and his followers have brought about an increase in size of tomatoes and now some of them are so large they are called "beefsteak" tomatoes.

Today tomatoes are a necessary food. They supply us the much talked-of vitamins which food experts tell us we must have to keep fit.

The juice of fresh or canned tomatoes is the best substitute known for orange juice, which is so essential to babies fed on artificial food and to invalids.

Tomatoes, like oranges, contain stored up sunshine, that is when they are gathered ripe. It is the warm sunshine that develops or makes vitamins. So, after years of growing and eating them, we have come to know the true value of tomatoes.

Tomatoes are colorful and beautiful and have enough tartness to sharpen the appetite.

Then, too, tomatoes help the housewife to change many a dish. There are numberless ways of using, from the first course, as an appetizer, soup, vegetable and salad.

### Raw Tomatoes

Select ripe tomatoes. Peel with a small paring knife just through the skin. Chill, slice in half inch slices or serve whole (cutting into eight sections half way through the tomato pulling sections slightly open). Have blossom end up. Serve with salt, pepper and vinegar; French dressing or mayonnaise.

When placed on lettuce it then serves as a salad.

### Broiled Tomatoes

Select firm, ripe tomatoes. Peel and cut crosswise in slices half an inch thick. Drain for a minute; dip in flour. Into a heavy fry pan put 2 tablespoons butter. Heat and broil tomatoes on both sides until brown. Turn with batter cake turner. Serve with broiled fish, steak, or poached eggs.

### Stewed Tomatoes No. 1

| | |
|---|---|
| 1 can or 1 quart of tomatoes | 1 teaspoon sugar |
| 2 tablespoons bread crumbs | 1 teaspoon salt |
| 2 tablespoons butter | Dash of pepper |

Stew tomatoes in their own juice until thick and done. Add seasoning and serve. Some prefer to leave out bread crumbs.

### Stewed Tomatoes No. 2

Stew tomatoes as directed in above recipe leaving out bread crumbs. Have 2 cups of toasted bread cubes about size of 1 inch, and when tomatoes are thick put toasted cubes in dish; pour hot tomatoes over them and serve.

### Grilled Tomatoes

| | |
|---|---|
| 3 large tomatoes | 1 green pepper |
| 6 slices of bacon | 1 white onion |
| 6 rounds of toast | 1 cup grated yellow cheese |

Run the pepper and onion through the food chopper. Place tomatoes in boiling water for 5 minutes, then slip off the skins and cut in half. Cut the bread in rounds a little larger than the tomatoes, and toast them. Place a half tomato on each round of toast. Place a heaping tablespoon of pepper and onion on each tomato, salt well, and top with a heaping tablespoon of grated cheese. Place on a baking sheet under a broiler flame until the cheese melts and browns. Garnish with crisp bacon and stuffed olives.

## Tomatoes and Macaroni

| | |
|---|---|
| 6 medium sized tomatoes | 2 tablespoons grated cheese |
| ¾ cup cooked macaroni | 3 tablespoons bread crumbs |
| ½ cup white sauce | Salt and pepper to taste |

From stem end take a slice from each tomato. Scoop out the inside, salt and invert to drain. Cook the portion taken out until quite thick, mix with the white sauce. Cut macaroni in short pieces, add seasoning, fill tomatoes, put crumbs over top. Place in a greased pan, bake in moderate oven 20 to 30 minutes, until tomato is done and top is brown.

## Creamed Tomatoes

Peel and cut thick slices of tomatoes, broil in lard or butter, place on platter, cover with cream sauce, sprinkle top with cheese.

## Stuffed Tomatoes

| | |
|---|---|
| 6 medium tomatoes | 1 cup cold rice, hominy or bread |
| 2 tablespoons of butter or bacon | crumbs |
| grease | ½ cup buttered crumbs |
| 1 tablespoon chopped onion | Salt and pepper to taste |

Select tomatoes of uniform size and from the stem end cut a slice; remove seed and part of the pulp, sprinkle with salt and invert to drain. Into a saucepan put the butter and onion and cook slightly, then add the tomato pulp and continue cooking for about ten minutes. Add the seasoning, cold rice and mix well, having it rather stiff; fill the tomato shells and cover the tops with the buttered crumbs. Place in a greased pan; add just enough water to prevent sticking to the bottom; bake in moderate oven about 20 minutes.

## Tomato Timbales

| | |
|---|---|
| 1 quart of tomatoes (canned or | 1 teaspoon salt |
| fresh) | 1 tablespoon sugar |
| 1 small onion | 2 whole cloves |

Boil until done, about ten minutes; put through a coarse sieve. There should be 2 cups. Add a half cup of stale bread crumbs and mix well. When cool, add 2 eggs slightly beaten and blend all together.

Pour into buttered timbale molds, place in boiling water and bake until firm. Place on several folds of paper before adding the water. Unmold on hot platter, pour cheese sauce over all, sprinkle with chopped parsley, and serve.

For cheese sauce make the usual white sauce, add a cup of grated cheese, blend together until cheese is well melted.

## Tomatoes a la Schreiber at Breakfast Time

3 good sized firm tomatoes          6 slices of buttered toast
1 cup white sauce

Peel and slice each tomato in about three slices. Make and butter slightly the toast. Into a skillet put enough butter to broil the tomatoes and when this is done make the white sauce in the same pan adding more butter if necessary. As the tomatoes are broiled lay on the pieces of toast and place in a platter. Make the white sauce, pour over all, garnish with parsley and serve piping hot.

## Tomato Rarebit

½ pound cheese chipped fine          Salt and pepper to taste
1 can tomato soup (medium size)

Heat slowly all together in double boiler, stir to mix well. Serve over hot buttered toast.

## Baked Tomatoes

6 tomatoes                          4 slices of bacon or the drippings
2 teaspoons salt                    2 tablespoons flour
1 tablespoon butter                 Pepper to taste
1 cup stock or milk

Cut tomatoes in halves without peeling, place in a baking dish with the cut side up making cups of the tomatoes, sprinkle with salt and pepper, cut the bacon and put a piece on each piece of tomato; bake in a moderate oven for 20 to 30 minutes; when done put on a platter and make a brown sauce as follows:

Melt butter, add flour and allow to brown, now add stock making a smooth sauce; mash one of the cooked tomatoes in the sauce, using any juice or brown part that accumulated in cooking, pour over the tomatoes and serve. Any seasoning liked may be added to the sauce; more bacon may be broiled and served crisp around the platter, which makes a heavier dish. Mushrooms added to the sauce would still increase the food value and would be a delicious luncheon dish fit for the king.

## Scalloped Tomatoes

6 tomatoes                          ½ cup hot water
4 strips bacon                      ½ cup bread crumbs
2 hard-boiled eggs                  Salt and pepper
2 cups oyster crackers

Broil and mince bacon, saving the drippings for seasoning. Peel and slice tomatoes, putting in a layer of tomatoes, a part of minced bacon and one egg, sliced thin. Add salt and pepper, then a layer of crushed crackers. Continue until all is used, having tomatoes on top.

Add bacon drippings to hot water and pour over all. Cover top with the crumbs, bake until brown. A green pepper or small onion is a nice flavor for a change.

## Tomato Mayonnaise

1 cup of mayonnaise           Salt and pepper to taste
1 cup of grated tomatoes

Select very red tomatoes, peel and grate, beginning at the blossom end. Make the mayonnaise and mix the two. This gives a custard-like mixture; freeze as you would ice cream. Serve over heart lettuce or a cucumber aspic. It should be seasoned well with red pepper and salt.

## Burr Artichokes

Wash well, and let stand in salt water for 30 minutes or longer; this will draw out any insects or bugs. Drop into boiling water and cook about 30 minutes or until tender; pierce with a fork. Lift out, drain; place on a small dish and serve hot or cold with drawn butter, or a French dressing.

The dressing should be in a small dish so the leaves may be dipped into the dressing as each one is pulled off and eaten.

The tough part is thrown away, and the tender end eaten with the dressing. The good part is at the root of each leaf.

These artichokes sell for something like 12 to 15 cents each, though in some cities they are 5 cents each.

To eat a whole artichoke, steady it lightly with the fingers of the left hand, pull the leaves off one at a time with the thumb and a finger of the right hand, dip the thick white end into the butter or sauce and gently pull it between the teeth, thus removing the delicate meat held in this end. When all leaves are removed, the bottom or choke is cut and carried to the mouth with a fork.

An artichoke may be served as an entree with a sandwich or cracker, or as a salad with French dressing, having it hot or cold.

## Burr Artichoke Bottoms or Chokes

This part of the burr artichoke may be purchased in cans, and is used generally for a cocktail.

## Mock Chokes

Cut slices of small white turnips ¾ inch thick. Cover with cold water and bring slowly to boiling point. Drain and drop into a French dressing highly seasoned. Add enough water to cover and simmer until they can be pierced with a straw. Serve hot with melted butter or chill and serve as a cocktail with plenty of cocktail sauce.

## Jerusalem Artichokes

These artichokes are commonly grown throughout the South in old fields, fence corners and gardens. They belong to the sunflower family. They are used generally for pickles and may be used as cucumbers peeled, sliced and served with vinegar, salt and pepper. They are very good cooked, but have been used this way very little.

## Jerusalem Artichokes Cooked

Scrape and drop in cold water to prevent turning dark. Cut crosswise in half inch slices, and boil in salt water until just tender enough to be pierced with a fork. Drain and serve with melted butter or white sauce.

If overcooked, they are not crisp and tasty, but stringy.

## Boiled Onions

Select onions of uniform size, peel, removing tops; let stand in cold water until ready to cook. Drain and cover with boiling salt water and cook gently, uncovered, until tender. Drain, return to the stew pan and dry slightly over a slow fire. Pour into a hot dish, cover with white sauce or melted butter, serve piping hot.

## Fried Onions

Peel and slice in half-inch slices, crosswise.

Put into a saucepan, cover with boiling salt water, simmer for ten minutes, drain well. Into a fry pan place two tablespoons of butter or cooking oil or bacon drippings for every cup of onions. When hot add onions and fry until done tender and a delicate brown.

Stir frequently to prevent burning. Season with pepper and more salt if needed. Serve with steak or liver.

## French Fried Onions

Cut onions in ¼-inch slices and pull ring loose. Soak in sweet milk for an hour (water may be used). Take rings from milk and cover with flour to which salt and pepper has been added; drop in deep fat and fry until brown. They should float in the grease.

They will go to the bottom at first, then come to top as they begin to get done. Don't fry too many at one time. A small batch often may be done quicker than too many at one time.

A kitchen stunt: Put flour in a paper bag, drop a handfull of onion rings in, shake well, and they are covered with flour. A thin batter of flour, sweet milk and egg with salt and pepper is sometimes used. However, the first is very simple.

## Fried Onion Rings

Peel, slice into quarter-inch slices as many onions as needed. Have a vessel of deep fat, when hot drop in a handful and fry a delicate brown, remove, drain, sprinkle with salt, fry slowly enough to cook done. Do not fry too many at one time; a small quantity often will finish the job in less time and have better results.

If liked crisp, fry longer. These may garnish a broiled steak or any meat, or be served as a dish.

If you wish these onions very mild, soak for 1 hour in sweet milk, drain well, dredge with flour and fry as directed above.

## Scalloped Onions No. 1

3 cups cooked onions
2 cups oyster crackers
½ cup buttered crumbs
¾ cup sweet milk

2 eggs
3 tablespoons butter
Salt and pepper to taste

Slice or quarter onions. Boil until done. Into a baking dish put a layer of onions, butter, salt, pepper. A layer of broken crackers, more onions and crackers until all are used. Mix milk and eggs together, pour over the mixture, cover top with buttered crumbs, bake just long enough to set the milk and eggs and brown top about 20 minutes. Serve in the dish in which it was baked. Have milk heated just tepid.

## Scalloped Onions No. 2

1 quart onions (medium size)
2 cups white sauce
1 cup buttered crumbs

2 cups crackers
1 tablespoon minced parsley
Salt and pepper to taste

Peel, quarter and boil onions in salt water until tender. Follow directions for other scalloped dishes. Sometimes a little pimento pepper gives flavor and color. Cheese might cover the top in place of the crumbs, or a little mixed in the dish gives variety.

## Glazed Onions

6 medium size onions
½ cup boiling water
3 tablespoons butter

¼ cup brown sugar
1 teaspoon salt
⅛ teaspoon pepper

Place peeled onions in covered baking pan or dish. Pour boiling water, butter over onions. Sprinkle with salt and pepper. Cover with brown sugar and bake in moderate oven one hour. Remove cover from dish for the last fifteen minutes. If large onions are used they may be quartered.

## Onions as a Relish

Remove tops and outside peel. Drop into cold water until crisp and tender. Drain; eat with salt.

A spring salad would be to slice and mix with cucumbers and tomatoes. Serve with salt, vinegar and pepper or a French dressing.

## A Southern Dish

1 quart peeled and diced shallots
6 eggs

¼ cup butter
Salt and pepper to taste

Boil shallots until done in salt water. Drain.

Into a fry pan put butter and melt gently. Add shallots and the eggs, which are broken but not beaten.

Stir gently as they cook to mix. Have a slow heat so the eggs will be tender. Cook the same as in scrambling eggs, and do not have them dry, but a soft creamy mixture; season, serve very hot. A bit of milk may be added. Any leftover meat, ham, or bacon, may be minced and added. This is a nice luncheon dish

### Onions au Gratin

Boil Spanish onions until done. Cut each onion in quarters. Put into baking dish a layer each of onions, white sauce, a sprinkle of grated cheese, crushed crackers, and repeat until dish is full. Cover top with buttered crumbs and slip in oven to brown on top and heat through. Serve in same dish.

### To Cook Turnips

Peel and slice or dice the turnips. Just cover with boiling water. Add salt and a bit of sugar, boil until tender, about 20 or 30 minutes, drain and serve with white sauce or melted butter and chopped parsley. The white turnip and rutabagas are both good cooked this way, and make a pretty dish when mixed together.

### Molded Turnips

2 cups of cooked and mashed turnips
1 cup of thick white sauce

3 eggs
Salt and pepper to taste

Cook, mash and put the turnips through a coarse strainer. Make the usual white sauce with milk, butter and flour. Mix the two together and add the eggs which have been beaten together just enough to break them well. Add salt and pepper. Pour the mixture into a buttered mold and set into a pan to cook in which several thicknesses of brown paper are put in the bottom. Pour boiling water to come half the depth of mold, bake or steam until firm. Unmold, garnish with parsley and serve hot.

### Turnips and Pork

Peel, wash and slice turnips needed; then drop in cold water. Into a pot put a pork hock and let boil until done. Remove, add turnips and boil until tender. Drain, mash, season with more salt if necessary and add one tablespoon sugar. Serve with a small piece of pork and cornbread.

Sometimes a few Irish potatoes are cooked and mashed with turnips. This gives a more delicate flavor.

Turnips are much better cooked quickly; this keeps them from turning pink.

### Rutabaga Turnip

This is a deep yellow turnip and requires much longer cooking than the white turnip, and is not so delicate. It may be boiled with a piece of pork, seasoning meat or served with melted butter or with sauce.

### Carrots

Scrape or peel off outer skin and put into cold water until ready to cook. Boil moderately in salt water until tender, season with melted butter or white sauce. A little sugar added to the water is quite an improvement.

## Uses

Carrots grated or diced, raw or cooked, may be used for salad.

Young, tender carrots are eaten raw the same as radishes.

Young, tender carrots with two or more tiny leaves left on are used for garnishes.

Carrots and beets, cooked separately and mixed and seasoned, may be used very effectively in carrying out a color scheme. Carrots and turnips may be used in the same way. (See recipe).

## Carrots and Turnips

2 cups peeled and diced carrots          2 cups peeled and diced white turnips

Boil carrots and turnips separately until tender in salt water to which a little sugar has been added. Drain, mix together, season with melted butter or white sauce.

## Carrots and Onions

Substitute onions for turnips. Follow recipe above.

## Carrots and Peas

Use the first recipe and substitute peas for turnips, using half the quantity.

## Carrot Mold

2 cups grated or shredded carrot          1 teaspoon salt
1 cup thick white sauce                   Pepper to taste
3 eggs

Grate the carrots and put mixture in cheesecloth and press out some of the water; then measure. Make the usual white sauce. Half milk and half of the juice of the carrots may be used for the sauce. Add sauce to carrots, add seasoning, beat eggs together and add to mixture. Pour in a well-buttered ring mold and steam in hot water until firm, about 30 minutes. Let cool a few minutes, then unmold on platter and serve.

## Parsnips and Salsify

The above are prepared, cooked and used similar to carrots.

## Beets

Beets (roots) must be put into boiling water, cooked until tender (boil moderately) the time depends on the size and age of beets, from one to two hours. Do not trim off root nor cut leaves too close; if cut they bleed and lose their color.

Beets are sliced or diced and served hot with melted butter.

## Beets as a Relish

Boil beets, slice or dice. Cover with a mild vinegar to which has been added a little salt and sugar.

## Boiled Potatoes

Peel potatoes, remove any eyes or dark spots and put in cold water until ready to cook.

Drop into boiling water and boil rapidly for five or ten minutes, then reduce to medium heat and boil until done. Add salt when half done. Drain and place vessel over gentle fire; shake several times to turn potatoes to dry them out well, having pot uncovered. When dry, white and snowy looking, put into hot uncovered dish, dot with butter and serve at once. Potatoes may be peeled or boiled in their jackets.

## Baked Potatoes

Select smooth, medium-sized potatoes, scrub well and with a fork stick several times (this prevents their bursting). Place in baking pan or on a rack (about center) in oven; bake forty-five minutes to one hour, according to size of potato. Have oven hot and reduce to medium.

To test, do not stick, but with a towel mash to see if soft. If done, continue to mash gently, but not hard enough to burst, until quite soft.

With a knife make a cross cut on each, about an inch and a half long, press hard to open. This sends out steam and meals the potato. Sprinkle with salt and paprika, add a lump of butter and place potatoes in platter on which is a folded napkin. If potatoes must wait, mash, open, and keep in warm oven until served. If potatoes are baked in too hot an oven the skins are heavy and hard and potatoes are not so good.

## Stuffed Potatoes

Select medium-sized potatoes, prepare and bake as directed for baked potatoes. Remove a slice from one side, scoop out the inside, mash, season and refill shells, leaving the top of filling rough, place in a pan and into hot oven to reheat and brown the top. Serve very hot. The seasoning is usually milk and butter; a bit of cheese added is good, also minced bacon and onion.

## Potato Puff

| | |
|---|---|
| 2 cups of hot mashed potatoes | 2 tablespoons butter |
| 1 cup milk more or less | 2 teaspoons salt |
| 1 egg | Sprinkle red pepper |

Cook, dry and mash potatoes. Add milk and seasoning and beat well. Beat egg light, add to mixture and pile in a baking dish roughly. Bake in moderate oven about ten minutes. Serve immediately.

More eggs (two) would make a richer dish. If whites are beaten stiff and added the mixture will be lighter but will sometimes fall. A little grated cheese gives a nice flavor.

## Potatoes au Gratin

| | |
|---|---|
| 3 cups diced potatoes | 1 cup rich white sauce |
| 1½ cups grated cheese | Salt and cayenne pepper |

Boil potatoes until just done—about ten minutes. Drain. In a baking dish put half of the potatoes, a sprinkle of salt and pepper, add half of the white sauce over this and half of the cheese. Repeat this, using all material, with cheese on top.

Put in a hot oven just long enough to melt cheese, and it is ready to serve. Sometimes buttered crumbs are used over the top. The white sauce has sufficient butter for seasoning. Minced parsley, pepper or onion may be used if liked.

## Duchess Potatoes

Boil twelve potatoes, peel and pass them through a ricer; mix with them two tablespoons of butter, three eggs, a little salt and some chopped parsley. Make into balls and fry in hot fat.

## Hungarian Potatoes

| | |
|---|---|
| 2 lbs. potatoes peeled and sliced as for chip | 2 medium tomatoes peeled and sliced |
| | 2 medium onions |
| 3 tablespoons butter or substitute | 1 teaspoon paprika pepper |

Put butter into sauce pan, slice and cook the onions, but do not brown, slice and add the tomatoes and potatoes, add salt and pepper, just barely cover with stock, cook gently until potatoes are tender and the stock is almost gone. Put into a platter and sprinkle with parsley. Serve very hot, or serve from the dish in which it was baked.

## Mashed Potatoes for Piping

Boil potatoes and put through a ricer in order to free of any lumps. Season with butter and a little milk, beat until light and fluffy. Have the potatoes soft enough to use through the tube, decorate around the edge of plank or dish, using other vegetables to cover and fill in the space. Sometimes as many as six vegetables are used on one plank. If you wish to brown the potatoes after they are on the plank, the yolks of several eggs are mixed with the potatoes before piping, then run into a hot oven to brown.

## Mashed Potatoes

Boil potatoes as directed in recipe for boiling, taking great care to dry out well and keep hot. When ready to mash put through a ricer or mash, add butter and have milk hot. Season to taste with more salt, if necessary, and white or cayenne pepper. Beat with spoon or mixer until light and fluffy. Put into hot dish. Do not cover unless a napkin is used. A china cover will make them soggy.

Do not put black pepper into the potatoes; if used, sprinkle over the top. Serve immediately.

An egg added, a grating of cheese and returned to the oven in a baking dish until brown gives a different taste.

## Baked Mashed Irish Potatoes

| | |
|---|---|
| 6 large potatoes | ⅛ teaspoon pepper |
| 2 tablespoons butter | 2 eggs |
| 1 teaspoon salt | ½ cup milk |

Boil and dry out potatoes, put through ricer or mash well, add seasoning, beat eggs together till light, add to potatoes; put into baking dish in which they are to be served, bake in oven until nice and brown, serve at once. Cheese sprinkled over the top is good for a change, also to use up a stale crust of cheese.

## Potatoes de Luxe

| | |
|---|---|
| 3 cups hot mashed potatoes | ½ cup grated cheese |
| 1 cup ground boiled ham | |

Cook, mash, season and beat light the potatoes. Line a shallow baking dish with part of the potatoes, using about two-thirds. Sprinkle the ground ham over top; put the remaining potatoes into a ricer and cover ham, having it very light. Over this sprinkle the cheese. Set in hot oven long enough to brown slightly and melt the cheese. Sprinkle a dash of paprika over top and serve.

## Mrs. K's Potato Balls

Boil six medium potatoes and put through the ricer while hot and allow to cool. Add two tablespoons butter, one egg, salt and enough flour to make stiff. Make into balls the size of walnuts. Have a large vessel of boiling salt water, and drop the balls in and boil moderately (about 20 minutes). Drain and place balls on platter, pour the sauce over them and serve piping hot.

### Sauce

Broil crisp four slices of bacon, remove and mince fine. Add two tablespoons minced onion to grease and cook, then add the minced bacon, two tablespoons flour, and water or milk enough to make a gravy as thick as cream. Serve over balls.

## Scalloped Potatoes

Peel and slice the amount of potatoes needed. Into a baking dish put a layer of potatoes, seasoning—salt, pepper,, butter and a sprinkle of flour. Repeat until all potatoes are used. Heat enough sweet milk to just cover potatoes, put all in moderate oven and let cook until potatoes are well browned. Onion may be added as part of seasoning.

## Chiffon Potatoes

| | |
|---|---|
| 8 or 9 medium Irish potatoes | 3 eggs |
| ½ cup warm milk (more or less as needed) | 4 tablespoons butter |
| | Salt and pepper to taste |

Peel, boil and mash potatoes. Add seasoning. Add milk as needed to have mixture to hold its shape. Separate eggs, add yolks to potatoes, mix and beat well. Have border mold well buttered, fill with mixture and let stand while beating whites stiff like meringue. Add a pinch of salt. Put stiffy-beaten whites into a forcing bag with tube. Unmold potatoes on a flat pot cover about 6 or 7 inches in diameter and cover top of mold with the whites coiling criss-cross like a rope.

Use all the white piling high. Place top on baking sheet and into a medium oven (350). Bake for twenty minutes until meringue is light brown and very lacy looking. Place top with potatoes on platter, fill center with a creamed meat or vegetable and serve. This is a beautiful dish for company dinner.

## Potatoes a la Kitty

Peel and cut potatoes as for French frying. Boil in salt water until they are just tender. Drain well, pour into a large flat baking pan, sprinkle with flour, dot with butter and pepper. Place in hot oven to brown and when browned sufficiently turn gently (use a batter cake turner), and sprinkle with flour again—add more butter if necessary. Brown and turn until all are slightly browned. Place on platter and serve.

These potatoes are similar to French fried but are not greasy. Use just enough butter to season, and the flour is used to make potatoes brown.

## Potato Cakes

| | |
|---|---|
| 3 cups mashed potatoes | 1 teaspoon salt |
| Yolks 2 eggs | ⅛ teaspoon pepper |

Mix all together and roll out on board, using a little flour; cut with a tea biscuit cutter ¾-inch thick; place on greased biscuit sheet and put small pieces of butter in center of each cake; put in broiler, brown on both sides, turning with cake-turner. Arrange tastily on a hot platter and sprinkle with chopped parsley and serve with any kind of meat.

## Irish Potato Pancakes

| | |
|---|---|
| 2 cups grated potatoes | ½ teaspoon baking powder |
| 2 eggs | 1 tablespoon milk |
| 1 teaspoon salt | 1 tablespoon flour |

Peel large potatoes and soak in cold water for several hours. Grate and drain. Beat eggs, add all ingredients, then mix with potatoes. Have batter slightly thick, and bake as pancake on well greased griddle over moderate heat until well done.

### Irish Potato Fritters

3 large potatoes
¼ cup flour
1 teaspoon salt

3 tablespoons butter
1 teaspoon baking powder
2 eggs

Boil the potatoes and put through ricer; add butter and other ingredients while hot; beat light; add yolks of eggs to mixture, which should be thick enough to cook. If thin, cook stiff over hot water until thick. Let cool while beating whites stiff; fold together and fry brown like cakes. Serve with chops or broiled ham.

### French Fried Potatoes

Select large, old potatoes; peel and cut in long, slim strips. Drop into cold water and when ready to fry dry well on a towel. Have a deep sauce pan (one which holds two or more quarts) with grease about two inches deep. Drop a handful of potatoes (10 or 12 pieces) into pan and fry until done and brown. Skim out and drain on a paper napkin. Fry in similar quantities until all are cooked. Serve immediately. If crisp potatoes are wanted they must go from the grease to the guest. To keep them crisp as they are served plunge the second time into the boiling grease, drain and serve. This recrisps and heats at the same time. Sometimes they are fried until done but not browned; when ready to serve plunge them again in very hot grease until hot and brown, about two minutes.

### Hashed Browned Potatoes

Dice cold potatoes (about one cup). Put into a pan, and with a biscuit cutter chop again, sprinkle with a little flour to hold together, and chop more; then add salt and pepper. In a heavy fry pan put about two tablespoons bacon drippings or butter, pour in the potatoes and chop and spread about the size of a saucer, having potatoes about half an inch thick. Cook over medium heat until the bottom is well browned, and the flour used is well cooked. Turn together, making a half circle, lift up with a battercake turner and place on a plate and serve. The flour mixes with the moisture of the potato and holds together but is not noticeable.

### Irish Potato Balloons

Peel medium size potatoes, cut as for potato chips, only a trifle thicker. Let stand in cold water for an hour. Fry in deep fat until they are about half done, remove and let them get perfectly cold. Place in frying basket again and fry until potatoes will puff like a balloon. Continue to cook until brown. Drain and serve the same as potato chips.

### Straw Potatoes

Cut potatoes in straws, wash and dry. Fry in deep fat until brown.

Sprinkle with salt. When ready to serve plunge them again into the hot fat to heat and crisp. Serve quickly.

## Potato Chips

Cut with a regular slicer or very sharp knife, medium size and well matured potatoes into slices as thin as possible. Place them in cold water and let stand for an hour before frying. Remove from water and place between towels to absorb as much moisture as possible. Have ready frying basket with sufficient grease to cover potatoes in the basket. Test grease by putting in a piece of stale bread which should brown in about 40 seconds. If a thermometer is used it should register 400 degrees. Place a layer of potatoes in the basket and lower basket carefully, lifting up and down until excessive bubbling stops. Stir chips while cooking and let brown delicately—about a minute and a half. Avoid frying very many at a time as this cools grease quickly. Drain in basket and then on paper. Sprinkle with salt at once.

## Baked Sweet Potatoes

Select potatoes of uniform size, wash and trim ends. Rub over each potato with a bit of cooking oil, place in pan and bake in moderate oven until done. The time depends on the size of potato. When done put into a pan where they will keep just hot enough to prevent sweating, but to puff the skin and make the syrup. This is a very simple thing and sounds as though it is harder to do than it really is.

Sometimes they are peeled and sent to the table ready to serve. Most people prefer them quite hot and to peel them at table.

## Mashed Sweet Potatoes

Bake or boil the amount of potatoes needed, three or four of medium size. When done, peel and mash while hot; put in a good sized lump of butter, pinch of salt and a small amount of milk, beat all together until light. Pile onto a baking dish and run into a hot oven until slightly browned over top and piping hot. This takes the place of candied potatoes. A bit of sugar and an egg may be added. This enriches the dish.

If the potatoes are peeled and cut crosswise into half-inch slices, they will cream well and the "strings" will not be noticeable. Some potatoes are more stringy than others.

## Meringue Sweet Potatoes

| | |
|---|---|
| 3 cups mashed potatoes | ¼ cup hot milk |
| 3 egg yolks | ⅛ teaspoon salt |
| 3 egg whites | Sherry or vanilla to flavor if |
| ½ cup sugar | desired |
| 3 tablespoons butter | |

Peel, cook, mash and measure potatoes. Beat egg yolks and half of sugar, add to potatoes. Add salt and flavoring. Melt butter in hot milk, add to potatoes and mix well. Put into buttered ring mold to set while making meringue of egg whites and remaining sugar, beating meringue until it holds a point. Unmold potatoes on flat buttered plate, or tin. Using forcing bag with tube having star end, pile meringue in high peaks over potatoes covering well. Bake in slow oven, 15 minutes until meringue is delicate brown. Place plate on large platter and serve hot.

### Candied Sweet Potatoes No. 1

4 good size potatoes
1 cup of sugar

½ cup of water (boiling)
2 tablespoons of butter

Boil potatoes until about half done; peel and slice lengthwise, about one-third of an inch thick. Into a baking-dish put a layer of potatoes, dot with butter and sprinkle with sugar until all is used; put in water and put sugar and butter on the top. Bake until well done and syrup is thick, using a medium heat for baking. The amount of sugar would depend on how sweet one likes the dish. A lemon is sometimes sliced and baked with the potatoes; also an apple used is a different flavor.

Use a little spice or not as desired. A small quantity of syrup used with the sugar is liked by many. About 30 to 40 minutes would be required to bake.

### Candied Sweet Potatoes No. 2

Peel and slice potatoes. Follow recipe in No. 1, using potatoes uncooked. Add one cup hot water and bake, uncovered, in slow oven one hour or until potatoes are done and syrup thick. If potatoes are cut crosswise no strings are evident.

### Broiled Sweet Potatoes

Peel and cut cold baked potatoes in half-inch slices. Roll in flour, fry in bacon drippings or butter until flour is browned and potatoes hot through. Have just enough grease to make them brown and turn easily. Serve with bacon or chops.

### Sweet Potato Croquettes No. 1

3 cups potatoes
½ cup sweet milk
1 egg

1 tablespoon sugar
2 tablespoons butter
1 teaspoon salt

Boil and mash and strain potatoes.
Mix well, roll into balls, then into cracker crumbs, beaten egg and crumbs again. Fry in deep fat, drain and serve.

### Sweet Potato Croquettes No. 2

Make as directed in No. 1. Roll into balls, then roll into shredded cocoanut, place on baking sheet, put into hot oven long enough to cook egg and brown the tip end of the shredded cocoanut. Serve hot. Nuts and raisins may be added to mixture. Make mixture soft enough to handle, using more or less of the milk.

### Sweet Potato Balls

To two cups of hot mashed sweet potatoes add three tablespoons of butter, salt and pepper to taste. Shape into small balls. Roll in nut meats; heat and serve.

### Celery

This vegetable is the most used of any in making salads. It is used almost daily as a raw vegetable. As a hot vegetable it is diced and served with white sauce, mixed with cream chicken, brains and served in soups.
Celery should be cleaned thoroughly and crisped before serving.

### Cucumbers

Cucumbers are mostly used raw as a relish or salad. Those not overlarge with small, tender seed are best to use. They are peeled, sliced and made crisp by standing in cold water or crushed ice. Salt water destroys the crispness.
See Salads for other ways of using.

### Lettuce

Another vegetable eaten raw and used in various ways as a salad.
The head is quartered and served with dressings of various kinds.
The leaves are shredded and mixed with hard-boiled, diced eggs, a dressing, and used as a relish or salad. The leaves are used for holding portions of salad and for garnishing.
It is considered necessary in the diet, belonging to the leafy vegetables and sometimes classed as one of the protective foods.

### A Head of Lettuce

Remove the bruised outside leaves that are not usable. Remove the next leaves which are tough and large, and add to the greens (turnip, spinach or kale) for boiling. The next leaves may be used for holding salad or be shredded and dressed. This brings the head down to the center or heart, which may be quartered and eaten with dressing.

### Radishes

The young, tender radish is eaten raw, used for garnishing, and mixed with other vegetables as a salad. The tops are used with other greens for boiling.

### Parsley

This plant is used for seasoning and garnishing both meats, vegetables and salads.

## Earl House Recipe for Rhubarb

Use small or medium firm red stalks.

Wash but do not peel rhubarb and cut in $\frac{1}{4}$ to $\frac{1}{2}$-inch pieces. Put rhubarb in a shallow pan, sprinkle with sugar and cook in moderate oven. Do not stir. Cook until done.

Rhubarb may be used in sauces, floats, rolls, shortcakes, pies and other dishes. May be used as a substitute for apple sauce.

## Mushrooms

Mushrooms must be used only when perfectly fresh and firm; in peeling them take a small knife and, holding the delicate fringe and the edge of the mushroom between the edge of the knife and the thumb, peel the paper-like skin off, pulling it toward the center of the mushroom. The stems should be cut or broken off without breaking the cup and should be scraped and used. When the mushrooms are white, small and freshly picked they can be quickly washed and cooked without peeling.

One pound of fresh mushrooms is equivalent to two cans. Fresh mushrooms have a most delicious flavor while canned ones have very little, and are added mostly for bulk and looks.

Broiling mushrooms first in butter brings out the delicious flavor which is so much liked, then they may be added to any cream sauce.

When using canned mushrooms, drain off the juice, boil in salt water gently for 20 minutes and add to any mixture desired. If wished to broil, toss and cook in melted butter about 10 minutes. Large ones should be chopped when added to creamed dishes.

If a bright or granite pan is used for broiling, the mushrooms will stay lighter in color. Iron fry pan turns them very dark, but they are just as good.

## Broiled Mushrooms

Peel, wash and drain large mushrooms; place, cup side up, in a shallow pan, sprinkle with salt and place small piece of butter on each; place in broiler about three inches from fire; broil about five minutes or till hot and done. Care must be taken *not* to spill the juice, which is delicious; place on rings of toast and serve; garnish with parsley and radishes.

## Pan Broiled Mushrooms

Peel, wash and remove stems. Into a heavy frying pan put enough butter to broil; place mushrooms in whole, brown and cook on both sides until tender (4 or 5 minutes).

Place on toast on hot platter. Into the fry pan pour two or three tablespoons of hot water, cook for one minute, pour over mushrooms, serve.

If for steak, cook as above, place mushrooms on the steak and pour the sauce over all. Sprinkle with salt and pepper.

To use the stems, cut off the part which is tough and woody. Slice thin and sear well in butter, cover with hot water and simmer until tender.

After broiling the mushrooms pour the stems and water into fry pan to make the gravy; pour this over the mushrooms.

If a sauce is wanted, add a little flour to the pan, brown in the butter and then add pieces and water. Cook just to thicken and blend together. Season with salt and pepper and pour over the steak or mushrooms, or both.

## Stewed Mushrooms

½ lb. mushrooms, washed, peeled and cut in quarters or 1 can mushrooms
2 tablespoons butter
4 tablespoons flour
1 cup sweet milk
1 teaspoon salt
⅛ teaspoon pepper

Melt butter, add flour and cook till a light brown; add mushrooms and broil till hot; now add milk, heated; blend together, season with salt and pepper and cook slowly ten minutes. Serve on toast or pour over broiled steak.

## Baked Mushrooms

Select 2 dozen large mushrooms. Drop into cold water to which has been added a spoonful vinegar. Wash and drain, remove stems, peel mushrooms.

Take 6 mushrooms and the stems and chop fine. Add 2 tablespoons of minced parsley, 2 shallots which have been blanched in boiling water for 10 minutes, chop fine.

Into a fry pan put 4 tablespoons of butter, melt, add chopped mushrooms, parsley and onion and sear all together well, being careful not to burn. Add 2 cups of stock, or milk and water; and cook until chopped vegetables are done. Season with salt and pepper. Into a buttered baking dish place the whole mushrooms tops down, pour over the sauce which has been reduced some. Cover top with buttered bread crumbs and bake in moderate oven until mushrooms are done and crumbs are brown (about 20 to 30 minutes). Have oven hot when dish is put in. Serve from baking dish.

## Tomatoes and Mushrooms

Select tomatoes of uniform size, cut slice from top, scoop out inside, salt and invert to drain. Make filling as follows:

In sufficient butter fry 2 tablespoons minced onion, 2 tablespoons minced celery, 2 cups chopped mushrooms. Add 3 tablespoons flour and brown all together. Add tomato pulp and sufficient water or stock to cook until thick enough to stuff tomatoes. Fill tomatoes, cover top with buttered crumbs, bake in moderate oven until tomato is done (about 30 minutes). Serve hot. One cup mushrooms may be used, adding dry bread crumbs after the mixture is cooked to stiffen—stuff tomatoes.

## Egg Stuffed with Mushrooms

Boil hard 6 eggs. Chop and broil 6 large (or the equivalent) mushrooms making a sauce. Cut egg in half, remove yolks and mix with the mushrooms using the juice or gravy to moisten. Season with salt and pepper. Refill eggs. Set into a buttered baking dish, surrounded with a highly seasoned tomato sauce, heat thoroughly, and serve at once from the baking dish.

## Mushrooms and Spaghetti

| | |
|---|---|
| ½ lb. spaghetti | 2 cups stock |
| ¼ lb. butter | 3 tablespoons chopped pimentoes |
| ½ lb. mushrooms or 1 can | 2 tablespoons chopped parsley |
| 1 medium onion | 2 tablespoons flour |

Boil spaghetti in salt water until tender, drain and blanch in cold water.
Remove stems from mushrooms, chop or slice fine, peel tops.
Into half of the butter put stems, onions, and pimentoes; and cook but do not burn. With the other part of the butter broil the mushrooms until nearly done—add flour, brown, add the stock and the stems to the mixture and cook until the sauce is of a creamy consistency and mushrooms done. Season with salt and pepper.
Pour over hot spaghetti, sprinkle parsley over top. Serve with bread, dill pickles and coffee. More mushrooms may be used.

## Mushroom Stuffing for Turkey

One-half pound fresh mushrooms broiled, then stewed in 2 cups water for 15 minutes. Cut stale bread in slices then in cubes, fry brown in half cup butter. Mix mushrooms and bread together, being careful not to break the cubes of bread. Fill turkey and roast as usual.

## Mushrooms with Peas

Fill the cups of large mushrooms with canned peas, which have been tossed for 5 minutes in hot butter; season and set in a hot oven in a covered pan for 10 minutes; serve on toast with white or brown sauce, as preferred.

## Filled Mushrooms

Select as many large, cup shaped mushrooms as needed, remove stems, peel and put in shallow pan, cup side up. Take the stems and enough imperfect mushrooms, chop fine and season with salt and pepper; fill the mushroom cups; put a teaspoon of butter into each cup; put into hot oven and cook for 10 minutes or till done; place on rounds of toast, garnish with parsley and serve hot.

## Mushroom Pie

| | |
|---|---|
| 4 tablespoons butter | 1 lb. fresh mushrooms |
| 2 hard boiled eggs | ½ cup cream |
| 1 teaspoon salt | ¼ teaspoon white pepper |

Melt butter in saucepan, add mushrooms, that have been peeled and washed, and cook gently for 10 minutes; add the sliced eggs and cream; pour into baking dish or casserole; cover top with pie crust and cook until crust is done or about 10 minutes in a hot oven. Buttered crumbs may be used in place of crust. This is especially nice used in ramekins and served as an entree, cutting crust to fit ramekins and baking quickly and serving. Oysters broiled and added to pie make a nice dish.

## Brown Mushroom Sauce

| | |
|---|---|
| ¼ cup butter | 2 cups stock (chicken or veal) |
| 1 slice onion | 1 can mushrooms or ½ lb. fresh |
| 1 small carrot sliced | mushrooms |
| 1 slice green pepper | Salt and pepper |
| 6 tablespoons flour | |

Into a saucepan put butter, melt and add vegetables. Brown to extract juices, but do not burn. Remove vegetables. Add flour and brown. Drain and add mushrooms and slightly brown. Add stock and cook until a creamy sauce, add seasoning and it is ready to serve over any broiled meat, or add diced meat to make a creamed dish—chicken, oysters or sweetbreads.

If mushrooms are large, chop before using. If fresh mushrooms are used, peel, chop and broil in small portions of butter to bring out the flavor, then add juice and all to brown sauce.

salads

# CHAPTER VIII

## Salads

While salads have been known and used for hundreds of years, yet it has remained for the last generation to recognize the value and importance of salads in our daily diet. A new adage says, "A salad a day keeps the doctor away." Salads, especially the raw varieties, contain mineral salts and vitamins which are so essential to our growth and general well being. Dietitians are advising families to reduce the quantity of other foods, especially the starches, and to increase the daily consumption of salads for every member of the household.

There is a general impression that salads are expensive and should be regarded as luxuries, but this is a mistake, since a little judicious planning will produce delicious and appetizing dishes of salads made wholly or in part of leftovers attractively arranged on lettuce leaves. The cost of the salad may be what you choose to make it, since coleslaw can be served in winter at about the cost of a dish of potatoes, and raw tomatoes in season at the cost of a dish of string beans. A sweet salad may take the place of a salad and dessert combined.

At the present time frozen and congealed fruit and vegetable salads are quite popular and certainly wholesome. It is far better to confine the meal to a few well selected balanced dishes than to too many. The mixtures are the cause of "lots" of indigestion.

The uncooked food should always be washed well since producers are often forced to spray their plants to kill the insects which infest them. Arsenic and Paris green are the poisons most generally used for this purpose and caution should be used in preparing the salad materials. Salads must be cold, crisp, well blended in selecting the combinations of materials, and attractive.

The simple French dressing for salads for the hearty meal (salads should be light) is far more acceptable than mayonnaise, the latter being used where a heavy salad is used for the main dish. The secret of the perfect salad lies in the dressing and the plainest dinner may be made delightful by a well selected salad and dressing.

There is scarcely any limit to the many valuable crisp vegetables, fresh and canned fruits that are so plentiful. America takes the lead in producing the greatest variety of delicious vegetables and fruits, and is now the greatest salad eating nation. This is true of the better class; but since it is a known fact that the humble cabbage, carrots, lettuce and other commonly grown vegetables and fruits give so much food value, it is the desire of every one who is preparing food to stress salads. Salads may be put in the protective class of foods.

## FRUIT SALADS

### Pear Salad

Use canned pears; take from the can and let stand one hour in a good lemon water. Place on crisp lettuce two halves, make five or six balls from cottage or Neufchatel cheese, roll in chopped nut meats or chopped parsley, place on and around the pears, cover with French dressing and serve.

### Porcupine Salad

Select large Bartlett pears, one for each serving. Have ready almonds, blanched and shredded lengthwise. Place pear on lettuce, with cut side down, stick almond pieces in rows like quills, put two cloves in small end for eyes. Serve with French dressing.

### Apple Ring Salad

Core and slice into rings without peeling, bright red apples, ring ¼ inch thick, drop into salt water to keep white. When ready to use, dry and cover with French dressing. Core and remove seed and veins from crisp green peppers, cut in very thin rings. Arrange apple and pepper rings on crisp lettuce, garnish with pimentoes. Serve with French dressing.

### Waldorf Salad

| | |
|---|---|
| 1 quart peeled and diced apple | 1 pint chopped blanched almonds |
| 1 quart chopped celery | 1 cup mayonnaise |

Blanch and chop the nuts, cut celery and sprinkle with salt; put where both will keep cool. Make mayonnaise. Peel and dice apples one at a time and mix with the mayonnaise until you have a quart. When ready to serve mix in the nuts and celery; add more seasoning if needed; drain the celery free from any water; put into apples or on lettuce and serve. When apples are cut and mixed at once with the mayonnaise they will not turn dark. Any nuts may be used. The almonds are white and pretty.

### Log Cabin Salad

Peel and cut bananas in fourths lengthwise, soak in orange juice one hour. Arrange on lettuce log cabin style, fill center with any fruit desired, cherries, pineapple, grapefruit. Serve with mayonnaise or French dressing. The bananas may be rolled in chopped nuts before piling, if liked.

### Pineapple and Cheese Salad

| | |
|---|---|
| ½ cup cottage cheese (or two Neufchatel cheese) | 4 slices canned pineapple |
| | ½ teaspoon paprika |
| 2 or 3 tablespoons top milk or sweet cream (more or less) | Pinch of salt |
| | Dash of cayenne |

Mash cheese and soften into firm paste, using sufficient milk or cream, and add seasoning. Wipe slices of pineapple dry, so cheese will stick to fruit. Put layer of cheese as deep as the pineapple, then another slice of pineapple, press together hard, let stand with a weight on top until cold. Cut in small pie shaped sections, pile on crisp lettuce. Serve with pineapple dressing. See recipe. This is a nice sweet salad.

## Pineapple and Cheese Salad

1 fresh pineapple
¼ pound of rich soft cream cheese
1 cup mayonnaise

1 cup whipped cream
1 head lettuce
Salt and cayenne pepper to season

Peel and remove the eyes of the pineapple. From the stem end pluck off the pineapple in nice size cubes, going round and round the stem until all is removed. Moisten the cheese with a bit of milk, if necessary, and make into balls about as large as a marble. Wash and have lettuce crisp. Pile pineapple and cheese balls on the lettuce. Mix the cream with the mayonnaise and put a generous spoonful over top. Serve at once after the dressing has been added. This will make eight or ten portions.

## Butterfly Salad

The arrangement of this salad in the form of a butterfly is not a new one, but the fruit mixture is a good one. Including raw apple in fruit salads not only improves the flavor, but makes the more expensive fruits go further.

2 slices canned pineapple
2 slices orange
2 slices unpared apples
½ pound Malaga grapes

Strips of pimento
Lettuce
Chopped nuts

Cut the pineapple slices in half and place the round edges together on the plate. Over this fit the slices of apple with the core removed. (If you wish to remove the skin pour boiling water on the apple and the skin will peel off, leaving the red coloring showing in the meat). On top of this fit the orange slices, which have been allowed to stand in sugar at least 20 minutes. Form the butterfly's body from the grapes and the antennae from the pimento strips. Sprinkle with nut meats and serve with mayonnaise.

## Stuffed Cherry and Pineapple Salad

1 cup white canned cherries
½ cup blanched almonds

1 cup diced pineapple

Drain fruit, dice pineapple, remove seed from cherries and into each one stick an almond. Pile together on crisp lettuce and serve with fruit salad dressing. Plain mayonnaise may be used, or mayonnaise with whipped cream.

## Peach Salad

Select 8 halves of firm peaches
2 Neufchatel cheese (about ½ cup)
½ cup nut meats or salted peanuts

1 cup whipped cream (more or less)
¼ cup French dressing

Place a half of peach on crisp lettuce. Make cheese into balls and fill centers of peaches. Mix French dressing into cream, which should be quite stiff. Add more seasoning if necessary. Put portion on top of cheese, add peach, sprinkle with nuts and serve.

## Mary Louise Salad

Peel grapefruit and remove sections whole, allowing 5 or 6 sections for each person. Have crisp lettuce and arrange grapefruit in shape of cart wheel. Fill center with chopped pecan meats and seeded cherries or Malaga grapes and serve wih French dressing, using the juice of the grapefruit in place of lemon. Have everything cold when served.

### Bessie Tift College Salad

2 cups diced apples
1 cup cherries (red or white)
1 cup diced pineapple

1 cup nut meats
1 dozen mint leaves, chopped very fine

Seed cherries, dice all fruit, mixing the first three, and add mint leaves. Arrange on lettuce, cover with dressing, sprinkle nut meats over top and serve.

For the dressing use:

⅔ cup sugar
½ cup water

2 eggs
3 tablespoons lemon or grapefruit juice

Boil sugar and water until it threads well, pour over the stiff beaten whites, as in making icing. Beat yolks light, add to mixture, place bowl over boiling water and cook (beating all the time) until thick. Remove from fire, add lemon juice, beat until cold. Serve over fruit salad.

### Southern Salad

2 cups diced tart apples, unpeeled
3 bananas, peeled and diced
Meat of 1 large grapefruit

1 cup white grapes, peeled and seeded
Season with salt and cayenne pepper

Mix all together and serve on lettuce, using a whipped cream dressing.

### Grapefruit Salad

Peel and remove sections of grapefruit, keeping sections intact, place five sections on a crisp lettuce leaf in melon shape. Have Neufchatel cheese softened to a stiff paste with a bit of milk, put into a forcing bag with star end pastry tube and make four or five roses around the grapefruit. Over all put French dressing and serve. This is a nice dinner salad.

### College Salad

1 can pineapple, cut in cubes

Equal quantity marshmallow, cut small

Make a fruit dressing (see recipe). Using about one cup, put this over the pineapple and marshmallow to stand about two hours. When ready to serve, add a cup of pecan meats, or any nut preferred. Add more dressing, if necessary. Serve on lettuce.

### Avocado Salad (Alligator Pear) No. 1

Select medium sized, firm avocados, chill, cut in half, remove seed. Make a French dressing and put a portion into the pear, place on plate and serve with crackers or sandwich. Grated onion added to the dressing is much liked by many. Russian or Thousand Island dressing is used also.

If the avocado is to be used with other ingredients, peel, remove the seed and cut into sections or cubes.

## Avocado Salad No. 2

Select ripe avocado, peel, cut and mash to a pulp, season with lemon juice, salt and pepper, make into small balls about the size of bird egg, roll in very finely chopped green pepper. Have crisp lettuce ready, on this place one thick slice of ripe tomato and five balls, leaving space in center to make a rosette of mayonnaise. Serve.

## Santiago Salad

Peel and cut in cubes as much avocado as needed, mix a small onion, grated, salt and lime or lemon juice, mix with avocado, pile on lettuce on platter. Over all sprinkle finely chopped hard boiled eggs. Use more dressing if desired. The eggs may be rubbed through a coarse strainer, which gives a pretty effect.

## Avocado Nut Salad

Mix two parts diced avocado to one part nut meats. Place on crisp lettuce and serve with any preferred dressing.

## Avocado Aspic

| | |
|---|---|
| 2 cups water | ½ box Knox No. 1 gelatine (1 en- |
| ¼ cup lemon juice | velope) in ¼ cup cold water |
| 1 good sized avocado | 1 tablespoon grated onion, if desired |
| 2 large firm tomatoes | Cayenne and paprika to taste |
| 2 tablespoons sugar | Green coloring to make green |
| 1 teaspoon salt | |

Put gelatine to soak for five minutes, then melt over hot water. Peel and dice avocado and tomato. Make a stock of the water and seasoning, add coloring and melted gelatine. Into a mold put a portion of stock, set on ice, put in a layer of fruit when beginning to get firm, then more stock and more fruit until all is used. Place on ice to get hard, unmold on lettuce, serve with mayonnaise.

An easy way is to pour all the stock into mold, and when it begins to get firm, drop in the fruit, stir gently to mix, let get firm.

## Avocado With Coral Dressing

Peel and cut the avocado in sections, pile on lettuce leaf, pour over two or three tablespoons of coral dressing. See recipe in Salad Dressings.

## Avocado and Tomato

Peel ripe, firm tomatoes, cut into sections lengthwise, peel and cut avocado same way, alternate the sections red and green on crisp lettuce leaf, serve with French dressing.

## Avocado and Egg Salad

If they are of the small Mexican variety, peel and mash avocados, one for each guest. The American avocado is larger, and one will serve two guests. Chop or mince 1 hard-boiled egg, mince 1 small onion, add vinegar, salt and pepper to taste. Serve on a lettuce leaf. This also makes a delicious sandwich filling.

### Reesie's Favorite Avocado Salad

Select medium avocados, peel, remove seed and inside skin. Make a French dressing. Into each avocado place three or four stuffed olives, put sufficient dressing, place on crisp lettuce, serve at once.

### Avocado Delicious

Chill, peel, cut in half lengthwise, remove seed, place on crisp lettuce, fill center with frozen tomato mayonnaise, serve with crackers.
See recipe for Frozen Tomato Mayonnaise.

### Avocado and Grapefruit

Prepare both fruits, alternate sections of grapefruit and avocado on a plate until sufficient for serving, pour over French dressing with lots of paprika, serve with cheese sticks.

## VEGETABLE SALADS

### Salsify Salad

Scrape and boil in salt water, that is strong with vinegar, sufficient salsify to make two cups, dice and have cold; have equal amount of tender diced cucumber, mix well with three-fourths cup of mayonnaise and serve with sliced tomatoes on crisp lettuce individually, or serve on a platter with a border of sliced tomatoes. Keep salsify in cold water till ready to use to prevent turning dark.

### Lettuce and Egg Salad

Arrange crisp leaves on plate, quarter or slice hard boiled egg, arrange on lettuce. Use French or Thousand Island dressing.

### Lettuce Salad

Wash and crisp lettuce and cut into quarters or less. Place a piece for each serving on a small plate, and cover with French dressing, allowing about one tablespoon for each service.

### Dressed Lettuce

| | |
|---|---|
| 2 hard boiled eggs | Salt, pepper, vinegar and prepared |
| 1 dozen leaves of lettuce | mustard |
| 1 small onion | Dash of sugar if liked |

Remove yolks from eggs and mash smooth in a bowl with a silver fork. To this add the mustard (about one teaspoon). Salt and pepper. Then add sufficient vinegar, about ½ cup, to make into a sauce. Grate and add onion to taste. Season well with salt and pepper. Chop whites of eggs, add to sauce. Prepare lettuce, add sauce, toss together in the bowl and it is ready to serve.

To prepare the lettuce, pile three or four leaves together, roll up lengthwise, being careful not to bruise the lettuce. Cut in narrow strips with a pair of scissors, repeat until all is shredded, then mix with the dressing. Use a good apple vinegar. This can be diluted with water if too sharp.

## Stuffed Lettuce

Have crisp hearts of lettuce, and after removing any coarse outside leaves, cut them in halves crosswise and remove a little of the center. The halved hearts will then have the appearance of nests. Make some small eggs from cream cheese, sprinkle with black pepper and paprika, and put five or six in each nest. Put a large spoonful of red jelly over each portion and serve with French dressing, seasoned with paprika.

## Head Lettuce with Roquefort Cheese Dressing

Make a French dressing, mash cheese until fine, add small portion of dressing to soften, continue until well mixed. Cut firm lettuce in quarters, put about two tablespoons of dressing over lettuce, serve.

## Lettuce Salad with Coral Dressing

Prepare lettuce as in above recipe and serve with coral dressing. See recipe in Salad Dressings.

## Okra Salad

Select small tender pods of okra about 2½ inches long. Allow about six pods to each serving. Do not cut off point, and trim stem end like a pencil point. Boil until tender in salted water to which is added a little vinegar and one teaspoon of paprika. When tender drain and chill. Serve with French dressing. Arrange okra pods on lettuce leaf with stem ends at center and each pod extending out like spokes in a wheel. Put radish rose or sprig of parsley in center.

## Tomato Salad

Select ripe and well shaped tomatoes and peel. Across the blossom end of tomato cut half way through into eight sections, pull open like a lily, leaving tomato intact at stem end. Serve with mayonnaise, cucumber mayonnaise, or French dressing.

## Another Stuffed Tomato

Prepare tomatoes as in above recipe. Use tomatoes and fresh or canned pineapple to fill centers, using French dressing for filling and topping with mayonnaise.

## Novelty Salad

| | |
|---|---|
| 6 hard boiled eggs | 1 cup finely chopped chicken |
| 1 tablespoon each, finely chopped green peppers and pimentoes | Sufficient mayonnaise to mix |
| | Salt and pepper to taste |

Cut eggs lengthwise, remove yolks and rub through sieve. Toss all ingredients together, add seasoning and enough mayonnaise to hold together, refill egg whites, arrange on crisp lettuce, serve with mayonnaise. Each egg may be placed on thick slice of tomato then on lettuce. Garnish with strips of pimentoes, celery, celery hearts or any other garnish.

## Vegetable Combination Salad

1 slice tomato (half inch thick)  
2 rings onion (Bermuda is best)  
2 rings green pepper  
2 stalks asparagus

Place on lettuce leaf, serve with French dressing. Over all sprinkle beets cut in small pieces.

## Another Vegetable Salad

Cooked beets, sliced or diced  
Cooked carrots, sliced or diced  
Chopped celery  
Chopped olives  
English peas  
Proportions to suit individual

Mix all together and serve on lettuce with French dressing.

## Creole Salad

4 cups macaroni cooked (about ½ lb. raw)  
2 cups diced tomatoes  
1 cup grated cheese  
1 cup mayonnaise  
¼ cup sliced stuffed olives  
2 tablespoons grated onion  
½ clove garlic chopped fine  
⅛ teaspoon cayenne pepper

Boil macaroni in salt water until tender, but not mushy, blanch (wash well in cold water), drain, cut in inch pieces and place on cheesecloth to drain and chill. Have very cold. Measure after cooked. Mix all together as any salad and serve on lettuce.

This is a good salad for Dutch Supper, served with dill pickles and rye bread.

## Miss Evelyn's Spanish Salad

1 dozen hard-tack or ship biscuit  
4 large ripe tomatoes (more if necessary)  
3 tender cucumbers  
4 canned pimentoes  
1 cup mayonnaise

Put hard-tack in cold water until soft. Drain, and through a potato ricer or colander, mash the hard-tack. This should look like potatoes when riced. Into a bowl put a layer of the riced biscuit, then a layer of the tomatoes, sliced very thin, a layer of mayonnaise, another layer of riced hard-tack, a layer of cucumbers, sliced very thin, a layer of mayonnaise; next comes hard-tack, pimentoes, minced, and mayonnaise. Over the top a layer of riced hard-tack, and over this place slices of tomatoes cut in fancy shapes. Place all in ice box until thoroughly chilled and seasoned. Serve from the bowl. A bit of grated onion may be added, or rub the bowl with a clove of garlic cut in half. The mayonnaise should be highly seasoned.

## Stuffed Celery

Select uniform pieces of celery, leaving the pretty leaves on; mash sufficient cottage, Neufchatel or cream cheese, soften with top milk, season with salt and cayenne pepper. Fill centers of celery with mixture, roll in chopped nuts, place on ice to keep cold and crisp. Serve as a salad or to accompany a salad.

Ham rolls and stuffed celery would be nice together. See recipe for Ham Rolls.

### Cucumber Boats with Shrimp

Select cucumbers of uniform size, take a slice from one side, scoop out the cucumber, leaving boatshaped. Drop in vinegar water to keep crisp and white. Use shrimp and the inside of cucumber, dice small, season with French dressing, fill centers of cucumbers, place the whole on lettuce leaf and serve.

Any fish or just vegetables may take the place of the one given above.

The whole may be topped with frozen cucumber mayonnaise if desired.

### Asparagus Salad

Select large white asparagus tips, allowing three or four stalks for each serving. Cut green peppers crosswise, making three rings, run asparagus through the rings and place on lettuce. Serve with French or Russian dressing.

### Coleslaw

Use fresh white cabbage, cut into quarters and let stand in cold water for an hour. When ready to make, drain and shred fine. Use the following dressing:

| | |
|---|---|
| ½ cup water | 1 tablespoon flour |
| ¼ cup vinegar | ½ teaspoon dry mustard |
| 1 tablespoon sugar | 2 hard-boiled eggs |
| 1 tablespoon oil or butter | Salt and pepper to taste |

Mix flour, sugar and mustard together. Mix vinegar, water and oil. Bring to a boil, pour over dry ingredients and cook until thick. Mash yolks of eggs with a little of the dressing, add mixture, and let cool. Chop whites with cabbage, pour the dressing on, season to taste, and serve.

## VARIETY SALADS

### Chicken Salad

| | |
|---|---|
| 1 fat hen | 1 cup of mayonnaise |
| 1 large bunch of celery | Salt and cayenne pepper to taste |

Boil the hen until very tender. Remove from the water and chill; pull from the bones, discarding all skin, gristle and veins. Cut with scissors in cubes about half-inch in size or larger. Salt. Clean celery and cut into small pieces about the same size as chicken. Mix together, add mayonnaise. Salad should have plenty of lemon juice in the mayonnaise and be seasoned well with salt and pepper, always using cayenne or white. There should be equal quantities of celery and chicken. Sometimes nuts are added.

### Mock Chicken Salad

2 cups diced lean pork or veal
2 cups diced celery
½ cup chopped stuffed olives or cucumber pickles

½ clove garlic to rub bowl
1 cup cooked mayonnaise
Salt and cayenne pepper to taste

Boil pork in salt water with small onion and sweet green pepper until
very tender. Let get cold, remove all fat and cut in cubes. Rub bowl with
the cut garlic before mixing salad. Mix all together, add dressing and
serve on lettuce.

### Esther's Salmon Salad

2 cups salmon
1 cup diced celery
¼ cup diced pickles

1 cup mayonnaise or cooked dressing
Salt and pepper to taste

Remove any bones and skin from salmon, drain well of any juice, mix
together, add mayonnaise and seasoning and it is ready to serve.

### Oyster Salad

1 pint oysters
1 cup tender celery, cut fine
¼ cup mayonnaise

2 tablespoons chili sauce
2 tablespoons sour pickles or olives
Salt and cayenne pepper to taste

Boil the oysters until they curl, drain and put on ice until very cold.
Mix with other ingredients and serve on lettuce.

### Shrimp Salad

2 cups shrimp
1 cup finely chopped celery
4 hard-boiled eggs, chopped

½ cup mayonnaise
Salt and cayenne pepper to taste

Break shrimps into small pieces, removing any shell or objectionable part.
Mix together, season and chill. When ready to serve, add mayonnaise, toss
together with fork, place on bed of crisp lettuce and serve.
Minced pickles, olives, pimentoes, capers, may be used if desired. Shredded lettuce or cabbage may take the place of celery. Thousand Island
dressing may take the place of plain mayonnaise.

### Potato Salad

4 cups cold diced potatoes
2 cups chopped tender cabbage
1 cup chopped celery
1 cup mayonnaise
½ cup chili sauce

⅛ cup Worcestershire sauce
2 tablespoons of grated onion
Salt, pepper and more lemon juice
   if needed

Cook potatoes and do not dry or meal them. Take from the water to
get cold so they will be waxy; when cold, dice. Cut the heart of cabbage
and let stand in cold water at least an hour. Cut celery very fine or use a
few celery seed or dry leaves to flavor.
Mix dry ingredients together. Have the usual mayonnaise. Mix with

the chili and Worcestershire sauce. Add all seasonings. Mix into salad and serve or place where it will keep cool until ready.

Celery may take the place of cabbage if preferred.

### Crab Flake Salad

Use fresh or canned Japanese crab meat. Mix two cups of flakes, one cup of very tender, finely diced celery, with one-half cup of mayonnaise. Line platter with lettuce, pour on the salad, sprinkle over top a few capers, garnish with slices of hard boiled eggs and strips of pickled beets or strips of pimentoes.

### Mexican Salad

| | |
|---|---|
| 1 cup celery (diced) | 1 green pepper |
| 1 cup cucumber (diced) | 6 stuffed olives |
| ½ Spanish onion | |

Chop fine all vegetables and mix with 1 cup of cooked mayonnaise.

This may be congealed, or used over a congealed salad.

A good salad to serve with broiled or baked fish.

## CONGEALED FRUIT SALADS

### To Make a Fruit Aspic

Select the fruit you wish to use, peel and remove from skin, saving all of the juices. Cut into medium pieces. Sweeten to taste with the juice of the canned fruit, season with salt to taste.

To every one and a half quarts use one box of Knox's No. 1 plain gelatine, which has been soaked in one-half cup of cold water for 10 minutes.

Then place the vessel containing the wet gelatine over boiling water and melt until thoroughly clear. Remove from the heat. To the gelatine add a cup of the mixture in order to thin, then add it to the mixture to be congealed, mix well and turn into a mold to get firm. If the mixture is to be clear, and firm enough to stand or slice (an aspic) one box of gelatine for every quart will be required. If the gelatine is to be used in soft texture, follow directions on the package.

Grapefruit, oranges, canned pineapple and canned white cherries make a good combination for a fruit aspic.

A stock from chicken or knuckle of veal with any vegetable liked will make a good vegetable aspic.

### Grapefruit Aspic

Peel and free from white skin enough grapefruit to make one and a half quarts juice and pulp. Dissolve one box gelatine in one-half cup cold water for five minutes, melt over boiling water; add to grapefruit. Add salt to taste and a little sugar if too acid. Pour into mold to jell.

Turn out on bed of lettuce, serve with mayonnaise.

Any fruits may be used with grapefruit if liked. Oranges, canned pine-apple, white canned cherries. Have mixture of fruit and pieces to measure one quart and a half for one box of gelatine, which is dissolved in one-half cup of cold water, then melted.

## Fruit Aspic

| | |
|---|---|
| 2 good sized grapefruits | 1 box Knox No. 1 gelatine |
| 6 large oranges | ½ cup cold water |
| 1 medium sized can white cherries | Salt to taste |
| 1 medium sized can sliced pineapple | |

Remove fruit from skins and have in good size cubes or leave in whole sections, saving all juices. Dice pineapple, remove seed from cherries. Mix all together and add as much of the sweet juice from the pineapple and cherries as desired, also salt. Dissolve gelatine in the cold water and let stand for 10 minutes. Heat over boiling water until thoroughly melted. Add to fruit mixture; put into mold or pan to jell. Serve with may-onnaise.

A nice way to mold is to pour into jelly glasses, cut into slices one inch thick; place on lettuce leaf and with a star forcing tube put a rosette of mayonnaise in center of each slice. The forcing tube should be put into a bag of rubber cloth having the end extending out to be clear of the edge of the pointed bag. A cornucopia of stiff writing paper may be used. Make cornucopia, pin together, cut off the point to allow the tube to go through about one-half inch. Fill half full of mayonnaise, fold together the top; press mayonnaise out through the tube onto the salad.

## Congealed Fruit Salad

| | |
|---|---|
| 1 cup diced pineapple | 1 cup banana, peeled and scraped |
| 1 cup apple, unpeeled | 1 cup diced marshmallow |
| 1 cup white cherries | Making 1 quart in all |

Make a cooked dressing using:

| | |
|---|---|
| 1 teaspoon salt | 2 tablespoons flour |
| ¾ cup fruit juices, pineapple and cherry juice | 2 tablespoons gelatine soaked in ¼ cup water |
| ¼ cup lemon juice | 2 egg yolks |

Heat fruit juice, mix flour with a little cold water, add egg yolks and strain. Add to this the hot juices, return to double boiler and cook until a thick custard. Add the gelatine and thoroughly melt. Set aside to cool. When cool, mix with fruits, turn into mold to get firm. Serve with mayonnaise on crisp lettuce.

## Pineapple and Cucumber Aspic

| | |
|---|---|
| 1½ cups diced cucumbers | 1 box Knox No. 1 gelatine in ½ cup water |
| 1½ cups diced pineapple | Salt, pepper and vinegar to taste |
| 3 cups water | A dash of green coloring |

Put gelatine in the half cup of cold water for five minutes, then melt over boiling water. Season the water with salt, pepper and vinegar to taste. Add cucumbers and pineapple, color a dainty green, add the melted gelatine, turn into a mold to jell. Serve on lettuce with mayonnaise.

### Molded Cottage Cheese Salad

2 cups cottage cheese
1 tablespoon gelatine (dissolved in ¼ cup cold water)

½ cup top milk
⅛ teaspoon paprika
½ teaspoon salt

Mash cheese, add seasoning and cream, add gelatine after it has been soaked and melted over hot water. Pour into a ring mold to get firm.
Have ready:

1 cup orange sections, from which all white skin has been removed
1 cup diced pineapple (canned)

½ cup diced dates
¼ cup mayonnaise

Mix together.
Unmold cheese on platter of lettuce, fill center with fruit and over top of fruit pile the following dressing:

1 cup whipped cream

1 tablespoon each orange, lemon and pineapple juice

Fold juices into cream.
Garnish top with red cherries, or bits of bright jelly, or a few pieces of the fruit.

### Ginger Ale Salad

1 pint bottle ginger ale
2 tablespoons gelatine (one-half box) in one-third cup cold water
2 tablespoons sugar
¾ cup diced apples

¼ cup lemon juice
½ cup diced celery
4 tablespoons diced canned pineapple
2 tablespoons diced preserved ginger

Mix seasoning into ginger ale.
Melt gelatine over boiling water and add to ale. Pour into mold and when it begins to thicken add the fruits. Let stand until firm. Serve with mayonnaise.

## JELLIED MEATS AND VEGETABLES

### Molded Chicken

Prepare and disjoint a medium sized hen. Put into saucepan, pour over boiling water to cover. Boil quickly for five minutes, reduce heat and simmer until tender. Pull meat from bones, removing skin and gristles. Return bones to the liquid in which chicken was cooked. Add a stalk of celery, sprig of parsley, one small onion into which two cloves are stuck. Boil and reduce liquid to three-fourths of a pint (1½ cups). Line a mold with paper, place meat, alternating white and dark meat. Into the center of meat place two or three hard boiled eggs. Pour over all the liquid which is salted and peppered to taste. Let stand until cool. Put a weight on, let stand over night or until firm. Cut into thin slices, serve as a meat or with mayonnaise as a salad.

### Molded Salmon

1 teaspoon salt
¼ teaspoon dry mustard
2 tablespoons sugar
1 tablespoon flour
2 tablespoons gelatine dissolved in
¼ cup water

¼ cup vinegar
¾ cup boiling water
2 egg yolks
1 can salmon or crab, (about 1½ cups)

Mix all dry ingredients together, beat egg yolks, add to mixture. Pour vinegar into hot water and pour over egg mixture, put into double boiler and cook until it coats spoon. Add gelatine, melt well, set aside to cool. When cool turn in the meat which has been pulled to flakes, all bones and skins removed. Pour into mold to jell. Serve on lettuce with mayonnaise.

### Cucumber Aspic

1½ cups water
2 cups grated cucumber

2 pimentoes chopped fine

Season with vinegar, salt and pepper to taste. Color with a few drops of Burnett's green color paste, having it very delicate color.
One box of Knox gelatine No. 1, dissolved in ½ cup of cold water.
Into a bowl put all the ingredients, season and color, soak the gelatine in cold water for five minutes, then thoroughly melt over boiling water, add to the mixture and turn into a mold to get firm. When ready to serve turn out on a bed of lettuce and serve with mayonnaise. Other vegetables, may be combined with the mixture if desired.

### Filling for a Clear Chicken Aspic Mold

2 cups cooked diced chicken breast
¾ cup creamed brains
4 tablespoons milk
2 tablespoons gelatine

1 tablespoon sherry jell in ¼ cup cold water
4 tablespoons mayonnaise
½ cup cream, whipped
Salt and pepper to taste

Soak gelatine in water for five minutes, melt over boiling water, remove from fire, add milk, cool. When cool add mayonnaise, add whipped cream then the meat. Fill center of a mold of clear chicken aspic, cover top with more aspic, set aside to get firm. Unmold on lettuce, serve with mayonnaise.

### Asparagus Mold

2 cups cottage cheese
½ cup sweet cream
1 teaspoon salt
⅛ teaspoon cayenne pepper

2 tablespoons gelatine, dissolved in ¼ cup water from the asparagus for five minutes, then melted over hot water

Mix all together. Have ready:

1 cup asparagus, cut fine
¼ cup celery, cut fine

2 pimentoes, cut fine

Fold into the cheese mixture, pour into bread pan to get firm, slice and serve, plain or with mayonnaise.

## Perfection Salad

| | |
|---|---|
| ½ cup vinegar | 3 cups shredded cabbage |
| 2 teaspoons salt | 1 box gelatine dissolved in ½ cup |
| Red pepper to taste | cold water |
| 3 pimentoes or sweet fresh green | 1 cup boiling water |
| pepper chopped fine | 1 cup cold water |

Soak gelatine in the cold water for 5 to 10 minutes. Add cup of boiling water to dissolve gelatine well. Add the cup of cold water to hasten the cooling. Add all seasoning, set aside to jell. When it begins to thicken stir in the cabbage and peppers, and let stand until firm. Unmold and serve with mayonnaise. Have the cabbage crisp, a bit of sugar may be added if a sweet flavor is liked. Any kind of vegetable may be added that will blend with cabbage.

## Bess' Party Salad

| | |
|---|---|
| 1 lb. can crushed pineapple | 3 egg whites |
| 1 lb. can sliced pineapple | ½ pint whipping cream |
| 1 lb. can white cherries | 2 tablespoons plain gelatine |
| ¼ lb. blanched chopped almonds or | 3½ cups pineapple juice or mixed |
| pecans | fruit juices |
| 1 pt. mayonnaise | |

Drain juice from fruits, cut in small pieces the sliced pineapple, remove seed from cherries. Soak gelatine in ½ cup of fruit juice, melt over boiling water, add juices and let cool. When cold add fruits, nuts, whipped cream, mayonnaise and stiffly beaten egg whites. Place in refrigerator, stir several times during the chilling to mix fruits evenly. Chill over night, or freeze. Serve on lettuce.

## Cheese Mousse Salad

| | |
|---|---|
| 1 pint cream | 2 tablespoons gelatine, dissolved in ¼ |
| 1 cup grated cheese (yellow, nippy | cup cold water |
| kind) | 1 teaspoon salt |
| 2 pimentoes | ⅛ teaspoon cayenne pepper (more or |
| 2 tablespoons lemon juice | less) |

Whip cream stiff, chop pimentoes fine, add to cream, add seasonings and cheese. Melt gelatine over hot water, let cool slightly, add lemon juice to this and beat into cream mixture. Pour into mold to get firm and serve with mayonnaise.

This is quite pretty cut in slices and served on lettuce with a rosette of mayonnaise in center.

## Jellied Beets

Boil, peel and quarter small beets, filling a mold lightly so there will be room for the jelly, which is made as follows:

| | |
|---|---|
| 1 cup water | ½ teaspoon salt |
| ½ cup vinegar | 2 tablespoons gelatine, dissolved in |
| ¼ cup sugar | ¼ cup water |

Dissolve gelatine over hot water, mix all together, pour over beets. Set aside to jell. Unmold on lettuce. Serve with mayonnaise. If canned beets are used, a cup of the red juice may be used if the whole dish is wanted red. Thin rings of green peppers may be mixed with beets which makes a pretty dish.

### Another Beet Jelly

| | |
|---|---|
| 1 can baby beets | 6 tablespoons sugar |
| 1 cup beet water | 2 tablespoons gelatine, dissolved in ¼ |
| ¼ cup vinegar (more or less to taste) | cup beet water |

Arrange beets in a ring mold. Mix all ingredients together, melt gelatine over boiling water, add to mixture and pour over beets to cover. Set in ice box to get firm; unmold on platter, serve as beets or as a salad with mayonnaise.

### Baked Banana Salad

Baked bananas are easily assimilated. Put two bananas in a shallow pan and bake until soft. Force through a coarse sieve. Soften two tablespoons gelatine in one-half cup cold water, dissolve in one cup boiling water. Cool and add to banana pulp, together with one-quarter cup lemon juice and three tablespoons sugar. Turn into very small cups, which have been dipped in cold water, and chill. Turn out, cut in slices and arrange on lettuce. Put a spoonful of mayonnaise dressing on each piece and garnish with a walnut meat.

### Surprise Pickle Jelly

Cherries, olives, gelatine, pickles and oranges. Cut white cherries and olives into rings, oranges into cubes and pickles into strips. Dissolve 1 tablespoon of granulated gelatine in a little cold water and add to the heated juice of the cherries and pickles. Cool. Pour a little at a time into a mold and add a little of the fruit, adding more as the jelly sets. Turn out on a plate and garnish with watercress. Serve with turkey.

### Cheese Jelly

| | |
|---|---|
| 1 cup white sauce | 1 teaspoon salt |
| 1 cup grated (or diced) cheese | ⅛ teaspoon cayenne pepper |
| ½ cup cream to whip | 1½ tablespoons granulated gelatine |
| 1 teaspoon prepared mustard | (dissolved in ¼ cup cold water) |

Make the usual white sauce; while hot, add cheese and gelatine and blend together, add all seasonings. Let cool slightly. Whip cream, fold into mixture.

Sprinkle a layer cake pan with grated cheese, pour mixture in to get firm. When cold, cut in squares or fingers, roll in more grated cheese and serve with salad.

Leave out the cream, and this makes a sandwich spread.

## Tomato Jelly Molded in Egg Shells

Make opening in large end of egg as large as a dime, pour out the egg, rinse well with water. If whites are wanted, remove white first by turning egg from side to side. After white is removed, with a small knife or ice pick break the yolk and it will pour out readily. Make tomato jelly, fill egg shells full to the edge and place in cartons or set in a pan of salt or meal to keep them standing. Put into refrigerator to get firm. To peel, crack shell well, dip in pan of ice water, peel the same as hard boiled egg, place on lettuce and serve with mayonnaise.

One egg made of tomato, another of cucumber (green) and served together for an Easter party is very pretty.

Jello may be molded this same way, using several colors. The mixture must be stiff enough to hold the shape.

One tablespoon of gelatine to every cup of mixture is a good rule to follow.

The tomato fez may be used to fill egg shells.

When anticipating the need of egg shells, just crack them carefully when using for several days, keeping them intact. Rinse with cold water before filling.

## Tomato Fez

| | |
|---|---|
| 2 cups tomato pulp, after being strained | 1 teaspoon salt |
| 1 tablespoon grated onion | ⅛ teaspoon cayenne pepper |
| 2 tablespoons vinegar | 2 tablespoons gelatine, dissolved in |
| 2 tablespoons chili sauce | ¼ cup water |

Mash tomatoes (canned or fresh) to a pulp and strain to remove seed. Add seasonings. Melt gelatine over boiling water, dilute with half cup of the mixture, then add and mix well. Pour into small round molds to get firm, or mold in jelly glasses. Unmold and cut in thick slices. Serve on lettuce with mayonnaise. The tomatoes are not cooked.

## FROZEN SALADS

### Frozen Fruit Salad No. 1

| | |
|---|---|
| 1 quart can of fruit salad mixture | 2 tablespoons lemon juice |
| 3 tablespoons flour | ¼ cup mayonnaise |
| 3 tablespoons sugar | 1 cup unwhipped cream |

Drain off the juice, dice fruit. Bring juice to a boil, mix flour and sugar together dry, pour over this the hot juice and bring to a boil until clear, let get cold. Mix with the fruit again, add mayonnaise, lemon juice and cream. Freeze, serve on lettuce leaf. No other mayonnaise is necessary.

### Frozen Fruit Salad No. 2

| | |
|---|---|
| 1 quart fruit, diced small, using white cherries, sliced pineapple, canned pears | 1 cup mayonnaise |
| | 2 cups juice from the fruit |
| 1 cup chopped pecan meats | 1 teaspoon salt |

Mix together, then freeze. Serve on lettuce with dressing made of equal parts of mayonnaise and whipped cream. Lemon juice may be added to salad if too sweet.

### Frozen Fruit Salad No. 3

| | |
|---|---|
| 1 can white cherries | 1 cup mayonnaise |
| 1 can Bartlett pears | 1 cup cream whipped |
| 1 small can sliced pineapple | Juice 1 lemon |
| 6 oranges | |

Cut cherries in half and remove seed, cut pears and pineapple in small thin slices. Remove sections of orange from hull and white skin. Use all the orange juice and juice of pears. Mix mayonnaise and cream with fruit, pour into freezer and pack well with ice and salt to freeze without turning, cutting it down several times. Serve on crisp lettuce with a spoonful of mayonnaise. The pineapple juice is left out, to prevent too much flavor of that particular fruit. It may be added if liked.

### Frozen Fruit Salad No. 4

| | |
|---|---|
| 2 cups canned pineapple, diced fine | 1 cup blanched almonds |
| 2 cups marshmallow, diced after measuring | ½ cup white grapes (or canned white cherries) |
| 1 cup mayonnaise | 1 tablespoon gelatine dissolved in three tablespoons cold water |
| 1 cup thick cream | |
| ½ cup red cherries | 2 tablespoons lemon juice |

Whip cream stiff. Put gelatine in cold water for five minutes, then melt over boiling water, let cool slightly, add lemon juice. Dice all fruit, cut cherries and almonds in half, peel, seed and cut in half the grapes. Mix all together. To the whipped cream add gelatine and lemon juice, add mayonnaise, then mix the fruit in lightly but well. Pour into mold, pack in ice and salt for three or four hours. Serve on lettuce with cheese crackers.

### Frozen Fruit Salad No. 5

| | |
|---|---|
| 1 quart of grapefruit, oranges, pineapple and white cherries | ½ cup mayonnaise |
| 1 cup fruit juice | 1 cup whipped cream |

Remove fruit, freeing from all white skin, cut into small pieces. Mix mayonnaise and fruit juices together, mix with fruit. Whip cream stiff, add. Freeze or pack in ice. Serve on crisp lettuce with mayonnaise.

### Frozen Pineapple Banana Salad

Soak one tablespoon of granulated gelatine in one-half cupful of cold water for five minutes, then dissolve it over boiling water. Cool it to tepid stage and add one-half cupful of canned crushed pineapple drained from its juice. Add also one banana thinly sliced. Now stir in one-third cupful of mayonnaise dressing and turn all into a tray of the electric refrigerator, or a mold, and chill one hour. It will then be firm and can be heaped onto lettuce for serving. This recipe makes five generous portions.

### Hyatt's Frozen Fruit Salad

| | |
|---|---|
| 20 apricot halves | 4 teaspoons maraschino syrup |
| 20 marshmallows | ¼ teaspoon salt |
| ¼ cup maraschino cherries | 2 tablespoons lemon juice |
| 6 slices pineapple | ¾ cup heavy cream whipped stiff |
| ¼ cup pineapple juice | ⅓ cup mayonnaise |

Dice fruit, cut marshmallows small, add fruit juices, whipped cream, mayonnaise and salt. Mix gently with fruit, turn into freezer and freeze as ice cream. Serve on crisp lettuce. No dressing unless desired.

### Frozen Cottage Cheese Salad

| | |
|---|---|
| 1½ cups cheese | ½ cup cream (whipped) |
| ¼ cup chopped pecans | 2 tablespoons salad oil |
| ¼ cup chopped green peppers | ¼ teaspoon paprika |
| ¼ cup chopped pimentoes | ¾ teaspoon salt |
| ½ cup mayonnaise | |

Blend cheese with oil, add other ingredients, add mayonnaise, then fold in cream. Pack in ice and salt for three hours. Serve on lettuce.

### Frozen Tomato Salad No. 1

| | |
|---|---|
| 1 quart tomatoes | 1 stalk celery |
| 1 small onion | 3 cloves |

Boil together until done, strain to remove seed and seasoning. There should be three cups. Add:

| | |
|---|---|
| 1 tablespoon vinegar | Salt and pepper to taste, and chill |
| 1 tablespoon sugar | |

Add one cup of thick cream which has been whipped stiff, fold into tomato mixture, pour into churn and freeze or put into ½ lb. baking powder cans, pack in salt and ice for three or four hours. Turn out, slice, put on lettuce, serve with mayonnaise. If frozen in churn, serve with ice cream scoop which gives a cone shaped portion. Place on lettuce. Serve.

### Frozen Tomato Salad No. 2

Select tomatoes of uniform size. Peel and from the stem end, cut a slice, remove the pulp and seed without breaking through the tomato; invert to drain, and place in refrigerator to chill. To the removed pulp add two or three whole tomatoes diced fine, a teaspoon of grated onion, salt and pepper to taste. To two cups of this add one-half cup of mayonnaise and half cup of cottage cheese which has been made smooth and soft with tomato juice.

Mix well and freeze as you would ice cream. When ready to serve, fill tomato shells (which must be cold), place on crisp lettuce. The filling should stand up high. No other dressing is necessary.

Green peppers, cucumbers, olives, celery, or pineapple may be used in the filling.

### A New Tomato Salad

Make the usual tomato aspic by any recipe liked, clear or a thick aspic. Fill individual molds and let it jell. Have ready some salmon salad (or any salad preferred). Scoop out the inside of each mold and place a portion of the salad into the opening. Heat the removed aspic until liquid, let chill and, just before it jells, refill and cover the entire opening.

Let jell again until quite firm. When ready to serve unmold on crisp lettuce and serve with mayonnaise.

The center may be of cheese and nuts, or cucumber and celery. Proceed the same.

### Molded Tomato Salad

Select nice tomatoes, peel carefully, so they will hold the filling. Make small opening in the stem end, removing the pulp and seed, fill with a green cucumber aspic and place on ice to jell; when ready cut in quarters, place on crisp lettuce leaves and serve with mayonnaise.

### Tomato Aspic

| | |
|---|---|
| 1 quart can of tomatoes | 1 tablespoon salt |
| 1 bunch of celery | 1/8 teaspoon of cayenne pepper |
| 1 small bottle of stuffed olives | 1 box of Knox gelatine |
| 3 tablespoons of vinegar | 1/2 cup cold water |
| 1 tablespoon of grated onion | |

Mash tomatoes to a pulp, removing any stem pieces; cut celery fine, slice olives thin; add all of seasonings. Put the gelatine in the cold water for 10 minutes, then heat over boiling water until melted; add to the tomato mixture, turn into a mold to jell or individual molds. Rinse the mold with cold water before pouring in the mixture, so it will leave mold easily.

A pretty individual salad is to fill jelly glasses to jell, unmold, cut in inch thick slices, put on lettuce with mayonnaise on top.

The aspic is not cooked at all. Asparagus or any kind of vegetables may be added in place of what is used.

Serve with mayonnaise on crisp lettuce.

### Tomatoes in Aspic

Select small, round tomatoes. Remove skin by plunging first into hot water, then into cold, when it will rub off easily. Cut a hollow in the blossom end of each, and stuff with celery and chopped sweet peppers, moistened with mayonnaise. Arrange the tomatoes in a circular mold, in the bottom of which one-half inch of rich, highly flavored meat stock, stiffened with gelatine, has been allowed to harden. The stock should be clear and transparent. Pour around the tomatoes enough of the same jelly to set them when hard, but not enough to float them. When the jelly is firm, add enough to cover the tomatoes to the depth of one-half an inch. When the whole is cold and firm, turn out on a round platter, surround with a wreath of shredded lettuce, and garnish with mayonnaise.

### Asheville Salad

| | |
|---|---|
| 2 medium size cans tomato soup | 1 cup celery, onion and green |
| 2 Philadelphia cream cheese | pepper, cut fine and mixed |
| 1 package plain gelatine | 1 cup mayonnaise |
| ⅓ cup cold water | ½ cup pecan meats |

Put cheese and soup together on stove to dissolve. Add gelatine which has been dissolved in cold water, and mix well. Cool. Add nuts and vegetables, and last of all add mayonnaise. Pour into a mold to congeal. Serve on lettuce with a portion of mayonnaise.

## GARNISHINGS FOR SALAD

### Curled Celery

Select nice stalks of celery, cut in sections one and one-half inches long. With a paring knife cut down each end in thin slices one-third of the stalk, leaving the center third intact; drop in ice water to which a little vinegar or lemon juice has been added, let stand until the celery is curled. Use to decorate salad.

### Calla Lily

Select white turnip of medium size (those not pithy), peel and slice very thin, drop in tepid water until very limp. Have several carrots peeled and cut in slender strips to represent the pistil, also parsley stems for the lily stems.

Take a slice of turnip, piece of carrot and parsley stalk, pinch the slice of turnip together at one edge, place the other two parts in position, and with a coarse needle and thread take one stitch and tie to hold all together. Drop in ice water until crisp and ready to use.

### Radish Roses

Select perfect, bright red radishes, leaving a small portion of the green for stem; remove the root, and with a small paring knife cut peeling to form petals, leaving the white radish inside of the petals. Drop into ice water to curl.

## SALAD DRESSINGS

### Mayonnaise and Salad Dressings

Mayonnaise is one of the most universal and most liked of any salad dressing. It is the dressing used for salads in its simplest form and is unlimited in its variations. It may be made and kept in the refrigerator for a week or more.

The ingredients consist of eggs, oil, lemon juice, salt and pepper. Some prefer the yolks of the eggs only, while many use the whole egg. We have our own domestic oils, made and refined in the South, and these are the most commonly used. Olive oil is used also, but this being an imported product, adds greatly to the cost.

The making of mayonnaise, at one time, was considered very tedious, but the improvement in materials and utensils today makes it an easy task.

The making of mayonnaise and other dressings is very easy and simple when once you start in the correct way. A pint of mayonnaise can be made in five minutes, while a quart would require two minutes more. The first part of the process is the particular part. After you have put in a cup of oil the other goes in very rapidly.

No special mixer is necessary, although there are several popular devices on the market. All that is needed is a well-shaped bowl, one sloping to the center and heavy enough to stand steady on the table; a wire mixer (sometimes called an egg-beater), a slitted spoon, or fork, will do the same work.

A great amount of ice is not necessary, as the ingredients work better when only moderately cold. Mayonnaise should be well seasoned to be tasty. A cooked mayonnaise is preferred by many. This has some flour in it to form a binder and is not as rich as the real mayonnaise. Cooked mayonnaise may be made with oil or butter, the oil being preferable. Cooked mayonnaise, like the real article, has many recipes, and I am giving those I have used for many years.

Any mayonnaise may be made into other dressings by adding various condiments and seasonings.

A salad dressing, made with whipped cream and fruit juices, is particularly adapted to fruit salads, but, like all other dressings, there are numerous recipes for it. The ones given are very dependable.

## Mayonnaise

| | |
|---|---|
| 1 pint of oil | 1½ teaspoons salt, more or less |
| 3 egg yolks | ⅛ teaspoon cayenne pepper |
| Juice of ½ lemon, more or less | |

Into a bowl or mixer put egg yolks, break well, add half of lemon juice and mix; this gives a thin mixture. Take one cup of oil and pour in the first quarter of it very slowly, stirring or beating; after which the remaining oil may be poured in much faster, stirring constantly until the oil is used. Add salt, pepper and the balance of the lemon juice. Now add the second cup of oil, pouring in quite rapidly and stirring constantly. Sometimes the dressing thickens very rapidly, or it may thicken slowly. If too thick to mix, add more lemon juice or a teaspoon of cold water. Continue stirring until salt is well mixed. This will make one pint of mayonnaise and requires from three to five minutes. The mayonnaise should be stiff enough to hold its shape. Put into a container, cover closely; if in an open vessel, cover with a piece of wax paper to prevent mixture separating.

## To Remake Curdled Mayonnaise

If the mixture should become curdled during its preparation it may be restored by the following method:

Into a bowl break a fresh egg, mix with a small portion of lemon juice or water. With a teaspoon add one at a time a spoon of the curdled mixture to the fresh egg, proceeding slowly, resting a moment if it looks greasy; continue until all is properly blended. Add any oil which has not yet been used.

## To Prevent Mayonnaise From Curdling

To be sure mayonnaise will stay smooth when broken after it has stood in the refrigerator for several days, put one teaspoon of water, lemon juice or vinegar on one side of the bowl and with a fork or spoon mix this liquid with a small portion of the mayonnaise. This will soon show whether it will be smooth or will separate. If it separates, continue adding and stirring the mayonnaise until the whole amount has been mixed.

## Mock Mayonnaise

### First Part

| | |
|---|---|
| ¾ cup hot water | 6 tablespoons flour |
| 2 tablespoons cold water | |

Mix the flour and 2 tablespoons of cold water till free from lumps; add slowly the hot water (strain if lumpy); cook in double boiler till very thick; set aside to cool. When cool—

### Second Part

| | |
|---|---|
| Yolks of 2 eggs | 2 tablespoons cold water |
| Juice of 1 lemon | 1 cup salad oil |
| 2 teaspoons salt | ⅛ teaspoon red pepper |

Add the second two spoons of cold water; then yolks of eggs slightly broken; slowly beat in a cup of oil just as in making mayonnaise; lastly add the salt, pepper and lemon juice. This is best for sandwiches because its thickness prevents bread becoming soggy.

Olive oil may be added if flavor is desired. This quantity is sufficient for two quarts of salad, such as chicken and Waldorf.

## To Decorate With Mayonnaise

Make a good stiff mayonnaise, fill bag and proceed to trim a mold of salad to suit your fancy. Must be cold and used in the rubber bag and tube. If mayonnaise is not stiff enough add more salt and beat until stiff and smooth. This makes it stiffer.

## Cooked Mayonnaise

1 cup vinegar
1 cup water
¾ cup flour
½ cup oil

Yolks of 4 eggs
1 teaspoon salt
⅛ teaspoon cayenne pepper

Mix the flour into a paste with part of the water, having it thin enough to strain; add yolks to flour and strain. Put vinegar, oil, salt, pepper and remaining water into a saucepan. Bring to a boil, then pour slowly over the flour and eggs. Return to a double boiler and cook until quite thick. Do not let boil as it would curdle, but keep just below the boiling point. Let get cold before using. This makes nearly a quart, and half the quantity may be used.

Use over potato salad instead of the real mayonnaise, as some do not like much oil.

## "Eat and Grow Thin" Dressing

2 teaspoons dry mustard
⅛ teaspoon cayenne pepper
2 tablespoons flour
2 cups boiling water
½ cup cold water

2 teaspoons salt
4 tablespoons sugar
¼ cup lemon juice
4 egg yolks

Mix the dry ingredients together; beat eggs and mix with the cold water and add to the dry mixture; strain to remove any lumps, now add the boiling water slowly, stirring all the while, then add lemon juice and put into a double boiler and cook till as thick as cream (do not let boil for it will curdle), take from fire, cover to prevent a crust forming and beat occasionally till cool. Put in covered jar and it will keep indefinitely. If too thick, thin with water or lemon juice. This is especially good for cole slaw or dressed lettuce. Add a diced hard boiled egg to dressing if it is to be used in dressed lettuce. Use dressing to suit individual fancy.

## Thousand Island Dressing

1 cup mayonnaise
¼ cup chili sauce
1 tablespoon chopped onion

1 tablespoon chopped pickles
1 tablespoon Worcestershire sauce
1 teaspoon paprika

Make mayonnaise as usual, add all ingredients, mix well and it is ready to use. A hard-boiled egg is sometimes added. Cucumbers may be used, too, if served with fish.

## Tartar Sauce

1 cup butter creamed until soft
⅓ cup lemon juice
¼ cup Worcestershire sauce

1 teaspoon salt
2 teaspoons paprika
Red pepper to taste

Add all seasoning together, beat into the soft butter.

## French Dressing

2 tablespoons of vinegar
4 tablespoons of olive or salad oil
½ teaspoon salt

¼ teaspoon of cayenne pepper or drop of tabasco

Put into large-mouthed bottle and shake until blended together. Use immediately. It separates if allowed to stand.

If the hostess is to mix the French dressing she does the measuring at table from cruets and stirs with a fork or spoon and serves it over the salad. Either taragon or plain vinegar may be used.

## Roquefort Cheese Dressing

Make a French dressing, crumble the cheese into small bits and beat into the dressing and pour over quarters of crisp lettuce. The cheese must be added to the dressing and all well mixed and served immediately.

## Russian Salad Dressing

2 tablespoons mayonnaise
1 tablespoon chili sauce
1 tablespoon of grated onion

1 tablespoon chopped pimentoes
1 tablespoon taragon vinegar

This makes enough for four guests when placed on the hearts of lettuce.

## Hungarian Dressing
### (for Potato Salad)

1 cup mayonnaise
1 teaspoon grated onion

2 tablespoons chili sauce
2 tablespoons Worcestershire sauce

Use equal parts of diced potatoes and celery. This mixture makes enough for twelve guests.

## Sauce Tartare

Mayonnaise with many condiments, pickles, cucumbers, nuts, onions, parsley, capers.

## Mayonnaise for Fish Salads

1 cup mayonnaise
3 tablespoons chopped pickles and olives

1 tablespoon chopped parsley
1 tablespoon chopped pimento
1 tablespoon capers, if desired

Blend thoroughly and mix with any fish salad (fish flakes and celery).

## Frozen Tomato Mayonnaise

1 cup mayonnaise
1 cup of grated tomatoes

Salt and pepper to taste

Select very red tomatoes, peel and grate, beginning at the blossom end. Make the mayonnaise and mix the two. This gives a custardlike mixture; freeze as you would ice cream. Serve over heart lettuce or a cucumber aspic. It should be seasoned well with red pepper and salt.

## Frozen Cucumber Mayonnaise

1 cup of mayonnaise
Enough coloring to make a delicate green

1 cup of grated cucumber
Salt, pepper and lemon juice to taste

Make the mayonnaise as usual. Add the grated cucumber, coloring, and extra seasoning. This will give a thin mixture. Freeze as you would ice cream. Use tender cucumbers, peel thick piece to remove any bitter. Grate the whole, using the meat and seed. This quantity will serve about ten. Use as you would regular mayonnaise, giving a more generous portion.

## Hot Water Mayonnaise

1 quart oil
1 cup hot water
5 tablespoons flour

Yolks of 3 eggs
Juice of 3 lemons
Salt and cayenne pepper to taste

Add juice of lemons to water and bring to boiling point. Mix flour with enough of the oil to pour. Pour the flour and oil into the boiling water, cook until a thick paste. Have egg yolks broken into a bowl, pour the hot paste into eggs, beating well. Immediately begin to add oil to the hot mixture, making exactly as with the raw eggs, only the oil may be added more rapidly. When all the oil is in, season with salt and pepper to taste, using cayenne pepper.

## Mayonnaise Made With Evaporated Milk

Use three tablespoons of evaporated milk to take the place of two egg yolks, add oil and season exactly as if using eggs.

## Mayonnaise With Gelatine for Fruit Salads

To 1 cup of mayonnaise add 1 tablespoon of gelatine which has been dissolved in 3 tablespoons of cold water for 5 minutes and melted over boiling water, add 1 tablespoon of lemon juice and mix into mayonnaise. When dressing begins to stiffen mix in a few spoons of any diced fruit desired, such as cherries, diced pineapple or both.

## Another Salad Dressing

1 teaspoon mustard
1 teaspoon sugar
1/4 teaspoon cayenne pepper
1/2 cup cream

4 teaspoons flour
1 teaspoon salt
2 egg yolks
1/2 cup vinegar

Mix flour, mustard and sugar and wet with a little water to form a paste; add the 2 egg yolks well beaten, then the cream and last the vinegar; put into double boiler and cook until thick; if too thick, thin with a little cream, milk or water. Milk and butter the size of a walnut may be substituted for cream. Add vinegar last.

## Sour Cream Dressing No. 1

1 cup sour cream
2 tablespoons vinegar
1 tablespoon sugar

1 teaspoon salt
1 teaspoon mustard (French)
1 teaspoon paprika

Whip cream about half, mix all other ingredients together, add slowly to cream and continue whipping until stiff enough to stand. Serve over sliced tomatoes.

## Sour Cream Dressing No. 2

1 cup sour cream
1 egg yolk
½ teaspoon salt
½ teaspoon paprika

½ teaspoon prepared mustard or
    half the quantity of dry
4 tablespoons vinegar

Mix seasoning with yolk of egg, add cream and mix well. Add vinegar slowly, cook in double boiler until it coats spoon. Chill and serve over salad or tomatoes.

## Hyatt's Coral Dressing

2 tablespoons paprika
½ tablespoon salt
½ teaspoon white pepper

¼ teaspoon cayenne pepper or less
2 cups oil
Juice of 2 lemons

Mix dry ingredients together, add lemon juice, mix well and slowly beat in oil. If made carefully, will stand without separating. Will keep for a week.

## Mrs. S's Pineapple Dressing

1 cup juice from can pineapple
¾ cup sugar
½ cup thick cream, whipped

2 tablespoons butter
1 tablespoon flour
2 eggs

Heat pineapple juice until warm, blend together the sugar, flour and egg yolks. Beat whites stiff, mix together and pour over this the warm juice. Put into double boiler and cook until thick. When cold, add whipped cream. Juice of lemon may be added if desired. Serve over fruit salad, pineapple salad or frozen salad.

## Fruit Salad Dressing

2 egg yolks
2 tablespoons vinegar
2 tablespoons sugar

2 tablespoons butter
½ teaspoon salt
Dash cayenne pepper

Mix and cook over fire until thick, cool and add 1 cup cream, whipped stiff.

## Another Fruit Salad Dressing

3 tablespoons vinegar
4 tablespoons sugar

3 egg yolks

Mix and cook over fire until thick, cool and add 1 cup cream, whipped stiff.

## Sour Cream Dressing
### (for Tomotoes or Slaw)

½ cup thick cream
1 egg yolk
1 tablespoon lemon juice

1 teaspoon prepared mustard
1 teaspoon salt
Dash cayenne pepper

Mix all into cream, chill and serve.

## Dressing for Fish Salad

1 cup cooked mayonnaise
¼ cup chopped pimento

½ cup chopped fresh crisp cucumbers
¼ cup chopped olives

Mix together, add cucumbers when ready to serve.

# bread

# CHAPTER IX

# Bread

Bread is called the Staff of Life and plays a very important role in our daily lives. A great deal depends on the breads used in the home—eating too much bread at the expense of other foods is harmful and should be avoided.

Flour may be classified into two general varieties, bread and pastry, or Spring wheat and Winter wheat. From soft Winter wheat the pastry flours are made; this wheat grinds finer and is more starchy. Spring wheat is a hard grain, has more gluten and is a grainy flour requiring more liquid per cup and is more suitable for yeast breads, as it contains more food on which the yeast can grow.

Usually the flour bag indicates or designates the flour—pastry (high patent) or bread flour. To test for pastry flour, squeeze tight a handful of flour and if it clings together and shows each finger print and wrinkle, it is a pastry flour. It should also feel smooth and starchy to the touch. Bread flour, when rolled between the finger and thumb will feel grainy, and when squeezed in the hand, will fall apart instead of staying tightly packed. Bread flour usually is about 60% of the grain; pastry flour or high patent is about 40% of the grain and sometimes less. Both flours have their places. From the various flour mills throughout the country, the milling and blending is done by many different formulas. For this reason flours vary and some require more liquid than others. Bread flour is more absorbent than pastry flour and therefore requires more liquid per cup.

The South is noted for its quick breads, such as its delicious hot biscuits, corn sticks, egg bread and many other varieties. The Southern housewife has always prided herself on the whiteness and flakiness of her biscuit, which calls for a pastry flour. The daily use of corn meal breads, hominy (grits), rice and other cereals has prevented any deficiency in our diet and offsets the general use of pastry flour.

The Southern housewife prefers pastry flour for biscuit, pastries, waffles and cake. Buttermilk is the preferable liquid used for quick breads as the lactic acid in the buttermilk, clabber or sour milk, acts on the starches, the result being a sweet, moist bread.

When using buttermilk and soda, the rule is a half teaspoon of soda for each cup (half pint) of tart buttermilk. Buttermilk a day old is preferable. If this rule is followed, there will never be any yellow soda bread, whether using half a cup or a gallon of buttermilk. The Southern woman has standardized the use of soda and buttermilk.

Quick breads should be baked in a hot oven, 450 to 550 degrees, the time and heat, depending largely on the thickness of the bread. All breads should be thoroughly cooked, otherwise they will be gummy or raw in the center. It is not so much hot bread, as underdone bread which is indigestible.

There are many who prefer sweet milk and baking powder. The standard measurement of baking powder, when using sweet milk, is two teaspoons for each cup of flour. In many of her breads, however, the Southern housewife prefers buttermilk with soda and a small quantity of baking powder, which gives a light fluffy result, lessening labor (beating) and the number of eggs.

## QUICK BREADS

### Buttermilk Biscuit

| | |
|---|---|
| 2 cups flour (2½ after sifted) | 1 teaspoon salt |
| 1 cup buttermilk | ½ teaspoon soda |
| 4 tablespoons shortening | |

Into the flour put salt, soda, and sift into bowl. Mix in shortening with tips of fingers, or chop in with spoon, add buttermilk, using spoon, and make into a dough. Lift onto a well floured board, knead just to get smooth and firm enough to handle. Roll or pat out to one-half inch thick, cut, place on baking sheet, bake in hot oven about ten minutes. Acid buttermilk is better for cooking, and for every cup of milk one-half teaspoon soda is necessary. Use a tea biscuit cutter.

### Drop Biscuit

| | |
|---|---|
| 1 pint flour | ½ teaspoon soda |
| 1 teaspoon salt | 4 tablespoons shortening (lard) |
| 2 teaspoons baking powder | 1 cup buttermilk |

Sift flour into which is put the salt, soda and baking powder, into a mixing bowl. Mix in the shortening with tips of fingers or chop in with spoon.

Mix into a dough with the buttermilk. Stir and mix well, but quickly. Drop with a spoon, pieces about as large as a walnut, leaving space between. Bake in quick oven about 10 minutes or until done.

### 20th Century Buttermilk Biscuit

Use recipe for Buttermilk Biscuit, add two teaspoons baking powder to flour. Follow first recipe exactly. Either white or brown flour may be used with any of these recipes.

### Baking Powder Biscuit No. 1

| | |
|---|---|
| 2 cups flour | 4 teaspoons baking powder |
| 1 cup sweet milk (more or less) | 1 teaspoon salt |
| 4 tablespoons shortening | |

Sift dry ingredients with flour, mix in shortening, add sweet milk and make into a dough, knead slightly, roll, cut and bake. Do not crowd in pan.

## Baking Powder Biscuit No. 2

Use first recipe, add 1 teaspoon sugar. Follow directions, making a firm dough. Knead until smooth and rather stiff, using extra flour if necessary. Roll out one-fourth inch thick and cut with small size cutter with stickers in center, or stick several times with fork. Place on baking sheet, leaving space so sides will brown. Bake in quick oven until a pretty brown. The tops may be brushed with sweet milk when nearly done if a glaze is wanted.

## Scotch Scones

| | |
|---|---|
| 2 cups flour (sifted before measuring) | 3 teaspoons baking powder |
| | 1/4 cup butter |
| 1/3 cup sugar | 2 eggs |
| 1/4 teaspoon salt | 1/2 cup milk, or more if needed |

Sift baking powder, salt and sugar with flour. Chop in the butter as in making pastry. Beat eggs together, add the milk and mix with the flour making a soft dough using a little more flour if necessary to handle. Lift to a well floured board, knead lightly, roll out to 1/4 inch thick. Cut, using a large biscuit cutter. Place on moderately hot griddle and bake as a hoe cake, turning when well brown. Cook slowly for thorough cooking. Serve immediately with butter and jam. Any scones left over may be split, toasted and served hot. This is something like English muffins.

## Party Biscuit

| | |
|---|---|
| 2 1/2 cups flour | 4 teaspoons baking powder |
| 1/3 cup shortening | 1 teaspoon salt |
| 3/4 cup milk | 1 tablespoon sugar |
| 1 egg | |

Sift sugar, salt and baking powder with flour. Break egg in cup and mix well; fill with sweet milk. Mix shortening into flour, mix into dough with milk and egg, using spoon. Turn onto a well floured board and knead until smooth, using extra flour if necessary. Roll out to one-fourth inch thick, cut with tea biscuit cutter, butter one-half, turn over (like Parker House rolls), place on baking sheet and bake in quick oven until done (10 to 12 minutes).

## Raisin Biscuit

Use recipe for Party Biscuit. Add 1 cup seedless raisins, knead until smooth, cut and bake.

These may be turned or left round. If round, roll dough half inch thick before cutting.

## Miss Mary's Beaten Biscuit

| | |
|---|---|
| 4 cups flour (sifted) | 1 teaspoon salt |
| 3/4 cup milk (more or less) | 1 teaspoon sugar |
| 1/3 cup lard | |

Sift sugar and salt into flour, mix in shortening and make a very stiff dough, using more or less milk—the dough must be very stiff. Roll until dough blisters, pops, and is very smooth. Roll out ¼ inch thick, cut, stick, bake in moderate oven 30 to 40 minutes. Have oven hot when biscuits are put into same.

### Mrs. M's Beaten Biscuit

6 cups flour (sifted)
¾ cup lard
½ cup ice water

2 teaspoons sugar
2 teaspoons salt

Dissolve sugar and salt in water. Sift flour four times. Mix in lard thoroughly and water little at a time, never getting any portion of flour very wet. The dough must be very stiff. Roll twenty minutes or until it blisters and pops.

Put into hot oven for few minutes then reduce heat and bake about 40 minutes at medium heat, about 350 degrees.

### Georgia Beaten Biscuit

1 quart pastry flour
6 tablespoons of lard
1 teaspoon salt

1 cup of sweet milk, ice cold, more or less, to make a stiff dough

Sift salt into the flour, mix in the lard, add the sweet milk, being very careful to have the dough very stiff, even if you leave out some of the milk. Beat or grind in biscuit break for 20 minutes. Cut one-half inch thick with a small cutter made for beaten biscuit with stickers in center (or stick with a fork), bake in slow oven 20 to 40 minutes until brown and crisp.

### Biscuit Fritters

Use recipe for biscuit made with sweet milk. Roll out dough thin, cut with large cutter, place spoonful of jam or stewed fruit on one-half wet edge, cover with other half, press together with fork or fingers, fry in deep fat, drain, sprinkle with powdered sugar.

### Sweet Potato Biscuit

To 20th Century biscuit recipe add 1 cup of mashed and strained sweet potatoes (hot or cold). 1 tablespoon of sugar, using more or less milk as necessary, have dough firm. Cut, bake in hot oven. Less shortening may be used. An egg may be added.

### Porter Puffs
#### (5 o'Clock Tea Puffs)

4 tablespoons butter
1 egg
1 cup sweet milk
2 tablespoons sugar

6 teaspoons baking powder
½ teaspoon salt
Sufficient flour to make a stiff batter

Beat egg together very lightly, add milk and all ingredients, add melted butter last.

Drop a teaspoonful into well greased muffin tins, sizzling hot, bake in hot oven. Have some butter melted and in a small pitcher. Puncture side of muffin with pitcher, pour in about a teaspoon of melted butter and serve at once.

## Quick Sally Lunn

| | |
|---|---|
| ½ cup butter, or shortening | ¾ teaspoon salt |
| ½ cup sugar | 4 teaspoons baking powder |
| 2 cups flour, sifted then measured | 3 eggs |
| 1 cup milk | |

Cream shortening and sugar together well, add eggs one at a time quickly, but well. Sift salt and baking powder with flour. Alternately add milk and flour to egg mixture, mixing quickly with as little stirring as possible until free of lumps and smooth. Pour into deep layer cake pan, bake at 425 degrees for 30 minutes. Serve hot with butter. This may be baked in large muffin pans for individual Lunns.

## Aunt Sweet's Quick Sally Lunn

| | |
|---|---|
| 2 eggs | 2 tablespoons sugar |
| ¾ cup milk | 1 teaspoon salt |
| 2½ cups flour | 4 teaspoons baking powder |
| 3 tablespoons butter | |

Beat eggs together until very light, add sugar, mix as in making cake, having baking powder and salt sifted with flour, add melted butter last. Drop in hot, greased muffin tins, or bake in round layer pans. Cut in pie shape sections, serve hot with butter. Use more or less flour to have batter as thick as muffin batter. Use hot oven.

## Cheese Biscuit

Roll out biscuit dough to one-fourth inch thickness. Spread generously with grated cheese, sprinkle with red pepper, roll up like a jelly roll. Cut one-half inch or more across the roll, place on greased baking sheet and bake in moderate oven until done and brown. They are good hot or cold. Leave space for biscuit to spread.

## BATTER BREADS

### Wheat Muffins No. 1

| | |
|---|---|
| 2 eggs | 1 teaspoon sugar |
| 1 cup sweet milk | 1 teaspoon salt |
| 1½ cups flour | 3 teaspoons baking powder |
| 1 tablespoon oil | |

Separate eggs, beat yolks light; add milk, oil, salt and sugar; now add flour; beat whites stiff; fold in; now mix in baking powder. Put into greased muffin tins; bake in hot oven, 15 to 20 minutes on top rack.

## Wheat Muffins No. 2

| | |
|---|---|
| 1 egg | 1 cup buttermilk |
| 1 tablespoon cold water | ½ teaspoon soda |
| 2 teaspoons baking powder | 1½ tablespoons oil or melted lard |
| 2 teaspoons salt | Flour enough to make drop batter |

Beat egg light; add milk, salt, flour and oil; grease pans and set in hot oven to get hot; sift in powders; dissolve soda in water, mix quickly; put into hot pans, sizzling hot or they will stick; put on top rack and bake 10 to 15 minutes until done, according to size of muffins. Have stove very hot.

## Graham Gems Without Eggs

| | |
|---|---|
| 4 cups graham flour | 4 teaspoons baking powder |
| 4 tablespoons oil | 1 pint sweet milk |
| 2 teaspoons salt | |

Sift powder and salt with flour; pour in milk; add oil; have a drop batter; grease pans and have hot. Bake on top rack, 15 minutes or until done. If batter is too stiff, muffins will be dry, if too thin, they will be sticky.

## Huckleberry Muffins

| | |
|---|---|
| 1 cup huckleberries | 1 cup milk |
| ½ cup sugar | 3 teaspoons baking powder |
| ½ cup shortening | ½ teaspoon salt |
| 2 cups flour | 2 eggs |

Cream shortening and sugar, add eggs and mix well. Sift dry ingredients together, add to mixture, alternating with milk. When smooth add berries which have been washed and well drained and sprinkled with a little flour. Fill well greased muffin tins half full, bake in moderate oven.

## Quick English Muffins

| | |
|---|---|
| 2 tablespoons butter | ½ teaspoon salt |
| 2 cups milk | 2 cups sifted flour |
| 4 egg whites | 1 tablespoon sugar |
| 1 teaspoon baking powder | |

Mix flour, sugar, salt, baking powder and milk making a batter. Add melted butter and fold in stiffly beaten egg whites. Place English Muffin rings on griddle, fill rings half full of batter, and bake until brown and done. Turn rings twice if necessary. Serve with butter and honey.

## Popovers

| | |
|---|---|
| ⅞ cup of sweet milk (a scant cup) | 1 teaspoon salt |
| 1 cup of flour sifted and measured | 2 eggs |

Beat eggs together until light; add salt and half of milk; mix into a smooth batter free of any lumps; add remainder of milk, which gives a very thin batter. Grease popover pans; have hot, fill each cup half full or less, have oven hot. Place in about the center of oven; cook with hot oven for 15 minutes, then reduce heat and continue baking at medium until dry and crisp.

Do not open oven for first ten minutes. When well popped lower heat to crisp and dry out. The popovers will be hollow inside and should be almost like a bubble. A real popover pan is best to cook them in. There is no grease or leavening in popovers. They must be made with sweet milk.

## Waffles

1 cup buttermilk
½ cup cold water
2 cups flour
3 tablespoons of cooking oil or melted lard

1 tablespoon of sugar
1 egg
1 teaspoon salt
4 teaspoons of baking powder
½ teaspoon soda in 1 tablespoon water

Beat egg, add milk, oil, sugar, salt and flour, beat smooth, thin the batter with half cup of water. When ready to begin to bake add the soda mixed in the water, sift in the baking powder, thoroughly mix, pour into a pitcher or quart cup and do not beat any more. Pour from pitcher into the center of molds until half full; spread out with a spoon; close irons and turn immediately. Cook 2 to 4 minutes, turn again, cook 1 minute. Remove the waffle and refill. Grease the irons for the first waffle, never any more. If made properly they will not stick or make any smoke. Do not have irons too hot; this causes them to stick. The irons should be heated over a low fire, turning several times, getting them ready to cook well.

This applies to the iron waffle mold used on top of gas or oil stove. The electric irons need no grease after once they are "treated," and the turning is not done, as the heat is in bottom and top. This recipe makes eight or ten waffles.

## Willie's Waffles

1 cup milk
1 egg
2 tablespoons sugar
1½ cups flour (sift before measuring)

1 teaspoon salt
¼ cup of cooking oil or melted shortening
3 teaspoons baking powder

Mix and cook as any waffle. To make chocolate waffle substitute ¼ cup of cocoa for ¼ cup of the flour.

## Griddle Cakes

2 eggs
2 cups buttermilk
1 cup corn meal
2 cups flour
2 tablespoons shortening

1 teaspoon salt
1 teaspoon soda, dissolved in a little cold water
3 teaspoons baking powder

Beat egg together until well broken, add milk, salt, shortening, meal and flour. Mix well, beating thoroughly. When ready to begin to bake, add soda and baking powder, beat well until batter is light and foamy, then do not beat any more. Pour on hot griddle, having batter thin enough to pour and shape cake. When top fills with broken bubbles (before it becomes dry), turn and cook other side. Remove to plate and serve.

All flours and meal differ, so that quantity is hard to give. If batter is too stiff, cakes will be tough; if batter is too thin, they will be sticky. A pour batter is necessary. It is not necessary to grease griddle if the right kind is used. A thick material cooks better. Have hot enough to sizz when batter is poured. Too much heat causes smoking and burning.

When using white flour, part meal makes a better cake. When using corn meal, whole wheat or graham, no other flour is necessary.

Cold hominy may take the place of the corn meal with white flour. Cold hominy and rice used in batter cakes with flour make good cakes and a nice way to use leftovers. Use one cup to two of flour.

### Whole Wheat Batter Cakes

Make same as griddle cakes, using whole wheat flour.

### French Pancakes No. 1

| | |
|---|---|
| 1 cup flour | ¼ teaspoon salt |
| 2 eggs | Sufficient milk to make thin batter |
| 2 teaspoons baking powder | |

Grease a griddle. Make medium sized pancakes. Spread with jelly or jam, roll up, sprinkle with pulverized sugar, run under gas flame and brown the sugar. Serve.

It takes two to make these: one to make the cakes and another to spread, roll, and get ready to brown.

### French Pancakes No. 2

| | |
|---|---|
| 3 eggs | 1½ teaspoons melted butter |
| ¼ cup sugar | Few grains salt |
| ½ cup flour | ½ teaspoon vanilla |
| ½ cup milk | 4x sugar for sprinkling |
| ⅛ teaspoon baking powder | |

Mix all together thoroughly. Batter should be very thin. Bake as crepes in a full size frying pan, having them very thin and turning almost immediately, greasing pan for each cake. When all are baked, fold each pancake in half, spread generously with some kind of jam and roll up beginning at large side. Place on baking sheet, sprinkle with 4x sugar. Run under blaze to heat and sear sugar. Serve. (Plain sugar and lemon juice may be used instead of jam.)

### Flannel Cakes

| | |
|---|---|
| 1 quart flour | ½ teaspoon salt |
| 3 eggs | Sweet milk to make medium batter |
| ½ cup butter | (about 3 cups) |
| 2 teaspoons baking powder | |

Make batter, beat egg whites stiff, add to batter. Bake on griddle, greased very lightly.

## CORNMEAL BREADS OF VARIOUS KINDS

### Cornmeal Muffins

| | |
|---|---|
| 2 eggs | 2 teaspoons salt |
| 2½ cups sifted meal | 1 teaspoon soda |
| 2 cups buttermilk | 3 teaspoons baking powder |
| 3 tablespoons melted shortening | |

Beat eggs together until light. Add milk, shortening and salt.

Add meal, being careful in putting in, as meal varies and the batter should be a medium batter. Beat smooth. Grease and heat pans. Sift in the baking powder and dissolve the soda in a spoonful of cold water. Add to mixture, stir well and pour into molds. Bake in good hot oven until brown and crusty—about 15 to 20 minutes.

This same recipe can be used for corn sticks or egg-bread.

If the batter is too thin, the muffins will be sticky; if too stiff, dry and tough. No flour is used in corn sticks, muffins or egg-bread. The real Southern cornmeal is sufficiently fine to hold the bread together. The bran is sifted from the meal.

### Corn Sticks

| | |
|---|---|
| 2 eggs | 1 teaspoon sugar |
| 2 cups sifted meal | 2 teaspoons salt |
| 2 cups buttermilk | 1 teaspoon soda |
| 3 tablespoons melted shortening | 3 teaspoons baking powder |

Beat eggs together until light. Add milk, shortening and salt.

Add meal, being careful in putting in, as meal varies and the batter should be a medium batter. Beat smooth. Grease and heat stick pans. Sift in the baking powder and dissolve the soda in a spoonful of cold water. Add to mixture, stir well and pour into molds. Bake in good hot oven until brown and crusty—about 15 to 20 minutes. Corn sticks need a batter some thinner than muffins.

### Egg Bread

Make the same as cornmeal muffins. Pour into baking pan, well greased and piping hot, bake in hot oven about twenty to thirty minutes, according to thickness. Egg bread should be about one and one-half inches thick when done, with a good brown crust bottom and top. Cut in squares to serve. If baked in pan with sides too deep, the top does not brown well.

### Cornmeal Hoecake

| | |
|---|---|
| 2 cups sifted meal | Cold water to mix |
| ½ teaspoon salt | |

Mix meal with water sufficient to handle, let stand a few minutes to see if more water is needed to spread. Have a heavy griddle greased and hot, pour on the mixture and pat out into a round cake, having about one-half inch thick; reduce fire and let brown, turn and brown other side. Cook altogether about thirty minutes. Serve hot with butter.

## Mrs. P's Pone Cornbread

| | |
|---|---|
| 1 cup cold hominy (grits) | 1 teaspoon baking powder |
| 2 cups meal | 2 tablespoons lard |
| ¼ teaspoon salt | |

Mix together with cold water, just stiff enough to hold the shape; put on a hot greased griddle, grease well the top of pones and bake 30 to 40 minutes, according to size, in a fairly hot oven, until a good brown.

## Fried Cornmeal Pones

| | |
|---|---|
| 2 cups meal | Hot water to mix |
| ½ teaspoon salt | |

Have meal sifted before measuring, add salt and mix with hot water, using spoon. Let stand a few minutes, add more water, if necessary. The dough should be stiff enough to hold its shape.

Into a heavy fry pan put sufficient grease to fry, about one-half inch deep. With a spoon drop into hot grease small pones, fry until brown on both sides and until well done. Have pones about as large as large eggs. Drain, keep hot until served. To be served with turnip greens.

## Cornmeal Batter Cakes
### (for Semi-Invalid)

| | |
|---|---|
| 1 cup sweet milk | 1 heaping tablespoon cornmeal |
| 1 egg | Salt to taste |

Cook meal and milk together for five minutes. Let cool, if too thick thin with more milk. Beat egg light, add to mixture, bake on slightly greased griddle.

## Mrs. Peters' Cornmeal Batter Cakes

| | |
|---|---|
| 1½ cups cornmeal | 1 teaspoon salt |
| 2 cups boiling water | 1 egg |
| 1 teaspoon sugar | 1½ cups buttermilk |
| 1 tablespoon butter | 1 teaspoon soda |
| 1 cup boiled rice | |

Mix salt, sugar, butter, meal and rice together and pour over this the boiling water stirring constantly. Let cool slightly, then add the buttermilk. Beat egg well and add, dissolve soda in one tablespoon water, add, mix well, bake on griddle, greased just enough to cook without sticking.

## Cornmeal Lace Cakes

| | |
|---|---|
| ½ cup southern ground cornmeal | ¼ teaspoon salt |
| ⅔ cup cold water | |

Mix into thin batter. Into a heavy fry pan or griddle put 2 or 3 tablespoons of shortening or cooking oil and let heat rather hot, but not smoking; pour batter onto pan, using 1 tablespoonful to make a cake as large as top of a teacup. Hold spoon 2 or 3 inches from pan so the batter will spatter, making a lacey cake. Brown, turn and brown top side; when a light brown and crisp like a wafer, they are ready to serve. 4 or 5 may be cooked at one time. Serve as any wafer. This will make ten wafers. It will require about 2 minutes to cook a wafer. Add more grease as needed to make them spatter. Remove any burnt crumbs while cooking to prevent clinging to others. These are particularly good with turnip greens, or with a salad.

### Cracklin' Bread

| | |
|---|---|
| 2 cups meal (sifted first) | 1 teaspoon salt |
| 1 cup cracklings | Water to mix |

Mash or break the cracklings into small pieces, over them pour half cup of hot water, pour into meal and add sufficient cold water to mix into a dough, add salt. Let stand five minutes and if too stiff add little more water. Shape into small loaves, place on hot pan, in hot oven until slightly browned on top, reduce heat to medium, bake from 30 to 45 minutes, according to size of pone.

During first part of baking place near top of oven, then lower and allow to cook.

### Bess' Virginia Spoon Bread

| | |
|---|---|
| 1 qt. buttermilk | 3/4 pint sifted meal |
| 1 teaspoon soda | 1 teaspoon salt |
| 3 eggs | 2 tablespoons butter or lard |

Add soda to buttermilk. Heat well, but do not boil. Add eggs slightly beaten. Stir meal and salt slowly into milk and egg mixture Melt butter and add. Bake 40 minutes in baking dish at 375 degrees. Serve from the baking dish.

### Virginia Spoon Bread

| | |
|---|---|
| 3/4 cup fine white meal | 1 teaspoon salt |
| 1 cup sweet milk | 2 teaspoons baking powder |
| 2 eggs | 1 tablespoon lard or cooking oil |
| 1 cup boiling water | |

Into a mixing bowl put lard, salt and meal; over this pour the boiling water, mix until smooth, free from any lumps. Add cup of milk, beat eggs light (not separated) and add to mixture, add baking powder, pour into greased baking dish and bake 30 to 40 minutes, in moderate oven.

Have oven hot when put in, then decrease to moderate.

### Netsy's Virginia Spoon Bread

| | |
|---|---|
| 2 cups meal | 2 teaspoons salt |
| 2 cups boiling water | 3 tablespoons butter |
| 1 1/2 cups sweet milk | 2 large eggs |

Sift meal twice and dissolve in the boiling water. Add butter and salt. Thin with the sweet milk.

Separate egg; beat light; add yolks, then whites, which are beaten stiff. Pour into a buttered baking dish, cook in a moderate oven 30 minutes.

Serve from the pan in which it is cooked. Often the eggs are not separated.

### Southern Spoon Bread

2 cups boiling water
1 cup white meal
1 tablespoon butter
1 teaspoon salt

2 teaspoons baking powder
2 eggs
2 cups milk

Pour boiling water over meal, stirring constantly, and boil five minutes. Remove from the fire, add butter, salt and milk. Mix well. Beat eggs light, add to mixture, sift in the powders, mix well, pour into greased baking dish and bake one-half hour in moderate oven. Serve from dish in which it is baked.

### Hush Puppies
#### (To be Cooked and Eaten with Fish)

2 cups cornmeal
1 tablespoon flour
½ teaspoon soda
1 teaspoon baking powder

1 teaspoon salt
1 whole egg
3 tablespoons chopped onion (fine)
1 cup buttermilk

Mix all dry ingredients together. Add onion, then milk and last the beaten egg. Drop by the spoonful into the pan or kettle, in which fish is being fried. Fry to a golden brown. Drain on paper, the same as fried fish. If a deep kettle is being used the hush puppy breads will float when done.

Hush puppy is a Southern dish cooked at all fish frys and hunting trips. At first they were made to feed the hungry, howling hounds or hunting dogs to keep them quiet, hence "hush puppy". Later they were more carefully made and eaten by the entire party. This old colonial custom has been handed down to the present day. Hush puppy Red Horse Devil No. 2 is used today to serve with barbecues.

### South Carolina Hush Puppies

2 cups meal
¼ cup shortening
1 teaspoon salt

Cold water to make a firm mixture to shape

Mix together with cold water to firm mixture. Take small portions, about two tablespoons, make in small long pones one inch thick by two and one-half long, roll in dry meal, then fry in deep grease, like a doughnut, until a golden brown.

### Southern Pone Cornbread

2 cups meal (water ground preferred)
1 teaspoon salt

1 tablespoon grease
Cold water to make into dough

Sift and measure meal, add salt and shortening, mix into dough with cold water and let stand a minute, adding more water if necessary. Shape into small pones and place on hot, greased shallow pan, leaving space so they will not touch. Put into hot oven for ten minutes, then reduce to medium, bake thirty to forty minutes. If gas oven is used, place under blaze until slightly browned, then into oven about center, with moderate heat. Serve with vegetables.

## BROWN BREADS

### Annie's Reliable Brown Bread

2½ cups graham flour
1 cup of white flour
1 cup of buttermilk
½ cup sugar

½ cup of molasses
1 cup of raisins
½ teaspoon salt
1 teaspoon soda

Mix all dry ingredients together, mix liquids, combine the two. Grease one-pound baking powder cans well, fill half-full, put on tops, steam two hours, or until done.

Place cans on rack or trivet so they will be entirely surrounded by water, let water come up half-way the depth of can. Keep a constant boiling.

### Steamed Bread

3½ cups cornmeal
1 cup flour
2 cups sweet milk (or water)
1 cup buttermilk

1 teaspoon soda
1 teaspoon salt
1 teaspoon baking powder
¾ cup molasses

If not thick enough, add more meal.

Steam three hours. Have water cold in steamer. Bread will rise while water heats.

### Mrs. H's Brown Bread

2 cups white flour
2 cups graham flour
½ cup molasses (black)
½ cup shortening, lard or oil
½ cup sugar

½ cup milk
1 cup raisins
1 cup nut meats
½ teaspoon soda
6 teaspoons baking powder

Mix soda and baking powder into the flour, mix all dry ingredients into flour. Mix syrup and milk with melted shortening, add the two mixtures together. Mix well and fill one-pound baking powder cans half full. Steam two hours. Have water come up half way the depth of cans, which must be set on a rack while boiling. When boiled, place in oven, dry out half hour.

## NUT BREADS

### Nut Bread

4 cups flour
1 cup chopped pecan meats
¼ cup sugar
2 cups sweet milk (or half water)

2 eggs
2 teaspoons salt
4 teaspoons baking powder
3 tablespoons melted shortening

Mix all dry ingredients together. Beat eggs together well; add liquid and shortening; combine the two, mix well and pour into a greased bread pan. Bake one hour in moderate oven.

### Pecan Brown Bread

2 cups buttermilk
½ cup molasses
¼ cup sugar
3 cups whole wheat flour

1 cup pecan meats, chopped
1 teaspoon salt
3 teaspoons soda

Mix all dry ingredients together. Mix syrup and milk together; mix the two. Put into greased pan, and bake in moderate oven 45 minutes. There are no eggs, no grease or baking powder in this recipe. It makes one loaf.

### Yellow Nut Bread

3 cups flour
½ cup sugar
1 cup pecan meats
¼ cup butter (or substitute)

1½ cups sweet milk
3 egg yolks
4 teaspoons baking powder

Mix all dry ingredients together. Beat eggs light, add milk, melted butter, then pour liquid into flour, mix well, pour into greased bread pan, let stand twenty minutes, bake in moderate oven forty-five minutes. This makes one nice loaf.

### Quick Nut Bread

4 cups flour
¾ cup sugar
1 egg
4 teaspoons baking powder

1 cup chopped nut meats
2 cups sweet milk
2 teaspoons salt

Mix all dry ingredients together; beat egg light, add milk; now mix the two and beat till smooth, but quickly, put into 1 lb. baking powder cans, filling ½ full, have cans well greased. Cook same as light bread, cooking 30 minutes with tops on and then 30 minutes uncovered.

### Mrs. P's Nut Loaf

½ cup sugar
½ cup New Orleans molasses
2 cups milk
2 cups flour
1 cup graham flour
½ cup raisins, seeded

1 cup chopped nut meats (walnuts or pecans)
1 teaspoon salt
1 teaspoon soda, dissolved in 1 tablespoon boiling water
2 teaspoons baking powder

Over raisins pour boiling water to plump. Drain, dry and dredge with flour. Mix all dry ingredients together, mix liquids and mix the two. Bake in loaf pan, same as loaf bread, until done. Time depends on the thickness.

### Miss Honey's Bran Bread

1 quart bran
2 teaspoons soda
2 cups thick buttermilk

1 pint white flour
½ cup molasses or syrup
1 teaspoon salt

Sift soda and salt into flour; add the bran; add syrup to milk and mix into a very stiff batter; put into a greased bread pan and bake in moderate oven 1 hour. A little shortening may be added if liked better.

### Peanut Butter Whole Wheat Bread

| | |
|---|---|
| 3 cups whole wheat flour | 4 teaspoons baking powder |
| ½ cup peanut butter | 2 teaspoons salt |
| ¼ cup sugar | 2 eggs |
| 1½ cups sweet milk | |

Mix all dry ingredients together. Make peanut butter soft with part of milk, beat eggs together light, add milk and peanut butter, mix well, mix into flour, pour into a greased bread pan, let stand twenty minutes, bake in moderate oven forty-five minutes.

## YEAST BREADS

For yeast breads, compressed, dry or liquid yeast may be used. For party rolls pastry flour is preferable, but for hungry people bread flour or certain blends of family flour gives a more satisfying roll.

Yeast breads are easily made after a few important facts are thoroughly grasped. A small amount of yeast is used when more time is allowed in the rising process, while for a quick method much more yeast is used at the beginning, which naturally makes the rising process shorter. All yeast breads must double in size whenever handled. Yeast dough may be "killed" and soured by getting too hot, but it is never injured by getting too cold. Cold retards the growth of the yeast, but as soon as the temperature is restored the rising process begins again. Bread made by the quick process should be kept warm. The rising may be hastened by placing the vessel containing the dough in another vessel of tepid water—about 88 degrees. If the vessel is placed on metal radiator or oven top the dough is likely to become overheated.

Yeast breads should be cooked with a medium heat, 350 to 400 degrees F. The oven should be hot when the loaves are placed in it. The length of time of baking depends on the thickness of the loaf or roll. A pound loaf will require about 45 minutes to bake, while one and one-half pounds will require 1 hour.

## LIGHT BREADS

### Everlasting Bread

| | |
|---|---|
| 1 quart milk, scalded and cooled | 1 teaspoon sugar |
| 1 cup melted lard (or substitute) | 5 teaspoons salt |
| 1 cake compressed yeast, softened in | ½ cup sugar |
| ½ cup water | Flour to make a soft sponge |
| 2 teaspoons baking powder | |

Let rise until full of gas bubbles, add flour to make a stiff dough, knead thoroughly and put in refrigerator. It will keep well four or five days and must be kept cold.

From this foundation can be made many kinds of bread and rolls, by rolling and shaping dough in desired shape, let rise in warm place until light and bake. For coffee cake for breakfast, roll out at night, leaving it in refrigerator over night and in the morning it will be ready for the coating of butter, sugar and cinnamon and the oven.

This dough is a great time saver, especially when preparing for guests, as hot Parker House rolls can be had with only the work of shaping and baking. Rolls will rise in about one hour. A six-quart covered kettle is needed to keep this dough in.

Dry yeast may be used. One cake.

### Perfection Light Rolls

| | |
|---|---|
| 1 quart liquid (potato water or milk and water) | 3 quarts of flour (more or less) |
| 1 cake compressed yeast dissolved in ¼ cup of water | 1 tablespoon salt |
| | 2 tablespoons sugar |
| | ½ cup shortening |

To get the potato water, peel and dice one cup of potatoes, cook, mash and strain with the water in which they are cooked, having one quart. Take one quart of flour and the yeast cake and make a sponge, let rise (which will require about two hours). When risen, sift another quart of flour into a bowl, add salt, sugar and shortening and mix sponge into dough, using more flour as needed. Knead for ten minutes until the dough is smooth and will pop. Return to the pan and let rise again, which will require about one hour. When risen, knead again just to get the gas out and to handle, using as little flour as necessary. Roll out about one-third inch thick, cut with a biscuit cutter, butter slightly one-half and fold over for Parker House rolls. Place close together, being careful to place them straight. They will rise up and not become larger. Let double in size and bake in moderate oven twenty to thirty minutes. When done, lift up the turned-over edge, place a piece of butter into each roll, return to oven to stand a few minutes to thoroughly cook and become piping hot. Serve at once. If desired, they may be buttered at table. This same dough can be put into other forms of rolls. If milk is used, use one pint of milk, scald and let become tepid, one pint of water, one yeast cake, one quart of flour and make as directed above.

When making over night, use three-fourths of compressed yeast cake. One dry yeast cake dissolved in half cup of water will be required.

### Quick Method Rolls

| | |
|---|---|
| 6 cups flour sifted and measured | 1 cup of milk |
| 4 tablespoons shortening | ½ cup of water |
| 1 tablespoon sugar | 3 yeast cakes dissolved in ¼ cup of water |
| 2 teaspoons salt | |

Scald the cup of milk and add the half cup of cold water. To the sifted flour add salt and sugar. Mix in the shortening same as for any dough. Mix with the yeast and liquid to a good firm dough and knead smooth and until springy (about five minutes); put in warm place and in 15 to 20 minutes it will be ready to punch or mash down. In about another 10 minutes it will be ready to make into rolls. Knead just enough to handle and knock out the gas, shape into rolls, let double in size and bake in a moderate oven 20 to 30 minutes. The rolls should rise in 10 to 15 minutes. The quickness of this method depends on the temperature in which the dough is kept, which should be warmer than for other methods—about 88 degrees—in a warm oven or over a pan of warm water. Another thing to remember is quickness in handling; the dough should not get too cold. It would only delay the time, not injure the rolls. Use sufficient flour to handle; reserve one cup for this. This will make about three dozen rolls.

## South Georgia Ice Box Rolls

| First Portion | Second Portion |
|---|---|
| 1 pt. milk | 1 teaspoon baking powder |
| ⅓ cup sugar | ½ teaspoon soda |
| ½ cup shortening | 2 teaspoons salt |
| ½ yeast cake | |
| 1 pint flour | |

Scald milk and pour over sugar and shortening. Set aside until tepid. Dissolve yeast in a little cool water and add to milk mixture. Fold in pint of flour measured after sifting, and beat to smooth, medium batter. Let rise for two hours in warm place. Then add baking powder, soda and salt and sufficient flour for soft dough. Knead and place in refrigerator until ready to make rolls. When ready for use make into rolls, let rise until double in size and bake at 350 degrees for 30 minutes.

## Mary's Rolls

| | |
|---|---|
| 2 yeast cakes | 1 cup scalded milk |
| 2 eggs | ½ cup sugar |
| 2 teaspoons salt | ½ cup luke warm water |
| 1 cup mashed Irish potatoes | ⅔ cup shortening |
| Flour to make medium dough | |

Put mashed potatoes into bowl, add shortening, sugar, salt and scalded milk. When this mixture is tepid, add yeast, which has been dissolved in the ½ cup of luke warm water, now flour to make a medium stiff dough.

Put this in the refrigerator to gradually rise until you are ready to make out the rolls. When made out at 4 o'clock, they are ready for 6 o'clock dinner. Make up the dough about 9 o'clock in the morning.

These rolls have a crust very similiar to Sally Lunn and are wonderfully tender.

## Butter Horns

| | |
|---|---|
| 2 yeast cakes (compressed) dissolved in 2 tablespoons from the cup of water | 1 cup water |
| | ¼ cup sugar |
| | 1 teaspoon salt |
| 3 eggs | 5 cups sifted flour |
| ½ cup shortening | |

Mix shortening, remaining water, sugar and salt together and heat until melted. Cool until tepid. Add the dissolved yeast cakes, beaten eggs and flour. Mix well. Turn on a floured bread board, knead for ten minutes, using flour as necessary. Let rise until double in bulk (about 2 hours at 78 degrees). Knead again for ten minutes, then roll out 1/4-inch thick in round sections as for pie crust. Spread with melted butter. Cut in pie-shaped sections (large or small), begin rolling at the large (or outer edge) like a jelly roll into horn shape. Place about one inch apart, let rise again until double in bulk (about one hour), butter when put to rise. Put in medium oven (375), bake about twenty minutes. Serve hot. This is a good ice box roll, to be made and kept until wanted. They may be made and shaped and placed in ice box overnight. When removed give two hours to rise before baking. Cinnamon and sugar may be used before rolling for afternoon tea rolls.

### Cloverleaf Rolls

Make the usual risen dough. When ready to shape, make three small balls as large as a hickory nut, touch one small portion of each ball in melted butter, put the greased part together in center, put all three in muffin mold, let rise and bake. This makes three tiny rolls in one and is quite pretty.

### Dimple Rolls

Make the usual risen dough. When ready to shape, roll out one-fourth inch thick, sprinkle generously with flour, cut with small cutter, put two together, one on top of another and let stand until all are cut. With the finger make a deep dimple to hold the two pieces together. Let rise, bake as any roll. When served, they come apart readily for buttering.

### Crusty Rolls

Take the risen dough, pinch off sufficient to half fill each muffin mold, let double in size and bake.

### Parker House Rolls

Parker House rolls are designated by the shaping of the roll. Any risen dough may be used.

Roll out a sheet of dough one-fourth inch thick and cut with a tea biscuit cutter. Have butter melted in saucer, dip one-half of the cut roll into melted butter, lap over the other half, leaving one-fourth inch of the lower side uncovered, and place in greased pan. Each roll should be placed in pan with the lap in the same direction, so the buttering will be easy. Let rise (double in size), bake as any roll. When done, have butter that is soft (not melted), with a fork lift up the turn-over, and with another fork put a portion of butter in the roll. Return to oven a few seconds before serving.

This is an easy and rapid way of making and buttering rolls for parties, and where quite a number is needed. The first buttering makes the turned lap easy to lift.

## Pocketbook Rolls

Use recipe for any risen dough. When ready to shape rolls, knead the dough sufficiently to remove gas, pinch off pieces of dough about the size of an egg, place on a floured board until all are shaped, and let stand at least five minutes to rise slightly. With the side of the hand mash right through the center of roll, brush with a bit of melted butter. Pick up each roll, turn together, place in pan side by side, let rise (double in size) and bake. Rolls after this method may be made and placed quicker than it takes to explain.

## Whole Wheat or Graham Bread

Start the sponge with white flour just as you do in Perfection recipe bread. When it has risen use the whole wheat or graham flour for making the dough. Use little less shortening, knead only four or five minutes, place in pans to rise and when double in bulk, bake.

This bread only rises one time. The yeast works much faster in the brown flours.

## Whole Wheat Bread

| | |
|---|---|
| 1 pint tepid water | 4 teaspoons sugar |
| ½ yeast cake compressed | ¼ cup shortening |
| 2 teaspoons salt | About 1½ quarts flour |

Dissolve yeast in water; add salt and sugar; mix shortening into flour and make dough; knead well; shape into loaves; put into pans; let double in size, bake in moderate oven. Have oven hot, place bread about center, cook 45 minutes, using medium heat. Dough should be about as any other bread. Whole wheat and graham breads are usually made with just one rising.

## Graham Bread

Make as above, using graham flour.

## Puffs

| | |
|---|---|
| 1 tablespoon salt | 1 yeast cake |
| 2 tablespoons sugar | 2 eggs |
| 2 tablespoons shortening | About 2½ quarts sifted flour |
| 2 cups boiling water | |

Put salt, sugar and lard into bowl; over this pour the boiling water; let stand until tepid; add yeast cake; beat eggs, and add to liquid; now add all the flour it will take; let rise 4 to 6 hours; knead the gas out; put into muffin pans. Let double in size, bake in moderate oven until done, 15 to 20 minutes.

## Rye Bread

| | |
|---|---|
| 2 cups tepid water | 4 cups white flour |
| 2 tablespoons sugar | 4 cups rye flour |
| 2 teaspoons salt | 1 yeast cake |
| 3 tablespoons shortening | |

Mix into a dough, knead for ten minutes, place in bowl to rise about three or four hours. Grease top to prevent a crust forming. When risen, knead again; put into pans, let double in bulk. Bake in moderate oven forty-five to sixty minutes for usual size loaf. Rye bread is made as any other bread, using rye and white flour, half and half.

### Liquid Yeast

| | |
|---|---|
| 2 large potatoes grated | ½ cup sugar |
| 3 pints boiling water | 1 yeast cake (or ½ cup liquid yeast) |
| 1 tablespoon salt | |

Pour 3 pints of boiling water over potatoes, stirring all the time, add salt and sugar, when cold add yeast, set in warm place to rise, then keep in refrigerator. When using, shake well. Use ½ cup to 1 quart flour.

### Loaf Bread—Using Liquid Yeast

| | |
|---|---|
| 1½ cups liquid yeast | 1 teaspoon salt |
| 2 tablespoons lard (more if desired) | Flour to make firm dough |
| 1 tablespoon sugar | |

Knead ten minutes. Shape into loaf or rolls, let stand until double in size, then bake, using moderate oven.

### Liquid Yeast for French Rolls

One large Irish potato boiled mealy and mashed smooth. Add 1 pint boiling water; 1 pint cold water; 1 cup sugar; 1 yeast cake dissolved in 1 cup tepid water.

Let stand in warm place for five or six hours, then put into refrigerator.

### The Rolls

| | |
|---|---|
| 1 quart flour | 1 teaspoon salt |
| 1 tablespoon lard | 1 tablespoon sugar |
| 1 egg | 1 cup of the liquid yeast |

Mix into a dough, using the yeast for the liquid. Knead well, make into rolls, put into refrigerator and let stand all night. Bake for breakfast. Use moderate oven.

### Yeast—Mrs. Earl's Recipe

Peel and boil 3 medium size Irish potatoes with half cup of peach or hop leaves. Remove potatoes, mash, and pour the water in which they were boiled back on them, having strained free of leaves. Dissolve 1 or 2 yeast cakes in half cup of tepid water. When potatoes and water are tepid add yeast, one teaspoon sugar, and ¼ teaspoon salt. Set in warm place to rise over night. In the morning, stir into the yeast enough sifted meal to make a very stiff batter.

Let rise again from 1½ to 2½ hours. Add more meal to make a dough, roll out to one-third inch thick, cut in two inch squares, place on bread board to dry in the shade, turning every day until dry.

Use one yeast cake to one quart or more of flour. Dissolve yeast in tepid water. Use as any yeast. (See yeast breads.) Commercial yeast may be used for starting the home made yeast. Compressed yeast is stronger than dry and when used the entire making may be done in a day.

## Buttermilk Yeast

| | |
|---|---|
| 1 pint buttermilk | 1 tablespoon sugar |
| 1 yeast cake (any kind) | Meal to make a very stiff batter |

Scald buttermilk, but do not boil; let cool. Dissolve yeast cake in a little cold water, make batter and cover top with meal; set to rise for 24 hours until risen and well cracked open. Make stiff with more cornmeal; make into yeast cakes, about two inches across and half inch thick. Place on board, in shade, to dry and harden. Turn during the drying. Use one cake to one or more quarts of flour, depending upon the quickness of the making.

## Old Time Buckwheat Cakes

| | |
|---|---|
| ½ yeast cake or 1 cup liquid yeast | Sufficient buckwheat flour to make |
| 2 cups tepid water | stiff batter |
| 1 cup milk | |

Scald milk and let cool. Dissolve yeast in a portion of the water. Mix all together, let rise overnight. Next morning add:

| | |
|---|---|
| 1 teaspoon soda | 2 tablespoons syrup |
| 2 teaspoons salt | |

Mix well and bake on griddle. One cup of meal, white or brown flour may be added when making batter at night.

Where buckwheat cakes are used often, the jar is kept with a portion of the risen batter for a starter and no other yeast is used; this will last all winter. Place jar in cold closet or refrigerator when not using and keep covered. Make up at night when wanted for breakfast next morning.

## Sally Lunn

| | |
|---|---|
| 1 pint milk | 3 eggs |
| 2 tablespoons of butter or substitute | ½ cake of compressed yeast |
| 2 tablespoons of sugar | Flour sufficient to make a good |
| 2 teaspoons salt | thick batter, about 3 or 4 cups |

Scald milk and, while hot, put into it the butter, sugar and salt. Let it stand until tepid. Dissolve yeast cake in ¼ cup of cold water. Beat eggs together until light; add milk and yeast, then flour; beat for several minutes to thoroughly mix. Set aside to rise. When risen, beat down. Let rise again and repeat the beating down. The beating takes the place of kneading and is done three or four times. The vessel should be kept at just a pleasant degree of heat, 68 or 70 degrees. When time to bake, pour into a greased pan and let double in size, which will require about an hour. Bake in a moderate oven from three-fourths to one hour, according to the depth of the loaf. It should be well cooked, with a thick crust. It may be put into muffin molds for individual lunns. The small ones will require about thirty minutes to cook the same as rolls.

## Coffee Rolls

When making rolls, roll out a sheet of dough ½ inch thick, cover with soft butter, sprinkle well with brown sugar, cover with chopped nut meats, roll up as you would a jelly roll. Make in circle, place in a round pie plate, make deep cuts with scissors two inches apart, let rise and bake.

## Crumpets

| | |
|---|---|
| 1 quart flour | 2 eggs |
| 1 cup milk warmed until tepid | 1 teaspoon salt |
| ¾ cup liquid yeast or 1 compressed cake dissolved in half cup water | |

Beat eggs together well. Add milk, yeast and flour, making a stiff batter. Let rise until light, covering bowl to prevent crusting over top. When well risen have a griddle hot and greased. Pour on a large spoonful carefully as large as batter cakes. Bake rather slowly turning when one side is browned. Butter and send to table.

## Coffee Cake No. 1

Make the usual light bread or roll dough, roll out, spread with soft butter, or substitute, sprinkle generously with brown sugar and cinnamon, roll up like a jelly roll, make in a circle, place in round cake pan. With scissors snip on the outer edge of circle, going half way through. Let double in size and bake. Raisins and nuts may be added.

## Coffee Cake No. 2

Into a deep layer pan put a layer of light roll dough, one-half inch thick. Cover top with soft butter, sprinkle heavily with brown sugar, sprinkle with nuts and seedless raisins, let rise, bake as any risen bread until done. Cut in squares and serve hot or cold.

## Mrs. C's Cinnamon Rolls

Roll out a piece of risen dough until one-fourth inch thick. Cover generously with soft butter, brown sugar and cinnamon, sprinkle currants or seedless raisins over top, roll up like a jelly roll and catch the ends and pull out long. Cut rolls about one inch or more thick, place in buttered pan on cut end and let rise until double in size. Bake as any roll, using medium oven.

## Banana Bread

| | |
|---|---|
| ½ cup shortening | 3 cups sifted flour |
| ½ cup sugar | 3 teaspoons baking powder |
| 2 eggs | ½ teaspoon salt |
| 1 cup mashed bananas | 1 cup chopped pecans |
| 1 teaspoon lemon juice | |

Cream shortening and sugar, beat eggs together and add. Put bananas thru ricer, add lemon juice and then add to creamed mixture. Sift flour with baking powder and salt. Mix quickly with banana mixture, add nuts. Pour into greased loaf pan, bake about 1 hour at 375 degrees, F.

### Date and Nut Loaf

| | |
|---|---|
| 1½ cups liquid yeast | 1 teaspoon salt |
| ½ cup warm water (or milk which has been scalded) | ⅔ cup chopped dates |
| | ⅔ cup chopped nut meats |
| ¼ cup sugar | Flour necessary to make loaves |
| 2 tablespoons shortening | |

Sift two cups flour, add shortening, sugar, salt, dates and nuts, mix together dry, add yeast to warm water, mix in a dough using more flour; knead slightly and put in loaf pan or two small ones; let rise double in size and bake as any loaf bread.

### Cornmeal Light Bread No. 1

| | |
|---|---|
| 1 quart cornmeal | 1 cup flour |
| 1 quart fresh buttermilk | 3 tablespoons sugar |
| 2 eggs | 2 teaspoons salt |
| 2 level teaspoons soda | |

Mix well, cover lightly with cornmeal, place in warm temperature and let rise 3 or 4 hours. When risen pour into hot well-greased pan and bake.

### Cornmeal Light Bread No. 2

Scald ½ or ¾ cup sweet milk and thicken with meal. Let stand about 24 hours or until sour and light (keep warm).

Next morning take a quart of warm water and stir this scalded meal into it. Put in ¼ cup sugar and thicken with meal again, real thick so you can just stir with spoon. Let stand in warm place until risen and cracked open; takes from 1 to 2 hours. Next, stir in ¾ cup molasses (more sugar if liked sweet), 1 pint graham flour or whole wheat, 1 teaspoon each of soda, and salt. Pour in baking pan, and keep warm again until it rises about 1½ to 2 inches. Grease pan. Bake in moderate oven. No lard used.

### Cornmeal Light Bread No. 3

Three pints of sifted meal, 2 teaspoons salt, make up with cold water as for plain bread; let stand all night. Next morning, add lard size of an egg; one pint of flour, one teaspoon soda, one teacup buttermilk, one half cup of sugar (more if you like sweeter). Mix and bake immediately. Don't have fire too hot at first, give time to rise, then bake. Use moderate oven.

### Staunton (Va.) Salt Rising Bread

| | |
|---|---|
| 4 small Irish potatoes | 1 teaspoon salt |
| 2 tablespoons sugar | 1 quart boiling water |
| 4 tablespoons cornmeal | |

#### First Part

Peel and slice potatoes thin, put into medium vessel and pour boiling water over them. Add meal, sugar and salt. Into a larger vessel put tepid water and set container with yeast starter into this. Let stand 24 hours. Start about 10 o'clock one morning, preparing the bread for the next morning. Bubbles will form on this starter, similar to soap bubbles, and the salt-rising odor will be unmistakable if the yeast starter is good.

### Second Part

Strain the first part and add:

2 cups warm milk                     Enough flour to make stiff sponge
¼ teaspoon soda

Let rise until light, which will be in about two hours. Again set in vessel of tepid water and keep just warm until light.

### Third Part

Into bowl sift: 1 quart flour with teaspoon of salt. Mix into flour thoroughly 4 tablespoons of shortening. Add sponge and more flour to make a soft dough. Knead just enough to handle and work quickly so dough will not chill. Put into greased bread pans, filling half full, let rise again till double in size, bake in moderate oven until done. A medium loaf requires between 45 and 60 minutes baking.

Placing the loaves over smaller vessels of tepid water, getting the warmth above the warm water is a good way to keep the loaves warm. This bread should never be allowed to get cold and in the last rising not too warm. If directions are followed carefully, success is certain. Use bread flour. The milk should be fresh, full milk, warmed but not scalded.

This recipe has been passed on to many a housewife with success. It is the Colonial yeast bread, wholesome and delicious.

### Flannel Cakes With Yeast

2 cups flour                          2 cups sweet milk
2 eggs                                1 yeast cake
1 tablespoon butter                   1 tablespoon sugar

Set to rise over night. Next morning add 2 teaspoons salt, ½ teaspoon soda. Beat well and bake on slightly greased griddle.

### English Muffins

1 yeast cake (compressed)             2 cups sweet milk
1 cup water                           ½ cup butter or shortening melted
1 teaspoon salt                       1 egg white
2 tablespoon sugar                    Flour to make soft batter

Scald milk, add water and when tepid mix into batter, let rise to light sponge. Add melted butter and egg white beaten stiff and sufficient more flour to make stiff batter. Let double in bulk and with greased spoon drop into greased muffin tins, filling tins three-fourths full. Bake immediately in moderate oven until done (about 20 minutes). The batter is already light and does not have to stand to rise after being put into muffin tins. These muffins are also baked on a griddle. Place rings on griddle, fill, let rise while baking, turn ring and all to cook top side. Delicious for lunch with butter and honey. Open, toast and serve with butter and marmalade.

# TOAST

Cut bread into slices of medium thickness, remove crust, have oven or toaster hot, toast to a golden brown on both sides. Serve hot. Bread a day old cuts and toasts best.

## French Toast No. 1

Cut slices of bread half inch thick, remove crust and cut into any shape desired. Beat two eggs together, add half cup of milk, mix well. Dip each slice of bread in the eggs to cover both sides and fry in butter just long enough to brown and cook coating. Serve hot with jam or jelly.

## French Toast No. 2

Cut slices of bread size and thickness desired. Beat two eggs together and add half cup sugar, two cups milk, one teaspoon nutmeg or cinnamon, dip in slices of bread, fry in butter until brown.

## Cinnamon Toast

Cut and toast slices of bread, spread with butter, cover with cinnamon sugar, return to oven close to blaze so as to caramel or brown the sugar, toast until sugar bubbles slightly and serve. For cinnamon sugar mix two tablespoons of cinnamon in one cup of sugar, sprinkle on toast. Have butter soft to spread. Butter, sugar and cinnamon may be mixed together and all spread at one time. There is a cinnamon sugar prepared, that comes in cans all ready to sprinkle on toast.

## Biscuit Toast

Split open stale biscuit and toast cut side until nicely browned. Have ready one cup or more of hot milk, to which has been added a piece of butter and a dash of black pepper. Place biscuit in dish, pour over them a cup or more of hot water and pour off immediately, then pour over the hot milk and serve at once. A sprinkle of salt may be necessary.

The hot water slightly softens biscuit to take the hot milk.

This is good for children and is a nice way to use up cold biscuit.

## Left Over Biscuit

Split biscuit in half (as many as needed). Into a heavy fry pan put enough butter to brown biscuit, placing inside down. Cook over gentle heat until the side is nicely browned and biscuit hot. Serve as hot biscuit.

## Browned Biscuits

Split open biscuit, place cut side up, toast until nice brown. Serve as hot biscuit, or as toast.

### Milk Toast

Make slices of toast the desired size and thickness. Heat fresh, full milk, add butter, salt and a dash of pepper. Pour over the toast and serve immediately.

When serving milk toast many prefer to have the seasoned hot milk in a pitcher to pour over the toast at the table. This prevents its being too soft.

### Toast for Soup

Cut bread in long strips, one inch wide by one inch thick, more or less, by four or five inches long. Toast on all sides and serve with any soup.

### Toasted Crackers

Place crackers on a baking sheet, in medium oven. Toast until crisp and slightly browned. Serve as any crackers.

### Toasted Crackers With Cheese

Arrange crackers on baking sheet, sprinkle with grated cheese and put in a medium oven until crisp and cheese is melted. A sprinkle of paprika is sometimes added.

### Jelly Toast

Make the usual toast, spread with butter, then with jelly. Add a sprinkle of grated cheese, run under gas blaze for a few seconds to melt cheese and serve immediately.

# desserts

ambrosia

# CHAPTER X

# Desserts

## PASTRIES

Ask the average man what he prefers for dessert, and almost invariably he will answer "pie." In a hotel or restaurant, when he looks over the menu, he usually chooses "pie." If there is an apple pie he usually goes no further, but stops there—and "pie" it is.

Pie is often called the American dessert, and from the great numbers shown in the cafeterias it must be true. Women are not such pie eaters as men—but aren't most of us trying to please the men and give them what they want?

There are certain essentials to be observed in making pies, which are necessary if one is to have the best results. First, pastry flour will make a better crust than a heavy flour, because it has little gluten left in it; next, the shortening should be chopped into the flour, using a spoon or a knife. The hands are apt to soften the shortening, and the success of the pastry depends on keeping all the materials cold. Chopping the shortening in large pieces, some as large as the end of the finger, is preferable to having it too fine.

The next important thing is a firm, cold shortening and ice water, which should be added very gradually, just enough to hold the mixture together, having it so dry and crumbly that you may wonder if it is moist enough. The dough should then be pressed together with the hands. It may be rolled and folded, but never kneaded. The less handling of the dough, the better. If there is time, the dough is more easily handled after being placed in the ice-box for an hour or so. In order to prevent a crust forming on the dough while it is being chilled, always cover with a cloth or with oil paper.

If the materials or the board on which the crust is rolled should be warm, the pastry is apt to stick, be hard to handle and shrink when baked.

Pastry should be rolled lightly from center to edge, back and forth from side to side, with light, quick movements, using flour necessary to handle. Handle as little as possible, lay the dough on the pan loosely and then press into shape, making sure that no air spaces are left at the side or bottom of the pan.

Attention should be called to the difference between a pie pan and a cake pan. A pie pan has a slanting side, with a flange or flat portion at the edge, about one-fourth inch wide, on which the two crusts may be stuck together. When the bottom crust is in place and the filling has been poured in and ready for the top crust, wet the flange with cold water and press the upper crust lightly to it. Then crimp the edges together to hold in the juices, and make generous cuts in the top crust to allow the steam to escape while baking and to prevent the boiling out of the juices.

A pastry shell should be baked with more heat than a pie. Pastry should be crusty through and through and a delicate brown in color. Scorched pastry is not only unattractive to the eye, but indigestible and unpleasant to the taste—therefore the baking is very important. The oven should be hot when the pie is first put in, to set the pastry, and then reduced immediately for the cooking, which is medium, 350° to 400°. A pastry shell will cook in about 10 to 12 minutes, while a pie takes 30 to 40 minutes. A pastry shell may be cooked with a hotter oven, since a filling may boil out if cooked too rapidly.

All pastry and pies should be cooked on or near the bottom of the oven. This is done to cook the bottom of the pie. Since the pastry is rich, the top crust will brown anywhere in the oven, but it is the bottom crust which must be considered. Individual pastry shells may be made over inverted muffin tins, if spaces are far enough apart.

Pies properly baked will refute the old argument that they are indigestible.

The above instructions cover particularly plain pastry, but if well made will answer the need of puff paste, with a few exceptions. Puff pastry is the finest of all pastries, but it is very tedious to make, the success is anything but certain—therefore, it would seem best to spend your time in learning to make excellent plain pastry, and buy from an expert your fancy pastry.

There is a hot water pastry (made with hot water), which is almost unbelievable. While it is not quite as flaky, some succeed best with this recipe, so one is given here. Do not be afraid to try it.

There is also another pastry which is more generally used for shortcake and is somewhat like a short biscuit dough.

### Plain Pastry

1¼ cups sifted flour  
4 tablespoons shortening  
3 tablespoons ice-cold water  
½ teaspoon salt

Sift salt with flour. Chop in shortening with a spoon until broken into small pieces. Add water in several places in order not to get any part too wet. Mix with a spoon into a ball, having it very dry. With the hands press together, place on a floured board and roll out until as thin as desired. Place on pie plate and proceed for a pastry shell or for a filled pie. Put into a hot oven, but reduce heat to little more than medium to cook.

For a pastry shell after rolled, press into the pan, stick with a fork so it will bake evenly (not pop up into large blisters). If a filled pie, brush the pastry well with melted grease to prevent the filling from soaking into the pastry. No sticking with fork.

All materials must be cold for a success, the shortening hard, and the water ice cold. This recipe makes one crust. Use extra flour for rolling.

### Easy Puff Pastry

4 cups pastry flour  
2 cups butter  
½ cup ice-cold water  
1 tablespoon sugar  
1 teaspoon salt  
2 eggs  
1 tablespoon lemon juice

Add salt and sugar to flour in mixing bowl; chop butter into flour as fine as possible, having butter very cold. Beat eggs together for five minutes, add lemon juice to them, add the cold water and mix flour into a stiff dough. Lift dough to well-floured board, roll out into rectangular shape, fold all four sides onto the dough, roll again; repeat this process four times. Fold again and wrap in a napkin, place on plate and stand on ice or let stand until thoroughly chilled. Roll out again and use for patties, pie crust or tart shells.

## Never Fail Hot Water Pastry

2½ cups flour  
½ cup boiling water  
¼ teaspoon baking powder

1 teaspoon salt  
½ cup shortening (half butter may be used)

Cream the shortening with the water by adding the latter only a little at a time. Mix the salt and baking powder with the sifted flour and stir this into the shortening and water. Turn out upon a floured board and roll thin. This amount will make upper and lower crusts for one large pie.

## Pastry for Shortcake

2½ cups flour  
⅔ cup firm cold shortening

6 tablespoons ice-cold water  
2 teaspoons salt

Chop shortening into flour until it looks like meal. With a spoon mix into a very dry, stiff ball, using less liquid if necessary to have it very dry. With hands press into a ball; do not knead at all.

Lift on a well floured board, using extra flour to handle. Divide into two parts, roll out thin and bake two pastry shells. Fill the shells with strawberries, putting one on top of the other, like layer cake. Top with whipped cream.

When ready to bake crust, prick with a fork in many places to prevent blistering. Do not have pastry very brown, have a light color but crisp.

## Individual Tart or Pie Shells

Roll and cut pastry with large cutter, or the desired size, stick with fork to prevent blistering, place carelessly over inverted patty pans or individual molds and bake as any pastry, a light brown but crusty. Fill with any desired filling, fruits or custards. Cover top with a soft icing, run under the blaze to brown quickly and serve hot or cold. Meringue may cover top (see baking of meringue).

Jelly glasses and empty spools may be used. Grease slightly before placing on pastry. Put molds on large baking sheet and many may be baked at once. Tiny shells filled with marmalade, topped with an icing, may be used as French pastry.

## Paté or Patty Cases of Puff Pastry

To cut patties: Roll dough ¾-inch thick, use tea biscuit cutter. Make another cut and remove center. Wet first piece with cold water and place ring on top, press together well. Place carefully on baking sheet, not too close, chill before baking. Bake tops, which are the removed pieces from ring. Remove the inside, which is a soft dough which refuses to get crisp, fill and replace top. Never brown too much. Puff paste must be light brown, but crisp. This may be used for pie crust.

Use more or less of the liquid, according to what the flour requires. Use extra flour for rolling. Everything must be ice-cold.

Place in center of hot oven which registers 500 degrees, reduce heat 50 degrees every five minutes until thermometer reads 300 degrees. Continue cooking until a golden brown (about 30 to 40 minutes).

Several thicknesses of paper placed in bottom of pan will prevent cases from burning. A bright pan does not burn easily.

## Timbales

Timbale cases are used to hold creamed dishes (meats or vegetables). Timbale cases and pastry patés are used for the same purpose; timbales hold the hot filling, while patés (or patties) and filling both must be hot.

Rosettes are another form of timbale, and may be sweet or plain. They are used for vegetables or fruit. (See recipe with wafers.)

### To Make Timbales

| | |
|---|---|
| 1 cup milk | 1 egg |
| 1 cup water | Flour to make a thin batter, about 2½ |
| 1 teaspoon salt | cups |

Into a bowl put the milk, half the water, salt and egg unbeaten, beat enough to mix the egg into the milk using a stirring motion to get as little air as possible into the mixture.

Add flour and mix well until free of lumps. Add the remaining water, which gives a thin batter. Cover and let stand until the bubbles come to the top, an hour or more. Pour a portion into a small bowl large enough to float the timbale iron, dip into batter, let dry, then fry in hot grease until a light brown. Slip out the iron, fill the shell with the hot grease and continue cooking until crisp; remove with a fork; drain on paper. Keep the iron in the boiling fat while finishing the timbale and repeat the process.

Before dipping into the batter, wipe off the mold on a piece of soft paper before cooking each timbale. As the batter is used keep filled with the cold portion. It's better not to use the entire portion because the hot iron makes the batter too thin. Have the hot grease just as deep as the timbale iron. Be careful to let the batter come within one-fourth inch of the top. Keep mold hot enough to sizzle. If too hot the timbale slips off, or if too cold it will stick.

Put mold into the grease and heat gradually when ready to cook. Have grease hot but not smoking. This will make three dozen. Use a small saucepan deep enough for the grease to boil up without running over.

### Individual Apple Pies

Make tart shells the size desired, baking over bottoms of patty pans (see tart shells). Fill with cold apple sauce, sweetened and seasoned. Top with whipped cream, or garnish with a rosette of mashed and seasoned cottage or Philadelphia cream cheese.

### Individual Peach Pie

Make tart shells, fill with canned peaches, or fresh ones, sliced thin and sweetened. Cover top with whipped cream, jelly meringue or cheese.

### Lemon Tarts

Juice and grated rind of 2 lemons. Grate 2 sponge cakes (2 large lady-fingers).

Beat 2 eggs light and add one cup of sugar. Mix all together. Mix rich pastry, line patty pans and fill with mixture. Bake.

This makes about 9 tarts in muffin pans.

### Chess Tarts

Make small shells. For filling use Janet's Chess Pie. (See recipe in Pies.)

### Cheese Straws

| | |
|---|---|
| 2 cups flour | ⅛ teaspoon cayenne pepper |
| 1 cup grated cheese | Ice-cold water to make very stiff |
| 1 teaspoon salt | dry dough |
| Butter the size of an egg | |

Mix salt, pepper and butter into the flour, add cheese and mix with the ice water. Cover and place in ice box for 30 minutes, roll out, fold and roll again. Repeat this four times. Roll out to ¼ inch thickness, cut in ¼ inch strips about 4 inches long, place on baking sheet and bake in moderate oven until a light, crisp brown.

Sometimes cut small biscuit about as large as a half dollar and bake as crackers or wafers. The oven should be very hot when put in, then reduced to medium heat.

## PIES

### My Favorite Lemon Pie

| | |
|---|---|
| cup sugar | 3 tablespoons of sugar for the |
| 1 cup of wet light bread | meringue |
| 3 eggs | Butter the size of an egg |
| Juice of 1 large lemon | |

Remove the crust from fresh bread and dip into a bowl of water until it will take up enough to be wet thoroughly. Squeeze out the water and measure in a cup—not packing too tight. Put the wet bread, sugar, yolks of eggs, lemon juice and butter into a double boiler and cook until thick enough to stand when cut. Pour into a baked crust. Make meringue of the whites and sugar, cover the top and bake in a slow oven for 10 minutes or until brown.

## Wilmington Lemon Pie

| | |
|---|---|
| 1 cup sugar | 3 eggs |
| 2 tablespoons butter | Juice of 1 large lemon |

Cook sugar, egg yolks and lemon juice in double boiler until thick. Make meringue of 3 egg whites using 3 tablespoons sugar. Pour filling in a baked pie crust, put meringue on top, and bake in a slow oven until meringue is brown (about 10 minutes).

## Lemon Sponge Custard (Pie)

### First Part

| | |
|---|---|
| 1 cup sugar | Juice and rind of 1 lemon |
| 1 tablespoon butter | |

Mix sugar and butter together and add lemon.

### Second Part

Beat yolks of 3 eggs with one cup sweet milk; mix parts 1 and 2.

### Third Part

Beat whites of 3 eggs stiff, fold parts 1 and 2 into part 3; pour in uncooked pastry; cook 30 minutes in moderate oven. Success depends on careful mixing.

## Mrs. McD's Lemon Pie

| | |
|---|---|
| 4 eggs | 1 tablespoon flour |
| 1 cup sugar | 3 tablespoons butter |
| 1 cup boiling water | Juice of 1 lemon |

Reserve 2 whites for meringue. Beat eggs together, then add flour to dry sugar, mix into eggs, add water and lemon juice, butter, pour into raw crust and cook until firm and crust is brown. Make meringue of the 2 whites and 2 tablespoons of sugar; put on top when nearly done, cook until meringue is done (about 10 minutes).

## Lemon Pie—in Uncooked Pastry

| | |
|---|---|
| 1 large lemon (grated rind and juice) | 2 tablespoons butter |
| 1 cup sugar | 3 eggs |
| ½ cup milk | 6 tablespoons of sugar for the meringue |
| 2 tablespoons corn starch | |

Mix together, using the yolks for the custard. Pour into an uncooked crust and bake; when nearly done make the meringue of the whites and the 6 tablespoons of sugar, put over top and bake until brown. The meringue should be cooked in a slow oven about 10 minutes.

### Lemon Cream Custard (Pie)

| | |
|---|---|
| 1½ cups milk | 1½ tablespoons corn starch dissolved |
| 1 tablespoon butter | in ½ cup of milk |

Cook together until thick like white sauce. Let cool. Beat yolks of 4 eggs with 1 cup sugar, add juice of 2 lemons and rind of 1 lemon. Mix into the cooked sauce. Pour into a half done crust, bake until firm and crust is brown.

Make meringue of the whites using 4 tablespoons of sugar. Put over the top during the last 10 minutes of baking.

### Angel Dream Lemon Pie

| | |
|---|---|
| 1 large lemon | ¼ teaspoon salt |
| 1¼ cups sugar | 4 eggs |

Separate eggs, divide sugar into two parts. Beat yolks until light, add lemon juice and one part of sugar. Put into double boiler, stir constantly until well cooked, let cool. Add salt to whites, beat stiff and dry, add the other portion of sugar slowly, beat two minutes after all is in. Fold into the yellow mixture, put into a cooked crust, place in medium oven, cook about 20 minutes. until puffed and a light brown on top. Serve hot or cold.

### Egg Custard

| | |
|---|---|
| 3 eggs | 1 tablespoon flour |
| ½ cup sugar | 1 teaspoon vanilla |
| 1 cup whole milk | 1 pie pan lined with a rich pastry |
| 1 tablespoon butter | |

Separate egg. Reserve 2 tablespoons of sugar to add to beaten whites. Warm milk, having just tepid. Mix flour with dry sugar. Beat yolks. Add sugar and flour. Add melted butter, then milk and flavoring. Beat egg whites stiff. Add sugar as making meringue. Fold into the mixture, pour into pastry which has been partly baked in quick oven, bake in moderate oven until custard is firm. If the pastry is brushed with melted butter or margarine before baking it will prevent custard seeping into pastry. Bake near the bottom of oven. This is an old-time custard put together differently.

### Foolish Pie

| | |
|---|---|
| Whites 4 eggs | 1⅓ cups pulverized sugar |
| 1 teaspoon lemon juice | |

Beat eggs fifteen minutes, then add sugar slowly, then lemon juice and beat again for fifteen minutes.

Grease pie pan (use pan with cutter), bake until a very light brown, using slow oven. Serve with any fruit, pineapple, orange or any of the berries, whipped cream on top.

## Angel Delight Pie

| | |
|---|---|
| 2 cups canned (or fresh) fruit diced and drained as dry as possible | 4 egg whites |
| | ¼ teaspoon salt |
| 1 pie shell | 1 cup sugar (fine grained) |

Dice and drain fruit. Make pastry, and while baking beat eggs stiff, add half of the sugar gradually; continue beating until very stiff. Now add the remaining sugar gradually but quickly folding in. Fold in the fruit with as little motion as possible. Pile into the hot crust as little mountain peaks. Sprinkle top with sugar (about 2 tablespoons). Bake in moderate oven 15 minutes or until a delicate brown. The success of this pie is fresh eggs that will whip stiff, and having the fruit dry, so it will not sink to the bottom in cooking.

## Macaroon Custard

| | |
|---|---|
| 1 dozen macaroons | ½ cup marmalade |
| 2 cups milk | 1 cooked pastry shell |
| 3 egg yolks | Meringue of the 3 whites and 3 |
| ½ cup sugar | tablespoons of sugar |

Dry and roll fine the macaroons. Sift and roll again the large pieces. Make a custard of the milk, sugar and yolks. Cook until quite thick, add macaroon crumbs, mix, pour into a cooked pastry. Over top spread marmalade or jelly. Make meringue of the 3 whites and sugar, put on top, bake for 15 minutes, until done.

## Chocolate Cream Pie

| | |
|---|---|
| 4 tablespoons corn starch | ½ cup sugar |
| 4 tablespoons hot water | 1 teaspoon vanilla |
| 2 squares melted chocolate | 2 eggs |
| 2 cups milk | |

Separate eggs. Mix melted chocolate and hot water. Mix sugar and corn starch together dry, beat yolks, add sugar then melted chocolate. Pour over this the heated milk and mix smoothly. Cook in double boiler until thick and quite stiff. Beat whites stiff and fold into the mixture, after letting the chocolate mixture cool slightly. Pour into a cooked crust. Serve cold.

## Chocolate Custard

| | |
|---|---|
| ½ cup sugar | 3 tablespoons corn starch |
| ¼ cup butter | 3 eggs |
| ¾ cup grated chocolate | 1 teaspoon vanilla |
| 1 cup sweet milk | |

Melt chocolate, add to sugar and butter. Dissolve corn starch in the sweet milk, add to butter and sugar and mix well, heating slightly to get smooth. Add yolks of eggs to mixture, also flavoring. Pour into a rich pastry, bake until firm with a moderate fire. Make meringue of the three whites and three tablespoons of sugar, place on top of custard and cook about 10 minutes, or until brown, in very slow oven. This should be put on when pie is nearly done.

### Cocoa Meringue Pie

½ cup cocoa  
¾ cup sugar  
3 tablespoons corn starch  
¾ cup milk  

¾ cup water  
1 teaspoon vanilla  
3 eggs  
Pinch of salt  

Mix cocoa and sugar together dry. Dissolve corn starch in small portion of water. Separate eggs, beat yolks, add sugar together, add corn starch. Heat milk and water, pour over the egg mixture. Return to double boiler, cook until thick, pour into a cooked crust. Make meringue of whites saving out three tablespoons of the sugar for meringue, bake until meringue is done. Serve cold.

### Syrup Custard

1 cup syrup  
½ cup sugar  
4 tablespoons butter  

3 eggs  
1 teaspoon vanilla  

Cook sugar, butter and syrup together until thick. Beat eggs together until light, pour over them the hot syrup, pour into a pastry (uncooked), and bake until the filling is firm and pastry well done.

The eggs are not separated. To make the custard better, sprinkle half a cup of pecan meats over top before baking. Have nuts in large pieces.

### Molasses Custard

1 cup syrup  
½ cup buttermilk  
3 eggs  
1 cup sugar  

½ teaspoon soda  
2 tablespoons flour  
Flavor with cinnamon  

Mix ingredients together, adding beaten eggs last. Boil until it begins to thicken, pour into a crust and bake slowly about 30 minutes.

### Brown Sugar Custard

2 cups brown sugar  
1 cup nuts  
2 tablespoons flour  
1 teaspoon vanilla  

2 cups cream  
4 eggs  
2 tablespoons butter  

Mix and pour into pastry, bake as any custard. Meringue may be made.

### Butter Scotch Custard

4 tablespoons butter  
3 tablespoons of corn starch  
½ cup sugar  
1 cup sweet milk  

1 teaspoon vanilla  
3 eggs  
Pinch of soda  

Into a skillet put the sugar and butter and cook until a deep brown.

Stir to prevent burning. Heat milk, add to sugar and butter, add soda and simmer until the sugar is all melted. Dissolve corn starch in one-fourth cup of cold water, add yolks of eggs, mix well. Pour the boiling mixture over the eggs and starch portion. Return to fire and cook until a very thick mixture, thick enough to stay in pastry shell when cut. Add vanilla and pour into a ready-cooked pastry shell, make meringue of the three whites and three tablespoons of sugar, cover top and bake in slow oven 10 minutes, or until done. Granulated sugar is used.

### Butter Scotch Pie

| | |
|---|---|
| 2 tablespoons of corn starch | ½ teaspoon nutmeg |
| ¼ cup flour | 1 teaspoon vanilla |
| 1 cup brown sugar | ½ cup pecan nut meats |
| 1 cup boiling water | 3 eggs |
| 4 tablespoons butter | ½ cup grapenuts |
| 1 cup scalded milk | |

Mix flour and brown sugar, add boiling water and butter, then add milk, and stir and cook over hot water until thick (double boiler). Cover and cook 10 minutes in double boiler. Add well beaten egg yolks and continue cooking for one minute and pour hot mixture over egg whites beaten until stiff. Add nutmeg, vanilla, pecans broken in pieces, grapenuts. Pour into a crust already baked. Serve with whipped cream on top when pie is thoroughly cold.

### Janet's Chess Pie

| | |
|---|---|
| 1 cup sugar | 3 tablespoons water |
| 1 cup butter | 1 teaspoon vanilla |
| 3 egg yolks and 1 white | |

Cream butter and sugar as if for cake. Add egg yolks and 1 white and beat until foamy; add water and flavoring, again beating until well mixed. Pour this into pan lined with raw pastry and cook.

This is delicious. When done the top is covered with damson preserves and meringue and slipped back in the stove to cook meringue. Or it may be served just as it is at first. It makes lovely tarts.

### Buttermilk Custard No. 1

| | |
|---|---|
| 1 cup buttermilk | 4 tablespoons cold water |
| 4 tablespoons flour | 2 tablespoons butter |
| ¾ cup maple syrup or brown sugar | Juice 1 lemon |
| 2 egg yolks | |

Mix flour with the water and add to buttermilk, put into a double boiler and cook until thick, add other ingredients and cook until thick or clear.

Make meringue of the whites, using 2 tablespoons of sugar or 4 tablespoons of maple syrup. Pour mixture into a cooked crust, put on meringue and cook in slow oven until done, about 10 or 15 minutes.

### Buttermilk Custard No. 2

| | |
|---|---|
| 2 cups butter milk | 3 tablespoons flour |
| ¼ cup butter | 3 eggs |
| 1 cup sugar | |

Mix flour and sugar together dry, beat yolks light, add sugar, add this to the buttermilk, melt and add butter. Beat whites stiff, add to the mixture last. Pour into pastry shell and bake about 30 minutes or until the crust is brown and the filling firm.

## Cottage Cheese Pie No. 1

1½ cups cottage cheese
2 tablespoons flour
1 tablespoon butter
½ cup sugar

2 tablespoons cream (top milk)
3 eggs
Pinch salt

Mix cheese, flour and cream together until smooth. Beat egg yolks light, add sugar and mix with cheese mixture, add butter and salt. Beat whites stiff, fold into mixture, pour into uncooked crust, bake 30 minutes until firm. Serve hot or cold.

## Cottage Cheese Pie No. 2

½ cup milk
2 tablespoons corn starch
2 eggs
¾ cup sugar

2 tablespoons butter
1 cup cottage cheese
Juice and rind 1 lemon

Heat milk, add sugar and corn starch, cook until thick. Now add yolks of eggs and stir until thick again, but do not boil. Remove from fire, put cheese through ricer and add to egg mixture, add lemon juice and rind. Pour into cooked crust.

Make meringue using the 2 whites and 2 tablespoons of sugar. Put on custard and bake in slow oven until done.

## Raisin Pie

2 cups seeded raisins
1½ cups boiling water
½ teaspoon salt

3 tablespoons corn starch
½ cup sugar
Rind and juice 1 lemon

Cook raisins and water in upper part of a double boiler for five minutes. Mix salt, corn starch and sugar, pour raisin mixture over them, stirring constantly; return to double boiler and cook five minutes longer. Add lemon rind and juice, cool, then bake between two crusts.

## New Pecan Pie

2 cups finely rolled vanilla wafers    ⅓ cup melted butter

Mix and press into a pie tin making sides well and firm. Place in refrigerator to chill.

### Filling

1 cup milk
¼ cup sugar
2 tablespoons corn starch
2 teaspoons gelatine

1 tablespoon sugar
1 egg
½ cup chopped toasted pecans
½ cup whipping cream

Soak gelatine in a little of the cold milk. Scald milk, add sugar, corn starch, and cook until thick, stirring often. Add beaten egg and cook one minute longer. Add soaked gelatine to hot mixture, stir until dissolved. Add half of nuts and cool until it begins to thicken. Whip cream, add sugar (1 tablespoon) and add to milk mixture folding in. Pour into chilled crust. Sprinkle top with remainder of chopped pecans and let chill thoroughly. Serve.

### Cocoanut Custard

¾ cup sugar
1 cup milk
2 cups grated cocoanut
2 tablespoons corn starch

1 tablespoon lemon juice
2 tablespoons butter
3 eggs

Mix corn starch, sugar and milk together. Separate eggs, add yolks to milk and sugar and cook in double boiler until it begins to thicken.

Add butter, cocoanut and lemon juice. Stir constantly, until thick enough for pie. Pour into a cooked crust, make meringue of the whites, using three tablespoons of sugar, put over top and bake in slow oven until brown, about ten minutes.

### Sweet Potato Custard

3 eggs
4 tablespoons butter
¾ cup sugar

1 cup mashed and strained potatoes
1½ cups sweet milk
Flavor with lemon or nutmeg

Boil, mash and strain potatoes, then measure, add butter and milk; separate eggs, beat yolks with sugar; add to potatoes. Beat whites stiff and add last.

Pour into a pie crust and bake 30 minutes in moderate oven, or until done. If gas oven is used bake near the bottom of oven in order to cook at bottom. Brush over the pastry with cooking oil or melted shortening before putting in the mixture. This prevents the crust getting soggy.

### Jam Custard

¾ cup sugar
⅓ cup butter
½ cup jam

2 eggs
Juice of 1 lemon

Cream butter and sugar together, add jam and beaten yolks to mixture, mix well.

Beat whites stiff and fold into mixture. Pour into a crust which is half baked; continue cooking until firm and brown, both crust and filling.

Serve with whipped cream.

### Nan's Pineapple Custard

¾ cup sugar
1 cup milk
1 small can grated pineapple
   (about one cup)

4 tablespoons corn starch
3 eggs

Separate eggs. Mix corn starch, sugar and milk together. Beat yolks and add to milk, put into double boiler and when it begins to thicken, add pineapple. Stir constantly until thick enough for pie. Pour into a cooked crust. Make meringue of the egg whites and three tablespoons of sugar, put on top, place in oven, cook with slow heat for 10 minutes or until brown. Serve cold.

## Pineapple Custard

| | |
|---|---|
| 1 cup grated pineapple | 3 tablespoons sugar (more or less) |
| ¾ cup sweet milk | 1 tablespoon flour |
| 2 eggs | Pinch of salt |

Mix as any custard; pour into a rich pastry, bake in a moderate oven (about 30 minutes) until done.

Remember, the pineapple is sweet, so little sugar is required. If cooked too fast it will whey.

## Pineapple and Raisin Pie

| | |
|---|---|
| ½ cup flour | 1 can crushed pineapple |
| ¾ cup sugar | ½ cup seeded raisins |

Mix together the flour and sugar, add pineapple and raisins. Stir and cook until the mixture boils and becomes thick; then add one well beaten egg and cook until smooth. Remove from the fire and add to a previously baked crust. Cover with marshmallows and heat in the oven until light brown.

## Transparent Custard

| | |
|---|---|
| ½ pound butter | 1 wineglass thick cream |
| ½ pound sugar | ½ teaspoon lemon flavoring |
| 8 egg yolks | |

Beat egg yolks and sugar together well. Place over a moderate heat (or in double boiler) and add butter, broken into small pieces, stirring constantly until butter melts. Remove from fire and add the cream, mixing well. Pour into a rich uncooked pastry and bake. Citron or other sweetmeats may be used, putting them on the pastry then pouring on the batter. This is much like a chess pie.

## Banana Custard

| | |
|---|---|
| 4 bananas | 1 cup milk |
| 3 eggs | ½ cup sugar |
| 1 tablespoon butter | 1 teaspoon vanilla |

Mash bananas, add milk, sugar, butter and yolks of eggs. Cook in double boiler until thick. Pour into a cooked crust, make a meringue of the whites using 3 tablespoons extra sugar. Put on top and bake meringue in slow oven 10 minutes or until brown.

## Cherry Pie No. 1

| | |
|---|---|
| 2½ cups flour | 8 tablespoons cold, firm shortening |
| 1 teaspoon salt | 6 tablespoons ice-cold water |

Make as directed in pastry for shell. Divide into two pieces, roll out thin (as thick as the tine of a silver fork), put into pan, press firmly over all parts. Brush top side of the bottom (not sides) with melted grease. Put in filling, wet edge with cold water.

Roll out top and place over pie, press edges together well, trim and crimp edge with a fork. Make generous opening in top and pie is ready to go into oven.

Bake on or near bottom of oven, have oven hot, reduce to medium heat, bake 30 to 40 minutes.

### Filling

| | |
|---|---|
| 2 cups of cherries after stoning | 2 tablespoons butter |
| ½ cup sugar (more if very sour) | 2 tablespoons flour |

Mix flour into sugar dry. Put half of cherries into pan. Add sugar and flour, then put the remaining fruit on top of sugar, dot with the butter, put on top crust as directed and bake. Any fruit may take the place of cherries, usually the small fruits furnish sufficient juice. Dry fruit such as apples may need a little water—half a cup to a pie.

## Cherry Pie No. 2

| | |
|---|---|
| 2 cups pitted cherries | ½ cup cherry juice |
| 3 tablespoons flour | Sugar to taste, about ½ cup |
| 2 tablespoons butter | |

Drain juice from cherries and heat. Mix flour with sugar and pour boiling juice to it, mixing well. Add butter and boil one minute. Add cherries and pour in pan lined with pastry which has been cooked for five minutes. This prevents pastry being soggy. Put on top crust or strips and bake in moderate oven 30 or 40 minutes till done. See recipe Plain Pastry.

## Mock Cherry Pie

| | |
|---|---|
| 1 cup cranberries | 2 tablespoons butter |
| ½ cup seeded raisins | 1 teaspoon vanila |
| 1 cup boiling water | 4 tablespoons of flour |
| ¾ cup sugar | |

Use seeded raisins. Cut cranberries in half before filling cup. Mix sugar and flour together dry, over this pour the boiling water and let boil one minute after it begins to boil; stir to prevent lumping.

Take from the fire, add all other ingredients and flavoring. Pour into a pan lined with raw pie crust. Put strips or solid top on; bake in moderate oven 30 to 40 minutes. Have oven hot to begin with. Have plenty of opening in top crust to prevent the juices boiling out.

Brush the pastry over bottom of pie with oil before putting in the filling, this prevents the bottom crust becoming soggy. Moisten the edges of the crust with water so the two edges will stick well. This is a delicious pie when directions are followed.

### Blackberry Pie

1 quart berries, picked over, washed    ¾ cup sugar or less
    and drained    2 tablespoons flour

Get ready the pastry; line pan; put in half the berries; then the sugar and sift flour over the sugar or mix together dry. Add the other half of the berries; place on the top crust; make a long cut in center; place in moderate oven to bake. Sometimes a small piece of butter is added. This makes a richer pie and kills the sharp tartness.

### Peach Pie or Cobbler

4 cups of firm sliced peaches    Enough pastry for a deep baking
1 cup sugar    dish or pie plate
¼ cup water

Slice peaches in usual slices, moderately thick. Make a syrup of the sugar and water; boil for three minutes; turn the peaches into the syrup and cook gently until tender. While peaches are cooking prepare the pastry, using two cups of flour. Line sides of baking dish or pan with pastry; lift the peaches out and line the bottom of dish; dot with butter and a dusting of flour; repeat until all is used. Pour on the juice and cover top with pastry, same as making pie. Make generous opening in top of center; cook in moderate oven 30 to 40 minutes. For the usual pie make same as blackberry.

### Georgia Deep Peach Pie

4 cups firm ripe peaches    ¾ cup boiling water
1 cup brown sugar    1 thick slice lemon from end, rind
2 tablespoons flour        and all.
2 tablespoons butter    Pastry

See recipe for Plain Pastry, using half recipe. Line sides of well greased deep baking pan with pastry, and put in peeled and sliced peaches. Mix dry flour with sugar, butter, lemon and water in saucepan. Bring to boil and pour over peaches. Roll balance of pastry ¼ inch thick, cut with large biscuit cutter, slit each piece in center and cover top, overlapping edges but leaving spaces for steam to escape. Bake in moderate oven 40 minutes until fruit is juicy done and pastry brown.

### Huckleberry Pie

Prepare same as for blackberries, using less sugar, about one-half cup for a pie.

### A New Huckleberry Pie

1 pastry shell    4 egg whites (large eggs)
1½ cups berries    ⅛ teaspoon salt
1 cup sugar

Make and bake pastry. While baking get filling ready. Wash and dry the berries well, taking care not to crush. Add salt to whites, beat very stiff, add half of the sugar slowly, beating constantly. Continue beating until very stiff, about three minutes.

Sprinkle in the remaining sugar, using a spoon, and cut and fold in with a quick choppy motion, putting in sugar gradually. When all is in, fold in the berries, pile the mixture on the cooked shell, using a spoon and have many peaks and valleys. When all is ready, sprinkle a few berries over the top and sprinkle one or two tablespoons of sugar (extra) over all. Put in slow oven (about the center) bake for 15 to 20 minutes until meringue is done and is a pretty brown.

Any dry fruit may be used—bananas, sliced canned pineapple, peaches or berries. Slice large fruit, cut into small pieces, drain on cheese cloth and use. Canned fruit makes this pie delicious when made right.

### Apple Pie a la Virginia

Make 2 pie shells.

Fill with cold, sweetened and flavored apple sauce. Place one on top of the other.

To serve cut in sections and put spoonful of whipped cream on top with sprinkle of nutmeg.

The crust *must* be crisp, and the sauce *cold*.

### Lilly May's Apple Pie

| | |
|---|---|
| 3 good size apples | 2 tablespoons butter |
| 1 cup sugar | 3 tablespoons water |

Peel and slice apples in medium slices, put into a sauce pan, add water and steam slightly until apples are hardly half done (they must be whole pieces).

Make pastry, line pie plate, put apples and sugar, layer of each until all apples are in, using ¾ of the sugar. Cover top with pastry strips; over the strips sprinkle the remaining ¼ cup sugar, dot butter all over top.

Bake as any pie (30 to 40 minutes) using medium heat. Have oven hot when pie is placed in, then reduce heat to medium.

By putting sugar and butter over the top a delicious, crusty surface is given.

### Mock Mince Meat

| | |
|---|---|
| 1 peck green tomatoes | 5 lbs. sugar |
| 3 lbs. seeded raisins | 2 tablespoons cinnamon |
| ½ lb. citron | 2 tablespoons salt |
| ½ lb. suet | 1 teaspoon cloves |
| 1 cup cider vinegar | |

Slice and scald tomatoes twice, fifteen minutes each time. Drain and put in bag to drip all night. Measure the dripped water and use the same amount of boiling water.

Grind raisins, citron and suet all together through food chopper, add sugar and spices, boil all together until thick. Just before it is done add

1 cup cider vinegar. Put in jars and seal while hot. Make into pies when ready to use.

## Boston Pumpkin Pie

| | |
|---|---|
| 1¼ cups cooked pumpkin | ½ teaspoon salt |
| ¼ cup sugar | ¼ teaspoon each, ginger, cinnamon |
| ⅞ cup milk | and nutmeg |
| 1 egg | |

Mix sugar and seasoning with pumpkin, beat egg together until light and add. Pour milk into mixture, gradually beating free of lumps. Pour into pie crust and place in hot oven for few minutes then decrease heat and cook until firm and crust is brown.

## Pumpkin Pie

| | |
|---|---|
| 1½ cups of cooked and strained | 3 eggs |
| pumpkin | 1 cup sugar |
| 1 cup of sweet milk | ½ teaspoon of salt |
| ¼ cup of butter | 1 teaspoon ginger |

Have the pumpkin cooked down dry. Mix all ingredients together thoroughly, beat eggs light and add to mixture.

Put into a crust and bake slowly about 40 minutes, or until done.

## To Make Meringue

| | |
|---|---|
| Whites of 3 eggs | 3 to 6 tablespoons of granulated |
| Pinch of salt | sugar |

Have whites chilled, add salt and beat until they are very stiff. Then gradually add sugar and when all is in beat long enough to thoroughly dissolve the grains of sugar. Spread half over the top of the custard and fill the forcing bag with the other half and proceed to decorate the top. Sprinkle the top with one tablespoon of sugar. When finished place in a slow oven and bake for ten minutes, or until brown. Meringue should cook slowly and long enough to make firm the egg cells, so when it comes from the oven, and the steam escapes from them, the meringue will hold its shape.

## Jelly Meringue

| | |
|---|---|
| 1 egg white | ½ cup jelly |
| A few drops of pink coloring | |

Into a bowl put the egg and jelly. Whip just as though you were frothing the white, continue until it is very stiff and the jelly is thoroughly mixed. Add the coloring and use the same as whipped cream. This is good to use with a short cake or fill cream puffs.

## Meringue Shells

| | |
|---|---|
| Whites of 4 eggs | Pinch salt |
| 1 cup fine grain sugar | ½ teaspoon vanilla |

Add salt to whites, beat until dry and stiff. Add sugar slowly, beating all the time, beat for 10 or 15 minutes or until meringue is very stiff. On a wet board place white paper, put meringue in round or oblong shape, as large as desired, with spoon or pastry bag. Sprinkle with sugar, bake in very slow oven from 30 to 60 minutes. They should be a light brown but firm. Remove from oven, let cool, take from paper, wet if necessary. Scoop out the soft inside, sprinkle with sugar, place again in warm oven to dry. Place together filled with ice cream, or use single. This will make about 8 halves. It depends on the size.

### Meringue Surprise

Use meringue shells for ice cream. Fill shells half full of cream, place in center some delicious sweet, figs, peaches or marrons. Cover well with more ice cream and serve.

### Meringue Tasties

| | |
|---|---|
| 2 egg whites | 1 teaspoon vinegar |
| ⅔ cup sugar | ½ teaspoon vanilla |
| ¼ teaspoon almond flavoring | |

Beat egg whites until stiff. Gradually add sugar, beating constantly until all of the sugar has been added. Add vinegar, beating in thoroughly, then beat in the vanilla and almond. Drop by teaspoonful on to a paper lined baking sheet two inches apart. Form into cup shapes using a small spoon. Bake at 275 degrees F. for 20-25 minutes. Remove from paper lined baking sheet immediately upon removing from oven. Place on cooling rack to cool. Fill with ice cream or fresh fruit. Makes 8 to 12 tasties.

### Meringue Kisses

Make the meringue by recipe given. Place oil paper on board, drop kisses on paper the size wanted, leaving space between. Use spoon or pastry bag and tube. Bake in slow oven until a delicate brown. Serve as cake.

### Three-Minute Meringue

| | |
|---|---|
| 2 egg whites, unbeaten | 2 tablespoons of water |
| ½ cup sugar | Few drops of flavoring |
| Dash of salt | |

Put egg whites, sugar, salt and water in upper part of double boiler. Beat with rotary egg beater until thoroughly mixed. Place over rapidly boiling water, beat constantly with rotary beater, cook 3 minutes, or until mixture will stand in peaks. Remove from fire and add flavoring. Beat well. Spread over top of anything that calls for meringue. Place under flame in broiler and brown lightly. It will burn easily so must be watched closely.

### Orange Surprise

Remove tops from navel oranges, cutting slice ¼ its height, remove pulp with sharp knife and spoon. Fill shells with orange ice, cover the opening with meringue. Set oranges into pan of crushed ice and set pan in very hot oven to brown meringue. Serve at once.

## Crepe Suzettes

Use popover batter for crepe. Into a moderately hot, large, heavy fry pan or skillet, about 9 or 10 inches across, put 2 tablespoons of cooking oil—pour in just enough batter to cover the bottom well, turning pan from side to side to cover almost the entire surface, cook until bottom is lightly browned, turn to cook top side, using a spatula or pancake turner. When done fold in half, then in quarter, place on platter until enough are made, then place each folded pancake in the suzette (sauce), cook over gentle heat until well saturated. Place on platter and pour over the remaining sauce. If brandy or liquors are used, California brandy and rum are preferable, the quantity to be determined by the individual.

### Sauce for Crepe Suzettes

| | |
|---|---|
| 1 cup sugar | 1 grated orange rind |
| 2 tablespoons butter | 1 cup orange juice |

Melt and cook together until consistency of syrup. Several liqueurs may be added for seasoning if desired.

## Baked Alaska
### First Part

| | |
|---|---|
| 5 egg whites | 10 tablespoons sugar |
| ⅛ teaspoon salt | |

### Second Part

| | |
|---|---|
| 1 layer of cake | 1 piece cardboard |
| 1 quart brick of Neapolitan ice cream | 3 pieces writing paper |
| 1 steak plank | |

Prepare plank, on this place cardboard, writing paper then cake.

Make meringue, being careful that eggs are fresh, and the meringue very stiff, beating after all sugar is in until smooth, glossy and stiff.

Place brick of cream on cake; having cake 1 inch larger all around. Cover generously with meringue—using about half. Put the remaining portion in forcing bag (this bag must be of rubber) with star tube, and decorate the loaf in any fancy way desired—making it very high and full in rosettes and peaks. Sprinkle well with sugar (about 1 tablespoon—this is extra). Have oven very hot (about 500 degrees), lower rack so the top of meringue will be just above the center. Place plank and all into oven, bake with hot fire (about 2 minutes) until the meringue is a delicate brown, and darker brown on the high points. Watch closely, remove, slip white paper, top layer and all on a platter.

Serve at once. Slice through meringue, ice cream and cake.

The dish is prettier if garnished with cherries, crystallized rose leaves or violets.

Sponge or butter cake may be used.

## Individual Alaska

Use rounds of cake, placing on this ice cream in ball shape (using round ice cream scoop) and putting the meringue on in any way preferred. Bake same as the large Alaska.

### Forcing Bag and Tube

The pastry tube is a small tin tube with a star or round shaped end which forms the shape of the icing or meringue. The bag is entirely separate, but the two must be put together to use either. For icing, meringue, creams and mayonnaise, you should have a rubber bag made of rubber sheeting. A 12-inch square sewed on the machine into a three-cornered bag, the small end cut large enough for the tin tube to extend out, the bag filled and mixture piped through the tube which forms fancy shapes. For potatoes or anything hot make bag of a piece of heavy unbleached drilling and use the same way. Hot potatoes would ruin the rubber. The tube can be purchased at any hardware store for ten cents, or so much per set, of many shapes. Sometimes the bag can be purchased. They can be made much cheaper. There are metal containers that come with the tubes if desired.

## DUMPLINGS AND SHORTCAKES

### Apple Dumplings

| | |
|---|---|
| ⅓ cup shortening | 1 egg |
| ¾ cup sweet milk | 1 tablespoon sugar |
| 1 teaspoon salt | Flour enough to make soft dough |
| 4 teaspoons baking powder | |

Roll dough ¼ inch thick, cover with slices of apple, chopped slightly, and bits of butter; roll like a jelly roll and cut in pieces about 1½ inch thick; drop into boiling sauce and bake 30 to 40 minutes.

#### The Sauce

| | |
|---|---|
| 1 cup sugar | 4 tablespoons butter, cinnamon |
| 3 cups boiling water | or nutmeg |
| 4 tablespoons sifted flour | |

Mix flour dry with sugar; add butter and then hot water; let come to the boil; put dumplings down in the sauce on the cut end and cook in sauce; sprinkle nutmeg over the top. This dumpling is good baked dry and served with hard sauce. This will make 12 large dumplings.

### Apple Pudding

Peel and slice apples as for a pie, put in a layer of apples, bits of butter, sugar to sweeten, and a sprinkle of flour (about 1 teaspoon), fill a pan half full, having apple about 2 inches deep. Make a batter as follows:

| | |
|---|---|
| 1 egg | 1 teaspoon vanilla |
| ½ cup sugar | 3 teaspoons baking powder |
| ½ cup sweet milk | 1 cup flour |
| 2 tablespoons of melted butter (or oil) | Pinch of salt |

Mix as for cake; pour over the apples. Bake in moderate oven 30 to 40 minutes. Serve with hard sauce or whipped cream. This will serve six. When turned out the apples are on top.

## Apple Torte

2 eggs
1 cup sugar
½ cup chopped nuts
3½ tablespoons flour

1½ teaspoons baking powder
⅛ teaspoon salt
1 teaspoon vanilla
1 cup chopped apples

Beat eggs well, add other ingredients and mix. Bake in shallow greased pan half an hour at 350 degrees. Serve with whipped cream.

## Peach Cobbler

For a family of six, use 3 cups of firm peaches, sliced in the usual way, having them of medium thickness. Use 1 cup of sugar, ¼ cup of water, bring to a boil and let boil for a few seconds. Add peaches and simmer slowly while making the pastry.

Line sides of pan or baking dish with pastry. Carefully lift out peaches and form a layer on bottom, dot with butter, put another layer until all is used. Cover top with pastry, make a generous slash in center both ways, bake in moderate oven 30 to 40 minutes.

If peaches are very acid, use more sugar.

Often a sprinkling of flour may be placed after each layer of peaches—this rather thickens the liquor and is liked by many. A layer of pastry may be put between each layer of peaches if liked.

## Peach Melba Shortcake

2 cups fresh peaches, or equal of canned
½ cup sugar
1 pint raspberries

½ cup 4x sugar
1 cup thick cream whipped and sweetened or a jelly meringue

Peel and slice thin, ripe peaches, cover with sugar for an hour. Crush raspberries, add sugar. Make the usual shortcake dough, open, butter and spread with peaches, then raspberries. Put on top layer, repeat. Cover top with whipped cream or meringue. Cut individual shortcakes with large biscuit cutter.

## Cranberry Shortcake

1 cup ground raw cranberries
1 cup grated apples
1 small bottle red cherries

⅓ cup grated (or crushed) pineapple
1 cup sugar

Grind and measure cranberries, also red cherries. Mix all together and let stand several hours. Make the usual rich biscuit shortcake dough, baking in two layers. Separate layers, spread with the mixture, putting together like a layer cake. Cover the top with the fruit mixture and cover again with whipped cream or jelly meringue. Serve immediately. The dough is made same as for strawberry shortcake.

## New Shortcake

6 egg whites (unbeaten)
2 cups granulated sugar

½ teaspoon cream tartar
1 teaspoon vanilla

Combine eggs and sugar and beat until mixture is not grainy and very stiff; add cream of tartar; beat 10 minutes; add vanilla, beat 5 minutes. Pour into 2 buttered and well floured tins and bake in slow oven about 1 hour. To be served as a shortcake.

## Strawberry Shortcake

⅓ cup shortening
¾ cup sweet milk
1 egg
2½ cups flour

1 teaspoon salt
4 teaspoons baking powder
1 tablespoon sugar

Put all dry ingredients together and sift. Mix shortening into the flour, put egg into milk and mix together and make into a dough. Turn on a floured board and knead until smooth.

Divide in two parts, pat or roll out to fit a pie pan, sprinkle generously with flour, roll out second piece and place on top. Bake in moderate oven until well done (about 30 minutes). Separate the layers, spread generously with soft butter. Have ready a box of berries sliced and sweetened. Spread the berries over the layer (half of them), then put the top layer on and more berries on top.

Cover the whole with whipped cream or jelly meringue, and serve. Use about ¾ of a cup of sugar to a box of berries.

## Willie's Strawberry Pie

1 cup of ripe berries cut
    in half
1 medium size baked pie shell
1 cup crushed berries

½ cup sugar
1 tablespoon corn starch
½ cup heavy cream
Few grains salt

Halve and measure one cup of ripe strawbrerries, and put into baked pie shell.

Crush and measure one cup of ripe strawberries, heat to boiling, add ½ cup sugar, 1 tablespoon corn starch, and few grains of salt. Cook five minutes. Cool and pour over berries in pie shell. Put in refrigerator for two hours before serving. Heap with whipped cream when ready to serve.

## Jelly Meringue

½ glass of firm jelly
1 egg white

Pinch of salt

Into a bowl place all ingredients and with a good egg whip begin to beat just as though you were whipping cream or eggs. Keep beating until quite stiff and it will hold its shape. Use same as whipped cream.

## Boston Cream Cake

Make two layers of cake and fill with the following cream filling.

1 cup sweet milk
½ cup sugar
3 tablespoons flour

2 egg yolks or 1 whole egg
½ teaspoon vanilla

Mix flour and sugar together dry; beat eggs light; add sugar; scald milk and pour over the mixture. Pour in a double boiler and cook until thick. Let cool, add vanilla and when cold put between two layers; it should be about an inch thick. Cover top with whipped cream which has been sweetened and flavored. Then make cake using:

| | |
|---|---|
| 1 egg | 4 teaspoons baking powder |
| 1 cup milk | 1 heaping tablespoon of butter |
| 1 scant cup sugar | 1 teaspoon vanilla or lemon |
| 2¼ cups flour | |

Mix as any cake, bake in two layers, put the filling between.

### Washington Cream Pie

| | |
|---|---|
| 2 eggs | ⅓ cup butter or substitute |
| 1 cup sugar | ½ cup sweet milk |
| 1¼ cups flour | 3 teaspoons baking powder |

Cream butter, add sugar, eggs and mix well; then milk and flour and beat till smooth, sift in powders; bake in 2 layers, same as layer cake. Make filling as follows:

| | |
|---|---|
| ⅓ cup cold milk | 1 cup hot milk |
| ½ cup sugar | ⅓ cup flour |
| 2 eggs or 4 yolks | ¼ teaspoon salt |
| 1 teaspoon vanilla | |

Mix flour and sugar together dry; add milk, eggs, and mix until smooth; pour hot milk into mixture and put into double boiler, cook until stiff enough not to run; add salt and vanilla and allow to cool; spread between layers and on top, or put whipped cream on top.

### Peach, Apricot and Banana Shortcake

Make same as strawberry.

### Pastry for Shortcake

See Pastries.

### Cream Puffs

| | |
|---|---|
| 1 cup water | ½ cup butter |
| 3 eggs | 1 cup flour |

Put water and butter together and when boiling add flour and cook until it is very thick and will ball to sides of pan (stirring all the time). Put into bowl, add one egg at a time until all are in, beating between each egg, thoroughly mix. Drop on a greased baking pan, brush top with egg mixture, and bake in moderate oven 30 minutes or longer, until light and dry. They should puff and not shrivel. When cold, make opening in side and fill with the cream filling. This mixture can be put into a forcing tube and put onto the pan from the tube, which makes them a little more fancy. This makes one dozen large puffs. Use 1 egg, 1 tablespoon milk mixed to brush tops.

### Filling for Cream Puffs

| | |
|---|---|
| 1 cup milk | 2 tablespoons flour |
| 2 egg yolks or 1 whole egg | ½ teaspoon flavoring |
| ½ cup sugar | |

Scald milk, reserving enough to mix the flour into a paste. Pour hot milk over this and cook in double boiler 10 to 20 minutes. When thick, add the eggs and cook about 2 minutes. Take from the fire, add flavoring. When cold put into puff.

### Sliced Sweet Potato Pie

| | |
|---|---|
| About three potatoes | ¼ cup spiced vinegar or spices, to |
| 1 cup brown sugar | taste, and grape juice |
| ½ cup butter | |

Peel and slice crosswise the amount of potatoes needed. Boil until half done.

Line sides of baking pan with a rich pie crust (the same as making a chicken pie).

Put a layer of potatoes, sprinkle with sugar, butter and spices.

Put a layer of pastry rolled very thin. Another layer of potatoes until all are used having potatoes on top. Cover with the boiling water in which potatoes were boiled, until the liquid comes near top of potatoes. Add grapejuice or spiced vinegar. Season highly. Cover top with a pastry, cut good openings in top to allow steam to escape and prevent boiling over.

Place in moderate oven, 30 to 40 minutes, cook slowly, until crust is done and brown. Just before taking from oven rub top with butter and sprinkle with sugar to add more to crispness of crust.

There should be plenty of juice on the inside so when served this juice is a rich brown sauce to serve with the seasoned potatoes, pastry, and hard crust. This pie tastes something like a mince pie and an apple could be added along with the potatoes. A few pieces of dried apple which have been soaked would answer. Use cloves sparingly.

## PUDDINGS AND SAUCES

### Angel Food Pudding

| | |
|---|---|
| 2 egg whites with pinch of salt | 1 cup powdered sugar |
| 1 tablespoon flour | 1 teaspoon baking powder |
| 1 cup English walnuts chopped coarse | 1 cup dates cut fine |
| | 1 teaspoon vanilla |

Beat eggs stiff; sift flour and baking powder with sugar; add to beaten eggs gradually; add fruits and pour into a buttered baking dish; place dish in hot water with several thicknesses of paper in pan of water; bake in moderate oven for 30 minutes, or until firm; let cool and serve with whipped cream.

## Date Whip

2 cups dates from which stones
   have been removed
⅓ cup water
Juice of 1 orange

1 cup diced marshmallows
1 cup thick cream
Pinch of salt

Mix cream, marshmallows and pinch of salt; and let stand 1 hour.
Stew dates slowly in 1/3 cup water until tender. Set aside to cool and
then cut into small pieces, and add orange juice.
Whip cream mixture stiff and fold in the dates.
Fill charlotte glasses and serve.

## Date Loaf

1 cup chopped dates
1 cup chopped walnut meats
1 cup sugar
3 eggs

1 tablespoon cream
1 tablespoon flour
2 teaspoons baking powder
1 teaspoon vanilla

Mix all dry ingredients together. Beat eggs light, mix together; bake
thirty minutes in moderate oven. When cold serve with whipped cream
which is slightly sweetened and flavored.

## Banana Pudding

2 dozen vanilla wafers
6 bananas
1 pint sweet milk
3 eggs

½ cup sugar
1 teaspoon vanilla
Pinch of salt

First make a boiled custard of the milk, sugar and yolks of eggs. To this
add vanilla and salt. Into a pudding dish put a layer of the wafers, then a
layer of sliced bananas. Over this put a portion of the custard. Repeat until
all is used; usually three layers of each is required, having bananas and
sauce on top. Make meringue of the three egg whites, using three extra
tablespoons of sugar; put on top and bake in moderate oven until brown,
about ten minutes. Serve hot or cold.

## Mrs. B's Bread Pudding

### First Part

½ loaf stale wholewheat bread,
   grated

1½ cups sugar
1 cup butter

Mix well, add—

### Second Part

2 cups seedless raisins
2 large apples, grated
1 teaspoon nutmeg
1 teaspoon cloves

1 teaspoon allspice
½ teaspoon salt
3 eggs

Mix well and bake in greased, covered 1 pound coffee cans four hours
at 250 degrees. Serve with hard sauce.

## Cottage Pudding With Brown Sugar Sauce

1 cup sugar
1 cup milk
2 cups flour
4 tablespoon butter

1 egg
4 teaspoons baking powder
½ teaspoon salt

Bake in deep layer pan in moderate oven. Cut in cubes and serve with following sauce:

1 cup brown sugar
2 cups boiling water
4 tablespoons flour
2 tablespoons butter

1 tablespoon sweet spiced vinegar
    left from pickles
1 teaspoon vanilla

Mix flour with sugar. Over this pour hot water, add other ingredients. Cook until clear and thick as sauce. Serve over pudding.

## Butter Scotch Rice Pudding

1 cup sugar
3 cups milk
⅓ cup rice
4 tablespoons butter

2 teaspoon vanilla
Pinch salt
2 tablespoons gelatine in ½ cup
    cold water

Into a saucepan put sugar and butter. Cook until a golden brown, add two cups of milk and let simmer. Wash rice well and drop into boiling mixture, cook until tender.

Let gelatine soak in water for five minutes, add the remaining cup of milk, which has been heated, to gelatine and thoroughly melt. Stir into rice mixture, turn into mold to get firm. Serve with boiled custard or caramel sauce, or sweet cream which has been sweetened.

## Banana and Pineapple Pudding

1 cup sugar
1 cup milk
1 tablespoon of flour
1 tablespoon butter

1 egg
Bananas
Sliced pineapple
Wafers or macaroons

Cook together the sugar, milk, flour, butter and egg until thick like custard. Put a layer of vanilla wafers or macaroons in a dish, then a layer of fruit cut fine. Alternate with the custard. Let stand three hours. Serve with whipped cream or ice cream.

## Blackberry Jam Pudding

4 eggs
1½ cups of flour
1 cup sugar
1 cup jam

1 cup sweet milk
1 teaspoon cinamon
½ teaspoon nutmeg
1 teaspoon baking powder

Beat eggs light and add all ingredients. Put in buttered pan, bake in moderate oven from 30 to 40 minutes. Dish out with spoon and eat with sweet cream.

## Blackberry Roll

Make a rich biscuit dough, knead well, having the dough very stiff and firm. Roll out to ¼ inch thick (or less) having it about 8 inches wide by 12 or 14 long. Spread well with berries, sprinkle lightly with sugar, dot with small lumps of butter, roll up like a jelly roll, mash well the edges to hold in fruit, place in baking pan, bake 30 to 40 minutes in moderate oven, 350 degrees, or until brown and done to center. Serve hot with hard sauce or any sauce desired.

### Blackberry Pudding
#### (From Kentucky)

1 quart berries, washed and drained in colander

2 or 3 cups flour

Place moist berries in a large bowl. Sift the flour over them, as much as will cling to them. Mix gently so as not to crush berries. Place mixture in empty sugar bag and tie securely, leaving a little room for expansion. Lay in colander that has been placed over vessel containing boiling water. Cover the whole with a cover, weighted. Steam one hour, turning bag every 15 minutes. Never let bag touch the water. Turn from bag on platter and serve hot with hard sauce.

### Blackberry or Huckleberry Kuchen
#### (From Virginia)

1½ cups flour
½ teaspoon salt and
2½ teaspoons baking powder, sifted
together twice

½ cup sugar
1 egg
¼ cup melted butter
¼ cup milk

Beat egg until light, add milk, sugar and butter. Add flour well. Pour into a well-greased, shallow pan about 8x8 inches and 2 inches deep.

Over top spread 3 cups of berries. Sprinkle with ½ cup of powdered sugar, bake in moderate oven (350 degrees) 30 or 40 minutes. Serve warm with whipped cream.

### Frozen Peaches With Cream

Peel and chop very ripe peaches, sweeten to taste. Pack in freezer or cans, pack in ice and salt for 3 or 4 hours until frozen. Turn out, slice and serve with whipped cream piled on top of each slice. Plain ice cream may take the place of the whipped cream.

This may be frozen in an electric refrigerator or any freezer where there is no turning.

### Chocolate Pudding

1½ cups milk
1 cup sugar
¾ cup flour
2 squares of chocolate (melted)
Butter the size of an egg

2 eggs
1 teaspoon vanilla
4 tablespoons of sugar for the
meringue

Mix sugar and flour together dry. Warm milk, add beaten yolks and all other ingredients. Pour into a buttered baking dish, cook in moderate oven until firm about twenty minutes. Make meringue and put on top. continue cooking until done or meringue is brown. It will take about ten minutes or less to make meringue and about the same length of time to cook, which will take the required 20 minutes. The heat should be a little less when the meringue is put in.

### Chocolate Cream Pudding

| | |
|---|---|
| 2 layers of cake | 1/3 cup sugar (more or less) |
| 1½ cups heavy cream | 1 teaspoon vanilla |
| ½ cup cocoa | |

Make sponge or one egg cake. Bake in two layers. Add cocoa and vanilla to cream. Whip stiff, sweeten with the 1/3 cup sugar. Put between the two layers, which must be cold, pile high on the top, serve. Sufficient cocoa should be used to color cream light brown. Sweeten to taste.

### Cantaloupes as a Desert

Chill cantaloupes. When ready to serve, cut in half, remove seed, fill with vanilla ice cream, piling quite high in the opening.

### College Pudding

| | |
|---|---|
| 1 cup sugar | 1 cup sweet milk |
| 1 egg | 2 tablespoons butter |
| 2 cups flour | 2 teaspoons baking powder |

Mix as any cake, bake in moderate oven. Eat with sauce.

### Miss C's Dandy Pudding

| | |
|---|---|
| 1 cup molasses | 1 teaspoon soda |
| 1 cup currants | 1 teaspoon salt |
| 3 cups flour | 2 teaspoons baking powder |
| ½ cup boiling water | 1 egg |
| 1 cup raisins | |

Into bowl put molasses; add soda to water and mix. Mix all dry ingredients together with fruit and put together, beat egg and add; pour into greased mold and steam one and one-half hours.

Serve with sauce made as follows:

| | |
|---|---|
| 2 cups boiling water | 1 tablespoon vinegar |
| ¾ cup sugar | ½ teaspoon vanilla |
| 3 tablespoons flour | ½ teaspoon lemon extract |
| 3 tablespoons butter | |

Add flour to sugar dry. Mix all together and cook in sauce pan or double boiler until thick, stirring constantly.

### Delmonico Pudding

| | |
|---|---|
| 2½ cups milk | 2 tablespoons gelatine |
| ⅛ teaspoon salt | ½ cup sugar |
| 1 cup thick cream | 1 cup macaroon crumbs |
| 3 eggs | |

Put the gelatine in ½ cup of the milk and let stand 5 minutes. Separate eggs and make a custard of milk, yolks and sugar. While hot add gelatine, mix well and let cool.

Beat egg whites stiff after adding the salt. Pour cool mixture over the whites. Let cool again and when beginning to set fold in whipped cream and macaroons. Put into glasses or large mold. When firm serve ice cold.

## Dorothy Pudding
### (For Children)

| | |
|---|---|
| 1 cup dry bread crumbs | 2 tablespoons butter |
| 2 cups milk | ½ cup seedless raisins |
| 1 cup sugar | Juice of 1 orange |
| 2 eggs | |

Put bread crumbs into 1 cup of milk to soften. Beat egg yolks with ¾ cup of sugar until light and creamy, add cup of milk and the butter, which has been melted, then the soaked crumbs and raisins. Bake in moderate oven until slightly firm. Make meringue of the two whites, using the remaining sugar (¼ cup), place on top of pudding and return to oven to cook meringue and finish baking the pudding. This last cooking should require about ten minutes.

## Mrs. Thompson's Eggless Pudding

| | |
|---|---|
| 1 cup raisins | 2 teaspoons baking powder |
| 1 cup "C" sugar | 1 teaspoon cinnamon |
| 1 cup water | ¼ teaspoon salt |
| 2½ cups flour | Butter or substitute, size of an egg |
| ½ teaspoon soda | |

Put raisins, shortening, sugar and water together and boil for 5 minutes. Cool, sift soda, baking powder, salt and spices into flour, add to the mixture. Mix well and smooth. Put into a greased pan, bake in moderate oven 30 to 45 minutes, serve with foamy sauce or any special kind liked.

## Kiss Pudding

| | |
|---|---|
| 1 quart sweet milk | 1 cup sugar |
| 6 tablespoons corn starch | 4 eggs |

Scald milk, mix corn starch with a little water, add to milk with sugar; add beaten yolks and cook until thick. Turn into a buttered pan.

Make meringue of the whites of eggs and 4 tablespoons sugar. Put on top and bake in oven until done (10 or 15 minutes).

## Lemon Pudding

| | |
|---|---|
| 3 eggs | 1 tablespoon butter |
| 2 tablespoons chopped nuts | ¾ cup sugar |
| (walnut meats best) | Juice of 3 lemons (rind if liked) |

Beat the yolks and mix with the sugar and butter, mixing well. Next add the juice of lemons and the chopped nuts; beat the whites very stiff and fold the yellow mixture into this; pour into buttered pan; place the pan in hot water; bake in a moderate oven 20 minutes; serve with sweet cream or plain.

### Grated Sweet Potato Pudding

| | |
|---|---|
| 4 cups grated potatoes (raw) | ½ cup chopped nut meats |
| 1 cup Georgia cane syrup | 1 cup raisins |
| ½ cup sugar | ½ teaspoon cloves |
| 1 cup sweet milk | 1 teaspoon each allspice and |
| ½ cup butter | cinnamon |
| 3 eggs | |

In a heavy iron skillet melt the butter. Mix all ingredients together, beating eggs and adding last. Pour mixture into the hot pan of butter, stir until heated. Put skillet into moderate oven to bake. When crusted around edge and top, turn under and let the crust form again. Do this twice, allowing the last to remain on sides and top. Time required to bake, 40 minutes. Serve with sweet cream sweetened and flavored to taste. The iron skillet bakes well and causes the pudding to be very dark, which is desirable. The pudding is much lighter and not so much like a plum pudding if baked in other wares. The cream is better served plain, not whipped.

### Rice Pudding With Raisins

#### First Part

| | |
|---|---|
| ½ cup rice | 1 quart milk |
| ½ teaspoon salt | ½ cup raisins |

Put together and boil slowly for one hour.

#### Second Part

Remove rice mixture, add yolks of 3 eggs and 1 cup of sugar beaten together, 1 teaspoon vanilla. Pour into buttered baking dish and bake until firm, using moderate oven. When nearly done, make meringue of the 3 whites and 3 tablespoons sugar, pinch of salt, place over top in spoonsful, leaving it quite rough like mountain peaks. Sprinkle top with 1 tablespoon of sugar, continue baking in slow oven until brown (about 10 minutes). Serve hot or cold.

When mixing for baking, chocolate or caramel may be added.

### Shannon Rice Pudding

| | |
|---|---|
| 1 quart sweet milk | 1 tablespoon of butter to butter |
| ⅓ cup rice (raw) | dish |
| ⅓ cup sugar | Flavor with nutmeg or vanilla |
| ½ cup raisins, seeded | |

Wash rice. Heat milk, but not to boiling point, put rice, raisins and flavoring into milk. Butter a baking dish, pour the pudding in and cook slowly for two or three hours, never letting it boil, keeping it below the boiling point. Two eggs added would make a richer pudding. This is especially good for children.

## Rice Divine

2 cups cold boiled dry rice (every  
    grain standing to itself)  
1 cup thick cream

¼ cup sugar  
1 teaspoon vanilla

Sweeten and flavor cream. Add rice, whip until cream is whipped and well mixed with rice. Fill charlotte glasses. Serve with chocolate or butterscotch sauce, marmalade or any fruit sauce.

## Willie's Syrup Pudding

2 cups syrup  
4½ cups flour  
2 teaspoons soda  
1 teaspoon nutmeg

1 cup hot water  
¾ cup lard  
3 teaspoons baking powder  
½ teaspoon salt

Into a bowl put syrup, hot water and the lard, which should be soft enough to mix. Add to the flour, soda, baking powder, salt and nutmeg, sift into the liquid, mix until smooth, pour into a greased pan and bake in moderate oven 30 to 40 minutes (time according to the thickness). Serve with any kind of sauce.

## Delicious Pineapple Dessert
### (Upside Down Cake)

1 cup brown sugar  
4 tablespoons butter  
1 can sliced pineapple (small slices)

1 small bottle maraschino cherries  
For the cake batter (see 1 egg  
    cake recipe)

Into a skillet or deep layer cake pan sprinkle the sugar. Dot butter; next place slices of pineapple just touching, with sections of slices filling any spaces. Put cherry in center of each slice. Make and pour over this the cake batter. Bake in moderate oven as any loaf cake (40 to 60 minutes). When done turn out on platter. Serve hot or cold with whipped cream. If baked too fast the brown sugar will scorch or become too hard, and be hard to remove. A square layer pan using small slices of pineapple will give 9 servings.

## Christmas Plum Pudding

2 lbs. currants  
2 lbs. raisins  
½ lb. each citron, almonds and red  
    cherries  
½ lb. pecan meats broken  
1 lb. brown sugar  
1 lb. flour, browned if liked  
1 lb. suet or butter  
½ lb. dry bread crumbs  
1 cup Porto Rico molasses

½ cup coffee  
½ cup grape juice  
2 teaspoons soda  
1 teaspoon baking powder  
1 teaspoon each cinnamon and  
    allspice  
1 grated nutmeg  
½ teaspoon cloves  
7 eggs

Cut citron and almonds, mix spices, baking powder and soda with flour and dredge fruit. Cream butter and sugar, beat eggs light, add to butter and sugar, add molasses and other liquid, mix in fruit thoroughly. Fill 1 pound coffee cans (well greased) half full and steam 3 hours. If suet is used, add 1 teaspoon salt.

Place cans on rack or trivet while boiling. Have water ¾ depth of cans. Replenish if necessary.

## A Flaming Plum or Christmas Pudding

When ready to serve place pudding on platter ready to set before the hostess. Saturate lumps of loaf sugar with lemon extract and place over and around the pudding, light with a match and beautiful blue flames will leap from the burning extract and sugar until the extract is consumed. Serve the pudding with the hard sauce or the latter may be passed. Red cherries dotted over the pudding will give the Christmas red. Be sure to have everything ready when the extract is poured and lighted so the burning flames may be effective. The extract must be lemon to burn. The lighted pudding is an English custom and was much used in our grandmother's time. They used brandy, and we use lemon extract.

## Hard Sauce

½ cup butter
2 cups light brown sugar, sifted

1 tablespoon of sherry jell or fruit juice to flavor

Cream butter until creamy. Gradually add the flavoring and sugar until creamy. Serve over pudding.

## Mrs. D's Plum Pudding

6 eggs
2 lbs. raisins
½ lb. citron
½ lb. almonds
½ lb. cherries
½ lb. pecans
1 lb. brown sugar
1 lb. browned flour

2 teaspoons baking powder
1 lb. butter
½ lb. bread crumbs
1 cup molasses
1 cup grape juice
2 teaspoons cinnamon
½ teaspoon cloves
1 teaspoon grated nutmeg

Mix butter and sugar together, add molasses, eggs and bread crumbs. Put the fruit in last. Steam 3 hours in buttered tins.

## Plum Pudding No. 1

5 eggs
1 cup sugar (brown preferred)
4 cups grated bread crumbs
2 cups flour
1 cup milk (sweet)
½ lb. beef suet
2 lbs. raisins seeded and cut in half

¼ lb. citron cut in thin slices
1 teaspoon cinnamon
1 teaspoon allspice
½ teaspoon cloves
2 teaspoons soda
1 teaspoon salt

Beat eggs light, add sugar. Chop suet fine, flour raisins and citron. Add milk and flour to eggs and sugar and mix well. Add all other ingredients and stir until well mixed. Soda and spices should be sifted into the flour.

Put into well greased molds and boil three hours, leaving plenty of room for mixture to rise. One pound coffee tins make nice molds. Fill two-thirds full, fit on top well, keep out any moisture by covering top first with

wax or brown paper, then pressing on lid. Place tins on a trivet or rack
to lift from bottom of pot in boiling. The boiling water must be three-
fourths of depth of tin or mold. The water must be kept boiling well and
be replenished when necessary. This will fill three or four one-pound cans.

## Plum Pudding No. 2

| | |
|---|---|
| ½ lb. each suet, raisins, currants, flour, citron | ½ cup milk |
| 4 eggs | 1 teaspoon soda |
| ½ cup molasses | ½ cup sugar |
| ½ tablespoon allspice | 1 tablespoon cinnamon |
| | ½ teaspoon cloves |

Mix as directed above.

Put into cloth or molds, boil 3½ hours. Dip cloth in hot water, cover
with flour to make paste, tie pudding in and boil.

## Sauce for Plum Pudding

| | |
|---|---|
| 1 cup sugar | ½ cup boiling water |
| ½ cup butter | Juice of 1 lemon with grated rind |
| 1 egg | |

Mix all together well, add boiling water last; put into a double boiler
and cook until it thickens.

## Foamy Sauce

| | |
|---|---|
| 1 cup sweet milk | 1 tablespoon of sugar reserved from the cupful |
| 1 cup sugar | |
| 1 tablespoon butter | ½ teaspoon vanilla |
| 1 egg white | ½ teaspoon lemon extract |

Put milk, sugar and butter together and boil for 5 minutes. Beat egg
white stiff, add the tablespoon of sugar. Pour boiling milk over the egg
slowly, flavor and serve at once over the pudding.

## Lemon Sauce for Pudding

| | |
|---|---|
| 1 cup boiling water | ½ cup sugar |
| 1 tablespoon flour | 2 tablespoons butter |
| 2 tablespoons lemon juice | Pinch salt |

Mix flour and sugar together dry. Pour over the boiling water, bring
to boil and cook 1 minute. Add other ingredients and serve.

## Chocolate Sauce

| | |
|---|---|
| 1 cup sugar | ½ cup milk |
| 2 squares chocolate (melted) | 2 egg yolks or 1 whole egg |
| 1 teaspoon vanilla | Pinch of salt |

Melt chocolate; mix with two tablespoons sugar; add a little milk to
mix to paste. Beat eggs and add to chocolate; add sugar and over all pour
the hot milk. Cook in double boiler until it will coat the spoon and be
glossy; add vanilla and salt. Serve over pudding or ice cream hot or cold.

## Marshmallow Sauce No. 1

1 cup sugar
½ cup water

18 marshmallows, cut fine
2 egg whites

Boil sugar and water together until a thick syrup (about five minutes), add cut marshmallows and pour over stiff beaten whites while hot.

## Hot Marshmallow Sauce No. 2

1 cup sugar
½ lb. marshmallows
½ cup water

1 teaspoon vanilla
Pinch of salt

Boil water and sugar until a thick syrup, remove from fire, add the cut marshmallows and seasoning, beat until marshmallows are melted. Keep hot, serve over any pudding.

## Marshmallow Sauce No. 3

Juice of 1 orange
2 tablespoons lemon juice
1 box marshmallows (about 12 marshmallows)
3 tablespoons water

1 tablespoon white Karo syrup
1 cup sugar
White of one egg
Pinch of salt

Put in double boiler and whip while cooking until thick; stir in marshmallow while mixture is hot. Stir until marshmallows are dissolved. Let cool.

When ready to serve fold in ½ pint cream.

## Hard Sauce

Cream ½ cup of butter and add one cup or more of powdered sugar, 1 teaspoon of vanilla or grated nutmeg for flavoring.

## Orange Sauce

Juice and pulp of 2 oranges
Grated rind of 1 orange

2 tablespoons corn starch
Pinch of salt

Put all this in sauce pan and cook, stirring constantly. Beat together 1 egg yolk, ½ cup sugar, 3 tablespoons butter and stir in hot mixture. Then beat 1 egg white stiff, add 1 tablespoon sugar, and stir into hot mixture.

Serve with scalloped apples.

## Lemon Curd

5 egg yolks
1 egg white
¼ cup lemon juice

1 cup sugar
3 tablespoons butter

Mix together well, cook in double boiler until thick and clear, stirring constantly. Store in jar for use as needed. Use over hot toast, hot biscuit or for small tarts.

### Fresh Fruit Sauce

1 pint fresh blackberries or     ½ pound 4X sugar
1 pint fresh strawberries

Mash through a strainer, add ½ pound 4X sugar (or pulverized). Mix well and serve over ice cream. Any juicy fruit may be used or several mixed.

### Delicious Sauce

½ cup butter     1 cup tart jelly melted to the
½ cup sugar         boiling point
2 egg yolks

Cream butter, add sugar, eggs, mix well and add hot jelly. Vanilla or lemon juice may be added if necessary for more flavor.

### Brown Sugar Sauce

4 tablespoons cream or milk     2 cups light brown sugar
¼ cup hot water

Mix all together and cook in double boiler till well melted. Serve on plum pudding or molasses pudding. Any flavoring may be used—1 tablespoon sweet spiced vinegar, 1 teaspoon vanilla is good.

### White Sauce for Puddings

2 egg whites     1 teaspoon vanilla
¾ cup sugar     ⅛ teaspoon almond extract
1 tablespoon vinegar     ¾ cup cream

Whip cream dry, whip egg whites stiff, add sugar and beat until an icing is made; add flavoring and when stiff and smooth fold in the cream. May be served on puddings and cake.

## CUSTARDS

### Boiled Custard No. 1

1 quart sweet milk     1 teaspoon vanilla or any special
4 eggs         flavoring wished
1 cup sugar

Into a double boiler put the milk to get hot, but not boil. Beat the eggs together until light. Add sugar and mix well, then pour a small portion of the hot milk into the eggs and sugar to warm, and thin this portion. Pour slowly into the hot milk, cook, stirring constantly until it will coat the spoon, add flavoring, set aside to get very cold before serving.

### Boiled Custard No. 2

1 quart sweet milk     2 tablespoons flour
4 eggs     1 cup sugar

Scald milk; mix flour with sugar dry; beat eggs together lightly and add sugar; pour over milk stirring constantly; pour into double boiler and allow to thicken but never boil (boiling will curdle); flavor to taste; serve with whipped cream in charlotte glasses. The eggs may be separated, whites beaten stiff, added to custard when cold.

## Tipsy Squire

1 round layer of sponge cake about one inch thick
1 quart chilled boiled custard
1 cup sherry

1 cup heavy whipping cream
½ cup blanched almonds cut in half lengthwise and stuck in cake with points sticking up

Into a large round glass bowl, larger than the layer of cake, put three cups of the custard. Place cake with nuts stuck in it on top of custard in the bowl, pour sherry over cake covering entire surface. Pour the remaining cup of custard over the cake then cover top with slightly sweetened whipped cream. Chill. Serve from bowl cutting down thru cake, custard and all. Red cherries may garnish the top. This may be made in individual dishes, cutting cake to suit the small dish, proceeding as directed for the large one. Use only sponge or angel cake.

## Floating Island

1 pint milk
½ cup sugar

3 egg yolks
½ teaspoon vanilla and lemon mixed

The pint of milk is heated first in a double boiler and used for cooking the meringue—it is later used for making the boiled custard. Make meringue of the 3 whites, using 3 tablespoons of extra sugar, add pinch of salt. Drop meringue by spoonful on top of hot milk, cook, turn over to cook the top side. When done lift carefully onto a platter to drain and continue until half the quantity is cooked, color pink the remaining half and finish cooking.

Now make a boiled custard of the milk, sugar and egg yolks, adding to the milk that which has drained from the meringue. Let get cold, place meringue in a glass dish and pour over custard. Serve very cold in charlotte glasses.

## Snow Balls

### First Part

Whites of 4 eggs
4 tablespoons sugar

Pinch of salt

Beat eggs as for meringue, add sugar and drop on hot milk. Cook, turning when one side is done. Do not let milk boil. Have portions of whites about as large as an egg. Lift out and drain.

### Second Part

1 quart sweet milk
½ cup sugar
1 glass red jelly

2 tablespoons flour
Yolks 4 eggs
Pinch of salt

Mix flour and sugar together dry, add yolks and mix well, add ½ cup of the hot milk to this mixture, then pour slowly into the hot milk and cook as for custard until thick, flavor with vanilla. Pour this over the egg ball, set aside to get ice cold. Serve in tall parfait glasses. The beauty of this is in making the snow eggs of pretty shape and cooking nicely, serving the white and yellow together. Dot top with jelly.

## Cup Custard

| | |
|---|---|
| ¾ cup sweet milk | ½ teaspoon vanilla |
| 1 egg | A few grains of salt |
| 1 tablespoon of sugar | |

Into a bowl break egg, beat enough to break well; add sugar, vanilla and salt. Heat milk tepid and pour slowly over the egg mixture. Mix well. Fill custard cups three-fourths full; place several thicknesses of brown paper on the bottom of a baking pan; place cups on the paper; fill pan half full, or rather have water come to half the depth of the cup, bake in moderate oven until firm; about fifteen or twenty minutes. To test, insert a silver spoon handle through the center of the cup of custard, if it comes out clean it is done; if sticky, cook a little longer.

When you wish to turn the custard out, butter the cups and let them get cold before turning out.

If a meringue is wanted, when custard is half done, make and place on top and continue the baking until the meringue is done, about ten minutes.

This should be eaten from the cup, either hot or cold.

## Cup Custard with Meringue

| | |
|---|---|
| 2¼ cups milk | 3 tablespoons sugar |
| 2 egg yolks | ½ teaspoon vanilla |
| 1 whole egg | Few grains salt |
| 4 teaspoons sifted flour | |

Make and bake the same as plain custard. When about half done, make meringue using the 2 egg whites with 2 tablespoons sugar. Drop irregularly over top like mountain peaks or use a pastry bag and star tube, arranging to suit individual fancy. Sprinkle sugar over top of meringue before baking to make a beautiful crust.

## Chocolate Cup Custard

Proceed in the same manner as for plain custard, but add 1 square melted chocolate to the eggs and sugar before adding milk. To be served hot or cold.

## Caramel Cup Custard

Add sufficient caramel to plain custard mixture to color and flavor, and follow the same recipe.

## Baked Custard—Large Pudding

| | |
|---|---|
| 5 eggs | ¼ teaspoon salt |
| ½ cup sugar | 1 teaspoon vanilla |
| 4 cups milk (1 quart) | |

Beat yolks and sugar until light and creamy. Beat whites stiff, heat milk until tepid, pour over yolks, mix with whites, fold together, fill cup or pudding dish, bake in moderate oven until firm. Place dishes in pan of boiling water on rack or paper. (See Cup Custard.) This may be made into caramel or chocolate using either one as desired. For chocolate use one square melted, add to yolks. For caramel, brown 2 tablespoons sugar, add one-fourth cup of water, cook until a syrup, add to milk.

### Quick Dessert

2 egg whites, with pinch of salt
4 tablespoons sugar
4 tablespoons sifted cocoa
1 teaspoon vanilla

Beat eggs stiff, add sugar, beat until quite stiff, then add cocoa and flavoring. Pile on slice of cake with a spoonful of jelly or marmalade on top. Stale cake may be used up this way. Cream may take the place of eggs. Cocoa added to thin cream will cause it to whip.

### Macaroon Custard

1½ cups milk
⅓ cup sugar
½ cup seedless raisins
3 eggs
6 macaroons rolled into crumbs
1 teaspoon vanilla

Beat eggs slightly; add sugar; scald and pour hot milk to this mixture; pour into double boiler and cook until it coats the spoon like custard; add raisins and macaroon crumbs; remove from fire at once; stir occasionally until cool; add vanilla; pour into bowl to get very cold. Serve in charlotte cups with whipped cream.

### Orange Rice Custard

2 cups milk
½ cup sugar
Pinch of salt
½ cup cooked rice (soft)
2 eggs
Peel and juice ½ orange

Scald milk with orange peel in it to get flavor. Beat eggs light, add sugar, salt and orange juice, mix into milk. Pour into a baking dish, place in pan of boiling water, bake until firm, using moderate oven. If meringue is wanted, add more rice (¼ cup). Reserve the two whites, make into meringue. When custard is nearly firm, put on meringue and continue baking until the meringue is done. Serve hot or cold.

Any other flavoring may be used; chocolate or caramel, using a little vanilla as flavoring.

## CREAM DESSERTS
### White Charlotte

1 quart whipping cream
1 cup sugar
Whites of 4 eggs
Juice of 1 large orange
1 teaspoon vanilla
2 tablespoons granulated gelatine
⅓ cup cold water

Put the gelatine to soak in the cold water.

Whip the cream until dry and stiff. Beat egg whites until stiff, add sugar
and beat until well mixed, then beat into the cream, add flavoring. Melt
the gelatine over hot water until perfectly clear and melted, add orange
juice, cool and pour quickly into the mixture, beating rapidly until mixed,
turn into a mold, set on ice or in cool place to jell.

Line a bowl or charlotte glasses with lady fingers and fill with the charlotte. Set aside to jell and serve. Sponge cake or angel food cake may
be used in place of the lady fingers. Sometimes tint the charlotte pink and
white and it is quite pretty. Any kind of crystallized fruit and nuts may
be chopped fine and added.

### Yellow Charlotte

| | |
|---|---|
| 1 cup sugar | 2 cups thick cream, whipped |
| 1 cup sweet milk | 2 tablespoons gelatine |
| Yolks 3 eggs | Flavor with sherry jell, vanilla |
| Whites 4 eggs | or fruit juice |

Beat yolks and sugar together. Put gelatine into milk for five minutes,
then heat and pour into sugar and egg mixture; cook in double boiler until
it coats spoon. Cool and pour over stiffly beaten whites; add whipped
cream and flavoring. Pour into mold to get firm.

### Marshmallow Charlotte

| | |
|---|---|
| ½ lb. marshmallows | ½ cup cherries |
| ¼ cup cherry juice | |

#### First Part

Chop marshmallows and cherries fine and soak in cherry juice one hour.
Dissolve 1 tablespoon gelatine in ¼ cup cold water, melt over hot water.

#### Second Part

Add 1 tablespoon lemon juice, 2 tablespoons orange juice or sherry jell.
Add to marshmallows.

Whip 1 pint cream, add ½ cup chopped nuts and mix with the marshmallows. Set aside to mold. Add a little sugar if not sweet enough.

### Orange Charlotte

| | |
|---|---|
| 1 pint thick cream | ¾ cup orange sections, cut small |
| ¾ cup sugar | and drained |
| 2 egg whites | 2 tablespoons gelatine in ⅓ cup |
| ½ cup orange juice | cold water |

Peel and remove all white skin from orange sections, drain and save
juice. Put gelatine to soak in cold water for five minutes, then heat
over boiling water, add orange juice and let stand until as thick as egg
whites. Beat egg whites stiff, add sugar and continue beating until well
mixed, then add whipped cream. Beat gelatine until it is foamy and light;
beat into the cream mixture, add the orange sections; turn into mold to
get firm. Unmold and decorate with orange sections, if desired.

Any fruit juices may be used.

## Mrs. P's Orange Charlotte

½ box granulated gelatine
¼ cup cold water
½ cup boiling water
1 cup sugar

1 cup orange juice and pulp
3 egg whites
Juice of 1 lemon

Soak gelatine in cold water for five minutes. Add boiling water and sugar, dissolve well, cool and add orange and lemon juice and set aside to thicken. When stiff as whites of eggs, whip mixture until frothy. Whip whites of eggs, mix the two, turn into mold to get firm. Serve with whipped cream.

## Angel Charlotte

1 tablespoon plain gelatine
¼ cup cold water
¼ cup boiling water
1 dozen marshmallows
¼ lb. blanched chopped almonds

¼ lb. crystallized cherries
1 cup sugar
1 pint heavy cream
½ dozen rolled stale macaroons
1 teaspoon vanilla

Soak gelatine in cold water, dissolve in boiling water. Add sugar. When mixture is cool add well beaten cream, almonds, macaroons, finely chopped marshmallows and cherries. Add vanilla and put into a mold which has been dipped in cold water.

## Mock Charlotte

### First Part

1 cup boiling water
½ cup sugar
⅓ cup cold water

4 tablespoons corn starch
Juice of 1 lemon
Whites of 3 eggs

Dissolve corn starch in the cold water. Add the boiling water and cook one minute after it comes to the boil. Beat whites stiff, add sugar and lemon juice. Pour the hot mixture over the eggs; fold in. Set aside to jell in mold or pan.

### Second Part—Sauce

Yolks of 3 eggs
Grated rind of the lemon

3 tablespoons sugar
1½ cups milk

Beat yolks and sugar, heat milk, add to the yolks and sugar, return to double boiler and cook until it will coat the spoon, add flavoring. Let get very cold, serve over the white part or charlotte as a sauce. This will serve six.

## Heavenly Hash

1 pint cream
25 candied cherries (or maraschino cherries)

1 cup chopped pecan meats
25 best marshmallows
Flavor to taste

Cut marshmallows in four pieces, slice cherries, leaving a few to decorate top. Mix marshmallows with cream and let stand an hour or more, then whip stiff. Mix other ingredients. At serving time, decorate top with cherries, serve very cold. Any other fruit may be added if desired, candied pineapple or ginger or any goodies.

## Delight

1 pint double cream  
½ lb. malaga grapes  
½ lb. marshmallows  
1 cup chopped nut meats

Cut marshmallows into four pieces and soak in cream until melted (about 1 hour). Peel, seed and cut the grapes in half. Whip cream stiff, add grapes and nut meats and little sugar, if needed. Mix well, pour into mold to get cold and firm. Serve as charlotte. This may be made over night.

## Pineapple Sponge

2 cups grated pineapple  
⅓ cup minute tapioca  
⅔ cup sugar  
½ teaspoon salt  
Juice 1 lemon  
Whites 2 eggs, beaten stiff

Heat pineapple over hot water. Mix sugar, tapioca and salt together, add to pineapple and cook until tapioca is transparent; add lemon juice. Fold in the whites, which must be beaten until they are very dry and stiff. Serve hot or cold with sugar and cream, flavor with sherry jell.

## Lemon Sponge

4 eggs  
1 cup sugar  
4 tablespoons cold water  
Juice of 2 lemons; grated rind of 1, if liked

Separate eggs; beat yolks light; add sugar; then add water and lemon juice. Put into a double boiler and cook until thick as custard. Beat whites stiff and pour the hot custard over the beaten whites, being careful to fold in order not to break down the stiff whites. Set aside to get cold. Serve in charlotte glasses. A spoonful of whipped cream on top of each glass adds to the beauty and richness. This in taste is much the same as a lemon pie, although it is very light and fluffy. Two tablespoons of gelatine would congeal it and you have a charlotte.

## Caramel Sponge

1 cup sugar  
½ cup boiling water  
3 eggs  
1 tablespoon gelatine in ⅓ cup cold water  
2 tablespoons lemon juice

Put gelatine to soak in cold water. Take half of the sugar and burn to a golden brown, add boiling water and simmer until caramel is melted. Add the gelatine, melt thoroughly, cool, add lemon juice. Beat egg whites stiff and dry, add the remaining sugar, beat two minutes. Add cold caramel, continue beating until quite stiff. Pour into mold to get firm. Make a boiled custard sauce of the three yolks and serve over top.

## Lemon Charlotte

4 eggs  
1 cup sugar  
1 cup water  
2 tablespoons granulated gelatine in ⅓ of the cup cold water  
Juice 4 lemons

Beat yolks of eggs light, add sugar, then water and lemon juice. Cook until thick, add gelatine and thoroughly melt. Remove from fire, beat whites stiff and fold into cooked mixture. Pour into mold to get firm. Serve with whipped cream.

### Pineapple Charlotte

1 pint cream, whipped stiff
1 cup milk
¾ cup sugar
1 small can (1 cup) grated pine-
    apple
3 eggs

1½ tablespoons of granulated gela-
    tine, in ⅓ cup cold water
1 teaspoon vanilla
Juice of half lemon
Pinch of salt

Drain pineapple, dissolve gelatine in 1/3 cup cold water. Heat milk, beat yolks and add sugar, add juice of pineapple, then hot milk, cook until it coats the spoon, using double boiler. Melt gelatine and add to mixture and thoroughly dissolve. Set aside until it gets as thick as whites of egg. Beat whites of eggs stiff, mix with whipped cream, add the pineapple and flavoring.

When gelatine mixture is thick enough to whip, beat with eggs, whip and mix with the cream mixture. Turn into a mold to get firm. Individual dishes may be used, lining with lady fingers or strip of angel food cake.

### Spanish Cream

1 quart milk
¾ box of gelatine (Knox)
½ cup cold water
1 cup sugar

4 eggs
½ teaspoon vanilla
½ teaspoon lemon
Pinch of salt

Put the gelatine in the cold water for 10 minutes, then add to milk. Put milk into a double boiler to get hot. Separate eggs, beat yolks with half of sugar, add to the hot milk and cook until it coats the spoon. Add salt to the whites, beat stiff and add the remaining one-half cup of sugar; beat very stiff and pour the hot milk mixture slowly over the whites, stir briskly, add flavoring and pour into a shallow pan or mold to get firm. The jelly will be at bottom, the custard on top. Cut in cubes and pile into a dish. Serve plain or with whipped cream.

### Marshmallow Pudding

1 scant cup blanched almonds
1½ cups sugar
Whites of 6 eggs

1 lb. white or pink grapes
1½ tablespoons cold water
1½ teaspoons granulated gelatine

Put water over gelatine; and let stand 10 minutes; melt over hot water and let partly cool; beat whites of eggs stiff, add cooled gelatine; now add sugar, beating all the time; divide this into three equal parts; color one portion pink and into this portion add the nuts and the seeded and peeled grapes (cut in half). Line a square mold or bread pan with paper, which must be wet; put in one portion white, then pink, then white and so on until you have used all; chill thoroughly and serve with whipped cream sweetened slightly, and flavored.

## Snow Pudding

| | |
|---|---|
| 1 tablespoon gelatine | ¾ cup sugar |
| ¼ cup cold water | ¼ cup lemon juice |
| 1 cup boiling water | Whites of 3 eggs |

Put the gelatine into the cold water to stand for 10 minutes. To this add the boiling water; add sugar and lemon juice.

Stir well to thoroughly dissolve; set aside to get cool. When it jells to the consistency of whites of eggs, beat with an egg whip until frothy, like egg. Beat egg whites until stiff; beat the two together, turn into a mold to get firm, or mold. Turn out as any mold.

## Syllabub

| | |
|---|---|
| 1 pint thick whipping cream | ½ cup sugar |
| ½ cup whole milk | ½ cup sherry |

Mix cream, milk and sugar until sugar is well dissolved. Let stand ten minutes, then add sherry. Whip with syllabub churn until foam is thick and heavy. Fill glasses and whip again until all is used or the quantity needed is whipped. An egg whip or nice clean willow switches or broom straws may be used. Syllabub does not stand very well, and should be whipped and served immediately. Keep mixture cold for best success.

## Syllabub With Fruit Juices

| | |
|---|---|
| 1 quart cream, 24 hours old | ½ cup grape juice, or the same |
| 1 cup fresh milk | amount of orange juice |
| 1 cup sugar | 1 teaspoon of vanilla |

Have everything cold and put into a large bowl. With a syllabub churn or egg beater, froth the cream and fill goblets. The cream and milk will blend, thus not being too rich. It must be done not too long before serving else it will fall. ¼ cup of sherry jell may be used as flavoring.

## Ambrosia

| | |
|---|---|
| 6 large oranges | ¾ cup sugar (more or less to suit |
| 1 large cocoanut | the taste) |

Remove the brown skin and put the cocoanut through the food chopper or grate. Remove the orange sections from the skin, being careful to remove all of the skin. Mix orange, cocoanut and sugar. Put in a cool place for one hour, and it is ready to serve. ½ cup sherry may be added.

To get the cocoanut out easy remove the milk and place in a hot oven until the shell is quite hot to the hand. With a hammer tap over the nut, then give a hard knock to crack the shell, which will break and come from the nut meat.

## Apple Float

| | |
|---|---|
| 1 pint apple sauce sweetened to taste | 6 tablespoons sugar |
| and very cold | Nutmeg |
| Whites of 2 eggs | Sweet cream or milk |

The apple sauce should be free from lumps. Beat egg whites stiff as for meringue, add sugar slowly and beat until stiff; beat into the apple sauce; serve with the sweet cream; grate nutmeg over top. Everything should be cold.

### Pineapple Souffle

| | |
|---|---|
| 1 tablespoon gelatine | 1 small can sliced pineapple |
| 1 cup cream | (about 1 cup) |
| 3 tablespoons sugar | Juice of half lemon |
| Whites of 3 eggs | |

Drain pineapple and chip fine. Pour juice over gelatine, let stand for 5 minutes, then melt over boiling water; let cool. Whip cream stiff. Whip egg whites stiff, add sugar and pineapple. The gelatine mixture should stand until as thick as whites of eggs. Whip until fluffy and add to eggs and pineapple. Add lemon juice and whipped cream. Place on ice to get firm. Serve as charlotte.

### Coffee Souffle

| | |
|---|---|
| 1 cup strong coffee | 2 tablespoons granulated gelatine |
| 2 cups thick cream | 1/3 cup cold water |
| 3/4 cup sugar | |

Whip cream and drip free of any milk. Put gelatine in cold water for 5 minutes then melt over boiling water. Add to coffee and sugar and set aside to get as thick as whites of eggs; beat until frothy, add to whipped cream and pour into mold to get firm.

### Williams Prune Souffle

Allow 1 egg white to each serving you wish to make, and 4 prunes to each egg white. Sugar to taste. Cook prunes, put through colander, add sugar, fold into the stiffly beaten egg whites. Bake in a slow oven, setting pan in water. Serve with custard or whipped cream. A spread of orange marmalade or pineapple preserve is nice on top of this souffle.

## FROZEN AND MOLDED DESSERTS

There is much to be said about frozen dishes since the mechanical refrigerators have made their advent. Many of the ice refrigerators have a freezer for still-freezing too. Ice and salt have to be put in and the entire pan slipped in the refrigerator until frozen and ready to serve. Another thing to remember is that churn freezers have improved along with the mechanical refrigerators and some require only fom 2 to 5 minutes turning for freezing.

Many women make the mistake of using too heavy whipping cream and using too much sugar, which has a tendency to prevent a smooth product when frozen. An important point to remember is that when ice cream is still frozen (that is without turning) it must have in the mixture something to act as a binder to prevent crystals forming, such as flour, corn starch or gelatine. This in turn blends with the water content and makes for a better, smoother cream. A turned freezer keeps in motion the mixture until blended which prevents formation of any crystals. It is then packed to mellow, get firm, and hard. Therefore, recipes necessarily vary for the type of freezing method used.

Frozen desserts may be put into six classifications, namely: ices, sherbets, mousses, parfaits and ice creams. Each and every one of these types has several variations or foundations, and the ice cream has two distinct bases —a custard base or cream with fruits added. In this cook book there are recipes for each type of dessert mentioned. There are also frozen puddings, frozen salads, frozen mayonnaise, which are not only good but popular. With the refrigerators of today all of these delicious dishes may be had with little labor and time. The timing element should always be considered so frozen dishes will be ready at the time desired.

Parfaits and mousses are packed in salt and ice for several hours until stiff enough to hold the shape, or put into freezing pan in refrigerator.

Frappes are a half frozen mass, a soft mushy substance.

Ices are frozen stiff, and usually contain fruit juices and a rich lemonade as a foundation.

Sherbets may have milk, gelatine or egg whites in the foundation, and frozen stiff. Milk and gelatine, or milk and egg whites are often combined.

Milk or egg whites should never be put into an ice; when added it becomes a sherbet.

## Maple Parfait

| | |
|---|---|
| 1 pint cream | ¾ cup maple syrup |
| 2 egg yolks | 2 egg whites |

Whip cream and drain. Heat syrup to boiling point and pour over beaten yolks. Let get cold. Beat egg whites stiff, add 2 tablespoons sugar, beat until it will hold a point, fold into syrup mixture. Fold in the cream and pack in freezer or mold 3 or 4 hours. It should be inverted at the end of 1 hour, to prevent syrup from settling at bottom. Serve as ice cream.

## Pineapple Parfait

Chop fine enough slices from a can of pineapple to fill a cup. With a wooden pestle press through a coarse, heavy strainer (not a sieve). If it is chopped fine and it is tender, it will pass through. Have ready:

| | |
|---|---|
| ¼ cup juice or syrup | ¾ cup sugar |
| Juice ½ lemon | 1½ cup cream, whipped very stiff |

Mix pineapple pulp, juice and sugar together until sugar is melted, then fold into the cream, mix thoroughly, pour in freezing pan or pack in ice and salt for 3 hours. When packed half the time, reverse the mold, or stir so there will be no syrup when served.

Unmold on a platter, garnish with half slices of pineapple, chopped pecans and whipped cream. Serve with angel food cake.

## Grape Juice Parfait

2 tablespoons gelatine in ⅓ cup
    water
1 cup grape juice
½ cup orange juice

½ cup sugar
2 tablespoons lemon juice
2 cups whipped cream

Soak gelatine in cold water for five minutes. Add hot grape juice and dissolve thoroughly. Add sugar and other juices. Set aside to get as thick as egg white. Beat until fluffy with egg beater, add whipped cream, fill charlotte glasses. Chill. Serve with a spoonful of whipped cream on top and candied violets.

## Angel Parfait

1 cup sugar
½ cup water
    Whites 4 eggs

1 quart cream, whipped stiff
Flavor with fruit or vanilla

Boil sugar and water until it spins a thread. Pour over the beaten whites and beat until cold; add the whipped cream and flavoring. Pour in freezing pan or pack in ice and salt same as a mousse for about four hours. If fruit is added, crush and sweeten and add when ready to pack in ice.

## Coffee Caramel Parfait

1 cup milk with 3 tablespoons coffee
    boiled and strained
½ cup sugar caramelized and added
    to milk

3 cups thick cream
¾ cup sugar
Yolks of 2 eggs
Pinch of salt

Beat eggs with sugar, pour over them milk mixture. Cook in double boiler until thick. Remove, add 1 cup thick cream. Let get cold. Add 2 more cups thick cream, which has been whipped, freeze. Serve as ice cream.

## Coffee Parfait

1 cup sugar
½ cup water
1 cup strong coffee

2 cups whipped cream
1 teaspoon vanilla
Whites of 3 eggs

Boil sugar and water until it spins a thread; pour slowly over the stiffly beaten whites and let cool. Add coffee, then whipped cream. Put in mold, cover tightly, pack in ice and salt for 3 or 4 hours, or pour in freezing pan and place mold in freezing unit.

## Frozen Lemon Sponge

4 eggs
1 cup sugar
4 tablespoons cold water

4 tablespoons flour
Juice of 2 large lemons
1 pint of cream

### First Part

Beat egg yolks light, sift the flour with half the sugar and mix well into the yolks. Add water and lemon juice. Put into a double boiler and cook to a thick custard.

### Second Part

Beat the whites stiff and add the remaining sugar and beat till it will hold a point. Fold the first into the egg whites and if not cold let stand till thoroughly cold before folding in the cream which has been whipped. Pour into a refrigerator pan and let it freeze. No stirring is necessary.

## Frozen Angel Food Pudding

One pint of whipping cream
2 cups crushed pineapple, juice included

8 slices of angel food cake ¾-inch thick
½ cup sugar

Whip cream, but not dry, and add half of the sugar. Add the rest of sugar to the pineapple.

Line the bottom of the freezing tray with whipped cream, then a layer of the cake, then a layer of the pineapple. Continue this, being sure to keep the cake between the fruit and the cream. Freeze, unmold and slice, and serve as a pudding.

Crushed and sweetened peaches or strawberries may take place of pineapple.

## Bisque

¾ cup sugar
½ cup water
4 eggs
1 teaspoon vanilla

1 tablespoon lemon juice
1 pint thick cream, whipped and drained

Boil sugar and water until it threads, pour over stiffly beaten whites. Beat yolks until light and creamy, beat into whites. Cook over boiling water for 10 minutes, stirring constantly. Place aside to get cold. Add whipped cream and flavoring. Pour in freezing pan or pack in ice and salt for 4 hours. Serve with crushed macaroons sprinkled over top, or crushed fruit.

## Cherry Mousse

1 cup cherry juice
1 pint cream

½ cup powdered sugar

Get very cold; whip cream and drain; mix with juice and sugar. Put into mold, pack in ice for two hours, or put in freezing pan, turn onto platter and serve.

## Orange Mousse

1 cup water
1 cup sugar
1 cup orange juice
2 cups thick cream

2 egg whites
Juice of 1 lemon
Few grains salt

Boil water and sugar until it threads, pour over the stiffly beaten whites, add the fruit juices and let cool. When cold, add the cream, which has been whipped stiff. Pack in ice and salt for several hours to freeze without stirring, or freeze in freezing pan.

### Pineapple Mousse

| | |
|---|---|
| 1 cup drained pineapple | ¾ cup pineapple juice |
| ¾ cup sugar | 1 can sliced pineapple |
| 1½ cups cream | Juice of ½ lemon |

Whip cream and drain well; mix sugar and juices and dissolve well; add grated pineapple and fold into the whipped cream; pack into a quart mold and pack on ice for 3 or 4 hours, or pour into pan and freeze in refrigerator; when packed 1 hour, invert mold or stir to prevent syrup from settling at the bottom; place on platter and garnish with half slice of pineapple. Serve with sponge cake or angel cake.

### Coffee Mousse

| | |
|---|---|
| 1 cup strong coffee | ¼ cup cold water |
| ¾ cup sugar | 2 tablespoons granulated gelatine |
| 2 cups cream, whipped stiff | 1 teaspoon vanilla |

Dissolve gelatine in the cold water. Add sugar to coffee; melt gelatine over hot water; add to coffee and sugar; add vanilla and set aside to thicken. When as thick as the whites of eggs, with an egg beater froth until stiff; add whipped cream; pour into a mold to jell. Serve same as a charlotte. Whites of two eggs may be used instead of cream, and serve with cream, either plain or whipped. Grapejuice may be used instead of coffee.

### Chocolate Mousse

| | |
|---|---|
| 3 squares chocolate | 1 cup sugar |
| ½ cup water | 1 pint whipped cream |
| Yolks of 6 eggs | 1 teaspoon vanilla |

Boil chocolate in water until smooth. Cook the egg yolks with one cup sugar until thick and remove from fire. Add chocolate and stir until cold. Add whipped cream and vanilla. Put into mold. Pack in ice and salt for 4 hours to freeze, or freeze in pan in refrigerator.

### Cafe Frappe

| | |
|---|---|
| 1 quart good coffee | 1 cup sweet cream |
| ¾ cup sugar | |

Make coffee and while hot add sugar. Let get cold, add cream. Freeze to a mush and serve in tall frappe glass with whipped cream on top.

### Cafe Mousse

| | |
|---|---|
| 1 quart strong black coffee | 1 cup sugar |
| 1 pint cream | |

Add sugar to coffee and have cold—whip cream stiff; mix; put into freezer and let stand 4 hours. Serve in tall glasses with a spoonful of whipped cream.

## Boiled Custard Cream

1 quart milk
1 cup sugar
4 eggs

2 teaspoons vanilla or any flavor desired
Pinch of salt

Beat eggs together, add salt and sugar, mix well, thin with a little of the warm or cold milk.

Pour the mixture into the hot milk, cook until it thickens enough to coat the spoon.

Be sure to cook in double boiler. Too much heat will cause the mixture to curdle. The water under inset should boil moderately to cook mixture. Six or eight egg yolks may take the place of the four whole eggs. When done, add flavoring. Let it be cold before freezing. Freeze as any cream.

## Caramel Ice Cream No. 1

1 quart of full milk
1 pint of cream
1¼ cups sugar
4 tablespoons flour

1 egg (or 2 yolks)
2 teaspoons vanilla
½ cup of sugar made into caramel
Pinch of salt

Put milk into double boiler to heat. Mix flour and sugar together dry. Moisten with a small portion of the milk, warm or cold.

Add the egg and mix well. Add about one cup of the milk (which by this time should be hot) to the sugar mixture to thin, then pour into the hot milk and cook until it thickens enough to coat the spoon. Remove from fire; add cream to hot mixture. Add caramel and vanilla. Set aside to get cold. Freeze as any cream.

## To Make Caramel

Into a saucepan or skillet put ½ cup of dry sugar. Cook until all is melted and a golden brown; stir to prevent scorching. When a brown liquid, add ½ cup of hot water, cook until all of browned sugar is melted and the mixture is a thin syrup.

Add to custard. If the sugar burns, a bitter flavor will be the result. There is a difference in browning and burning the sugar.

A helpful way is to make a large quantity and keep in a fruit jar. Add sufficient to custard to color and flavor.

## Caramel Ice Cream No. 2

Use recipe for boiled custard, adding sufficient caramel (see Caramel) to flavor and color. Either custard or rennet recipe may be used.

## Rennet Ice Cream

1 quart sweet milk
1 pint sweet cream
1¼ cups sugar
1 tablespoon rennet

1 teaspoon vanilla
1 teaspoon lemon extract
Pinch of salt

Put sugar into milk and heat until lukewarm or tepid. Remove from fire, add flavoring, mix well. Add rennet and give one good stir, place in cool, dark place to set or clabber.

When firm, pour into freezer, add cream and freeze as any cream. Junket tablets may be used in place of rennet. Caramel, chocolate or sweetened fruit may be used with this. Add chocolate or caramel to milk before heating, as the milk must be quiet after the rennet is added. More sugar may be added if a very sweet cream is desired.

### Chocolate Ice Cream

Make same as caramel, adding melted chocolate in place of caramel, using two squares, more or less, to taste.

### Another Chocolate Ice Cream

Use recipe for boiled custard, adding melted chocolate to custard.

### Peach Ice Cream

| | |
|---|---|
| 1 quart of sweet cream | 3 cups sugar |
| 1 quart of soft peaches | |

Peel and mash the peaches or put through a strainer; to them add two cups of sugar; to the cream add the other cup of sugar and the vanilla. Put the cream into the freezer and when it begins to freeze add the fruit; continue freezing until hard enough to pack. The amount of sugar depends somewhat on how much acid the fruit has. Less cream and some milk makes a good cream, but not quite so rich. Some like a custard with the fruit added. When this is used make one quart of custard for one quart of peaches after peeled and mashed. Let the custard be cooled before using and follow the directions as in the other recipe.

### Strawberry Ice Cream

| | |
|---|---|
| 1 quart strawberries | 2 cups sugar |
| 1 quart sweet cream | |

Pick, wash, crush and sweeten berries with one cup sugar, let stand an hour. Sweeten cream with the other cup of sugar. Turn into the freezer and when beginning to freeze add the berries and continue to turn until stiff. Remove dasher, pack to mellow and harden.

Real cream is not apt to curdle, and when chilled first this prevents it entirely. Use less sugar if fruit is sweet or the cream is not liked so very sweet.

### Fig Ice Cream
#### (South Carolina Recipe)

| | |
|---|---|
| 1 pint milk | ¾ cup sugar |
| 1 pt. cream | 3 tablespoon sherry |
| 4 egg yolks | 1 qt. crushed figs |
| 4 egg whites | |

Mix egg yolks and one half of the sugar, beat lightly. Scald milk and pour over mixture. Heat until quite hot but do not boil. Pour slowly over stiffly beaten egg whites to which remainder of sugar has been added. Cool, and add sherry and cream. Add crushed figs and freeze.

### Sweet Potato Ice Cream

| | |
|---|---|
| 1 cup mashed potatoes | 2 egg whites |
| 1 cup thick whipping cream | 1 teaspoon vanilla |
| ¾ cup sugar | ½ teaspoon salt |

Boil, mash and strain potatoes, then measure and let cool. Add to this half of the sugar, the salt and vanilla. Beat egg whites stiff, add the remaining sugar, and beat until it will hold its shape, a perfect meringue. Whip cream, add meringue and cream to potato mixture, folding together until well mixed. Pour into pan. Place in freezing zone of any mechanical refrigerator until frozen. This will freeze smooth. If the small pan is used it will freeze in about 60 to 90 minutes. More sugar may be added if a very sweet mixture is desired. Too much sugar makes the cream icy when frozen in refrigerators. This will serve six or eight. Chopped nuts and maraschino cherries may be used if desired.

### Peppermint Candy Ice Cream

Use any recipe for plain ice cream. Use sticks of peppermint candy to sweeten and color, using a half pound to take the place of one cup of sugar. Pound the candy fine and dissolve in a little hot water or milk; add same as sugar. Raisins cut fine and chopped nuts may be added.

### Pineapple Sherbet No. 1

| | |
|---|---|
| 1 quart water | 1½ cups of sugar |
| 1 can grated pineapple | Whites of 2 eggs |
| Juice of 3 lemons | |

Boil sugar and water together until clear, let cool, add lemon juice and pineapple. Pour into freezer and when a soft freeze, add the stiffly beaten whites, mix well and freeze until hard. Pack until ready to use.

### Pineapple Sherbet No. 2

| | |
|---|---|
| 1 quart milk | 1 cup sugar |
| 1 tablespoon powdered gelatine in | 1 large can grated pineapple |
| ⅓ cup water | Juice 2 lemons |

Put water on gelatine to soften, then melt over hot water and add to milk and sugar. Pour into freezer and when it begins to freeze, add the pineapple, to which has been added the lemon juice.

### Grapejuice Sherbet

| | |
|---|---|
| 6 lemons | 2 cups grapejuice |
| 2 cups sugar | 1 quart water |

Heat two cups of the water and dissolve the sugar. Let cool and mix with all the other ingredients, using just the juice of the lemons, none of the rind, freeze and serve.

More grapejuice may be used and less lemons if you wish a sweeter dessert.

### Peach Sherbet

1 quart mashed peaches
3 cups milk

1 cup cream
3 cups sugar

Scald milk and add sugar and let cool, add cream, turn into freezer and when partly frozen add peaches; freeze till hard and pack to ripen for at least one hour.

### Mrs. Singer's Lemon Sherbet

2 lemons, sliced very thin
4 cups sugar
Juice of 3 lemons

½ gallon of full milk
1 tablespoon gelatine in ¼ cup cold water

Mix lemons, juice, and 3 cups of the sugar together and let stand for two hours.

Soak gelatine for 10 minutes, melt and add to milk. Add remaining cup of sugar and mix well. Have freezer ready, then blend the two mixtures. Turn into freezer and freeze.

If you work fast the sherbet will be smooth. However, if it curdles, it is not ruined.

### Orange Ice

1 quart water
2 cups sugar
2 cups orange juice

½ cup lemon juice
Grated rind of 2 oranges, just the yellow part

Boil water and sugar together until thick, about ten minutes. Cool. Get juice from fruit; strain and add to syrup while a little warm. Grate orange rind before removing juice. Add all together and freeze. Use plenty of salt and ice, one cup of salt to four of ice.

If you wish a deep color rinse the oranges well before cutting, pour the quart of water to be used over them, bruise and mash the rinds well in this water, then strain and boil with sugar. This increases the color and flavor of oranges.

Many people wish a slightly deeper color and so add a few drops of orange vegetable coloring.

plenty of salt and ice, one cup of salt to four of ice. If you wish a deep color rinse the oranges well before cutting, pour the quart of water to be used over them, bruise and mash the rinds well in this water, then strain and boil with sugar. This increases the color and flavor of oranges. Many times orange coloring is used.

### Apricot Ice

1 can of apricots (large)
2 tablespoons granulated gelatine in ¼ cup of cold water

2 lemons (juice)
2 cups of sugar
2 cups of hot water

Put the gelatine to soak in the cold water for five minutes. Pour over this the boiling water, add the sugar and let cool. Mash apricots through a colander. Mix with the sugar and gelatine. Add lemon juice. Freeze until a soft ice. Pack and let stand to ripen and become firm. Serve with whipped cream or as a plain water ice.

## Mint Ice

| | |
|---|---|
| 2 quarts of water | 1 bunch of fresh mint or 1 dozen |
| 2 cups sugar | sprigs of mint |
| Juice of 6 lemons | A few drops of green coloring |

Add enough water to the sugar to boil and make a syrup. Add to the water and let cool. Add the juice of the lemons and enough coloring to make a pretty delicate green. Strip the leaves from the mint and put into a strong cloth, pound until beaten to a pulp. Dip the cloth holding the mint into the lemon water, shake well until as strongly minted as liked. Pour into freezer and freeze. Serve in ice glasses with tiny tender sprigs of mint on top.

This is nice to serve with a salad course or put a large spoonful into a glass of iced tea which is to accompany a salad course.

## Lemon Ice

| | |
|---|---|
| 2 quarts of water | 12 lemons, the juice only |
| 3 cups of sugar | |

Over the sugar pour 1 quart of water and bring to a boil until clear. Cool. Add lemon juice and the remainder of water. It is then ready to freeze.

If this is to be served in a cup (not in the tea) add one more cup of sugar where the recipe calls for three. This will also serve twenty glasses of tea.

## Ginger Ale Ice

| | |
|---|---|
| 1 quart ginger ale | 1 cup water |
| 1 cup sugar | Juice of 3 lemons |

Boil sugar and water until a syrup, cool, add lemon juice and ginger ale. Freeze as any ice.

## Watermelon Ice

| | |
|---|---|
| 1 quart ripe red meat watermelon | ⅛ teaspoon salt |
| juice | Juice of 1 lemon |
| ¾ cup sugar. | |

Mix and freeze to a soft frozen ice. Have ready some cubes of red watermelon which have been chilled—put 4 or 5 cubes in a sherbet glass, fill with the frozen ice and serve immediately.

## Cherry Ice

Wash, seed and mash 1 quart of ripe cherries, put through a coarse strainer, pressing the pulp through. Take 2 cups sugar and 2 cups water and boil to a syrup. Cool, add cherry juice and freeze as any ice. Serve in ice glasses with a few whole cherries on top.

### Dewberry Ice

Make same as cherry ice, using a strainer fine enough to remove seed Use more or less sugar to taste. Frozen dishes need to be quite sweet, for they lose some of the sweetness in freezing.

sweet potato pie

fritters

# CHAPTER XI

## Fritters

### Plain Fritters

½ cup milk
1¼ cups flour
½ teaspoon salt
1½ teaspoons baking powder

1 tablespoon sugar
1 tablespoon melted butter
1 egg

Mix as any batter, beating very hard. Put in baking powder after the beating is done, then mix well. Drop small pieces in deep fat and fry until done (like doughnuts). Drain. Serve with sauce.

#### Sauce

2 cups water
1 cup brown sugar
4 tablespoons butter

1 tablespoon corn starch
½ teaspoon vanilla
1 tablespoon spiced pickle vinegar

Dissolve corn starch in a little water. Mix all together, bring to boil, add corn starch, boil until clear and thick enough for sauce, add flavoring.

### Fritter Batter for Fruits

2 cups flour
1 tablespoon oil or butter
2 eggs
Pinch of salt

2 tablespoons sugar
1½ cups sweet milk
4 teaspoons baking powder

Make batter, leaving out whites of eggs. When ready to fry, add baking powder to batter and stiffly beaten whites. Drain fruit on napkin. Dip each piece of fruit in dry flour, then in the batter, fry in hot fat until a golden brown. Place on napkin or brown paper to drain. Sprinkle well with powdered sugar, run into a very hot oven or under the blaze of the gas stove, and glaze or brown sugar. Serve at once. Use apricots, pears, peaches, pineapples or bananas.

### Banana Fritters

1 cup flour
½ cup milk
1 tablespoon butter

1 tablespoon sugar
2 eggs
2 teaspoons baking powder

Mix into batter, let stand until ready to use. Add whites beaten stiff, slice bananas in half lengthwise, cut each half in two pieces, dip in batter, fry in deep fat. Serve with sauce made as follows:
One-half cup sugar, one-half cup water, boil together for three minutes. Add half cup tart jelly flavor with sherry jell. Serve over hot fritters. Orange or other fruit may be used.

### Pineapple Fritters

One can pineapple drained and wiped dry. Dip in fritter batter, fry in deep fat, drain on soft paper, serve with pineapple sauce, made from juice. Serve hot.

### Fritter Batter

| | |
|---|---|
| 1 egg | 1 teaspoon sugar |
| ½ cup milk | 2 teaspoons baking powder |
| 1 cup flour | ½ teaspoon salt |

Mix into a batter beating thoroughly, let stand for fifteen minutes before using. This same batter may be used for fish if sugar is left out.

### Portuguese Fritters

Put into a saucepan one pint of milk and 6 ounces of rice; when hot, add 2 tablespoons of butter and 3 of sugar, a pinch of cinnamon and the grated rind of a lemon. Cook slowly until the rice has absorbed all of the moisture; beat in the yolks of 2 eggs, form into round balls; make a deep impression in each and put ½ teaspoon of orange marmalade, closing over the opening; roll in egg and bread crumbs and fry in deep fat.

### Queen Fritters

Put 1 tablespoon of butter with half a cup of water over the fire; when boiling, add half a cup of flour. Beat rapidly until smooth, and the dough forms into a round loaf. Take from the fire and when a little cool, beat in 1 whole egg, then add a second egg and beat until smooth. Drop this dough, by small spoonfuls, into smoking hot fat and cook slowly. They will keep turning and bursting until done. Serve with any sauce desired.

### Puff Balls

Beat yolks of 2 eggs light; add ¾ cup chopped fruit (soft peaches or bananas best) and mix well; 1 tablespoon of melted butter; ⅓ cup sweet milk; ½ cup flour; 1 teaspoon baking powder and pinch of salt. When ready to fry fold in lightly the beaten whites of two eggs (beaten stiff). Drop by spoonfuls into deep, hot fat. Cover with powdered sugar and serve at once.

# beverages

## afternoon tea

# CHAPTER XII

## Beverages

### COFFEE

### Coffee Tips

Always keep coffee in a closed container.

To clear coffee use egg shells, which should be rinsed well before breaking. The white or whole egg, shell and all, will serve the same purpose.

Do not boil coffee long—from two to five minutes is sufficient for a few cups.

Never start coffee in a pot with cold water, bring water to boil and pour on the coffee grounds already in the pot. This way prevents boiling over.

When starting coffee in a percolator, use cold water. Hot water may be used but it is not necessary, for the percolator is so constructed that it begins to spray the coffee long before the entire amount is hot.

Adding water to coffee, already made, often causes its flavor to deteriorate. Measure correctly and adding water will not be necessary.

One pound of good coffee usually makes about thirty-two cups of good strength, the strength desired to be determined by the individual taste.

Two tablespoons (level) of coffee for every cup desired, and one portion (2 tablespoons) extra for the pot is a good rule to follow, adding or taking less to suit taste.

Extra water must be allowed for moistening the coffee when making if you wish the exact number of cups. For five cups allow one extra cup of water and one portion of coffee.

Black coffee requires a generous portion of coffee, and extra percolation until black.

Demi-tasse means literally a small cup, or a half cup, and is served usually without cream. Many take it without sugar.

Coffee is better served with plain sweet cream. It is not considered good taste to have cream whipped for coffee. Even for iced coffee, the cream is not whipped but used plain.

When making coffee to be iced it should be strong enough to allow for the melting of the ice. This also applies to iced tea.

When necessary to reheat coffee, *never* let it stay on the grounds or percolate through them. Pour off coffee and reheat in another vessel.

Have a vessel that never has been used with grease to be used in reheating coffee or heating water for coffee. All vessels when generally used will show signs of grease, thus spoiling coffee.

Never wash the coffee pot in the dish pan or with same cloth used for dishes, as this method will leave its trace of grease. Rinse well, scald and air, allowing the sun or air to reach all parts of the pot. A real scrubbing occasionally will keep it clean and sweet.

*Never* allow the grounds to stay in the pot from one using to the next. Pots *must* be aired, scalded and kept clean.

When making large quantities of coffee an urn is best. Often there is no urn. Then a large vessel is put into use with coffee tied in a bag. Many times not sufficient room is allowed for swelling of coffee grounds, consequently no strength is obtained. Always allow plenty of room for this.

In making large quantities, try this. For one pound of coffee wash an egg and break into coffee, using shell and all; mix well using hand or spoon. Now add sufficient cold water to wet. Continue to mix.

Cover with one quart of boiling water, put over good fire, stir and bring to boiling point and boil for 5 minutes. Have a colander ready over another vessel. Over this spread two thicknesses of cheese cloth and pour the liquid through, allowing it to drip without pressing the grounds. Add the second quart of water, repeat the process.

This gives a coffee extract. When ready to serve add sufficient freshly boiled water to get the desired strength. One quart will serve 5 ordinary cups because a coffee or tea cup does not hold a full half pint, nor should the cups be filled too full.

In making the extract, do not allow the grounds when boiling to settle in the vessel too long. They will scorch if not stirred. Use medium ground coffee. If made properly, liquid will be clear, eggs clinging to grounds.

### Iced Coffee With Orange Juice

1 quart strong coffee
¼ cup sugar

¾ cup orange juice which has been strained

Mix together. Serve in parfait glasses with crushed ice. Serve spoonful of whipped cream on top. For other uses see desserts.

### Iced Coffee

Fill glasses with ice cubes, pour over rather strong coffee to allow for the melting ice. Sweeten to taste, and add unwhipped cream.

### TEA

Most of the tea sold contains several kinds of grades blended to produce the most pleasing results.

The tea leaf contains caffeine, oil and tannin.

The average tea, if rightly made, is not harmful. Of course, too much of anything can be taken, and tea may be made harmful by drinking too much strong tea or that which is poorly made by allowing the water to stand on the leaves, or boiled.

Freshly brewed tea, after three to five minutes' infusion, is essential if a good quality is desired. The water, as for coffee, should be freshly boiled

and poured over the tea for this short time. The tea in the individual bag
or container is decidedly the nicest and most satisfactory way for making a
cup of hot tea.

The tea leaves may be removed when the desired strength is obtained.
Any bag or ball should be agitated several times to be sure the leaves are
throwing off the strength and to avoid any waste which might be left in the
leaf, if not thoroughly wet. Tea leaves when left in the pot or cup too
long bring out the caffeine and tannin, which makes this beverage harmful.

Tea, when it is to be iced, should be made much stronger, to allow for
the ice used in chilling. A medium strength tea is usually liked. A good
blend and grade of black tea is most popular for iced tea, while green and
black are both used for hot. The variety used depends on the individual.

The only recipe for making tea is, use a good grade of tea, freshly boiled
water, to make the tea quickly, and never leave it standing on the leaves.

It is poor economy to buy cheap tea as it requires more leaves for a
cup, and the flavor is not so good. Good tea may be spoiled in the making.
It is not necessery to buy expensive blends put up in fancy containers, just
be sure to get a reliable brand and then make it *right*.

Some water makes poor tea, because of the minerals it contains.

Earthenware or glass is best for brewing tea.

Teapots, like those for coffee, should never have any greasy cloth used
about them.

To sweeten tea for an iced drink—less sugar is required if put in while
tea is hot, but often too much is made and sweetened, so in the end there
is more often a waste than saving.

A slice of lemon, cream or full milk may be used in hot tea, according
to the individual taste. Iced tea is served with or without lemon, with
a sprig of mint, a strawberry, a cherry, a slice of orange, or pineapple.
This may be fresh or canned fruit. Milk is not used in iced tea.

## CHOCOLATE DRINKS
### Hot Chocolate

| | |
|---|---|
| 2 squares of chocolate | 1 cup boiling water |
| 5 tablespoons sugar | 3 cups milk |

Chip chocolate and melt over boiling water, add sugar and boiling
water, mix together until smooth and glossy. Cook for two or three
minutes, have milk scalded, add slowly, mixing well. Beat well with egg
whip to form a froth so no scum will form.

A few grains of salt and a few drops of vanilla may be added if liked.
Do not add milk until ready to serve. Drop a spoonful of whipped cream
or a marshmallow on top.

### Chocolate Milk
#### To Make the Syrup

| | |
|---|---|
| ⅓ cup cocoa | 1 tablespoon vanilla |
| 2 cups sugar | Pinch of salt |
| 1 cup boiling water | |

Mix cocoa and sugar together dry, add water, mix well and boil for five minutes. Cool, add vanilla and salt. The syrup may be made and kept on hand ready for use.

### To Use the Syrup

To make a drink of chocolate milk use one large glass and:

¾ cup milk                         2 tablespoons syrup
¼ cup crushed ice

Mix well and serve plain or with whipped cream.

## Cocoa

3 cups milk                        3 tablespoons sugar
1 cup boiling water                Few grains salt, if liked
3 tablespoons cocoa

Mix sugar, cocoa and boiling water together, stir and cook until smooth. Scald milk, add a small portion to cocoa mixture to thin and smooth, then pour to hot milk, beat vigorously with egg whip to form a coating of bubbles so no scum will form. Serve with more sugar if necessary, and a spoonful of whipped cream.

Children like a marshmallow dropped in to float on top, in place of the cream.

# FRUIT DRINKS

## Fruit Punch

4 dozen lemons                     4 cups sugar (2 pounds)
1½ dozen oranges                   6 quart bottles of carbonated water
2 cans grated pineapple            About 25 pounds of ice
1 bottle of maraschino cherries

Get juices from fruit; open pineapple cans and strain through cheese cloth or fine strainer. Put two cups of water on sugar and bring to the boiling point; let cool and add to the juices. Use one-third of the mixed juices for a medium-size punch bowl, adding plenty of ice for chilling, and when ready to serve pour two bottles of the carbonated water into the portion to be used. Fill punch bowl and serve. Have another portion ready when needed. If the charged water is opened too soon it loses the gas and one might just as well use plain water. Usually one large piece of ice is placed in the bowl to keep the punch cold.

## Tea Punch

2 dozen lemons                     1 gallon cold tea, just medium
½ dozen oranges                        strength
1 can grated pineapple             1 bottle of maraschino cherries
3 cups sugar                       2 bottles carbonated water
3 cups water                       1 large block ice

Get juice from fruits and strain, having perfectly clear. Boil sugar and water to a syrup, cool and add to fruit juices. Add syrup from cherries. Add sufficient ice to chill before mixing.

When ready to serve, chill tea, place a large block of ice in a punch bowl, add half of tea and half of fruit juices—put in a few cherries and a few slices of lemon. More sugar may be added, but punch should be quite tart. This will make 2 punch bowls full, about enough for 25 guests.

## Ginger Ale Punch

Use recipe for Fruit Punch or Tea Punch, substituting ginger ale for carbonated water or for tea.

## Mint Punch

| | |
|---|---|
| 1 quart mint leaves | 2 cups white grape juice |
| 2 cups boiling water | 1 quart strong lemonade |

Pour boiling water over mint leaves and let stand until cold. Strain and add other ingredients.

Mix all together, sweeten to taste. Into a punch bowl place a large block of ice, pour over the mixture. Serve.

To serve individually, fill glasses with crushed ice, fill with punch, place a sprig of mint in glass, slice of lemon, or orange.

## Russian Tea

| | |
|---|---|
| 2 lemons | 1 quart water |
| 3 oranges | 2 cups sugar |
| 12 cloves | 2 quarts strong tea |

Extract juices from lemons and oranges. Boil rinds with cloves in quart of water for 5 minutes. Strain, add juices, sugar and the tea. Serve piping hot.

## Apple Cider Punch

| | |
|---|---|
| 1 quart sweet cider | ½ cup lemon juice |
| 1 quart White Rock | Sugar to taste |

Mix together cider, lemon juice and sugar.

Into punch bowl put large piece of ice. Over this pour the mixture, add one quart of white rock or charged water. Serve.

## Cranberry Punch

| | |
|---|---|
| 1 quart cranberries | 1 cup orange juice |
| 1 quart water | Juice of 1 lemon |
| 2 cups sugar | Small bottle carbonated water |
| 1 cup water | |

Cook cranberries in quart of water until tender. Strain through cheese cloth. Boil 2 cups of sugar and 1 cup water until thin syrup. Add to cranberry juice, chill.

When ready to serve, add 1 cup orange juice which has been strained. Juice of one lemon. Place in punch bowl a block of ice, pour in punch, add small bottle of charged water. Serve.

## Cranberry Nectar

Place in saucepan, 2 lbs. of cranberries, 3 quarts of water, 2 lbs. of sugar. Stir well, and heat slowly to boiling point, then cook for 25 minutes;

strain through jelly bag or filter; place when cold in the punch bowl, add 3 bananas cut in thin slices. ¼ lb. marshmallows cut in tiny bits. 2 quarts of crushed ice. Stir to blend and serve.

This is an economical punch to serve when entertaining, and one the guests will insist upon for second and third helping.

### Fruit Cup

| | |
|---|---|
| 1 quart white grape juice | 2 cups of chopped candied grapefruit |
| 1 quart ginger ale | or orange peel |

Serve in tall glass with plenty of crushed ice. This is suitable for a salad plate to take the place of an ice or iced tea. Other fruits may be substituted.

### Another Fruit Cup

| | |
|---|---|
| 1 quart grape juice | 1 cup shredded pineapple |
| 1 quart water | 1 cup diced bananas |
| Juice of 6 lemons | 2 cups sugar (more or less to taste) |
| Juice and crushed pulp of 6 oranges | |

Dissolve sugar in water and grape juice; add the other ingredients and chill. Serve in tall glass with plenty of crushed ice. A slice of orange and a sprig of mint to garnish. Serve as a drink or an ice.

Grapefruit, sliced peaches, cherries, strawberries may be used.

### Grape Juice

Remove stems from 6 quarts of grapes. Add 1 quart of boiling water and place over fire and cook slowly until the pulp separates from the skins. Pour into a jelly bag and let drip without squeezing. Sweeten to taste, boil a few minutes and remove any scum, put into jars and seal while hot. When ready to serve, add water and sugar if necessary.

### Scuppernong Grape Juice

For five pounds of grapes use one pint of water, put grapes to heat and crush while heating. Do not boil on account of seed, but the heating will cause the juice to flow readily. When the fruit is soft strain as for jelly.

Measure, add one-half cup of sugar to every quart of juice; bring to the boiling point, fill sterilized bottles, cork and seal. When ready to use add crushed ice and more sugar if desired.

### Scuppernong Nectar

Four quarts of scuppernongs washed and put into a stone jar, over them pour one quart of vinegar and let stand three or four days; cover top with cheese cloth and stir once each day.

Strain through heavy cloth without squeezing. Add one pound of sugar to one pint of juice, bring to boil and continue boiling slowly for five minutes, bottle boiling hot, cork and seal. Serve same as grape juice.

## Mrs. T.'s Blackberry Shrub

2 gallons berries                          5 ounces of tartaric acid
3 pints cold water

Crush berries slightly. Mix acid in water until dissolved, pour over berries and let stand for forty-eight hours. Strain, do not press, but allow to drip.

Measure. To each pint of juice put three-fourths of a pint of sugar. Mix well, let stand for a week or two, lightly covered. Bottle, cork and store in cool place.

When using, add one glass of shrub to four of plain water, using crushed ice and more sugar if necessary.

## Blackberry Shrub

Select sound fruit, wash, measure and place in stone jar. For every gallon of berries use ¾ quart of vinegar. Cover jar with cheesecloth, tying over top. Let stand three or four days; only three days if weather is very warm. Stir daily. Strain without squeezing and put into kettle, allowing one pound of sugar for every pint of juice.

Boil slowly for five minutes, bottle, cork and seal. Dilute with cold water, use crushed ice to suit the taste when serving.

Blackberries, cherries, muscadines or scuppernongs may be used the same way.

# SOUTHERN HOSPITALITY

## Tom and Jerry
### (A Hot Drink)

1 egg                                      2 tablespoons brandy
¾ cup whole milk                           Few grains salt
1 tablespoon sugar                         Nutmeg if desired

Beat egg well, add sugar, brandy and salt mixing well. Heat milk in double boiler and add to egg, mixing gradually. Serve immediately. This makes one glass. Have egg room temperature so it will not chill milk. Drink should be hot to be good. A quick, nourishing and stimulating drink for a sick or feeble person.

## Southern Eggnog

3 eggs                                     Nutmeg
4 tablespoons sugar                        Few grains of salt to whites of
6 tablespoons brandy                           eggs
½ cup whipping cream

Whip cream stiff and add 1 tablespoon of the sugar. Separate eggs, beat whites stiff, using a bowl, adding remainder of sugar slowly, beating constantly until they hold a point. Let stand while beating yolks. Beat yolks until light. Add brandy slowly stirring all the time. When well mixed pour yolk mixture to whites folding in (over and over motion, never beat.) When well mixed fill glasses and top with large spoon of whipped cream, and a sprinkle of nutmeg. The cream may be folded into the egg-nog before serving. Eggnog is best served immediately. This makes 3 medium sized glasses. Rye, bourbon or other liquors may be substituted for the brandy.

### Blackberry Wine

Use ripe berries. To every gallon of berries pour one quart of boiling water. Let stand 12 hours. Strain and to every gallon of juice add 2 pounds sugar stirring until sugar is well dissolved. Put in jugs filling to the brim, so as the juice ferments the scum will flow off. Each morning refill the jugs with juice from a bottle kept for that purpose. Repeat for five days or until fermenting ceases, then close the jugs lightly. After another five days cork tight and let stand in a cool place for four months, then drain off carefully, put in bottles and seal.

### Scuppernong Wine

Gather ripe but firm grapes. Wash and to every gallon pour one quart of boiling water. Let stand 24 hours. Strain off juice and to every gallon add 2½ pounds of sugar. Mix thoroughly and let stand again 24 hours. Skim and strain and put in jugs covering each one with thin muslin cloth. Retain bottle of juice and from time to time remove cloth and fill with extra juice to flow off the skim, replace the cloth to keep out dust. Let mixture stand six to eight weeks, strain again thru flannel bag, bottle, and cork with new corks. It will be ready to use in a few weeks.

syllabub

cakes

# CHAPTER XIII

## Cakes

### CAKE MAKING

Cakes are put in two classes—butter and sponge.

Cakes are made light in two ways—incorporating air by beating, the use of eggs, and by another leavening agent, baking powder which releases carbon dioxide gas.

In making cake it is quite essential to use good materials and correct measurements.

Pastry flour is preferable—being lighter than bread flour, it gives better results.

In making butter cakes the important point is to cream thoroughly the butter or butter substitute. This should be done until soft and fluffy; never melt butter. Butter may be chipped and dropped into tepid water until soft, mashed to extract excess salt, drained and creamed until soft. Add sugar gradually and continue creaming until mass is light and fluffy. This is the greatest task of the entire process. After this has been done the remainder may be put together in a few minutes.

It has been my experience that cakes made with water in place of milk, and egg whites used unfrothed, will keep moist longer. I find the grain of the cake just as fine with eggs unbeaten as with eggs frothed. In sponge cakes, where there is no butter and often no baking powder, the eggs *must* be beaten well, usually separated, for this is the only means of making it light. Grease has a tendency to break air cells in eggs.

When baking powder is used it is well to let it do the work, therefore little beating is necessary for the family cake—it is simply a matter of putting it together properly.

After the butter and sugar have been creamed, only 3 to 5 minutes will be required to complete the cake. Only by beating will the large holes be made into small ones giving a fine grain, but there are short cuts which eliminate labor with good results.

After flour and liquid have been well mixed until smooth, by stirring instead of beating, large air cells will be broken.

Put batter in pan and pound the pan on the table 5 or 6 times. This will send large holes to the top, some will break while others that are left will be started upward and heat will cause them to break.

In baking always put cakes in oven just warm. A hot oven causes cake to bake at the edge and stick to pan and not rise at the sides, consequently it will be compelled to rise up in the center. A cool oven allows the cake to rise with the heating of the oven and becomes level before oven is hot enough to bake.

A layer cake should be baked in a quicker oven than a loaf. A thick layer will require less heat than a thin one. A layer one inch thick will require about 20 minutes at 425 degrees. A thick layer 30 to 40 minutes at 375 degrees. A loaf from 60 to 90 minutes at 300 degrees, the time depending on the thickness. A cake with much butter requires more time than one with a little butter.

The cooking of a loaf cake may be divided in three periods of thirty minutes each—the first, batter warms and begins to rise; second, batter continues to rise and begins to bake; third, finishes baking, settles and slightly leaves the sides of the pan. Cake may be turned while baking if it is cooking unevenly.

To test a loaf or layer cake—touch lightly with the finger, if done cake will spring back leaving no impression. If not done print of finger will be quite evident. Another test—stick a straw into the thickest part of cake and if it comes out clean cake is done, otherwise straw will have raw dough clinging to it. This last test is best for coal or wood stove—the first test for gas, electric or oil stove. Every woman must know her oven to succeed unless she has something by which heat is gauged.

It is well to select a few good recipes and become familiar with them, then vary the fillings instead of using various recipes. For example—try and succeed with a white batter; one with the whole egg; one with chocolate. These then may be converted into any number of cakes.

After years of experience I find a greased paper at the bottom of the pan is the surest and safest to prevent sticking and tearing. Grease lightly with a firm fat, bottom and top, just enough to cause paper to adhere to the pan. Sides and tubes of cake pans should not be greased. The cake is supposed to stick to these parts of the pan, which will help to hold it up and insure a smooth edge.

Never remove a cake the moment it leaves the oven. Allow to cool slightly so it may be handled with the bare hands. Run knife around the sides, invert pan, give a hard knock and cake comes out perfectly. Have paper one-fourth inch smaller than pan so there will be no sticking of the corners.

Some of the recipes in this book call for the frothed egg whites, some not. Being the original recipes they were left just as they were. I use these recipes without frothing or separating eggs, with success.

If an electric mixer is used, care should be taken not to over beat or to use too fast a speed. Should the mixture become warm or hot, the texture will not be good. The use of an electric mixer will require a little practice. Follow directions given with appliance.

Any recipe may be made by hand or in a mixer if one knows how to use the mixer. Many users cream the butter, sugar and eggs, then fold in by hand the liquid and flour or whipped egg whites.

My last word to cake makers is correct measurements, good material and well creamed butter and sugar.

## LOAF CAKES

### Old-Fashioned White Pound Cake

| | |
|---|---|
| Whites of 14 eggs | ½ pound butter (without coloring) |
| 1 pound sugar | 1 teaspoon lemon extract |
| ¾ pound flour | |

Cream butter and flour together, beat whites and sugar together until they look like icing, mix the two well and bake in slow oven (about 300 degrees) until done. No baking powder used.

### Mother's Wedding Cake Made in 1860

| | |
|---|---|
| 1 pound flour | ¾ pound white butter |
| 1 pound sugar | 1 teaspoon soda |
| Whites of 16 eggs | 2 teaspoons cream of tartar |

Bake in loaf pan in slow oven. No directions are given for mixing, but I think the directions given for the first cake were the general way of making cake then.

### White Loaf Cake

| | |
|---|---|
| 2 cups sugar | ½ teaspoon each of vanilla and lemon |
| ⅞ cup water or milk | 4 cups flour |
| 2 teaspoons baking powder | 1 cup butter |
| Whites of 8 eggs | |

Cream butter until soft—add sugar and continue creaming until soft and fluffy. Sift baking powder with flour. Add whites unbeaten to sugar and butter, then add flour and water alternately until well mixed and free from all lumps. Add flavoring. Bake 1½ hours at 325 degrees. See Cake Making.

### Canton's Prize Cake

| | |
|---|---|
| 1 cup butter | ½ teaspoon soda |
| 2 cups sugar | ½ teaspoon baking powder |
| 4 cups flour | Whites 10 eggs |
| 1 cup buttermilk | |

Cream butter and sugar; add milk and flour alternately. Beat stiff and fold in whites of eggs last. Bake in loaf or layers. See Cake Directions. Use pastry flour, and into that sift the soda and baking powder.

### William's Pound Cake

| | |
|---|---|
| ½ lb. butter | 1 cupful eggs (usually 5 eggs) |
| 2 cups flour | Lemon flavoring |
| 1 teaspoon baking powder | About ¾ teaspoon mace |
| 1½ cups sugar | Pinch of salt |

Cream butter with flour. Add baking powder and salt to the eggs and beat light. Add sugar gradually and beat well. Combine the two mixtures and beat thoroughly. Add flavoring. If mace is used, sift it with flour at the beginning. Bake in moderate oven 1 hour.

## Mrs. P's Reliable Pound Cake

Weigh as many eggs as you wish to use. Have equal weight in flour, sugar and butter. Also have:

½ teaspoon lemon
½ teaspoon vanilla

Add pinch of salt to egg whites

Cream butter and flour together. Beat yolks very light—add sugar and continue beating until light and creamy. Beat whites very stiff and add to yolks and sugar, then add creamed flour and butter and flavoring.

No baking powder is used. If properly weighed and mixed this recipe never fails.

Bake slowly at first and increase heat slightly when well risen.

Four eggs will make a medium size loaf.

## Twentieth Century Pound Cake

4 cups flour, sifted
2 cups sugar
1 cup creamery butter (½ lb.)
1 cup water or milk

6 eggs
½ teaspoon vanilla extract
½ teaspoon lemon extract
2 teaspoons baking powder

Cream butter and sugar well, add eggs one at a time, beating constantly between each egg. Add flour and water alternately until all is in and smooth. Add flavoring. Sift in the baking powder. Mix well. Put into a greased and papered pan. One with a steeple is best. Bake in moderate oven one hour and a half. This can be made into layers and baked as layers in a quick oven.

By using ½ teaspoon of soda and 1 cup of buttermilk, some like it better leaving out all of the baking powder. Use the buttermilk in place of the water or sweet milk. Dissolve soda in one tablespoon of cold water, add last and mix well; put into pans.

This cake I consider better than the old-fashioned pound cake which calls for a pound of everything with no liquid. Just try it.

## 1, 2, 3, 4 Cake

1 cup butter
2 cups sugar
3 cups flour
4 eggs

1 scant cup milk or water
2 teaspoons baking powder
½ teaspoon each lemon and vanilla

Cream butter, sugar and egg yolks; sift powders with flour, add alternately with liquid, add flavoring, fold in stiffly beaten whites last. Bake in loaf pan at 300 degrees 1¼ hours, or until done. A pan with tube will cook a little quicker than one without.

## Marble Cake

Use recipe for 1-2-3-4 cake. Mix the same. When all together divide batter, and to one portion add 1 teaspoon each of cinnamon, allspice, mace and nutmeg; and ¼ teaspoon cloves. Into a loaf pan put a layer of white batter then about 4 large spoonfuls of the spice batter. Add more of each until all is used. With the handle of spoon stir zigzag once around the cake to blend the 2 batters. Bake. When cut it is quite effective.

White batter may be used and part of it colored pink. Fill pan in the same manner. Bake as any loaf cake.

## LAYER CAKES

### White Layer Cake

| | |
|---|---|
| 3 cups sifted flour | 6 egg whites |
| 1½ cups sugar | 4 teaspoons baking powder |
| ¾ cup butter | 1 teaspoon vanilla or lemon |
| ⅔ cup cold water | |

Have butter soft, cream, add sugar and continue to cream until light and fluffy. Add whites of eggs unbeaten. Mix well, add water and flour in two portions, and beat until smooth and free of lumps. Sift in the baking powder, stir quickly, put in three layers; cook on top rack of gas oven 15 to 20 minutes in quick oven. See directions on how to bake and test cake.

Put together with any desired filling. Baking powder may be sifted with flour if preferred.

### My Favorite Chocolate Cake

| | |
|---|---|
| 3 cups flour | Whites of 6 eggs |
| 1½ cups sugar | 1 scant teaspoon vanilla |
| ¾ cup butter | 4 teaspoons baking powder |
| ¾ cup of water (or sweet milk) | |

Make as White Layer Cake. Bake in 3 layers.

#### Filling

| | |
|---|---|
| 3 cups of sugar | 2 squares of melted chocolate |
| 1½ cups cold water | 1 teaspoon of vanilla |
| Yolks of 6 eggs | |

For method see Cake Fillings.

### Lane Cake

| | |
|---|---|
| 8 egg whites | 4 cups flour |
| 1 cup butter | 3 teaspoons baking powder |
| 2 cups sugar | Pinch salt |
| 1 cup milk | 1 teaspoon vanilla |

Mix as any cake, and bake in three layers.

#### Filling

| | |
|---|---|
| 8 egg yolks | 1 cup pecans |
| 1 cup sugar | 1 wineglass of wine |
| ½ cup butter | 1 teaspoon of vanilla |
| 1 cup raisins | |

Beat yolks, add other ingredients, mixing well. Cook in double boiler until thick. Spread filling between layers. Cover the cake with white icing.

## Puff Cake

½ cup butter
1¾ cups sugar (fine grain preferred)
1 cup milk
2⅔ cups pastry flour

5 egg whites
6 teaspoons baking powder
¼ teaspoon salt
½ teaspoon vanilla or lemon extract

Cream butter well, add the sugar and cream slowly until very light. Add flour and milk alternately. Beat whites stiff, add last. Bake as any layer cake. Use any filling desired.

## Premium Cake

1½ cups sugar
½ cup butter (or substitute)
⅔ cup water
3 cups flour
Whites 7 eggs

3 teaspoons baking powder (sifted with flour)
½ teaspoon each vanilla and almond
½ teaspoon salt (if butter substitute is used)

Cream butter and sugar together, add unbeaten whites, add flour and water in two portions and beat well about two minutes, then stir to break any large bubbles, put into greased pan and bake in a moderate oven one and one-quarter hours.

## Orange Cake

½ cup butter
½ cup milk
1 cup sugar
7 egg yolks

1¾ cups flour
2 teaspoons baking powder
Grated rind of 1 orange

Mix as any cake and bake in two layers.

### Filling

½ cup sugar
3 tablespoons flour

Grated rind and juice of 1 orange
1 tablespoon butter

Cook all together until thick. Spread between layers.

## White Mountain Cake

1¾ cups sugar
½ cup butter
½ cup milk or water
2½ cups flour (pastry)

2½ teaspoons baking powder
½ teaspoon each vanilla and lemon
Whites of 8 eggs

Cream butter and sugar until very light and fluffy. Add milk and flour to which has been added the powders. Beat whites stiff, fold in last. Bake in loaf or three layers.

## Chocolate Cake

⅓ cup butter
¼ cup cocoa
1¾ cups flour
1 teaspoon vanilla

1 cup sugar
½ cup water
2 eggs
3 teaspoons baking powder

Cream sugar and butter, add eggs, mix well, add cocoa. Sift powders into flour, add to mixture alternately with water. Bake in two large layers or loaf pan.

## Jam Cake

| | |
|---|---|
| 1 cup butter or substitute | 2 cups sugar |
| 4 cups flour | 1 cup buttermilk |
| 2 cups jam | 6 eggs |
| 2 teaspoons each soda, allspice, cinnamon, nutmeg | 1 teaspoon vanilla |
| 1 teaspoon cloves | Juice 1 lemon |

Mix as you would any cake, sifting spices and soda into the flour. Bake into 3 layers. Put together with a white caramel as follows:

| | |
|---|---|
| ½ cup butter | 3 cups sugar |
| 1 cup sweet milk | |

Boil together until the soft ball, beat until creamy, put layers together and ice top.

If more of a fruit cake is wanted, add 1 cup raisins and 1 cup chopped nuts.

## Another Jam Cake

| | |
|---|---|
| 2 cups flour | 1 teaspoon soda |
| 1 cup sugar | 1 teaspoon each allspice, nutmeg and cinnamon |
| ½ cup butter | |
| 3 eggs | 1 cup jam |
| 2 tablespoons sour cream | |

Make as any cake, add jam, bake in two layers, put together with white icing. This may be baked in a loaf pan if desired. See Cake Making for baking.

## One-Egg Cake

| | |
|---|---|
| ⅞ cup sugar (scant cup) | 2¼ cups flour |
| 1 cup sweet milk | 1 egg |
| 1 heaping tablespoon butter, or substitute | 1 teaspoon vanilla |
| | 4 teaspoons baking powder |

Make as any cake. Bake in two layers about 20 minutes in quick oven.

## Devil's Food Cake

### First Part

| | |
|---|---|
| ½ cup milk | ½ cup cocoa or grated chocolate |
| 1 cup brown sugar | 1 egg |

Mix cocoa and sugar then add egg; beat all together and add milk. Cook until thick. Let get cold.

### Second Part

| | |
|---|---|
| 1 cup brown sugar | 2 eggs |
| ½ cup butter (or ⅓ cup substitute) | 3 teaspoons baking powder |
| ½ cup milk | 1 teaspoon vanilla |
| 2 cups flour | |

Cream butter and sugar, add eggs and beat vigorously. Add milk and flour alternately. When well mixed add first part. Bake in layers or loaf. Mix baking powder with flour. If butter substitute is used add ½ teaspoon salt.

### Marie's Devil's Food Cake

½ cup butter  
2 cups sugar  
4 eggs  
1 teaspoon vanilla  

1 cup milk  
2½ cups flour  
4 teaspoons baking powder  
2 squares chocolate  

Cream butter with 1 cup sugar. Beat yolks lightly and add one cup of sugar. Mix to butter mixture. Add milk and flour in two portions. Melt and add chocolate, then baking powder. Beat and fold in whites last. Bake in three layers. Put together with white or chocolate icing.

### Cecilia's Devil's Food

1 scant cup butter  
2 cups sugar  
1 cup buttermilk  
Yolks of 11 eggs  

¼ cup melted chocolate  
2¾ cups flour  
1 teaspoon soda dissolved in 2 table-  
spoons boiling water  

Cream butter and sugar together until light. Beat eggs light and add to butter and sugar. Add milk, and flour, alternating; add soda. Add melted chocolate last.

Bake in layers, put together with white or chocolate icing. Vanilla may be added, if desired.

### Mahogany Cake

1 cup grated chocolate  
2 cups brown sugar  
¾ cup butter  
3 cups flour  
½ cup boiling water  

½ cup buttermilk  
4 eggs  
1 teaspoon baking powder  
¾ teaspoon soda  
1 teaspoon vanilla  

Mix sugar, chocolate, boiling water and butter, and cream well. Add one egg at a time, mixing well. Then add buttermilk and flour, with powders and soda in flour. Add vanilla, bake in layers. Two whites for icing may be left out, using instead two tablespoons cold water to take their place.

### Filling

3 cups light brown sugar  
⅔ cup sweet milk  

½ cup butter  

Put all together and let cook until creamy when tested in a saucer. Beat hard until creamy and thick enough to spread between layers.

### For the Top

1 cup grated chocolate  

2 tablespoons melted butter  

When melted add enough milk to make the right consistency to spread well. Cover top with this or any icing liked.

### Chocolate Fudge Cake

#### First Part

1 cup grated bitter chocolate  
1 cup sugar  

½ cup milk  

Boil until thick and let cool.

### Second Part

½ cup butter
1 cup sugar
½ cup milk
3 cups flour

3 eggs
2 teaspoons baking powder
1 teaspoon vanilla

Cream sugar and butter well, add egg yolks. Add chocolate mixture, sift baking powder with flour and add alternately with milk, beat until smooth. Whip egg whites stiff and fold in last.

Bake in loaf or layers.

A cup of finely chopped nut meats may be added to batter.

### Chocolate Ice Cream Cake

5 eggs
1 cup milk
1 teaspoon baking powder
1½ cups sugar

2 cups flour
1 teaspoon vanilla
¼ lb. chocolate

Beat eggs and sugar until very light. Melt chocolate in milk, cook until thick, let cool. When cold add to egg mixture. Sift baking powder with flour and add last.

Bake in 2 layers as directed in baking. Put together with soft white icing.

### Cecilia's Ice Cream Cake

#### First Part

1 cup milk
1 cup sugar

1 egg yolk
¼ lb. unsweetened chocolate

Cook together until thick, cool, add to batter.

#### Second Part

½ cup butter
½ cup milk
2 eggs
1 cup sugar

2 cups flour
1 teaspoon baking powder
1 teaspoon vanilla

Cream sugar and butter. Separate eggs; beat yolks, add to sugar mixture. Sift baking powders into flour and add with milk, alternating. Beat whites stiff, fold into batter. Add first part. Mix well, bake in two layers. Put together with white icing.

### Meringue Cake

½ cup butter
½ cup sugar
1 cup flour
3 tablespoons milk

2 teaspoons baking powder
1 teaspoon vanilla
4 egg yolks

Make as any cake, pour into a deep layer pan lined with greased paper. Make meringue of the 4 egg whites and 4 tablespoons of sugar. Pile on cake, sprinkle top with chopped nuts. Bake in moderate oven 45 minutes. Let cool, cut in blocks and remove from pan. This is sometimes called Sunshine and Snow cake.

## Orange Cake

| | |
|---|---|
| ½ cup butter | 2 teaspoons baking powder |
| 1 cup sugar | ½ teaspoon salt |
| ½ cup milk | 8 egg yolks |
| 2 cups flour | Grated rind 1 orange |

Mix as any cake, bake in two layers. See directions.

### Orange Filling

| | |
|---|---|
| 1 large orange, juice and grated rind | 1 tablespoon lemon juice |
| ½ cup sugar | 1 tablespoon butter |
| 3 tablespoons flour | 1 egg |

Cook in double boiler until thick, stirring constantly, let cool, put between layers.

## Mrs. D's Japanese Cake

| | |
|---|---|
| 1 cup butter | 3 cups flour |
| 1 cup milk or water | 4 eggs |
| 2 cups sugar | 2 teaspoons baking powder |

Make as any cake. This is sufficient for 3 layers. Divide batter taking out enough for one layer. Into this put ½ teaspoon each of spice and cinnamon, ⅛ teaspoon cloves. Into the other two layers put 1 cup seeded raisins, 1 cup dates, ½ cup citron, 1 piece each of orange and lemon peel, 2 dried figs, 1 cup mixed nut meats; cut all very fine or put through food chopper, and mix well into batter. Bake layers in moderate oven, about 40 minutes.

### Filling

| | |
|---|---|
| Juice of 3 oranges, grated rind of 1 | 2 cups sugar |
| 1 medium cocoanut, juice and ground meat | Pinch of salt |

Boil all together until thick enough to spread, beat until cool, spread between layers, putting spiced layer in center.

## Japanese Fruit Cake

| | |
|---|---|
| 1 cup butter | 4 eggs |
| 2 cups sugar | 1 teaspoon baking powder |
| 3¼ cups flour | 1 teaspoon vanilla |
| 1 scant cup water or milk | |

Make as any cake. Divide batter into two parts. Into one part put 1 teaspoon each of cinnamon and allspice, ½ teaspoon cloves, ¼ pound of raisins, chopped fine. Bake into two layers. Bake the white part into two layers.

### Filling

| | |
|---|---|
| Juice of 2 lemons | 2 cups of sugar |
| Grated rind of 1 lemon | 1 cup boiling water |
| 1 good-sized cocoanut, grated | 2 tablespoons corn starch |

Put all together into saucepan, except corn starch. When the mixture begins to boil, add the cornstarch dissolved in half cup of cold water; continue to cook, stirring constantly until the mixture drops in a lump from the spoon. Cool and spread between the layers. Cover top with a white icing.

### Raisin Fudge Cake

½ cup butter or substitute
2 cups sifted brown sugar
2½ cups flour
½ cup buttermilk
½ cup water
2 eggs
1 cup chopped raisins
1 cup chopped blanched almonds

4 ounces grated chocolate or 5 ounces cocoa
1 teaspoon baking powder
½ teaspoon cinnamon
½ teaspoon soda
¼ teaspoon cloves
Juice and grated rind of 1 orange

Cream butter, add half sugar, then egg yolks, orange juice and rind, then add the other half of sugar. Mix all ingredients together, cocoa too, if used. Mix milk and water; add liquid and dry ingredients alternately together. Add chopped raisins and nuts, lastly the beaten whites. Bake in deep layer at 350 degrees, if baked in loaf at 300 degrees.

#### Filling

Yolks of 8 eggs
2 cups 4X sugar

¾ cup butter

Beat eggs light, add sugar and butter melted. Cook in double boiler until thick and remove from fire. Add 1 cup pecan meats, 1 cup grated cocoanut, 1 cup raisins cut in half, mix, let stand until cold, and spread between layers.

## FRUIT CAKES
### White Fruit Cake

1 lb. sugar
1 lb. flour
½ lb. butter
1 cup water (scant cup)
Whites of 8 eggs
2 teaspoons baking powder
1 teaspoon lemon extract
1 teaspoon of cloves

2 lbs. white raisins
1 lb. almonds, blanched and chopped
½ lb. white (light color) citron, sliced fine
½ lb. red crystallized cherries, cut in half
1 medium cocoanut, grated

Make cake as usual. Sprinkle fruit with 1 cup of flour. Add to the batter. Bake at 300 degrees Fahrenheit, for 2 hours. The depth of the pan should have something to do with the time of baking.

This cake is best made about two weeks before using. The cocoanut may be left out.

### Poor Man's Fruit Cake

½ cup of shortening
1 cup sugar
1 cup dried apple sauce unsweetened, strained and cold
1 cup raisins cut in half
2 cups flour
½ cup nut meats
½ cup citron

1 egg
1 teaspoon cinnamon
1 teaspoon nutmeg
½ teaspoon cloves
½ teaspoon soda in tablespoon of water
½ teaspoon salt

Cream sugar and shortening together, add egg. Sift spices and salt into flour. Use a portion of extra flour to dredge the fruits. Mix all together well; add soda last. Put into a greased paper lined pan, bake in a moderate oven 45 to 60 minutes. The nuts and citron may be left out if desired to make less expensive. If much fruit is used bake slower.

### Cephalie's Fruit Cake

3 cups dark brown sugar
½ lb. butter
6 eggs
½ cup molasses
½ cup buttermilk
1 tablespoon cinnamon
1 teaspoon cloves
1 teaspoon mace

1 teaspoon nutmeg
4 cups flour
1 teaspoon soda
1 package seeded raisins
1 package currants
1 lb. English walnuts
½ lb. citron
1 package dates

Cream butter and sugar together. Add beaten yolks of eggs, then the spices, molasses and sour milk. Beat all together well. Add the flour and then the stiffly beaten whites of eggs. Beat in the soda that has been dissolved in a few tablespoons of water. Last add the fruit that has been floured. Bake at 250 degrees for 4 or 5 hours.

### Black Fruit Cake

1¼ lbs. flour
1¼ lbs. sugar
1 lb. butter
14 eggs
¾ cup of Porto Rico molasses
3 teaspoons of soda in 1 tablespoon
of water
3 tablespoons of cinnamon
3 tablespoons allspice
1 tablespoon mace
1 tablespoon grated nutmeg

1 teaspoon of cloves
1 tablespoon of vanilla
1 cup of grape juice or black coffee
6 lbs. raisins
2 lbs. currants
1½ lbs. of citron
1 lb. dates
1 lb. almonds
½ lb. crystallized cherries
½ lb. of candied orange and lemon
peel mixed

Prepare all fruits the day before, dredge with extra flour. The raisins should be cut in half. The currants washed and dried. Almonds blanched, dried and chopped. All fruit cut into small pieces to suit the individual taste. The citron in thin slices about as large as the thumb.

Make cake as any pound cake, add spices to flour, mix soda and water into molasses and add to the batter. When all ingredients are in, add the floured fruits, mix thoroughly and fill pans, leaving an inch or little more for rising. Bake in slow oven 250 degrees, ¾ of an hour for every pound. This makes 14 pounds.

It is best to bake in two pans, having pans deep with tube. Grease and line with two pieces of brown paper.

### A Good Fruit Cake

6 eggs
1 lb. sugar
1 lb. flour
½ lb. butter
1 saucer of molasses
3 teaspoons of soda
1 tablespoon of cold water
3 lbs. raisins
2 lbs. currants

½ lb. citron
1 lb. dates
3 tablespoons cinnamon
3 tablespoons allspice
3 tablespoons mace
1 teaspoon cloves
2 nutmegs, grated
1 cup of coffee, wine or grape juice

Make and bake as directed in Black Fruit Cake.

## Mrs. W's Date Cake

### First Part

| | |
|---|---|
| 1 package dates, seeded and cut | 1 cup hot water |
| 1 package raisins, cut in half | 1 teaspoon soda |
| 1 cup English walnut meats | |

### Second Part

| | |
|---|---|
| 1 cup sweet milk | 1 egg |
| 1 cup sugar | 1 teaspoon baking powder |
| ¾ cup butter | 1 teaspoon vanilla |
| 2¾ cups flour | |

Into bowl place the first part all together, pour hot water over it, let stand while mixing second part. Cream sugar and butter, add egg, mix well, then add the first part and blend all together. Sift baking powder into flour, add, alternating with milk. Put in vanilla, bake in three layers.

### Filling

| | |
|---|---|
| 3 tablespoons butter | Warm coffee sufficient to mix to |
| 1 lb. 4X sugar | spread between layers |
| 3 tablespoons cocoa | |

Cover top with icing if desired.

## Loaf Date Cake

| | |
|---|---|
| 1 package dates, seeded and cut | 1 egg |
| 1 cup boiling water | 1 teaspoon soda |
| 1 cup shelled nut meats | 1 teaspoon baking powder |
| 1 cup sugar | ½ teaspoon salt |
| 2 cups flour | ½ teaspoon nutmeg |
| 3 tablespoons butter | |

Into boiling water put soda and pour over dates, let stand. Cream butter and sugar, add egg, mix in the dates, add flour and other ingredients. Bake in loaf pan in moderate oven.

## Georgia Date Cake

| | |
|---|---|
| 3 cups dates, cut fine before measuring | 6 eggs |
| | 1 teaspoon salt |
| 2 cups pecan meats chopped medium | 2 teaspoons cinnamon |
| 3 cups flour | ½ teaspoon mace |
| 2 cups sugar | 3 teaspoons baking powder |
| ¾ cup of water or milk | |

Sift salt, spices and baking powder into flour. Beat eggs together until light, add sugar, then flour and water, beat until smooth. With a little extra flour dredge dates and nuts; mix into batter and bake in moderate oven 2 hours at 300 degrees.

There is no butter or shortening in this cake. The batter should be quite stiff.

## Another Date and Nut Cake

| | |
|---|---|
| 1 cup stoned and chopped dates | 1 egg |
| 1 cup chopped nuts | 1 teaspoon soda |
| 1 cup sugar | 1 teaspoon salt |
| 1 cup boiling water | 2 tablespoons shortening |
| 2¼ cups flour | 1 tablespoon baking powder |

Put dates, sugar, shortening, into a bowl, over this pour the boiling water, let cool a little. Sift salt and soda with flour, mix in nuts while dry, then mix into first mixture. Add beaten egg. Bake same as any loaf. This makes a good date nut loaf bread to use plain or for sandwiches.

## Nut and Raisin Cake

### First Part

| | |
|---|---|
| 2 cups brown sugar | 2 cups warm water |
| ¾ cup butter (or substitute) | ½ lb. seeded raisins |

Put all together, boil six minutes; let get cold. Have ready:

### Second Part

| | |
|---|---|
| 4 cups bread flour | 2 teaspoons soda |
| ½ lb. nut meats | ½ teaspoon cloves |
| 2 teaspoons allspice | 1 teaspoons baking powder |
| 2 teaspoons cinnamon | 1 teaspoon vanilla |

Mix all ingredients into flour, mix into first mixture. Put into a greased paper lined pan, bake in slow oven about 2 hours. If substitute for butter is used, add 1 teaspoon salt. Bread flour makes a stiffer dough than pastry, so if the latter is used, add sufficient to make stiff batter.

## Bess' Nut Cake

| | |
|---|---|
| 1 lb. bread flour | 1 teaspoon grated nutmeg |
| 1 lb. sugar | 1 teaspoon baking powder |
| ½ lb. butter | 1 quart shelled nut meats (halves |
| ⅓ cup sweet milk | and quarter pieces, not fine) |
| 6 eggs | |

Make as any cake. Flour nuts with a little of the flour; bake in moderate oven about 300 degrees for two hours.

## Spice Cake

| | |
|---|---|
| ½ cup butter | ¼ teaspoon cloves |
| 1 cup sugar | 1 teaspoon cinnamon |
| ½ cup buttermilk | 1 teaspoon allspice |
| 1½ cups flour | 2 eggs |
| 1 tablespoon molasses | 1 teaspoon baking powder |
| ½ teaspoon soda | |

Sift spices, soda and powders into flour. Cream butter and sugar, add egg yolks, flour and liquids. Beat whites stiff, fold in. Bake in deep layer, in moderate oven. Ice top, cut into blocks.

## Mary's Spice Cake

| | |
|---|---|
| 7 egg yolks | 2 cups sugar |
| 1 cup butter | 1 cup molasses |
| 1 cup sour milk | 5 cups flour |
| 1 teaspoon ground cloves | 2 nutmegs (grated) |
| 1 tablespoon allspice | 1 teaspoon soda |

Mix soda in flour. Mix as any cake. Bake 1½ hours in tube pan.

## Cheap Spice Cake

| | |
|---|---|
| ½ cup of shortening | 1 cup sweet milk |
| ⅔ cup sugar | 2½ cups flour |
| ⅔ cup Georgia cane syrup | 2½ teaspoons baking powder |
| 1 egg | 1 teaspoon each of cinnamon, all- |
| ½ teaspoon cloves | spice, nutmeg and mace |

Sift all dry ingredients together; beat eggs and add milk, syrup and shortening. Mix together and bake in two layers. A cup of buttermilk and ½ teaspoon of soda will take the place of sweet milk. Use half of baking powder.

## Rosa's Potato Cake

| | |
|---|---|
| 2 cups sugar | 1 cup nuts |
| 1 cup slightly warm mashed Irish | 1 cup butter |
| potatoes | ½ cup cocoa |
| 2 cups flour | 1 teaspoon cinnamon |
| 1 cup sweet milk | 1 teaspoon nutmeg |
| 1 teaspoon cloves | 1 teaspoon lemon extract |
| 1 teaspoon vanilla | 4 eggs |
| 2 teaspoons baking powder | ½ lb. raisins |

Cream sugar, butter and potato; add yolks of eggs. Put all the spices and cocoa into 1 cup flour and mix with first part; add milk, mix baking powder with other cup flour and add. Flour the nuts and raisins and stir in. Lastly add beaten whites of eggs; add flavoring. Cook in slow oven 50 to 70 minutes.

## Dried Apple Cake—C's Favorite

### First Part

Soak 2 cups dried apples in water over night. Next morning chop fine and boil slowly for 1 hour with 1 cup brown sugar and 1 cup molasses. When done add:

### Second Part

| | |
|---|---|
| 1 cup butter | 3 cups flour |
| 1 cup sweet milk | 3 teaspoons soda |
| 2 cups raisins | 1 egg, beaten together and added last |

Mix well and bake in loaf pan for about 2 hours in slow oven. Spices may be added.

### Mrs. P's Pecan Cake

1¼ cups sugar
3 cups flour
1 cup molasses
1 cup pecan meats chopped fine
¼ lb. citron, cut thin

½ lb. grated chocolate
1 teaspoon each cinnamon, allspice and baking powder
½ teaspoon cloves
8 eggs leaving out 2 whites for icing

Make as any cake. Bake in deep layers or biscuit pan in moderate oven. Flour nuts and citron with portion of flour, before adding. Make white icing, cover top and cut in squares.

## SPONGE CAKES

### Louise's Angel Food Cake

1⅓ cup sugar (granulated)
1 cup flour, after sifting once
1½ teaspoons cream of tartar
1 teaspoon vanilla

¼ teaspoon salt
Whites of 11 large eggs or 12 medium

Sift sugar and flour before measuring. Use a measuring cup (one-half pint). To whites of eggs add the salt. Beat until foamy or white, then sift in cream of tartar and continue beating until firm. Invert beater, and if the eggs will stand erect in a point without turning over, it is ready.

Now fold in the sugar, sifting in a small portion at each fold, using long, gentle strokes. About seven minutes will be required to do this. Put in the flour the same way. Add vanilla, and when mixed in well, turn into a shiny, ungreased pan. Bake 45 minutes, or until done. Have heat very low for 30 minutes—225 degrees if thermometer is used. At the end of the time increase heat to 450 degrees and bake until done. When taken from the stove, invert pan and let stand until cold. When ready to take out, run knife around the edge, invert the pan, give a hard knock on the table with edge of pan and cake will drop out. The brown may be rubbed off, or not before icing. If no thermometer is used, and an oil stove used, try the following method:

Light one burner under oven and have burning medium. Have oven cold. Place in cake about center of oven. Cook 30 minutes. At the end of the time light the second burner and burn both lights to their greatest heat. Use this heat for 15 minutes or until done. To test: When it does not show the impression of the finger it is done. Test in the thickest place. Quick cooking at the last makes a more tender cake, even if it scorches a little on top. Never use a dark, or granite pan. One with a tube is better to learn with.

### Henrietta's Sunshine Cake

1½ cups flour
1½ teaspoons vanilla
1½ teaspoons cream tartar
Whites 11 eggs

1½ cups sugar
⅛ teaspoon salt
Yolks 8 eggs

Beat yolks until light and lemon color. Add salt to whites, beat until foamy, add cream of tartar and beat until stiff. Add yolks, mix the same as angel cake. Bake in large steeple pan 1 hour, same as angel cake. Invert pan until cold.

## Mrs. H's Sunshine Cake

Whites of 7 eggs
Yolks of 5 eggs
1¼ cups sugar
1 cup flour

1 teaspoon vanilla
⅓ teaspoon cream of tartar
⅛ teaspoon salt

Separate eggs, add salt to whites, beat until foamy, add cream of tartar and beat until stiff enough to stand, but not dry. Fold in the sugar; now beat yolks light and fold into the whites. Fold in the flour, add vanilla. Put into an ungreased pan and bake as an angel cake.

## Mrs. Singer's Sponge Cake

3 eggs beaten together for 2 minutes
Add 1½ cups sugar, beat 5 minutes
Add 1 cup flour, beat 2 minutes
Add ½ cup water with rind and juice of half large lemon, beat 1 minute

Add 1 more cup flour into which 2 teaspoons baking powder have been sifted, beat 1 minute

Pour into a pan, allowing space to double in depth, bake in moderate oven about 30 minutes, time depends on the thickness. This may be removed from pan when slightly cool. Grease and flour pan for baking. To be broken and eaten fresh.

## Delicious Angel Cake

Make angel cake. When cold remove from pan and rub off all brown; split through the center, making two thick layers. Have fresh cocoanut grated, medium size, and 1 cup of white seedless raisins, cut in half. Make white icing, using the creamy recipe, using half the quantity, when done and quite stiff add fruit, mix well and put thick between the cake layers. Cover top and sides with white icing. Three cups of sugar will fill and cover a large cake.

## Cooking School Dish

1 large sponge cake, baked in tube pan
½ lb. soft marshmallows, cut in pieces

¼ lb. pecan meats
¼ lb. each, candied cherries and pineapple
1 pint thick cream

Take out center of cake, leaving wall all round outside and center. Cut marshmallows in fourths and soak in cream for 2 hours. Whip stiff, add diced fruit and nuts. Fill center with mixture, having smooth at top. Cover with icing made as follows:

Boil together until it threads:
2 cups sugar (reserve 3 tablespoons)
1 cup water
1 tablespoon vinegar

Have ready:
1 tablespoon gelatine in ¼ cup cold water
3 egg whites

Beat eggs stiff, add the reserved sugar and beat for 2 minutes. Do this while syrup is cooking. Melt gelatine over hot water. When syrup is done, pour slowly over eggs, add melted gelatine, beat until nearly cold, pile on top and sides, decorate with red cherries and blanched almonds. The whole must be cold. Place on platter. Cut through all and serve as any dessert.

A slice of cake one inch thick may be first removed from top before taking out inside; after filling is in, replace top, then ice.

## Perfection Sponge Cake

| | |
|---|---|
| 6 eggs | ½ teaspoon cream of tartar |
| 1¼ cups flour | ⅛ teaspoon salt |
| 1¼ cups sugar | Juice of ½ lemon |

Sift sugar and flour before measuring. Add salt to whites and beat until foamy, add cream of tartar and continue beating until stiff; add sugar gradually beating all the time. Beat for 3 minutes or until it will hold its shape. Let stand while beating yolks until light and creamy, add lemon juice then add whites beating all together. Fold the flour into the mixture, putting in lightly a little at a time. Pour into a bright ungreased pan, bake 50 minutes in loaf pan at 300 degrees.

The depth of the cake will determine the length of time to bake. When done invert pan and let stand until cold.

This cake is much like an angel cake, no baking powder used. This may be baked and treated as any sponge cake.

## Jelly Roll

| | |
|---|---|
| 5 eggs | 1 cup flour |
| 1 cup sugar | 1 tablespoon lemon juice |
| Pinch of salt | |

Put eggs into bowl, add sugar and salt, beat for 15 minutes, add lemon juice, fold in flour. Line pan with paper, pour in batter, bake in hot oven 10 minutes. Remove from oven, dust top generously with sugar, turn out on cloth. Wet paper to remove easily. Spread with jelly and roll. Roll in cloth for ½ hour. If edges are crusty, cut off before rolling. The cake should be about ½ inch thick when baked.

## Quick Sponge Cake

| | |
|---|---|
| 2 eggs | ⅓ cup sugar |
| ½ teaspoon baking powder | 2 teaspoons lemon juice |
| ⅓ cup flour | ⅛ teaspoon salt |

Beat eggs together until light. Add lemon juice and continue beating, add sugar slowly, beating continually. Sift powders and salt with flour and fold into the mixture. Pour into a shallow oblong pan which has been greased and floured. Bake in quick oven about 5 minutes, or until done. Turn out on a damp cloth, cover with another for 5 minutes. Cut off crust on sides and spread with jelly, roll up and let get cold.

Cut in slices across the roll. This will make 10 slices.

## Mrs. Baldwin's Sponge Cake

4 eggs
1½ cups flour
1¼ cups sugar
1 teaspoon vanilla

Pinch of salt
2 teaspoons baking powder
½ cup cold water
1 tablespoon cold water

Separate eggs, add 1 tablespoon water to yolks, beat until very light, add sugar and salt and beat well. Add flour and half cup water alternately, beat whites stiff, fold into mixture last. Put into cold oven, start at 250 degrees for 10 minutes, then turn to 275 degrees and bake for 45 minutes. Invert pan until cold.

## Miss Fannie's Cream Cake

3 eggs
1 cup sugar
1½ cups flour

6 tablespoons water
4 teaspoons baking powder
Pinch salt

Separate eggs, beat yolks light, add sugar and beat again, add water. Add salt to whites, beat them stiff, add to sugar mixture. Fold in flour. Bake in two layers using quick oven. Put together with cream filling:

1 egg
1 tablespoon flour

3 tablespoons sugar
1 cup milk

Heat milk, mix other ingredients together, pour over the hot milk and return to double boiler. Cook until thick. Let get cold, put between layers. Serve with whipped cream or cover top with soft, spongy icing.

## Orange Sponge Cake

¾ cup sugar
¼ cup water
⅔ cup flour
¼ cup orange juice

½ teaspoon cream of tartar
4 eggs
Pinch of salt

Boil sugar and water together until it threads, pour over whites beaten stiff, beat five minutes. Then beat yolks in separate bowl until thick and light colored, to this add the orange juice, beat until thick, fold this into the white mixture. Sift flour and cream of tartar together, fold into the whites, pour into angel pan, bake in moderate oven about 300 degrees, about 40 minutes. Invert pan. Wait until cold, turn out like angel cake.

# SMALL CAKES AND COOKIES
## Mother Dull's Tea Cakes

2 cups sugar
1 cup of lard and butter mixed
½ cup buttermilk
3 eggs
½ teaspoon soda

2 teaspoons baking powder
1 teaspoon vanilla
Flour sufficient to make a soft dough

Cream butter and lard, add sugar then the beaten eggs. Into one cup flour sift soda and baking powder. Add this to the sugar mixture. Add milk and vanilla, now sufficiently more flour to make a soft dough.

Turn onto a floured board, knead until smooth, roll out one-fourth inch thick, cut into any shape, bake in moderate oven until brown and done, about ten minutes. Do not put close enough to touch, as this would spoil the shape. This recipe makes 120 cakes.

If a hard brittle cake is liked, by kneading into the dough dry sugar this will give a brittle cake. Divide dough into two parts, using half cup of sugar, half cup of flour for one part roll, cut and bake and you will have some of both.

If these cakes are iced over top or two put together with icing, they are unusually good.

This is without any exception the best tea cake or cookie recipe I have ever used.

### Filled Tea Cakes

Make dough for tea cakes. Roll out quite thin, cut tea cakes with a large biscuit cutter, put a teaspoon of the filling on one half, near the center, fold the other side over, crimp with a fork, stick tops, place on baking sheet and cook as tea cakes. Make filling as follows:

1 cup chopped seedless raisins
1 tablespoon orange juice
Grated rind 1 orange

2 tablespoons fine cracker or cake crumbs

Mix together and put a teaspoonful or more on the cut tea cake. More orange juice may be used if needed.

### Mrs. W's Ice Box Cookies

1 cup butter
2 cups brown sugar
1 cup chopped nuts
3½ cups flour

½ teaspoon salt
1 teaspoon soda
2 eggs

Cream butter and sugar, add eggs and mix well. Sift salt and soda with flour, add nuts, mix into first part. Roll out into a round roll, put into ice box over night. Turn out on floured board, slice very thin, bake in moderate oven until crisp. This makes five dozen, and they are delicious.

### Crescents

2 cups flour
¾ cup butter
1 cup chopped nuts; chopped rather
    fine

3 heaping tablespoons 4X sugar
2 teaspoons ice water
1 teaspoon vanilla
½ teaspoon salt

Have butter cold and mix with flour until it looks like fine crumbs. Add sugar, nuts and salt. Add the ice water and make into stiff dough; add vanilla, knead lightly. Roll out on floured board ¼-inch thick. Cut into crescent shapes. Bake in rather quick oven, about 350 degrees, until light brown. Roll while hot in granulated sugar.

Use a tea biscuit cutter, cut one and remove; place cutter ¾-inch over the curved edge, cut again and this gives a perfect crescent. The left over pieces may be kneaded together and cut. This will make 100 small crescents.

## Russian Rocks

3 cups flour
3 eggs
1 cup butter
1 pound raisins
1 cup pecans or English walnuts

1¾ cups brown sugar
2 teaspoons cinnamon
1½ teaspoons soda dissolved in a dessert spoon of warm water

Cream butter and sugar, add eggs beaten together, then add cinnamon, nuts and raisins well floured; add soda and flour. Have the batter so stiff that it will hardly mix. Take up in teaspoon and place on buttered tins and bake a pretty brown. Use moderate oven.

## Muffin Cakes

¾ cup sugar
1 cup sweet milk
2¼ cups flour
1 egg

1 heaping tablespoon butter, or substitute
1 teaspoon vanilla
4 teaspoons baking powder

Make as any cake. Bake in muffin tins or two layers.

## Marguerites

Make a soft white icing, cover crackers, butter thins or graham, with icing. Place 5 whole plump raisins like petals of a daisy with half a nut meat in center. Place in hot oven until icing is dry over top. Serve as sandwich or cake. The crackers may be placed under the blaze until a light brown, this will only take a few seconds.
Nice for tea. For small children's party, leave off fruit.

## Peanut Cookies

1 cup sugar
½ cup of peanut butter
2 eggs
1 cup buttermilk

1 teaspoon baking powder
½ teaspoon soda
Flour to make soft dough

Beat eggs, add sugar and peanut butter, then milk and flavoring. Put the soda and baking powder into some flour and sift into the mixture. Add enough more to handle. Turn onto a floured board, knead smooth and cut, bake in moderate oven about seven and one-half minutes.

## Angel Food Drop Cakes

Whites 2 eggs
¼ cup sugar
¼ teaspoon cream of tartar

¼ cup flour
¼ teaspoon vanilla
Few grains salt

Beat eggs till frothy; add cream of tartar; then beat stiff; add sugar slowly, beat 2 minutes; fold in flour; add vanilla.
Cover the bottom of an ungreased pan with ungreased paper. Drop about a teaspoonful 1½-inches apart. Sprinkle top with granulated sugar. Bake in moderate oven from 10 to 15 minutes.

## Hermits

| | |
|---|---|
| ⅓ cup butter | 2 teaspoons baking powder |
| ¾ cup sugar | ½ cup raisins cut in half |
| 2 cups flour | ½ teaspoon cinnamon |
| ½ cup bran | ½ teaspoon nutmeg |
| 3 tablespoons milk | ¼ teaspoon cloves |
| 1 egg | 1 teaspoon salt |

Sift spices, powder and salt with flour. Add bran and raisins, mix well. Cream butter and sugar, add beaten egg and milk, mix in flour. Mix well, drop on greased baking sheet, leaving space to spread. Bake in moderate oven. Flour varies so use more or less to make a stiff dough just able to stir with spoon. Half graham, half white may be used,. leaving out the bran, add more or less milk as needed to make stiff dough.

## Delicious Cakes

| | |
|---|---|
| 1 lb. sugar, fine grain | 1 lb. almond paste |
| 3 eggs | 1 tablespoon coffee |
| 1 teaspoon lemon juice | ½ teaspoon cinnamon |

Beat eggs light, add sugar, coffee, almond paste and lemon juice. Make into balls, dent with finger and into each dent put a small portion of jelly. Put on buttered baking sheet, bake in moderate oven until crusty.

## Addie's Syrup Cakes
### (16 small cakes)

| | |
|---|---|
| 1 cup Georgia cane syrup | ½ cup shortening |
| ½ cup sugar | 2 teaspoons soda |
| 1 cup boiling water | 2½ cups flour |
| 1 teaspoon cinnamon | 1 teaspoon allspice |
| ½ teaspoon cloves | |

Mix together syrup, sugar and melted lard; mix soda in hot water and add to syrup; mix in flour and spices. Bake in muffin pans in moderate oven. No eggs used.

## Oat Cookies

| | |
|---|---|
| ½ cup lard | ½ cup sugar |
| ½ cup raisins | ½ cup nuts |
| 1 cup oat flakes | 1 cup flour |
| 1 egg | 3 tablespoons sweet milk |
| ½ teaspoon soda | ½ teaspoon cinnamon |
| ½ teaspoon salt | |

Cream lard, add sugar, then egg and milk. Sift soda and cinnamon with flour, then mix the fruit into the flour, then the oats. Combine the two mixtures, drop on baking sheet and cook in moderate oven, or roll and cut, using extra flour to handle.

## Oatmeal Cookies

| | |
|---|---|
| 4 tablespoons butter | 2½ cups raw oatmeal |
| 1 teaspoon salt | 1½ cups flour |
| 2 teaspoons baking powder | 1 cup sugar |
| 2 eggs | 1 cup seedless raisins |

Mix butter and sugar together, then eggs, salt, baking powder, oatmeal and raisins. Now add the flour or enough to make a very stiff batter. Sometimes it does not take all of the flour. Have a baking sheet and with a fork and spoon put on pieces about as large as a walnut, leaving plenty of room so in cooking they will not touch. Bake in moderate oven.

Nut meat may be used if liked. A flavoring of spice may be added.

## Scotch Cookies

| | |
|---|---|
| 2 cups oatmeal uncooked | 1 cup sugar |
| ½ teaspoon salt | ½ teaspoon vanilla |
| 1 tablespoon melted butter | 2 eggs |

Beat eggs light, add sugar and other ingredients, drop from spoon onto a well greased and floured baking sheet, spread thin with a spoon. Bake in moderate oven about 12 minutes. Let cool, then remove from sheet.

## Highland Cookies

| | |
|---|---|
| 1 lb. brown sugar | 1 grated nutmeg |
| 2 eggs | Flour enough to make dough roll |
| ¾ lb. butter | |

Mix butter and sugar, then the beaten eggs. Sufficient flour to roll out and cut, roll thin. Bake in quick oven.

## Pearl Cookies

| | |
|---|---|
| 1 cup sugar | 1 egg yolk |
| 2 cups flour | 1 egg white |
| ½ lb. butter | 2 teaspoons vanilla |

Cream butter, add sugar and cream well. Add sifted flour, egg yolk and vanilla. Mix thoroughly. Divide dough and spread very thinly on greased cookie sheets. Paint top of dough with unbeaten egg white, sprinkle with nuts. Bake at 375 degrees until light brown. Cut while hot but do not remove from cookie sheets until cold.

## The Best Doughnuts

| | |
|---|---|
| 2 eggs | ⅛ teaspoon salt |
| 1½ cups sugar | 1½ cups buttermilk |
| 3 tablespoons shortening (butter or lard) | ¾ teaspoon soda |
| | 2 teaspoons baking powder |
| ½ teaspoon nutmeg or 1 teaspoon vanilla | Flour to make soft dough but stiff enough to roll and cut |

Fry in deep fat, drain on soft paper, sprinkle with sugar.

## Doughnuts

| | |
|---|---|
| 1 cup sugar | 4 teaspoons baking powder |
| 1 cup sweet milk | ⅛ teaspoon salt |
| ¼ cup butter | Flour to make a soft dough stiff enough to handle |
| 2 eggs | |

Beat eggs together until light, add sugar and mix well; add butter which has been softened. Into a portion of flour add salt and baking powder, add to mixture; then add milk and sufficient flour to handle; flavor if liked. Roll out one-quarter inch thick, fry in deep boiling fat, roll in pulverized sugar while hot.

### Doughnuts with Irish Potatoes

2 good-sized potatoes
3 tablespoons of shortening
3 eggs
4 teaspoons baking powder
1¼ cups sugar
¾ cup sweet milk

1 teaspoon salt
1 teaspoon vanilla
Flour enough to make a soft dough that is stiff enough to handle

The potatoes should be pared, cooked and put through ricer. Add shortening while the potatoes are hot, also sugar; beat eggs light and add; then add other ingredients and lastly flour. Turn on board and knead smooth using flour as needed. Roll out ¼-inch thick and fry in deep fat.

### The Best Ginger Snaps

1 cup molasses
½ cup shortening
1 tablespoon ground ginger

½ cup sugar
½ teaspoon soda
½ teaspoon salt

Bring molasses to boil, add sugar, shortening and seasoning. Use enough flour to handle. Let ripen over night in refrigerator. Roll out thin, using sufficient flour to handle, cut and bake in moderate oven. Will keep for weeks.

### Willie's Ginger Snaps

2 cups syrup
½ cup water
2 teaspoons soda

1 cup butter and lard mixed
1 teaspoon ginger
Flour enough to roll

Put syrup and water to boil. Add shortening, boil 15 minutes slowly. Remove from fire, add ginger, let get cold. Sift soda into a portion of flour and mix into a dough, using as much more flour as necessary. Roll thin, cut and bake in moderate oven.

### 1850 Ginger Cakes

1 cup syrup
¼ cup lard
1 teaspoon soda
¼ cup sour milk

1 tablespoon ground ginger
Flour to make dough roll
Pinch of salt

Do not knead much, roll out ½-inch thick, brush over with white of egg, bake in moderate oven. The yolk may be added to the mixture, the whites for brushing the top.

### Old-Fashioned Ginger Cakes

1½ lbs. flour
¼ lb. lard or butter
1 tablespoon soda

1 tablespoon ground ginger
Sufficient black molasses to make dough to roll

Make dough, roll out ½-inch thick, cut in squares 4x8 inches. Cook in moderate oven 20 minutes or until done. When half done, brush over tops with sweet milk or white of egg to give the glaze.

## Mrs. W's Ginger Cakes

| | |
|---|---|
| ½ cup butter and lard mixed | 2 eggs |
| ¾ cup sugar | 1 teaspoon cinnamon |
| ¾ cup black molasses or syrup | 1 teaspoon allspice |
| ½ cup buttermilk | ½ teaspoon ginger |
| 1 cup nutmeats | 1 teaspoon baking powder |
| ½ lb. raisins | 1 teaspoon soda |
| 3 cups flour | |

Mix all dry ingredients together. Beat eggs together light. Add sugar, then shortening. Add milk and syrup. Mix the two together well. The batter should be stiff. Drop on baking sheet two inches apart. Bake in moderate oven 20 to 30 minutes.

## Good Ginger Cakes (Without Eggs)

| | |
|---|---|
| 1 cup shortening | 1 tablespoon ginger |
| 2 cups molasses | 2 teaspoons soda, sifted with the flour |
| 1 cup water | enough to roll and cut |
| 1 teaspoon salt | |

Bake in moderate oven.

## Ginger Bread

| | |
|---|---|
| ⅔ teacup butter and lard mixed | 1 teacup chopped raisins |
| ⅔ teacup sugar | 1 tablespoon ginger |
| ⅔ teacup molasses | 2 teaspoons soda in ½ cup cold |
| ⅔ teacup buttermilk | water |
| 3 cups flour | 2 eggs |

Beat eggs, add sugar and butter. Put raisins into flour dry. Mix all together, add soda last. Bake in moderate oven until done, the length of time depending on the depth of the pan. Peanut butter may be used in place of the shortening. Bacon drippings will make good ginger bread.

## Lewis Ginger Bread

| | |
|---|---|
| 2½ cups flour | 2 teaspoons soda |
| ½ cup sugar | 2 teaspoons ginger |
| ¼ cup butter | 2 teaspoons baking powder |
| ½ cup syrup and black molasses mixed | ¼ teaspoon salt |
| ¼ cup buttermilk | 2 eggs |

Mix same as cake, beating eggs together, adding to creamed butter and sugar. If too stiff, add a tiny bit more buttermilk. Bake in slow oven.

Bake in deep layer pans, having about two inches deep when done (about forty-five minutes).

Cut in blocks, serve hot with butter.

## Peanut Butter Syrup Cake

1 cup peanut butter
1 cup syrup
1 cup sugar
3½ cups flour
½ cup buttermilk

1 teaspoon soda
3 teaspoons baking powder
2 eggs
½ teaspoon salt

Mix as any cake, bake in deep layer pan in moderate oven, about 30 minutes, break and serve hot. Use moderate oven.

## Miss Rosa's Kisses

Whites 2 eggs
1 cup pecan meats (chopped)
Pinch of salt

1 cup sugar
1 cup dates (cut into fourths)
½ teaspoon vanilla

Add salt to whites, beat stiff, add sugar and continue beating until sugar is dissolved and mixture quite stiff; add fruits and flavoring. Butter sheet of paper well and put on baking sheet. Drop from a spoon small portions not too close together. Bake in slow oven until brown. This will make 30 medium kisses.

## Macaroons

¼ lb. almond paste
1 egg white

¼ to ½ cup powdered sugar

Crumble the almond paste and mix with the egg white until smooth and stiff. Gradually add sugar until it is stiff enough to roll into balls. On a baking sheet spread an ungreased paper and put the balls, leaving room to spread. Bake in moderate oven about 30 minutes. Brush the underside with water to remove the paper.

## Cocoanut Macaroons

2 cups prepared cocoanut
1 cup 4X sugar

1 tablespoon flour
1 egg white beaten stiff

Mix dry ingredients together, mix with beaten egg, drop on buttered paper, bake in rather moderate oven about 30 minutes, until browned nicely. For almond macaroons use almond paste in place of cocoanut, using less of the paste.

## Cup Fruit Cakes

⅓ cup shortening
2 egg yolks
1½ cups flour
1 cup chopped dates
1 teaspoon orange extract
2 egg whites

1 cup sugar
⅔ cup coffee
1½ teaspoons baking powder
1 cup chopped nuts
½ teaspoon vanilla

Cream shortening and sugar; add egg yolks and beat until light, thick and lemon-colored. Add coffee; sift dry ingredients; add fruit and nuts. Fold into first mixture and add flavoring. Fold in stiffly beaten egg whites. Half fill gem pans and bake in moderate oven (350 degrees) 15 to 20 minutes.

## My Neighbor's Date Bar

1 cup sugar
1 cup dates
1 cup flour
1 cup nuts

3 eggs
2 teaspoons baking powder
1 teaspoon vanilla

Mix sugar and yolks, add nuts and dates, mix well, add flour and well beaten whites. Spread as *thin as possible* and *cook very slowly*. Cut in bars. Roll in powdered sugar.

## Drop Nut Cakes

½ cup butter
1 cup brown sugar
2 cups flour
1 cup nut meats
½ cup raisins

2 eggs
1 teaspoon cinnamon
1 teaspoon baking powder
½ teaspoon vanilla

Cream butter and sugar, add eggs. Mix spices and baking powder with flour, add nuts and raisins, mix well and add to sugar mixture.

Drop on well greased pan, pieces about the size of a walnut, leaving space between for spreading. Bake in moderate oven until done, about ten or fifteen minutes. The batter must be stiff enough to hold the shape, so more or less flour may be needed, according to the size of the eggs.

## Nondescripts

½ teaspoon salt
1 cup 4X sugar

Yolks of 4 eggs
Flour to make a medium stiff dough

Mix salt and flour into egg as for making noodles, having the dough stiff. Roll out just as thin as possible; cut into round pieces, using a saucer; fold together, making a half circle; fold again, making a fourth circle; slash up into fingers, leaving all together at the center or point. Catch by the point or center, shake open the cut pieces and drop into boiling fat and cook like a doughnut, shaking the pan constantly to make the strips open and curl, having enough fat to float them. Do not have fat too hot, as they should cook, but not brown, cooking one at the time. When it looks like a large chrysanthemum, lift out carefully onto brown paper and sprinkle with 4X sugar. Try the left-over ends first, leaving the round circles after you try the fat. These are most delicious for a tea or afternoon party.

If dough is too stiff the petals will not curl, if too soft they will stick.

## Sweet Wafers

2 cups flour
1 cup sugar
2 tablespoons of butter

3 eggs
1 teaspoon lemon extract

Beat eggs together until light; add sugar and butter; mix in flour and beat smooth. This gives rather stiff dough. With fork pull off piece about as large as good sized marble; bake in wafer irons. When coloring wafers they must be baked more slowly, so as not to brown too much. Roll while hot.

## Sweet Wafer Cones

Make and bake sweet wafer. While hot shape over a mold which comes for the purpose, or roll into a cone with the fingers.

## Sweet Wafers for Ice Cream

Make as for plain rolled wafers, and cook. Have two glasses ready with bottoms up. Place the hot wafer over the bottom of one glass; with the other glass press down over hot wafer gently. Remove glass instantly, remove wafer, turn up and you have a cup-shaped wafer for ice cream or charlotte. The more irregular the prettier the cup.

## Dixie Sweet Wafers

| | |
|---|---|
| 3 eggs | Pinch salt |
| 1 cup sugar | Flour enough to make thin batter, |
| 1 teaspoon vanilla | about as thick as buttermilk |
| 1 cup top milk | |

Beat eggs together until light; add sugar and half of the milk, enough flour to make a stiff batter. When smooth, add the remaining milk. This will give a thin batter. Bake in wafer irons and roll while hot.

## Zephyr Wafers

| | |
|---|---|
| ½ pint milk | ½ pint flour |
| 1 teaspoon salt | 1 teaspoon melted butter |

Cook in wafer irons.

## Cheese Wafers

| | |
|---|---|
| 2 cups flour | ¼ pound butter |
| 1 teaspoon salt | 1 pound grated American "bitey" |
| ¼ teaspoon cayenne pepper | cheese |

Mix and sift dry ingredients. Cut in butter with a pastry blender. Add the cheese. Roll out thin and cut in desired shapes. Bake in hot oven (400 degrees F.) for ten minutes. This makes fifty.

## Rosettes

| | |
|---|---|
| 2 eggs | 1 cup milk |
| 1 tablespoon sugar more or less | 1 cup flour (more if necessary) |
| ¼ teaspoon salt | |

Beat eggs slightly with sugar and salt; add milk and flour, beat until smooth.

Cook the same as timbales.

# ICINGS

## Spongy White Icing

| | |
|---|---|
| 1½ cups sugar | 1 teaspoon vanilla |
| ¾ cup cold water | 2 teaspoons lemon juice |
| Whites of 2 large eggs | Pinch of salt |

From the sugar reserve two tablespoons. Put sugar and water to boil until a long thread is given when tested.

Beat whites stiff, to which has been added the salt; add the reserved sugar, the same as making meringue. Beat egg while sugar is boiling. When ready pour the hot syrup slowly over whites; continue beating until thick, add flavoring, pour over cake, spread and let dry.

If icing does not thicken, place bowl over a saucepan of boiling water and steam. It will at first get thin, then thicken; remove and beat until stiff.

Do not let bowl touch water, have a heavy steam and let bowl fit top of saucepan very tight. This makes a soft, spongy icing.

## Glossy Icing

| | |
|---|---|
| Whites of 2 eggs | 1 teaspoon lemon juice |
| 1½ cups sugar | 1 teaspoon vanilla |
| ¾ cup cold water | |

Put sugar and water into pan and cook until it gives a good thread. Have ready the eggs beaten to a *soft* froth. When syrup is ready pour slowly over whites. Continue beating until icing is thick enough to spread over cake. It should be soft enough to spread smooth, but not run off the sides. A little practice will give perfect results.

## Fluffy Icing

| | |
|---|---|
| 2 egg whites | 2 tablespoons white corn syrup |
| ½ cup water | 1 teaspoon vinegar |
| 1 cup sugar | ½ teaspoon vanilla |

Put water, sugar, vinegar and syrup together, mix, and boil, without stirring, until it gives a long thread. Pour slowly over the stiff beaten whites and beat until cool and stiff enough to hold its shape.

## Seven Minute Icing

| | |
|---|---|
| ⅞ cup sugar | 1 egg white unbeaten |
| 3 tablespoons cold water | |

Put all together in double boiler, cook seven minutes, stirring constantly. Remove from fire, beat until right consistency to spread.

## Chocolate Seven Minute Icing

| | |
|---|---|
| 3 egg whites | 2 tablespoons white corn syrup |
| 2¼ cups sugar | 1½ teaspoons vanilla |
| 7½ tablespoons water | 5 squares chocolate |

Combine egg whites, sugar, water and corn syrup in top of double boiler, beating with rotary egg beater until thoroughly mixed. Place over rapidly boiling water, beat constantly with rotary egg beater, and cook 7 minutes or until frosting will stand in peaks. Remove from boiling water; add vanilla. Cool. Melt chocolate and cool. Fold chocolate into cooled frosting. Do not heat mixture.

### Orange Icing

Grated rind and juice 1 orange
1 egg yolk
2 tablespoons butter

Sufficient 4X sugar to make into paste

Grate orange rind and pour juice over it, let stand 1 hour, then strain. Mix butter into 1 cup of sifted sugar with tips of fingers, drop in the egg yolk, then mix with the orange juice. Use sufficient more sugar to make a paste easy to spread.

### Lemon Icing

1 cup 4X sugar, sifted and measured
Butter, the size of a walnut

1 egg yolk
Juice of lemon to make thin enough to spread

Rub the butter and sugar together, add egg yolk and lemon juice, mix to a paste and spread. This makes a nice icing for small cakes.

### Strawberry Icing

Crush berries until quite smooth leaving fruit and juice together. Add sufficient 4X sugar to make stiff enough to spread. This is pretty and good on small cakes or blocks.

### Refrigerator Icing

2 cream cheese
3 oz. chocolate
1 box 4X sugar

5 to 6 tablespoons milk
Pinch of salt

Add milk to cheese, add sugar one cup at a time and smooth out all lumps. Add chocolate which has been melted in double boiler. Place on cake and put in refrigerator for icing to harden.

### Butter Icing

¼ cup butter
2 cups 4X sugar which has been sifted

Flavor to taste
1 egg yolk

Cream butter until light and fluffy, add egg yolks and sugar. Use more or less sugar to make the right consistency to spread.

Two squares of melted chocolate give a chocolate cream icing. Two tablespoons of strong coffee give a mocha icing, using sugar to make the right consistency. Lemon or orange juice may be used for a fruit icing.

This icing may be used very effectively in decorating.

## Icing for Decorating

2½ cups sugar
1 cup water
½ teaspoon cream of tartar

Juice of ½ lemon
Whites of 4 eggs

Put 2 cups sugar and 1 cup water and cream of tartar on to boil until it threads. With a damp cloth wipe well the sides of the pan to prevent any crystals from forming. Boil over a brisk fire until it gives a short thread about 2 inches long. While the sugar is boiling beat whites stiff, and add ½ cup sugar, just as for making meringue. Keep beating until syrup responds to necessary test (short thread). Pour syrup slowly over the beaten whites.

Have ready a saucepan ¼ full of boiling water, over which the bowl will fit without touching the water.

Place bowl over boiling water, keep over water boiling very hard so the steam will cook the icing. Add lemon juice, cook, folding from side to side, being very careful not to scrape any hard crust which will form on the bottom of the bowl.

Continue cooking until the icing will stand in a small peak when pulled up with spoon or beater. When cooked to this point, remove from the steam and continue folding until cold.

When cold it will hold its shape and is ready to use. Keep bowl covered with a damp cloth to prevent any crust from forming. If different colors are desired, take a portion from the bowl to color, keeping everything covered with a damp cloth.

It is now ready to put into cornucopia tubes, the implements for decorating. This icing will keep and may be used several days if kept covered so no crust will form.

## A Simple Icing for Decorating

1 teaspoon of lemon juice
4 cups 4X sugar

White of 1 egg

Roll and sift the sugar so it will be very smooth, put egg into a bowl and without beating mix in the sugar until quite a stiff icing is formed to hold its shape, add lemon juice and beat until smooth and white. Fill forcing bag and proceed to decorate cake. This icing will get dry and firm and is quite satisfactory. If you wish to color, use a few drops of any color desired, adding to the icing when finished. Use more or less sugar as needed.

## FILLINGS

### Caramel Filling No. 1

1 cup brown sugar
½ cup butter

1 cup white sugar
½ cup sweet milk

Put all ingredients into pan and let boil hard for 2 minutes by the clock. Remove from fire and beat until cold.

Nuts may be added to vary the filling.

### Caramel Filling No. 2

| | |
|---|---|
| 1 cup sweet milk | 1 teaspoon vanilla |
| 3 cups sugar | ¼ cup sugar burned |
| ½ cup butter | ¼ cup boiling water to make the |
| ¼ teaspoon soda | caramel |

Burn the one-fourth cup of sugar in a saucepan or skillet until melted and dark brown.

Add the boiling water and cook until well blended, and there are no lumps.

Into the large saucepan put the caramel (burned sugar), and all other ingredients and boil rapidly, stirring constantly. Cook until it leaves the trace of spoon (about ten minutes on gas).

When thick like candy, place pan in vessel of cold water, stirring and beating until thick and creamy—when it begins to look creamy it is ready to go between the layers. Beat a little more, and have it stiffer to cover top. This will put together three layers and cover top and sides. If thermometer is used boil to 238 degrees.

### Brown Sugar Caramel Filling

| | |
|---|---|
| 1 cup dark brown sugar | ½ cup butter |
| 2 cups white sugar | ⅛ teaspoon soda |
| 1 cup milk | 1 teaspoon vanilla |

Put all together, stir well. Boil rapidly, stirring constantly until it leaves a good trace of the spoon. Remove from fire, place in cold water to cool, beat constantly until creamy and thick enough to put between layers and over top. Use large saucepan so it can cook rapidly, about eight or ten minutes from the time it begins to boil. Use giant burner.

### Easy Caramel Filling

| | |
|---|---|
| 3 cups sugar | ½ stick of butter (⅛ of pound) |
| 1 cup milk (or ½ cup evaporated | Pinch of baking soda |
| milk and ½ cup water) | 1 teaspoon vanilla |
| 1 tablespoon corn syrup | |

Put 2 tablespoons of sugar in saucepan and brown. Heat milk and soda and add browned sugar, and let dissolve. Add remainder of sugar and the syrup and cook until a firm ball will form in cold water. Remove from fire, add butter and vanilla and let cool before starting to cream. Cream until consistency to spread. If icing should be cooked too much add pure cream until consistency desired.

### Caramel

| | |
|---|---|
| 1 cup sugar | ½ cup water |

Into a saucepan or iron fry pan put the dry sugar and melt until a dark brown liquid, like syrup. After it begins to melt be careful not to burn, but stir to remove from the hot spots until all is brown. Then add the water and continue cooking until a thin syrup is formed. Add enough of this to your ice cream to flavor or the sugar and milk for a cake filling.

If too lightly browned it will require more to get the right color and flavor. If burned it will be bitter. I prefer the made caramel to brown sugar for custard, layer cake filling and butter scotch pie. This can be made and kept indefinitely.

## Marshmallow Filling

| | |
|---|---|
| 3 dozen marshmallows | 2 cups of icing, hot |

Snip the marshmallow with a pair of scissors, which are buttered so they will not stick, and cover well two cake layers. Have this done before making the icing. When the icing is still hot, very thick and spongy, cover the marshmallow well and, with a spoon or knife, mix and spread so every piece will get its portion of icing. Put on a second portion, spread quickly and add the second layer, covered with the marshmallows.

Repeat the process as on the first one. Add the last layer, cover top and sides with the icing, smooth evenly over top with back of the spoon, putting on enough to flow over the sides. Now with a knife bring this up on the sides, and smooth well. Cut a few strips of the marshmallow and decorate the top.

Candied cherries mixed with the marshmallows, chopped fine, make a pretty Christmas cake. A few whole ones over the top add to the Christmas spirit.

## Lady Baltimore Filling

| | |
|---|---|
| 1½ cups of sugar | ¼ cup of orange juice or 2 table- |
| ¾ cup of water | spoons sherry jell |
| 1 cup of chopped raisins | 1 teaspoon of vanilla |
| ½ cup of chopped pecan nuts | Yolks of 4 eggs |

Boil sugar and water until it spins a thread, pour over the beaten yolks, beat until it begins to thicken. Add all other ingredients, stir until thick, spread between the layers; cover the top with white icing.

## Cocoanut Filling

Make a spongy icing using the recipe given in Icings.

Have one fresh cocoanut of medium size, grated. Spread to dry out slightly. When icing is ready mix with cocoanut and spread on layers. Put together with a plain icing and sprinkle cocoanut over the top. A little lemon juice added gives a very delightful flavor.

## Orange Filling

| | |
|---|---|
| 3 cups sugar | 2 tablespoons flour |
| 4 oranges | 1 small cocoanut |

Squeeze juice of oranges, grind peeling of one through meat chopper, add sugar and cocoanut, pour one cup of boiling water over mixture, thicken with flour and boil the whole mixture until thick, set aside to cool, spread between layers.

### Perfection Orange Filling

| | |
|---|---|
| ¼ lb. butter | 2 eggs |
| 1 cup sugar | Juice and grated rind 2 oranges |

Grate rind of oranges then extract juice. Beat eggs and sugar together, add butter and orange juice, put into double boiler, cook until thick. Let get cold then spread between layers.

Chopped nuts, raisins and citron may be added if liked.

### Banana Filling—Mrs T's Recipe

Peel and put 4 bananas through potato ricer. Take 3 tablespoons sugar, 2 tablespoons corn starch, and 2 tablespoons lemon juice and blend together. Mix with mashed bananas and cook in a double boiler until corn starch is cooked—cool. Put between layers of cake when cold. This fills three layers.

### Sponge Cake Filling

| | |
|---|---|
| 3 egg yolks | 2 cups 4X sugar |
| 3 tablespoons black coffee | 2 tablespoons butter |

Mix butter well into one cup sugar, beat egg light, mix in sugar with butter, then coffee. Add sufficient sugar (the remaining cup) until the consistency to spread, using more or less sugar as needed.

Use two layers of sponge cake with filling between. Cover top with white icing or sprinkle 4X sugar over top.

### Japanese Filling

| | |
|---|---|
| 2 lemons grated, rind and juice | 1 cup boiling water |
| 1 good-sized cocoanut, grated | 2 tablespoons cornstarch |
| 2 cups of sugar | |

Put all together into a saucepan, except corn starch. When the mixture begins to boil, add the cornstarch dissolved in half cup cold water; continue to cook, stirring constantly until the mixture drops in a lump from the spoon. Cool and spread between the layers. Cover top with a white icing.

### Tutti Frutti Filling

| | |
|---|---|
| 2 cups sugar | 2 tablespoons granulated gelatine |
| 1½ cups water | Flavor to taste |

Boil sugar and 1 cup water until it spreads.

In ½ cup cold water put 2 tablespoons granulated gelatine and let stand 5 minutes. Melt over boiling water. Pour into a bowl and pour over this the boiling syrup, beating constantly.

Place bowl in cold water and continue beating until cold. Add flavoring. Add 3 tablespoons of any chopped candied fruit, and 3 tablespoons of chopped meat nuts. (Blanched almonds are good as they are white and prettier).

Put between layers of cake.

## Spanish Cream Filling

3 cups sugar  
1 cup milk  

¾ cup butter

Boil ingredients together until when dropped from a spoon the liquid will flake off like jelly.

Have ready whites of 2 eggs beaten stiff, pour over them the hot syrup and whip continually until thick. Add 1 teaspoon vanilla. Nuts and crystallized fruit may be added if desired.

## Maple Filling

Into 2 cups of 4X sugar mix butter size of a walnut, add 1 egg yolk; mix to a paste using maple syrup. Flavor with vanilla.

Chopped pecan meats may be added if wanted.

## Almond Cream Filling

¾ cup sugar  
1 cup of blanched and chopped almonds  
2 egg whites  

1 cup thick cream  
¼ teaspoon almond extract  
½ teaspoon lemon extract

Whip cream dry, whip egg whites stiff, add sugar and beat until an icing is made; add flavoring and when stiff and smooth fold in cream and nuts. Put between layers, ice top and sides with white icing.

## Chocolate Filling

3 cups sugar  
1 cup sweet milk  
2 squares chocolate  

½ cup butter  
⅛ teaspoon of soda

Grate or cut chocolate, put all together, put over a brisk fire and cook until thick, stirring constantly—if gas stove is used it takes about 8 to 10 minutes to cook. If thermometer is used boil to 238 degrees.

If it is tested in cold water it should be boiled to a soft ball. When taken from the fire set pan in cold water, stir and beat constantly until creamy. It should be put between the layers while much softer than for the top.

If at all uneasy after it becomes creamy and thick, leave for a few minutes to see if it will get firm  Then melt over a very gentle fire or hot water until thin enough to spread between the layers and top. If it is still thin recook and let boil two minutes, cool, beat and use.

If it becomes too hard, before using, add a little water or milk, bring to the boil, cool and beat as directed above.

## A New Chocolate Filling

3 cups sugar  
1½ cups of water  
2 squares of chocolate  

Yolks of 6 eggs  
1 teaspoon vanilla  
⅛ teaspoon of salt

Melt chocolate. Boil sugar and water until it spins a thread; pour slowly over the beaten eggs; when all is in add the chocolate and vanilla, beat constantly until creamy, put between layers and over top. This will fill and cover a three layer cake.

Make the cake with the whites, using the yolks for the filling. When properly made this is delicious. It does not get hard and is quite economical.

### Soft Chocolate Icing

3 cups sugar
1 cup milk
2 eggs
¼ cup butter (½ stick or ⅛ of lb.)

4 ounces unsweetened chocolate
1 teaspoon vanilla
⅛ teaspoon soda

Beat eggs together, add to sugar, milk and butter. Add soda. Cook stirring constantly until a soft ball will form in cool water. Cool slightly. Beat until creamy and consistency to spread.

### Another Chocolate Icing

Make the usual white fluffy icing, and while still hot, add melted or grated chocolate beating until stiff enough to use.

### Cream Chocolate Filling

2 squares of unsweetened chocolate
1 cup boiling water
¾ cup sugar
1 tablespoon butter

2 tablespoons cornstarch dissolved
in ¼ cup water
1 teaspoon vanilla

Melt chocolate in double boiler, add sugar, water and butter. Add cornstarch and cook for 5 minutes or until it becomes a thick jelly, stir constantly. Cool, add vanilla, and spread between layers.

### Cocoa Filling

6 tablespoons butter
6 tablespoons cocoa
1 tablespoon strong coffee

Sufficient 4X sugar to make it the
right consistency to spread

Cream butter, add cocoa and coffee. When well blended, add as much sugar as is necessary.

### Mocha Frosting

¼ cup butter
1½ cups sugar (4X)
¼ teaspoon vanilla

1 tablespoon cocoa
Coffee infusion

Cream butter, add cocoa, add coffee and sugar gradually to make right consistency to spread.

### Mocha Filling

Wash and cream ½ cup butter until very light. Add 4X sugar, about 1 lb., which is rolled and sifted, beat until very fluffy. Dissolve 3 tablespoons cocoa in ¼ cup hot strong coffee, add 1 teaspoon vanilla, let cool and gradually add to butter and sugar. Add more or less sugar as desired to spread between layers and over top. It will be quite soft over top, but good.

## Pineapple Cake Filling

| | |
|---|---|
| 1 cup drained crushed pineapple | 2 egg yolks |
| ½ cup pineapple juice | Juice of 1 lemon |
| ¾ cup sugar | Few grains of salt |
| 2 tablespoons cornstarch | |

Mix all together, cook in double boiler until quite thick. Cool, spread between layers of cake. Cover top with white icing using the 2 whites of eggs. See White Icing recipe.

## Lemon Filling No. 1

| | |
|---|---|
| 1 cup sugar | 1 apple |
| 1 egg | Juice and grated rind of 1 lemon |
| Butter the size of walnut | |

Grate apple and mix all ingredients together well; put in double boiler and cook till transparent and thick enough to drop from spoon; spread between layers of cake, ice the top of cake with white icing.

## Lemon Filling No. 2

| | |
|---|---|
| Yolks of 5 eggs | ¼ lb. butter |
| 1 cup sugar | ¾ cup milk |
| 5 tablespoons flour | Juice and grated rind of 1 orange |
| Juice of 1 lemon | |

Mix sugar and flour together dry. Beat eggs, add sugar and flour, and mix well. Add all other ingredients, put in double boiler and cook until thick, stirring constantly. It should cook long enough to cook flour. Cool slightly, spread on layers while warm.

## Lemon Cheese Filling

| | |
|---|---|
| 1 cup sugar | 3 tablespoons of butter |
| 4 tablespoons corn starch, dissolved in a little water | 2 eggs |
| | 2 egg yolks |
| Juice of 2 lemons | |

Put all together; cook in double boiler until thick; let cool before spreading between layers of cake.

## Butterscotch Filling

| | |
|---|---|
| ¾ cup sugar | 1 cup chopped pecan meats |
| 1 cup sweet milk | 4 tablespoons butter |
| 3 tablespoons cornstarch dissolved in a little cold water | 2 egg yolks |
| | 1 teaspoon vanilla |
| ⅛ teaspoon soda | |

Into a skillet put butter and sugar and cook together until a golden brown.

Heat milk, add soda and pour into sugar mixture. Simmer until there are no lumps. Mix cornstarch and egg yolks; pour over the hot mixture and cook in double boiler until quite thick. Let cool, add vanilla and nuts; spread between layers. Cover top with plain caramel icing or white icing.

# canapes and sandwiches

# CHAPTER XIV

# Canapes and Sandwiches

## Canapes

Canapes are made from old bread old enough to slice and toast nicely. The slices are usually ¼-inch thick, and the canapes cut into small rings, circles, cubes or diamonds, or any fancy shape (not more than 2 bites). These portions of bread are toasted, or fried a golden brown in butter or deep fat. They are then covered with any mixture preferred. The mixture is usually of some rich, tasty relish. Canapes are served in place of a cocktail, usually at formal dinners before the soup.

## New Canape

To one-half cup boiled salad dressing add two teaspoons gelatine which has been softened in one-fourth cup cold milk and dissolved by standing over hot water. Add two tablespoons each of finely chopped onion and green pepper. Mold in tiny cups. Toast thin slices of stale bread cut in square or in fancy shapes, spread with melted butter, and place on this a thin slice of peeled tomato. Unmold gelatine mixture, cut in thin slices and top the tomato. Serve as a first course at luncheon.

## Anchovy Canape

Boil hard 2 eggs, mash yolk, add seasoning and anchovy paste, keeping mixture stiff enough to shape in ball as large as a bird egg. Roll in chopped parsley.

Prepare toast, spread with soft butter or mayonnaise; place ball in center, and cover edge with grated egg white. Sprinkle white generously with paprika or drop tiny flakes of pimento over.

## Cheese and Anchovy Canape

Work some soft American cheese into a paste with some anchovy sauce, season with a dash of salt and some paprika, spread rather thickly upon round slices of toasted bread and put in a hot oven until the cheese bubbles, then serve quickly, garnished with a sprig of watercress.

## Cheese Canape

Cut the bread either in round circles or strips like fingers. Toast or fry in butter. Cream the cheese and soft butter together enough to make the required number, having the cheese grated if hard. Cover the toast and over the top put rings of stuffed olives, or the olives may be minced and arranged. The canape may be served on a small plate on the table when the guests are seated, or passed before they come into the dining room. They take the place of a cocktail.

### Tomato Canape

Prepare toast. Peel and cut slice of very firm tomato to fit toast.

Butter toast, place tomato, spread with mayonnaise. Cover center with grated egg yolk and border with the grated white. Drop a small portion of mayonnaise in center and stick a small stuffed olive in top.

### Caviar Canape

One small jar caviar. Add lemon juice and salad oil until a smooth paste is made. Spread on slice of bread and cover top with grated hard boiled egg.

### Caviar and Cream Cheese Canape

1 small jar caviar            1 package cream cheese

Mix caviar and cream cheese, whipping the mixture until light. Use for canapes.

### Ham Canape

Grind cooked lean ham. Prepare toast and cover with minced ham.

Have ready a cup of whipped cream. Add to cream freshly grated horseradish to flavor highly, salt and pepper. With a forcing bag and tube make a rosette on the ham and sprinkle with more ham or paprika.

The toast must have something to hold the ham in place—soft butter or mayonnaise.

Any other tasty meat may be used in place of ham.

### Artichoke Canape

Use the canned artichoke bottoms. Soak in highly seasoned French dressing about 1 hour. Rub butter soft with minced pimento until smooth.

Spread toast with butter, place choke, and decorate top with strip of pimento or rings of stuffed olives.

## SANDWICHES

The sandwiches given in this book are more for afternoon teas than for feeding real hungry people.

Sandwiches should be made of bread 24 hours old and of a sandwich loaf. The sandwich loaf gives better slices, is whiter, and the grain closer than in the ordinary loaf bread.

Brown, white and rye breads are those generally used. Nut breads are easily made at home and very effectively used with a light spread—sweet or plain.

Bread should be cut in thin slices and all crust removed. The shapes are cut to suit the individual. When using cutters if they are kept damp by dipping in warm water, the slices are not ragged around the edges, and the work is more easily done.

A cooked dressing (or cooked mayonnaise) is better for most sandwiches, especially meats. Cooked dressing acts as a binder, allows a generous filling, and never gets soggy. The kind of dressing has been specified in the different recipes.

See Dressings for cooked mayonnaise.

## Chicken Sandwiches

| | |
|---|---|
| 2 cups ground chicken | ½ cup cooked mayonnaise |
| 1 cup chopped and ground celery | Salt and cayenne pepper to taste |

Boil or roast chicken; pull from bones and grind. Chop fine and grind celery. Mix and add seasoning and mayonnaise, more or less as needed.

Cut bread in thin slices,, and in any shape desired. Spread filling generously between bread.

## Tongue Sandwiches

Make the same as chicken, using tongue instead.

## Ham Sandwich No. 1

| | |
|---|---|
| 1 cup ground boiled ham | Season well with salt and pepper |
| 1 cup ground celery | if needed |
| 1 cup thick cooked mayonnaise | |

Remove fat from ham. Cut celery before putting through chopper. Mix with the dressing, using more or less dressing. Have bread one day old, cut into thin slices, trim crust and spread with mayonnaise. Cooked dressing or mayonnaise will make a filling which will hold together and not get soggy but be very moist. The dressing is rich enough without spreading with butter or mayonnaise.

## Ham Sandwich No. 2

Cut thin slice of bread, spread with butter, put slice of baked ham to cover, two slices of dill pickle and place on top another slice of buttered bread. The bread may be left in full size slices or cut into smaller size. Sometimes prepared mustard or mayonnaise is used in place of the butter. The crust may be removed or left on the slices of bread.

## Ham Sandwich No. 3

Spread biscuit or slices of bread with soft butter and place slice of ham between.

## Sandwich Filling of Sardine

| | |
|---|---|
| ½ cup sardines free from skin and bones | 1 teaspoon lemon juice |
| ¼ cup soft butter | 2 hard boiled eggs |
| ½ teaspoon salt | ½ cup cooked dressing or mayonnaise |
| | Dash of pepper |

Blend sardines and butter, grate eggs and add with all other seasoning and spread between thin slices of bread.

### Italian Sandwiches

1 lb. calves liver                    Salt and pepper to taste
Stuffed olives                        Rye bread for sandwiches

Boil liver in salt water, put through food chopper, using fine knife, measure and use same amount of stuffed olives also ground, moisten with mayonnaise to consistency to spread, season with salt and pepper, spread between rye bread.

### Club Sandwich

Three slices of hot toast buttered.

On first slice of toast place leaf of lettuce, a slice each of white chicken meat, pickle, strip of crisp bacon; spread lightly with mayonnaise and place on top of this a piece of toast. On top of the second piece of toast place a leaf of lettuce, spread with mayonnaise, then a slice of tomato, more chicken meat, pickle, bacon and more mayonnaise. Top with third piece of buttered toast.

Cut in triangles and serve while bread is hot and fresh.

### Asparagus Sandwich

Cut thin slices of fresh bread. Spread with mayonnaise, place a stalk of white tender asparagus on one edge, having it the length of the bread; roll up like a jelly roll and stick with a tooth pick to hold. Wrap a narrow strip of pimento (canned) round and round the roll. Remove tooth pick before serving.

### Spanish Cucumber Sandwich

1 cup cucumber                        1 green pepper
1 cup celery                          6 stuffed olives
¼ cup Spanish onion

Chop fine and add sufficient cooked dressing and seasoning to spread between thin slices of bread.

### Cucumber Sandwich

Take tender cucumbers—those with small seeds—and peel and cut into thin slices lengthwise.

Cut sandwich bread in slices and cut each slice in half giving a long sandwich—about 1½ inches by 3 inches long. Spread with mayonnaise and put cucumber between.

Cucumber sandwiches are not good if made too long before eating.

Have mayonnaise highly seasoned and no other seasoning will be necessary. Do not use cooked mayonnaise.

### Russian Sandwich

Use equal amounts of canned pimentoes, stuffed olives and sour cucumber pickles. Have ready rye bread, cooked dressing.

Rinse peppers, and with them grind olives and pickles in food chopper.

Drain in strainer, and when dry add sufficient dressing to make a mixture to spread.

Cut rye bread in round shapes, using doughnut cutter for the top slice. Spread and place slices together putting a ring of sliced olive in the hole in top slice.

### Tomato Sandwich

Select firm, not over ripe tomatoes of medium size. Peel and cut in quarter inch slices. Place on cheese cloth to drain. Cut bread in round pieces using a tea biscuit cutter. Spread one side of bread with mayonnaise, place on the slice of tomato, cover with another slice which has been spread with mayonnaise. Real mayonnaise must be used with tomato.

### Cottage Cheese Sandwich

Make the cheese quite dry; add enough full milk or cream to make a stiff paste. Season with salt and pepper, cut five slices of bread a little thicker than for plain sandwiches, spread between the layers like a layer cake until the five are used. Let stand about an hour, then slice into six slices and you have a layer or ribbon sandwich which is quite pretty. This filling should be colored any color to carry out the color motif, pink, green or red to make them effective. I use Burnett's color paste. Pimentoes chopped fine may be added, also parsley chopped fine will give the green color. Plenty of paprika will make them pinkish.

### Celery Sandwich

Mash 1 cup of cream cheese to a paste, using milk, mayonnaise or soft butter. Have 1 cup of tender celery and stuffed olives chopped very fine. Mix the two and spread between thin slices of bread.

### Ribbon Sandwiches

| | |
|---|---|
| 1 loaf brown bread | 4 tablespoons cream or milk |
| 1 loaf white sandwich bread | Bit of pink coloring |
| 4 Neufchatel cheese or ½ lb. cottage cheese | Salt and pepper to suit taste |

The brown bread should be large enough in size to make a slice to fit with the square sandwich white loaf, or better still, if it is made to order, use a square pan for cooking.

Moisten the cheese with the milk and have the mixture thin enough to spread between the slices, add the coloring to make a pretty pink, season highly with salt and pepper. Cut bread in slices ¼ inch thick, remove any crust. Use 2 brown and 3 white slices. Build up the squares, using a white for the center, this gives a white, pink and brown layer. Stack together and cover with damp cloth until all are made. Then cut into 6 slices and you have a beautiful as well as a good sandwich.

Brown nut bread is easily made at home and when used to make the sandwiches is delicious.

## Rolled Sandwiches

To make rolled sandwiches you must use very fresh bread. Cut the slices thin and as they are cut place on a damp cloth and cover with another. Spread with a soft, sticky filling, roll up and wrap each one in wax paper until set; unwrap and pile on a platter.

Soft butter and chopped parsley; ground ham moistened with dressing; sardines boned and mixed with dressing, or cottage cheese seasoned, all make good fillings.

If you cut the slices the long way spread roll and wrap; let stand still next day, or several hours, then cut into slices like a jelly roll. You have a pretty sandwich and not hard to make. They will look like a slice of jelly cake when cut. Remove the crust before cutting the slices.

## American Cheese Sandwich

½ lb. cheese grated                          1 egg
1 cup white sauce                            Salt and cayenne pepper to taste

Make the usual white sauce, add cheese while hot and stir until melted. Add seasoning and egg and cook over hot water until thick. When cold spread between thin slices of rye bread.

Pimentoes, stuffed olives or 2 tablespoons tomato catsup may be used to vary the filling.

## Hot Cheese Sandwich

Rub soft American cheese to a paste, moisten with tomato catsup and a little butter. Spread between thin slices of bread, cut any shape desired, and toast slightly in hot oven. Serve immediately.

## Open Pimento Toast

Cut slices of whole wheat bread one-fourth inch thick, trim off crust and toast both sides. Butter one side and spread with pimento cheese. Cut each slice in three fingers, place on baking sheet, put in hot oven until cheese begins to melt.

Serve immediately with coffee.

Nice for last course at dinner.

## Beet and Cheese Sandwich

Spread bread with creamed cheese, then a layer of finely chopped beets seasoned with French dressing.

Use as an open sandwich.

## Tasty Sandwich

Spread a slice of brown bread with butter mixed with a pinch of mustard; for top layer spread with butter and cheese. Put the two slices together.

White bread may be used.

## Open Sandwich

Cut thin slices of bread, cut round with tea biscuit cutter. Mash season and color pink, cream or cottage cheese. Put into bag with star tube. Press large rosette in center of round, using tiny ones around edge. This completes sandwich.

## Tutti Frutti Cheese Sandwich

| | |
|---|---|
| 1 Philadelphia cream cheese | 1 tablespoon of minced crystallized |
| 1 tablespoon of minced maraschino | pineapple |
| cherries | 1 tablespoon salted, finely chopped |
| | nuts |

Mash cheese with a fork and add enough cream or mayonnaise to moisten, add all the other ingredients and mix well. Spread between thin slices of bread.

Canned pineapple may be used but is drained very dry. The juice of the pineapple or cherries may be used in place of the cream to moisten the cheese.

## Pineapple Sandwich

Use sliced, canned pineapple, large size and split each slice. Spread square slices of bread with mayonnaise, place slice of pineapple, cut in triangular shape, this gives two sandwiches.

Sandwich loaf should be used.

## Orange Sandwich (Sweet)

| | |
|---|---|
| Yolks of 4 hard-boiled eggs | 1 cup soft butter |
| 1 tablespoon more or less of orange | 1/3 cup 4X sugar |
| juice | Grated rind of 1 orange |

Spread on bread or cake.

## Honey Sandwich

Moisten cottage cheese or cream cheese with honey. Spread bread with soft butter, then the honey mixture; put on top slice.

Maple syrup or sugar makes a maple sandwich. Spread between thin slices of bread.

## Maraschino Cherry Sandwich

Cream cheese, moisten with maraschino juice and the sliced or chopped cherry. Spread between thin slices of bread.

## Pineapple Sandwich (Sweet)

| | |
|---|---|
| 1 cup grated pineapple | Juice 1/2 lemon |
| 1/4 cup sugar | |

Cook until thick, cool and spread on bread or angel cake.

### Date and Ginger Sandwich

1 cup dates chopped        ¼ cup preserved ginger

Cook together to a paste, chopped dates and preserved ginger. Moisten with syrup from the ginger, and spread between thin slices of bread.

### Date Sandwich

1 lb. dates        1 cup water
1 cup sugar        Juice of 1 large lemon

Stone dates and cut in pieces, cook all ingredients together until thick, cool. Spread between thin slices of bread. Other fruits or nuts may be used.

### Date Loaf for Sandwich

1 cup milk        2 cups whole wheat flour
¼ cup sugar        ½ teaspoon salt
1 cup chopped dates        3 teaspoons baking powder

Bake in small loaf and cut for sandwiches.

### Fig Sandwich

¼ lb. figs ground        ¼ cup water

Cook together to a paste and add nut meats.
Raisins, dates or marmalade may be used in place of figs. Spread between thin slices of bread.

### Salad Sandwich Loaf

1 loaf sandwich bread        Grated raw carrots
  Cottage cheese        Cooked salad dressing
  Chopped watercress (or green        Shredded raw cabbage
    pepper)        Hard-boiled eggs

Remove crusts from loaf. Cut lengthwise into 4 thin slices. Spread first slice with cottage cheese mixed with a little chopped watercress or green pepper; the next slice with grated raw carrots mixed with cooked salad dressing; and the third slice with finely shredded cabbage mixed with the chopped whites of hard-cooked eggs and cooked salad dressing. Top with remaining slice of bread. Cover whole loaf with cooked salad dressing and sprinkle top and sides with the sieved yolks of hard-cooked eggs. This makes 12 or 14 servings.

*fruits*

# CHAPTER XV

# Fruits and Ways of Serving

## Fruits

Fruit and vegetables are Nature's own protective foods keeping our bodies sound and aiding the resistance to ill health. Fruits should be used freely thus supplying the needed mineral salts, vitamins and cellulose which is so necessary. Fruits often stimulate the appetite to take other necessary food.

## Peaches

Being one of Georgia's prize products peaches are served morning, noon and night. Raw, with cream; made into ice creams; baked, in pies and cobblers; preserves, pickles, canned and dried. In different sections of the book will be found various recipes for peach dishes.

Do not ice or chill peaches. They are much sweeter when kept from the ice but put in a cool place. Being kept on ice will prevent too rapid ripening but circumstances will determine what to do.

## To Serve Fresh Peaches

Select ripe fruit, rinse quickly and dry. Place several peaches on a fruit plate with a fruit knife. Finger bowls should be used afterwards. Peaches may be placed in a fruit dish and passed. The finger bowl is then set in the fruit plate with the knife. The guest removes the bowl placing at the top of service until needed. Finger bowl may be placed on a mat or not, depending on the service. Bowl, mat and all are placed above the plate. When used the finger bowl is replaced in plate or used just where it stands.

Any fresh fruit after washing and drying may be served on a fruit plate the same as peaches.

## Figs

Select soft, ripe figs. Peel, taking off the very thin skin. Serve plain or with cream.

Figs may be served unpeeled the same as peaches or other fruit.

## Watermelon as a First Course

As a first course for luncheon, select a perfect melon; remove the meat that is best in rather large sections. Cut into one-inch cubes. Pile on an attractive plate, sprinkle with crushed ice; serve with a fork. Grape leaves make a pretty foundation for the red melon and ice. Grapefruit glasses holding the red cubes, with the crushed ice in the outer glass is an attractive way also.

To use a French baller, making the watermelons in the shape of pink marbles is very pretty—each ball a bite. These potato ballers are in several sizes, made of steel with a good, firm handle. The cutter is just half of the ball—it is pushed into the melon or potato and turned to form a perfect marble. All seed should be removed—just the firm meat used.

### To Serve Watermelon at Table

Cut slices crosswise, remove rind and white down to pink. Place slice on plate and serve with a fork.

### Watermelon a la Georgia

Select good, cold melon. Cut lengthwise into quarters, place slice on plate and serve with a fork. Nothing less than a quarter slice would satisfy a real Georgian, thus allowing the privilege to eat the heart and red meat only, leaving ends and pink meat.

At a watermelon cutting not even plates are used. The guests gather around a long table and are served.

### Watermelon as a Dessert

Select a good cold melon. Cut in slices crosswise, about ¾ of an inch thick. With a heart sandwich cutter, cut through the slice, making pink hearts. Pile on a cold plate, sprinkle with crushed ice and serve. The cutter should be dainty in size. Any fancy cutter or several shapes on one plate would be pretty. This is used as a dessert or a fruit course.

### Cantaloupes

This fruit grows to perfection in Georgia and is enjoyed greatly during the season for breakfast, lunch or dinner.

### To Serve Cantaloupe

Wash, dry and chill. Cut in half serving each guest a half. Salt, pepper or a sprinkle of sugar is used on them.

### Cantaloupes Served Fancy

Select small melons, remove a slice from the top (about ¼ of melon). From another melon, peel and cut enough cubes to fill the one to be served.

### Cantaloupe Balls

With a vegetable French baller make balls the size of a marble from the cantaloupes. Serve in small glass dish placed in crushed ice. Often glass fruit sets come for the purpose. These balls may be served plain, or with lemon juice or cocktail sauce used over them.

### Pineapple

Peel, slice and core pineapple. Pack in sugar for several hours before serving.

### Pineapple for Lunch or Dinner

Wash, scrub, and slice in ¾ inch slices. Remove core and cut in small triangular sections leaving the peel on. Place 5 or 6 sections around a mound of pulverized sugar. Each section is picked up by the peel, stuck into the sugar and eaten.

### Canned Pineapple

This is a most adaptable fruit being used as fruit, in salads, desserts, sandwiches and to garnish.

The canned pineapple should always be used in a congealed salad, as the fresh fruit contains an element which destroys the gelatine. Canned pineapple is preserved thus correcting the gelatine destroying property.

### To Serve Oranges

Wash and dry fruit. Cut in half and remove seed. Cut sections from skin at the outer side so the spoon may enter easily. The spoon will free the rest of pulp.

### Orange Juice

Cut oranges in half, ream or squeeze out juice. Remove seed and serve in fruit juice glass. No sugar.

### To Peel Oranges

Peel the same as grapefruit saving all juice to add to sections. Large oranges are easier to work with.

### Grapefruit

This is a fruit almost as valuable as oranges, and is used as a first course for breakfast, lunch or dinner; either as a cocktail or plain, cut in half.

### To Prepare Grapefruit

Cut in half, remove seed and take out core with scissors or core cutter. With a small paring or grapefruit knife cut each section of meat or pulp free from the white skin sections, leaving skins still clinging to the rind. When eaten each section can be lifted out with spoon and no juice will fly. Grapefruit may be eaten with salt or sugar.

### To Peel Grapefruit for Cocktails, Etc.

Peel the fruit as you would an apple taking off the rind, going through the white skin to the meat or pulp and removing every particle of the white membrane. With a large, stiff pointed paring knife go down to the center just inside the section and lift it out. The first section is the hardest to remove. For other sections stick paring knife between skin and section cutting edge up at the very core, entirely through grapefruit from right to left. Slowly bring knife to the outer surface thus freeing the skin from section of pulp. Turn cutting edge down and place edge at the very core, turn edge gently and pull or push section free from white skin on the far side. This removes the whole section and seed. Take out seed and a perfect section of fruit is obtained. Continue until all sections are removed. This leaves core and skin, which is called the rag, intact.

A large grapefruit may be peeled and sections removed in 2 or 3 minutes or less.

### Grapefruitade

Use equal parts grapefruit juice, water and crushed ice. Sweeten or use plain.

### Baked Bananas

Peel and cut the banana in half, then lengthwise. Dip in milk, then roll in bread crumbs, place in buttered baking dish and cook in hot oven 15 minutes. Serve as a fruit or dessert; the latter calls for cream.

### Broiled Bananas

Peel and cut bananas in half, then crosswise. Roll in flour, then broil in butter for several minutes, turning to brown on both sides. Use just enough butter to brown and turn well.

### Lemons

The lemon belongs to the citrus family and plays a large part in our daily diet for seasoning and drinks. Many recipes call for lemons.

### Apples

Apples contain an abundance of potassium and sodium salts, and the acids are beneficial to almost every one. An apple with much acid contains more sugar than a sweet one.

Fruit juices purify the blood and are essential to our health. Of course, young children have to have their apples cooked in order to digest them; this has to be tried out and determined by the mother. Don't oversweeten the cooked apples. If the sugar is added to apple sauce after it is cooked, less will be required.

A tart apple cooks quicker and smoother than a sweet one. A bit of lemon juice or cream of tartar to very sweet apples will help them become tender.

In using apples for salad, do not peel them. The red skin adds to the dish. If you must remove the skin, dip them into boiling water for a moment, then peel. This method will make them peel easily, like a tomato, and a red apple will still retain some of its color.

Fried apples for breakfast is a great Southern dish especially served with broiled crisp bacon. Usually the apples are fried in the bacon grease.

Apple pie is sometimes called "America's favorite dessert," and you seldom see a man pass it up uneaten. A piece of cheese seems to be the finishing touch to a good apple pie.

## Apples Just Different

Select medium and uniform size apples; peel and core an apple for each guest. Put them into a light syrup and let boil until tender, but still hold their shape. Place around a roast of pork and serve. The apples may be hot or cold.

If you wish the apples colored, make the syrup a pretty green, pink or red, using same coloring as that for cakes or icings; a few drops in the syrup will be sufficient.

Do not crowd the vessel when cooking; turn apples during the boiling so both sides will get into the syrup. Use sugar to taste according to the apple. Apples cooked in this way serve as a relish with meat or as a salad, filling center with nuts and celery.

## Christmas Apples

Peel and core apples of medium size, fill center with sugar and place in a baking dish.

Make a syrup of two tablespoons of red drop cinnamon candy and two cups of water. Let the candy dissolve in the water; cover apples with the red syrup, cover the dish and bake in a slow oven until soft and clear. Serve hot or cold with any kind of meat.

## Scalloped Apples

| | |
|---|---|
| 3 cups soft bread crumbs | ½ teaspoon nutmeg |
| ¼ lb. melted butter, poured over bread crumbs | ¼ teaspoon cinnamon |
| 6 apples, peeled and sliced thin | 1 cup sugar |

Mix apples, sugar and spices. Put layer of buttered crumbs into saucepan, then layer of apples until all are used, with crumbs on top, cover and cook in moderate oven about forty minutes.

## Fried Apples

Wash and core apples, then cut into quarters or smaller. Into a fry pan put a small quantity of bacon drippings; when hot put in fruit; fry until brown. Drain off the excess grease, keeping the pan hot. Replace over fire, and into the pan put a small quantity of water (three or four tablespoons), cover tight. Steam until tender and almost dry. Sprinkle with sugar and serve.

## Another Way to Fry Apples

Peel and core apples; cut into slices crosswise about ¼ inch thick.

Have a saucepan with deep fat; drop in a few pieces at a time and cook until brown and tender. Drain on paper and while hot, place on hot platter. Put on a small dot of butter and sprinkle with sugar. Continue frying until all are cooked. Place apples close together, one layer upon another as they are cooked and seasoned; they are better kept hot. Serve with broiled bacon.

## Apples for Breakfast

Peel and core large apples and cut crosswise in half-inch slices. Make a light syrup of sugar and water, drop a few slices in at a time and cook until they are tender. Remove and continue until they are all cooked. Serve cold with a small amount of thin syrup. Serve two rings with a large prune in center. These apple rings may be colored pink or green in the cooking.

## Baked Apples

Select apples of uniform size, wash and core, taking care not to go through the apple, as you want the place where you remove the core to form a cup. Make a cut around the center of the apple with a knife, going just through the peel. Fill the center (left by coring) with sugar and raisins. Bake in moderate oven until done, for medium size about 30 minutes. A bit of butter may be placed on each apple if desired. When ready to serve remove the peel from the top half of apple, which leaves the other part as a cup holding the raisins. Serve with cream or milk.

## Ring Mold of Apples

| | |
|---|---|
| 1 quart sliced apples | 1 tablespoon gelatine |
| 1½ cups sugar | Lemon juice or nutmeg |
| ¾ cup water | |

Cook sugar and water until it threads. Have ready 1 quart of apples peeled, cored and sliced. Add apples and cook to thick marmalade. Flavor with lemon juice or nutmeg. Soak 1 tablespoon of gelatine in ¼ cup cold water for five minutes, add to hot apples. Pour into ring mold until cold. Fill center with whipped cream or jelly meringue, over all pour 1 cup melted red jelly. Sprinkle top with toasted nuts chopped fine and serve.

## Apples and Cranberries

| | |
|---|---|
| 1 pint cranberries | 4 or 5 apples |
| 1 cup sugar | ¾ pint water |

Cook cranberries in the water until cranberries are done; put through strainer; add one cup of sugar to berries; pare, core and quarter apples; put apples into berries and cook till apples are tender but not cooked to pieces; pour into dish and serve as any fruit or jelly.

## Cranberry Relish

| | |
|---|---|
| 1 lb. cranberries | 2 apples |
| 2 oranges | 2 cups sugar |

Wash and pick cranberries. Remove core and seed from apples. Remove seed and center membrane from oranges. Put fruit, peel and all, through food chopper using medium knife, saving all juice. Add sugar, mix well and put in jar. Keep in refrigerator. Will keep for weeks. Add more or less sugar as desired.

# cereals

# CHAPTER XVI

## Cereals

The average person thinks of cereals as a breakfast food made from grain. These may be put into three classes: raw, partly cooked and ready to serve. They are made from oats, corn, wheat, barley and rye, and are known by name as hominy (grits), oatmeal, oat flakes, cream of wheat and many other mixtures, cooked and uncooked, prepared by food manufacturers. Some cooked cereals need to be stirred constantly, while others do not, and I have tried to make my recipes explicit so as to avoid confusion.

Southerners do not class rice as a cereal but as a starchy food or vegetable, taking the place of potatoes and bread.

### To Cook Oatmeal

| | |
|---|---|
| 1 cup oat flakes | 1 teaspoon salt |
| 2 cups boiling water | |

Have water boiling, add salt and sprinkle oat flakes into water. Stir until thoroughly mixed and the mixture begins to boil well. Have ready the lower part of double boiler with water hot. Place the boiler into the outer one and continue to cook until done, about one hour. Once or twice during the cooking turn the oatmeal from the sides to the center. Keep covered and have plenty of water for the cooking.

### Leftover Oatmeal

| | |
|---|---|
| 1 cup cold oatmeal | 3 eggs |
| 1 can pimentoes | Salt and pepper to taste |
| 2 tabespoons butter | |

Into a skillet put butter, oatmeal and milk; heat and stir until well blended, using a gentle heat. Add eggs and stir as if cooking scrambled eggs. Add seasoning and serve. This is sometimes called mock brains and is a good substitute for meat. Particularly good for small children.

### Cream of Wheat

| | |
|---|---|
| 1 cup of cream of wheat | 1 teaspoon of salt |
| 4 cups of boiling water | |

Into the upper part of a double boiler place the boiling water and salt, place over the fire and pour the cereal in slowly, stirring constantly until it comes to a hard boil, then place over the bottom part of the double boiler, which is well filled with boiling water. Cover, lower the fire and cook as long as needed. Stir occasionally.

## Hominy

| | |
|---|---|
| 1 cup of hominy (grits) | 2 teaspoons of salt |
| 4 cups of boiling water | |

Pour the hominy into the boiling water and stir until it comes to a good boil. Lower the fire or pull to a slow boiling point on range. Cover and boil slowly for one hour, stir frequently. When ready to serve, put a small lump of butter into the hominy and beat well for several minutes.

The beating whitens and makes the hominy much lighter.

Half a cup of hot milk or thin cream in place of butter can be used.

An asbestos mat is a good thing to place under the hominy pot to prevent burning.

To grease the pot with a small piece of lard or cooking oil will prevent scorching or sticking.

Hominy to be the best must be stirred often while cooking.

## To Fry Hominy

Cook as directed and while warm fill jelly glasses to mold. When ready to fry unmold and cut into slices one-half inch thick, which gives round circles.

Dip into flour then into an egg which has been beaten just enough to mix well with one tablespoon of water or milk. Into a skillet put just enough lard or bacon grease to make the circles of hominy brown and turn easily; brown on both sides. Serve on a hot platter or garnish a dish of chops with a border of the circles.

A spoonful of cranberry jelly in the center of each slice adds to the garnishing. A half of a canned peach may be used instead of the jelly. A slice of fried apple with the hominy will go nicely with broiled bacon for breakfast for a change.

## Baked Hominy

| | |
|---|---|
| 2 cups cold boiled hominy | 2 eggs |
| 1 cup milk | ½ tablespoon salt |
| 2 tablespoons butter or bacon drippings | ⅛ tablespoon pepper |

Heat milk and butter, add hominy and mix until smooth; add beaten eggs, seasoning and pour into a buttered baking dish.

Bake until firm and brown on top (about 30 to 40 minutes).

## Lye Hominy

Into a fry pan put two or three tablespoons of butter or bacon drippings, pour in the hominy, stir until seasoned, add a little milk or water, let cook slowly until well seasoned and very little moisture. Use 2 or 3 cups of lye hominy.

## Dry Rice

| | |
|---|---|
| 1 cup rice | 2 teaspoons salt |
| 6 cups boiling water | |

Wash and scrub the rice between the hands. Have water boiling hard add salt. Add rice slowly so as not to stop the boiling. Boil hard until rice is done, 20 to 30 minutes, test with a grain between the fingers, and there is no hard center. Pour into a colander to drain. Rinse with hot water, place colander over boiling water to steam, cover with cloth, toss with a fork if necessary to fluff.

### Steamed Rice

1 cup rice  
1½ cups water

½ tablespoon salt

Wash rice well, pour into top of steamer, sprinkle the salt over rice, and add the cup of cold water.

Bring water to a boil in the bottom of the steamer and boil rapidly for an hour or longer, until rice is done and fluffy.

Rice should be washed in several waters.

A rice steamer will have to be used to obtain good results.

### A Border of Rice

After rice is cooked and drained, add butter and white pepper to season. Have a border mold well buttered and pack the rice in good and firm.

Place mold in hot water or place where it will keep hot. When ready to serve unmold on platter, fill center with vegetables or creamed meat. Still another food may be placed around the rice border—chops, stuffed tomatoes, squashes or peppers. Garnish platter. This holds almost the entire meal, rice, vegetables and meat.

### Rice Pilau

1 large fryer  
¼ cup butter

2 cups rice  
Salt and pepper to taste

Prepare a large fryer or young hen as for frying, and put into a sauce pan with several pieces of bacon, white seasoning meat or ⅛ lb. butter. Cover with boiling water and season highly with salt and pepper. Cover and cook slowly until chicken is done. Remove any scum.

When chicken is tender, add rice, and continue to cook for 30 to 40 minutes, until rice is done and mixture is thick. There should be no liquid, and the mixture thick enough to be eaten with a fork. An asbestos mat or thick plate should be put under the stew pan to prevent scorching.

### Scalloped Rice

1 cup of rice cooked dry  
3 eggs boiled hard  
Salt and pepper to taste

1 tablespoon chopped parsley  
½ cup of buttered crumbs  
2 cups of chicken stock

Into a baking dish put layer of rice, then one of eggs until all are used, putting in the seasoning as the layers are put in. Pour over all the chicken stock, cover top with the buttered crumbs, bake until crumbs are brown and the dish gets very hot, serve from the dish in which it is cooked.

White sauce or cold gravy will take the place of the chicken stock.

### Brown Rice—Carrot Casserole

| | |
|---|---|
| 1 cup brown rice | ½ cup top milk or cream |
| 3 slices bacon | 2 tablespoons butter |
| 1 small onion | ½ teaspoon salt |
| 1 cup shredded carrot | ⅛ teaspoon pepper |
| 1 egg yolk | |

Cook unpolished brown rice in 3 cups of salt water until done. Drain. In fry pan broil bacon, remove and mince. Put minced onion in bacon grease and sear till light brown. Mix bacon and onion with rice, add carrots and seasoning. Mix egg yolk with milk and pour over rice, dot top with butter, cover baking dish and cook in moderate oven 40 minutes. Serve from baking dish. White rice, wild rice, or lye hominy may be used.

### Rice and Pimentoes

| | |
|---|---|
| 1 cup rice | 1 can pimentoes |
| 1 cup grated cheese | 2 eggs |
| 1½ cups milk | Salt and red pepper to taste |

Boil rice in salt water until tender, using plenty of water. Drain, add chopped peppers, cheese, milk, which has been warmed, and well beaten eggs, season. Pour into a buttered baking dish, bake 20 minutes in moderate oven.

### Spanish Rice

| | |
|---|---|
| 1 cup rice | 2 sweet red peppers |
| 1 cup tomatoes | 2 tablespoons lard or butter |
| 2 onions | Salt and pepper to taste |

Wash rice and brown in hot lard in fry pan, stirring constantly. Add 3 cups boiling water, peppers and onions which have been sliced thin. Add tomatoes, salt and peppers. Cook slowly until rice is tender and water absorbed—about 30 minutes.

### "Hopping John"

| | |
|---|---|
| 1 cup rice | ¼ lb. of seasoning meat or pork |
| 2 cups white peas | Salt and pepper |
| 2 tablespoons butter | |

Cook peas, being careful to keep them whole in the cooking, using the piece of meat to season. When done have only a small quantity of liquor left in them. Cook rice as you would in recipe for dry rice or use left over. Mix peas and rice together, season with salt, pepper and butter, serve with bread and butter. This is a good and a very nourishing dish.

# nuts and candies

# CHAPTER XVII

## Nuts and Candies

### To Shell Pecans Easily

Pour boiling water over nuts and let stay until cool or shells are soft. Use crackers and crush from end to end. This causes the sides to crack and the meat is loosened and comes out whole. Do not wet too many at a time, a small quantity will be more easily shelled.

When using a hammer crack first on the end.

### Salted Pecans

Shell the nuts, keeping the half meats whole. Into a baking pan place nuts and just enough butter to make them shiny. Toast in moderate oven until crisp, stirring often, and do not scorch. When done, sprinkle generously with salt. Serve as any salted nut.

Pecans require only a short time to toast and will burn easily, so do not have oven too hot.

### To Blanch Peanuts

Shell and cover the peanuts with boiling water; let stand about five minutes, or until the brown skin will slip. Pour off water. With thumb and finger slip off each brown skin; rub well with a towel until all water is gone. Let the nuts stay spread out for several hours. If cooked while damp the oil will sputter.

### Blanched Almonds

Use same recipe as for blanched peanuts.

### Salted Peanuts

Shell and blanch the peanuts and thoroughly dry them. It is better to let them dry overnight or for a day.

For toasting, use a saucepan with salad oil and a frying basket, a flat strainer, which fits into the saucepan. Cover the bottom of basket or strainer with a layer of peanuts about two deep. Plunge into the hot oil and fry until a golden brown. Drain on paper napkin; sprinkle well with salt. Repeat until all are toasted. Get oil hot enough to brown a piece of bread in forty counts. Let the oil reheat between each lot of frying.

### To Peel Chestnuts

With a small paring knife make a half-inch cut into the shell of each chestnut. Into a skillet put one tablespoon of cooking oil or lard, place the chestnuts into the pan, stir and heat thoroughly. Remove from the fire and proceed to remove the hulls. The dark skin will come off with the hull, thus blanching and hulling is done at one time. Try one to see if they are sufficiently heated.

### Salted Almonds

Use same recipe as for salted peanuts.

### To Cook Chestnuts

After chestnuts are peeled, boil in salted water until tender. Mash and use or serve whole.

### Deviled Chestnuts

Roast one pint of chestnuts and remove the shells; sprinkle them over with salt; cook for 3 minutes in butter; dust them with pepper and serve with lettuce salad.

### Peanut Butter

Shell and parch peanuts, remove the skins. Put through a food chopper using the fine knife. Do this twice, to make very fine. To the ground peanuts add oil or butter to make the right consistency to spread. Add salt to taste.

### Peanut Brittle

| | |
|---|---|
| 1 cup sugar | ½ teaspoon vanilla |
| 1 cup toasted peanuts | Few grains salt |

Into a heavy iron skillet put the sugar and stir until melted and a light brown; add the peanuts, vanilla and salt; mix quickly and pour into a buttered dish or marble, spread the mixture thin; when cold, lift from the marble and crack into medium size pices.

### Glace Pecans

| | |
|---|---|
| 1 cup sugar | ½ teaspoon vanilla |
| 1 cup pecan meats whole | Pinch of salt |

Put sugar into a heavy skillet to melt. (No water used). When a golden brown add nuts, flavoring and salt. Mix well and pour into a buttered dish. When cold break into pieces convenient to handle.

### Sugared Pecans

| | |
|---|---|
| 2 cups of pecan nuts | 1 cup water |
| 3 cups sugar | ½ teaspoon vanilla |
| 1 teaspoon butter | Pinch of salt |

Cook sugar and water until it threads; remove from fire. Stir until it becomes creamy; add vanilla, salt and nuts; pour into a buttered dish to harden; cut into squares. Use butter to grease dish.

If you prefer nuts separated, continue stirring until nuts separate but are covered with a white coating.

## Puffed Rice Candy

1 cup of sugar
2 cups of puffed rice

½ teaspoon of vanilla
Pinch of salt

Put sugar into a heavy iron frying pan to melt. (No water at all). Stir all the time until melted and a light brown. Add the salt and puffed rice and vanilla. Mix together and pour at once on a buttered slab or dish. With a wet rolling pin roll out flat, when cold break into small pieces.

## Alma's Date and Nut Cream Candy

3 cups sugar
1 box dates
1 teaspoon vanilla

1 cup milk
1 cup nuts

Boil sugar and milk together until soft ball will form when dropped into cold water. Have dates cut into small pieces, put into sugar and stir until dates are melted. Remove from fire, add vanilla and beat until nearly thick enough to pour out; add nuts (broken in small pieces) and beat until thick enough to pour so it will spread good. Pour into dish and when cool cut into squares.

## Lizzie's Date Loaf Candy

1 lb. package dates
1 cup nut meats (pecans preferred)

2 cups sugar
1 teaspoon vanilla

Seed dates and have these and nut meats ready in mixing bowl, also have wet cloth ready to put mixture on. Boil sugar moistened with ¾ cup water until it spins a good long thread, then pour onto nuts and dates and stir until very stiff, then putonto wet cloth, fold cloth over and flatten out, patting gently with hands. When cold, cut in blocks.

## Concord Cream Mints

3 cups sugar
3 level tablespoon butter
¾ tablespoon vinegar
2 tablespoons heavy cream

½ cup water
1 teaspoon vanilla
Few drops mint

Mix sugar, butter, vinegar, cream and water and cook until hard ball will form in cool water. Do not stir while cooking. Pour on slightly buttered slab. Sprinkle with vanilla and mint, (coloring if used). Let cool to handle. Pull until hard, clip with scissors and put in air tight container for 24 hours.

## Pralines

1½ cups sugar
½ cup sweet cream

1 cup maple syrup

Boil together until a soft ball will form when dropped in cold water.
Remove from fire and beat until creamy then add 2 cups of pecan meats (some broken). Drop on buttered paper from point of spoon to get firm.

## Spanish Cream Candy

| | |
|---|---|
| 1½ cups sugar | 1 teaspoon vanilla |
| ½ cup milk | 1 cup pecan meats |
| ⅓ cup butter | ¼ cup crystallized cherries |
| White of 1 egg | ¼ cup crystallized pineapple |

Boil sugar, milk and butter together until it drops like jelly (flakes off two drops together). Beat whites stiff and pour sugar over egg, beating until stiff and fluffy like icing. This requires lots of beating.

Add fruit and nuts; stir until thick; pour into a buttered pan or dish, let stand until cold and hard, cut in squares; dust with 4X sugar.

## Uncooked Candy (Margaret's Recipe)

| | |
|---|---|
| 2 egg whites | 2 tablespoons water |
| ¼ lb. butter | 4X sugar to make cream |

Flavor with mint, vanilla or any flavor desired. Color to suit fancy.

Cream butter until soft and smooth. Beat eggs until foamy. Add butter, then a portion of sugar. Add water and flavoring. Continue mixing in sugar until creamy and stiff as desired. About one and a half or two pounds of sugar will be required. The batch may be divided, some colored, some made as centers and rolled in melted chocolate. If a portion is thinned with water, marshmallows may be dipped in the coating. This recipe may be used in many ways, flavors and colors.

## Chocolate Nut Truffles

| | |
|---|---|
| 1 cup condensed milk | 1 teaspoon vanilla |
| 4 ounces chocolate | 1 cup nut meats |
| 2½ cups 4X sugar | |

Melt chocolate in top of double boiler. Add milk; let cook two or three minutes, stirring constantly. Remove from fire, add sugar, stir constantly, blending thoroughly the sugar with milk and chocolate. Add vanilla and nuts. Shape as desired. Then the candy may be dipped if desired. This candy can be made quickly.

## Mary Frances' Chocolate Fudge

| | |
|---|---|
| 1½ cups sugar | ⅛ teaspoon soda |
| ½ cup milk | 1 teaspoon vanilla |
| 4 tablespoons butter (half a stick) | 2 squares of unsweetened chocolate |

Put all together, except vanilla, and cook over a brisk heat, stirring constantly. Cook until the mixture leaves a heavy trace of the spoon when stirring.

Remove from the fire, set saucepan into cold water and beat until creamy; add vanilla during the beating.

Pour into a buttered platter, let get cool, cut into squares; when very cold remove; nuts may be added, put in when it begins to cream.

## Betty's Chocolate Fudge

| | |
|---|---|
| 3 cups sugar | ¼ teaspoon salt |
| 2 squares bitter chocolate or 6 table- | ¾ cup milk |
|     spoons cocoa | 1 tablespoon butter |
| 2 tablespoons corn syrup | 1 teaspoon vanilla |

Cook together sugar, chocolate, syrup, butter, salt and milk until it forms a soft ball when dropped in cold water. Set aside until cool. Add vanilla and beat until it creams. Pour into oiled pan and cut into squares.

## Fruit Fudge

| | |
|---|---|
| 2 cups sugar | ⅔ cup corn syrup |
| ⅓ cup hot water | ½ cup raisins |
| ½ cup chopped nuts | Pinch of salt |
| 1 teaspoon vanilla | Whites 2 eggs |

Boil sugar, syrup and water together until it forms a hard ball when dropped into water, add salt and vanilla. Pour slowly over stiffly beaten whites, add nuts and raisins, pour into a buttered pan to harden. The last mixing must be done quickly to prevent graining. Cut into blocks when cool.

## Cocoanut Fudge Candy

| | |
|---|---|
| 1 cup grated cocoanut | ¾ cup whole milk |
| 1 box marshmallows | 1 teaspoon lemon juice ¹ |
| 2 cups sugar | 2 tablespoons butter |
|     Soda the size of a pea | |

Cook to the hard ball. Remove from fire, add 1 cup of grated cocoanut and 1 teaspoon lemon juice. Beat until creamy, pour over marshmallows.

Arrange marshmallows in a buttered pan one inch apart. Pour the candy over marshmallows and let stand until cold and firm. Cut between each marshmallow into squares.

## Uncooked Fondant

| | |
|---|---|
| 3 cups of 4X sugar | ½ teaspoon fruit juice or flavoring |
| 2 egg whites | |

Beat egg whites slightly, add sugar gradually, beating until stiff; add flavoring, knead with the hand until well mixed. The size of eggs varies; more or less sugar may be necessary.

## Chocolate for Dipping

| | |
|---|---|
| 3 squares unsweetened chocolate | 1 teaspoon paraffin |

Cut chocolate and paraffin into small pieces. Melt slowly in double boiler, having the lower part three-quarters full of luke-warm water (110 degrees F.). Do not let temperature of chocolate register above 90 degrees F. Drop candy into chocolate, immersing completely by pressing down with a long-tined fork. Lift out quickly, scraping fork two or three times on side of boiler to remove excess chocolate. Turn fork over to drop candy on waxed paper, giving a slight twirl to make a professional looking curlicue on top.

## Fondant

2 cups granulated sugar                ¾ cup cold water
¼ teaspoon cream of tartar

Put into a saucepan over a gentle fire and stir until the sugar is melted. Let boil moderately without stirring until it reaches 238 degrees or until it spins a short thread.

Remove from fire and pour into a buttered platter, let stand until the hand can stand the heat when placed under the platter. When cool beat rapidly until it becomes creamy.

Then knead until smooth.

Place in a bowl, cover with a wet cloth, put into refrigerator until ready to use. To color and flavor take out a portion; add flavoring and coloring; knead until smooth; shape and finish by dipping in melted, unsweetened chocolate. Press half of nut meats on each side for another variety or roll in chopped nuts.

## To Crystallize Fruit

First, the fruit to be candied should be washed, peeled, or pared if necessary, cut in slices and dropped into boiling water for two or three minutes. Drain well, cover with a syrup made by boiling together one pound of sugar and one cup of water for each pound of fruit. Add fruit, boil rapidly for fifteen minutes, remove from the fire and allow to stand overnight. Next morning boil again for ten or fifteen minutes, repeating the heating and cooling for four to six days. The time depends on how rapidly the water is drawn out and the syrup absorbed. The fruit plumps slowly and the gradual increase in the density of the syrup caused by the many cookings insures tender fruit which is filled with the syrup. After the fruit is transparent and bright, lift from the syrup and dry in the sun or in a cool oven. Fresh trays and constant turning are necessary. Sometimes the fruit is rolled in sugar and wrapped or placed in layers on waxed paper.

## Crystallized Grapefruit Peel

Cut, peel into strips and boil until tender. By changing the water several times the bitter is removed. Make a syrup of equal weights of sugar and water; boil until it spins a thread, then to this add peel equal to the amount of sugar used, boil until the peel is transparent. If the syrup becomes too thick before peel is clear add one or two tablespoons of boiling water to thin the syrup and continue cooking.

When clear (transparent) lift out and drain well, then roll in granulated sugar, let dry slightly and it is ready to serve or pack.

A good test when cooking the peel is to bend one strip and place on a plate, if it stays bent, the cooking is sufficient, if it opens continue cooking. It is quite a nice idea to color some of the peel, pink, green or red.

Add a few drops of coloring to the syrup. Let the coloring be very delicate; vivid coloring is not attractive.

Orange peel may be used same as grapefruit peel.

## Apple Crystals

2 cups sugar  
2 large firm apples  
1 cup water

Granulated sugar to roll when dry-  
ing

Peel, core, quarter, and cut into slices about one-half inch thick; this gives rather crescent shaped slices. Put sugar and water to boil. Drop one dozen pieces at a time into syrup and boil gently until clear, transparent and tender when tested with a straw. Remove and place on platter to drain and dry slightly. Repeat until all are used, not crowding the syrup. Let apples stand for twenty-four hours, drain again and roll in granulated sugar. Repeat the rolling three times at intervals of twenty-four hours.

### Crystallized Field Citron

Take young tender field citrons and cut lengthwise four times, or in four parts. Trim off outer edge close, and remove seed. Put in strong salt water from early morn until noon, and then put in alum water, using ½ cup alum to 1 gallon of water. Let soak until about 6 o'clock. Change to clear water and let soak all night. Take 1 pound of fruit, or as many pounds as you like, and let boil until tender. In another vessel make a syrup of sugar and water, use 1 pound sugar to each pound of fruit, let come to a boil, and take out of clear water and put in this syrup, and let boil as low as you can, not to burn. Take out and spread on a platter and sprinkle each side with sugar, and repeat sugar two or three times.

# pickles and relishes

# CHAPTER XVIII

## Pickles and Relishes

### To Brine Cucumbers and Other Vegetables

Use one pound of salt to one gallon of water.

This gives about a forty-five degree brine. If a sixty degree is called for, use one and a half pounds of salt to a gallon. Keep vegetables under the water by weighting down.

It is better not to wash cucumbers for brining. The washing takes place when making them into pickles. Keeping them under water prevents mold and softness. The brine excludes air and germs which cause the spoiling. Cucumbers for dill pickles should be washed or wiped well.

### To Green Cucumbers

Line a kettle with grape leaves or spinach, put in cucumbers and cover well with leaves. Pour over boiling water and allow to stand until cold. Drain and cover with a hot vinegar and water solution, one part vinegar to three parts water. Let stand over-night or several hours. This vinegar and water bath may be repeated. It is thought this method greatly improves the pickles. Make according to recipe being used.

### To Green Cucumbers With Soda

Use one tablespoon of soda to gallon of hot water. Pour over cucumbers; let stand until cold. Then give a water bath or a vinegar and water bath.

### To Crisp Cucumbers

After the cucumbers have been soaked in fresh water to remove the salt, then soak for two hours in a lime bath. The lime used is calcium oxide and can be obtained at any drug store. Use 1 to 2 ounces to gallon of water. In using calcium oxide, the cucumbers may be soaked over-night. More lime may be used. Some recipes call for two ounces to one gallon of water for over-night, some say soak for two hours. Soak in fresh water after using lime, about two hours. This bath is usually done before the greening.

### Spiced Sour Vinegar

3 cups vinegar
3 cups water
1 ounce each stick cinnamon, whole allspice, black pepper, whole mace

½ ounce each of whole cloves and dried ginger
2 small pieces horseradish

Boil together for five minutes. Allow to cool and it is ready to use.

### Sweet Spiced Vinegar

| | |
|---|---|
| 6 cups vinegar | 3 long sticks of cinnamon |
| 3 cups sugar | 1 teaspoon cloves |
| 1 tablespoon of allspice | 1 tablespoon white mustard seed |

Boil together for twelve minutes, pour over the pickles, let stand overnight. Drain and boil for ten minutes and pour again over pickles; let stand two hours. Boil pickles and vinegar until pickles become clear, about twelve minutes. Cool, arrange pickles in jar, pour over the spiced syrup. Seal.

### Spice Vinegar

| | |
|---|---|
| 1 lb. of sugar | 1 teaspoon of whole allspice |
| 2 quarts vinegar | 1 teaspoon of mace |
| 2 long sticks of cinnamon | ½ teaspoon cloves |

Boil together for five minutes.
Pour over cucumbers while hot. Seal at once. One onion and a few pieces of horseradish may be added. Cucumbers must be soaked in fresh water to remove the brine before pickling.

### A Good Vinegar for Pickles

| | |
|---|---|
| 2½ cups sugar | 2½ cups cider vinegar |
| ½ cup olive oil | 2 tablespoons celery seed |
| 4 tablespoons black and white mustard seed | 2 tablespoons each whole spice and stick cinnamon |

Mix together well and pour over pickles cold.
Mix pickles after standing in salt over-night or cucumbers soaked fresh. Fill jars and cover with the vinegar.

### Uncooked Pickles

| | |
|---|---|
| 1 gallon medium size cucumbers | 2 cups sugar |
| 1 quart onions | 2 quarts vinegar |
| 1 cup white and black mustard seed | ½ pint olive oil or substitute |
| ½ cup celery seed | 2 cups salt |
| 1 tablespoon black pepper corns | |

Slice cucumbers and onions and sprinkle with salt; let stand over-night; next morning drain well, and, if too salty, rinse and drain again.

Mix sugar with dry ingredients, then stir into vinegar until well mixed. Beat oil gradually into vinegar. Put pickles into jars, fill to overflowing with vinegar and cover or seal.

### Olive Oil Pickles Uncooked—Mrs. O's Recipe

| | |
|---|---|
| 1 peck cucumbers, sliced thin | Cover with 1 cup salt |
| 5 large onions, sliced very thin | |

Let stand over-night. Next morning drain and mix with the following:

| | |
|---|---|
| 5 cups sugar | 1½ tablespoons white mustard seed |
| 5 cups cider vinegar | 1½ tablespoons black mustard seed |
| 2 tablespoons celery seed | ½ cup olive oil |

Mix and bottle cold.

## Artichoke Pickle Uncooked

Wash and scrub well 1 peck of artichokes. Drop into a weak salt water solution (½ cup salt to 1 gallon water) for 2 hours.
Make the following spiced vinegar:

| | |
|---|---|
| 5 cups sugar | 1 tablespoon whole cloves |
| 5 cups vinegar | 1 medium onion cut in rings or |
| 2 tablespoons celery seed | quarters |
| 2 tablespoons each white and black | 1 garlic clove, if desired |
| mustard seed, whole allspice and | Several, small red-hot peppers |
| stick cinnamon | ½ cup olive oil or substitute |

Mix all together, stirring to melt sugar.
Fill jars with artichokes, selecting those of uniform size, putting all of one size in a jar. Cover with the vinegar to the very brim. Seal until ready to use.
Artichokes may be sliced if desired.

## Artichoke Relish

Wash, scrub and dice artichokes, and fill quart or pint jars with cubes. Into 1 quart of cider vinegar put ½ cup salt. Stir until dissolved, cover with the vinegar and seal until ready to use.
This is good as a relish with meats, or to use in tomato aspic in place of celery.
Any pickle or relish if put into medium size jars or containers and sealed will keep better.

## Mrs. M's Cucumber Pickles

| | |
|---|---|
| 2 dozen medium cucumbers | 2 quarts small white onions |

Slice and cover with 1 cup salt. Let stand over-night. Drain well, if too much salt, wash and drain again.
Make the following dressing:

| | |
|---|---|
| ½ gallon vinegar | 1 tablespoon curry powder |
| 5 cups sugar | 1 tablespoon celery salt |
| ½ cup flour | ¼ tablespoon cayenne pepper or less |
| 1 tablespoon tumeric | |

Mix all to a paste, add to vinegar, boil together for a few minutes; add pickles, boil together for half an hour. Put into jars and seal.

## Cucumber Pickles

| | |
|---|---|
| 7 lbs. ⅛ inch slices of cucumbers | 1 teaspoon each of cloves, allspice, |
| 2 gallons lime water | ginger, celery seed, mace, cin- |
| 5 lbs. sugar | namon |
| 5 pints vinegar | |

Soak cucumber slices in 2 gallons of lime water (3 cups lime to 2 gallons water). Drain and soak for four hours in plain water, changing the water every hour. Drain well. Make syrup of sugar, vinegar and spices, bringing to a boil. Then pour over cucumbers and let stand over night. Boil all together next morning for one hour, stirring often so as to cook evenly. Put in small jars and seal.

## Plain Cucumber Pickles

Soak cucumbers in fresh water several hours or over-night to remove the salt. Drain and cover with a weak vinegar and water solution for several hours. Drain again and cover with a spiced vinegar, sweet or sour. Sometimes this vinegar is boiled and poured over the cucumbers hot and sealed immediately. Others boil the spiced vinegar, let cool and pour over cucumbers and seal up.

## Quick Cucumber Pickles

Into a bowl put layer of cucumbers and layer of salt, using one cup of salt for one gallon of cucumbers; cover with boiling water and let stand until cold. Drain.

Mix with sufficient vinegar (about two quarts) the following seasoning: a few pods of hot red pepper, whole, two cloves of garlic, several small onions or the equivalent, half cup of white and black mustard seed mixed, sugar to taste. Bring to boil, cool slightly, pour over cucumbers, which have been put into jars. Cover well, let stand several days and they are ready to use.

The seasoned vinegar may be used again and again.

## Mother Pope's Cucumber Pickle

| | |
|---|---|
| 4 cups vinegar | ¼ teaspoon celery seed |
| ½ teaspoon red pepper | 2 tablespoons salt |
| 1½ cups sugar | 1 gallon medium size cucumbers |
| 1 teaspoon white mustard seed | |

Cut up cucumbers. Put in the spiced vinegar and let come almost to a boil. Pack in hot sterile jars, fill with vinegar and seal. Should always use sufficient vinegar to cover cucumbers.

## Aunt Ella's Cucumber Pickles

Quarter cucumbers, lengthwise, and let stand in salt water for several hours; remove, drain and drop into apple vinegar, which has been seasoned with salt, sugar, red pepper and spices. Good in 12 hours; this is delicious for breakfast with broiled bacon, nice served with an entree, or to serve with broiled fish. They will keep several days. The idea is to use fresh cucumbers and have them fresh all the summer. Use the same vinegar.

## For Quick Pickles

For brining use 1 cup salt to 3 gallons of cucumbers. Let stand three days. Soak over-night in clear water.

Take 2 quarts vinegar, 1 lb. sugar. Bring to boil, put in half of cucumbers and keep them hot until they are heated through. Cool, heat the next portion and remove. Add to vinegar 1 tablespoon each of mustard seed, allspice, half spoon of celery seed and cloves. Add a few pods of red pepper. Bring to the boil, cool. Pack cucumbers into jars, cover with the cold vinegar. Cover well or seal.

## Green Tomato Pickles

| | |
|---|---|
| 1 peck green tomatoes | 1 dozen red peppers |
| 1 large cabbage | 1 cup salt |
| 12 large onions | 1 dozen green peppers |

Chop and sprinkle with the salt; let stand over-night.

In the morning, drain well, let drip in muslin bag, squeeze dry. Then add the following seasoned vinegar:

| | |
|---|---|
| 10 cups vinegar | 1 tablespoon whole allspice |
| 4 cups sugar | Enough tumeric powder to color as |
| 1 cup whole mustard seed | yellow as desired |
| 1 tablespoon celery seed | |

Put all together, pour over the chopped vegetables, let come to a boil, stir well, get every part well heated. Put into jars. On the top of each jar place a piece of horseradish; seal.

## Brined Cucumbers Made Into Dill Pickles

Soak cucumbers to freshen. Into a crock or jar put a layer of cherry or grape leaves, then a layer of cucumbers which have been soaked, a few cloves, a few pieces of hot red pepper, a few spices and a few switches of dill. Repeat the process until jar is full.

Into a weak vinegar solution (1 pint vinegar to 3 pints water), put ½ cup each, mustard seed, horseradish, and salt. Pour this over cucumbers. Put a weight on top and let solution cover top well, seal.

This seasoning is sufficient for about 100 cucumbers.

## Mrs. Thompson's Green Tomato Pickles

| | |
|---|---|
| 1 peck green tomatoes | 2 quarts onions |
| 2 lbs. cabbage | 1 dozen bell peppers |

Slice vegetables, shred cabbage, sprinkle well with two cups of salt. Put into bag and hang to drip overnight. Next morning, make spiced vinegar as follows:

| | |
|---|---|
| 1 gallon vinegar | ½ cup mixed white and black mus- |
| 1 lb. sugar | tard seed |
| Lump of alum the size of a hickory | 1 heaping tablespoon of mixed spices |
| nut, crushed | |

Mix into vinegar and pour over vegetables and cook slowly until vegetables look a little clear (about two hours). Stir often. When done, mix six tablespoons of dry mustard, two tablespoons of tumeric to a paste with cold vinegar; add to pickles, cook ten minutes longer.

This pickle will keep without sealing, although it is always safe to seal.

## Crystallized Green Tomato Pickles

Select firm green tomatoes not larger than a dollar. It is necessary to keep sliced tomatoes in refrigerator during the soaking period, and they must be weighted down. If a few slices float all will be ruined.

Slice tomatoes ¼ inch thick. Soak in lime water 3 days. Use 1 cup sifted lime to 1 gallon water. Lift tomatoes each day so as to get top ones on bottom. Cover and keep in refrigerator. Fourth day soak in clear water. On the fifth, sixth and seventh days soak in alum water—using ½ cup of alum to 1 gallon of water. On the eighth day wash tomatoes in clear water and cover again with water, using a small amount of alum, place this on fire, let come to a boil, remove from fire onto sink, add 1 tablespoon soda. (This will foam over when soda is added.)

Drain tomatoes and boil in strong ginger tea four minutes only. Now make syrup: For each pound of tomatoes use one pound of sugar, cover sugar well with white vinegar. Add one teaspoon mace, one teaspoon cloves, one tablespoon allspice, all whole, boil syrup until thick, add tomatoes and boil about four minutes. Seal while hot.

### Dixie Green Tomato Pickles

| | |
|---|---|
| 2 gallons green tomatoes | 3 quarts vinegar |
| 8 large onions | 2 tablespoons whole black pepper |
| 6 green peppers | 2 tablespoons allspice |
| 2 lbs. sugar | 1 tablespoon cloves |
| ½ cup celery seed | 1 cup white mustard seed |

Chop all vegetables and mix with ½ cup of salt, put into a bag and let drip over night. Next morning mix all together. Let come to a boil and cook long enough for every piece to be hot to the center. Put into a jar and seal while hot.

### Iced Green Tomato Pickles

Soak for 24 hours seven pounds sliced green tomatoes in two gallons of water in which three cupfuls of lime have been dissolved. Drain and soak in fresh water for four hours, changing water every hour. Drain, place in kettle five pounds of sugar, three pints vinegar and one teaspoon each of cloves, ginger, allspice, celery seed, mace and cinnamon. Bring this syrup to boiling, pour over tomatoes and let stand overnight. In morning boil for an hour and seal in glass jars. One cupful of raisins may be added ten minutes before canning if desired. The lime makes the tomatoes crisp. Like the name the pickle is wonderful.

### Dill Pickles

| | |
|---|---|
| 1 gallon water, soft if possible | 1 lb. (1 pint) of salt |

Wipe cucumbers well, place in the brine and weight them down so as to keep them well under the brine. Cover top of jar with cheese cloth.

When the brine becomes acid, test (turns blue litmus paper red). It is ready then to add a few whole spices.

Allspice, cloves, whole red pepper pods and the dill switches. This must be done to suit the individual taste. The same jar may be used or packed into smaller jars, the seasoning put in and the jars sealed. The cucumbers must be kept well under the liquid or they become soft and will spoil. A cool, dark place is best to keep them. If glass jars are used cover with dark brown paper when finished.

If the dill pickles are packed into small jars and sealed it would mean greater success.

The same liquid, that is already in them, is strained and used for packing into small jars.

It takes from seven to twenty-one days to become acid. Cool weather requires the longest time—about twenty-one days.

### Dill Spices

Allspices, black pepper grains, coriander seed, bay leaves and dill switches.

### Sauerkraut

Three pounds salt for every 100 pounds of shredded cabbage.

Remove outside leaves and stalk of cabbage.

Cut fine. Line the bottom of barrel with the outside leaves, also line the sides as the cabbage is packed in. Put in three inches of shredded cabbage, sprinkle over this five tablespoons of salt. Repeat until the barrel is full, or all of the cabbage used. Pound down several times during the packing. When finished, the water extracted from the cabbage should cover the cabbage. Spread over top more of the large leaves. Fit a top of wood down on the cabbage and on top place some heavy weight to keep the brine above the cabbage.

Keep in cool dry place for three or four weeks.

Remove the scum. If warm weather, less time is required. When the fermenting gets quiet, or the acid seems right, test with litmus paper. The blue paper will turn red, or pinkish red. Put in jars and seal, using plenty of the liquid to fill jar to overflowing.

It may be put into crocks and sealed with a cloth dipped in melted paraffin.

The cabbage must always be kept well under the brine. Use a hard flint rock or iron for weight. A limestone will spoil the brine and cause all to spoil.

### Making and Canning Sauerkraut all at the Same Time

To a quart of chopped cabbage add 2 level teaspoonfuls of salt, stir, and pound with pestle. Pack sterilized jar with mixture to within ¾ inch of top of jar. Fill to overflowing with boiling water. Seal with rubber and top. It may "work out" after a few days, but that does no harm.

This kraut has been pronounced the best ever eaten.

### Sauerkraut (Cold Pack)

Cut up cabbage and pack in fruit jars.

For 1-quart jars take 1 round teaspoonful of sugar and place on top of jars, then fill jars with cold water to cover; then place rubber and top on jars and seal air-tight.

Kraut fixed in this manner in warm weather is ready for use in three days.

## South Carolina Pickled Onions

Peel small white onions, cover with brine, using 1½ cups of salt with 2 quarts boiling water, let get cold. Let stand 2 days. Drain. Make new brine, cover onions and bring to boil and keep boiling for three minutes. Drain, fill jars, placing between layers bits of mace, whole white pepper corns, cloves, bay leaves, and slices of red pod pepper. Have ready vinegar, using one cup of sugar to half gallon, pour over hot onions, boiling hot, fill to overflowing, seal while hot.

## Suffed Green Peppers

Take large sweet bell peppers and open them at end or side to remove seed. Drop in cold water. For filling use:

| | |
|---|---|
| 1 gallon cabbage cut as for slaw | 1 quart sliced onions |

Sprinkle with a cup of salt and let stand 3 hours. Drain out all water then put into a saucepan and add:

| | |
|---|---|
| 1 quart of cucumber pickles cut small | 1 tablespoon ground mustard |
| 2 cups sugar | 2 teaspoons of tumeric |
| 4 tablespoons white mustard seed | ½ teaspoon ground cloves |
| 1 tablespoon black pepper (ground) | Vinegar to cover |

Boil for half hour. Fill peppers with hot mixture, pack in jars and cover with vinegar. See that the peppers are kept under the vinegar. The vinegar to cover may be made sweet or used plain. The vinegar may be diluted (with water) if less acid is desired.

Red peppers may be used.

## Chow-Chow

| | |
|---|---|
| ½ gallon green tomatoes | 6 medium onions |
| 12 cucumbers that are small enough to have tender seed | 6 bell peppers |
| | 1 lb. cabbage |

Slice, or grind, all vegetables and place in stone or enamel pan, a layer of mixture, a sprinkle of salt, using one pound of salt and having a generous amount of salt on top.

Let stand overnight. Drain well. For the seasoning use:

| | |
|---|---|
| 1 gallon vinegar | 1 ounce tumeric |
| 1 cup sugar, white or brown | 2 tablespoons flour |
| ¼ lb. ground mustard | |

Bring the vinegar to boil. Mix the seasoning to a paste with a little of the vinegar, put into vinegar, boil together and pour over vegetables. Stir constantly until hot through and through. Put into jars and seal while hot.

## Spartanburg Cabbage and Artichoke Pickle

| | |
|---|---|
| 1 peck or more tomatoes | 2 quarts or more of artichoke |
| 1 large cabbage | 1 dozen onions |
| 1 dozen green bell peppers | |

If you cannot get pepper and artichoke, make without.

Sprinkle two tea cups of salt over vegetables, let stand twelve hours, squeeze dry and cover with half gallon vinegar and same of water. (Cold). Let stand twenty-four hours, squeeze dry and cover with vinegar in which has been dissolved.

| | |
|---|---|
| 1 box Coleman's mustard (10c size) | 1 ounce celery seed |
| 2 lbs. granulated sugar | ½ lb. white mustard seed |
| 1 ounce tumeric | |

Cover well with brown paper and tie up. Will be ready to use in one week.

### Georgia Relish

| | |
|---|---|
| 1 large cabbage | 1 dozen large onions |
| 1 dozen green peppers (sweet) | 2 quarts artichoke |
| 1 dozen red peppers (sweet) | 2 cups salt |

Shred vegetables, cut artichokes fine, mix and put layer of vegetables and layer of salt; let stand twelve hours.

Drain and cover with weak vinegar, using equal parts of vinegar and water; let stand twenty-four hours. Drain again.

Drain again and cover with the following vinegar. To one quart vinegar add:

| | |
|---|---|
| 1 box mustard medium | 1 ounce tumeric |
| 2 lbs. sugar | ½ lb. white mustard seed |
| 1 ounce celery seed | |

Mix all together well, make sufficient vinegar to cover vegetables. Use cold; no cooking is done at all; mix well, put into jars. Ready to use in a week.

One cup of oil may be added to the mixture. More or less sugar to taste.

### Georgia Cabbage Relish

| | |
|---|---|
| 1 large cabbage shredded | 1 cup salt |
| 1 quart white onions sliced fine | |

Mix and let stand over-night.

In morning squeeze dry and cover with vinegar. Add 3 tablespoons each of white mustard seed, whole allspice and tumeric; 1 tablespoon celery seed, a few pods (small) red pepper, 1 cup sugar. Mix, bring to a boil and boil hard for 5 minutes. Put into jars and seal.

### Mixed Pickle—Mrs. Mixon's Recipe

| | |
|---|---|
| 1 peck tomatoes | 1 large cabbage |
| 1 dozen green peppers | 12 large onions |
| 1 dozen red peppers | |

Cut and grind all this together, add 1 cup salt, let stand over-night; next morning squeeze dry, then add:

| | |
|---|---|
| 1 cup white mustard seed | 2 lbs. sugar |
| 1 tablespoon celery seed | 10 cups vinegar |
| 2 tablespoons allspice | Enough tumeric to color as you like |

Put on stove and let come to a boil, put in jars with a piece of horse-radish on top of each jar, and seal.

### Pepper Relish—Mrs. Mixon's Recipe

| | |
|---|---|
| 1 dozen red peppers | 3 large onions |
| 1 dozen green peppers | 1 hot pepper |

Grind all this together, put into boiling water for 20 minutes, drain thoroughly, then pour boiling water over again and let boil 15 minutes. Drain well, then add 1 tablespoon salt, 1 cup brown sugar, 1 quart white vinegar, boil 10 minutes and seal while hot.

### Pepper Relish

| | |
|---|---|
| 2 lbs. cabbage | 1 dozen hot peppers |
| 1 dozen green bell peppers | 1 dozen medium onions |
| 1 dozen red bell peppers | |

Grind cabbage and onions, pour boiling water to cover well and let stand half hour. Drain.

Grind peppers and mix with cabbage and onions; add the following seasoning—

| | |
|---|---|
| 1½ quarts vinegar | 3 tablespoons salt |
| 1½ lbs. sugar | 2 tablespoons crushed celery seed |
| 4 tablespoons ground mustard | |

Cook until tender, put into glass jars, and seal.

### Minnie's Corn Pickle

| | |
|---|---|
| 18 ears tender corn | 4 red bell peppers |
| 2 lbs. cabbage | ½ gallon vinegar |
| 3 bunches celery | ¾ lb. sugar |
| 4 large onions | ¾ cup salt |
| 4 green hot peppers | 4 tablespoons dry mustard |

Cut corn, keeping grains whole; cut all other vegetables rather fine. Mix sugar and mustard together dry, dissolve in vinegar until free of lumps. Mix all together. Cook slowly, keeping it boiling one hour.

Put into jars and seal while hot.

### Mustard Pickles

| | |
|---|---|
| 1 quart cucumbers sliced (large ones) | 1 large cauliflower broken into flowerets |
| 1 quart green tomatoes, sliced | 4 green peppers cut fine |
| 1 quart small whole cucumbers | |
| 1 quart small onions | |

Mix together and cover with a brine made of one gallon of water and one pint of salt. Let stand twenty-four hours.

Heat just enough to scald, pour into colander and drain well. Make the following:

| | |
|---|---|
| 1 cup flour | 2 quarts vinegar |
| 6 tablespoons dry mustard | 1 cup sugar |
| 1 tablespoon tumeric | |

Mix sugar, mustard, tumeric and flour together dry; mix to a paste with sufficient vinegar. Heat vinegar, pour over mixture, boil until it thickens, have free of lumps.

Pour over vegetables and cook until well heated through and through, stirring all the time. Put into jars, seal. More sugar may be used if sweeter pickles are wanted.

Green tomatoes may be used instead of cucumbers and cauliflower.

### Neighborhood Pickles

| | |
|---|---|
| 5 lbs. cabbage | ½ teaspoon red pepper |
| 1 dozen dill pickles | ¼ cup salt |
| 4 large white onions | ¼ pound mustard seed |
| 2½ cups sugar | ½ small pkg. celery seed |
| ¼ cup mustard | 1 quart vinegar |
| ½ of 5c pkg. tumeric | ¼ cup flour |
| 1 tablespoon black pepper | |

Make a paste of the flour and mustard with a little vinegar. Grind cabbage and onions and cut up dill pickle. Put all together and boil half an hour. Put in jars and seal.

### Spanish Pickle

| | |
|---|---|
| 1 large cabbage chopped | 3 or 4 bell peppers |
| 1 gallon green tomatoes cut up | 1 bunch celery |
| ½ dozen large onions | 4 cucumbers |
| 3 or 4 green peppers | |

Sprinkle cabbage and tomatoes with salt and let stand over-night. Press all water out of them and mix with other vegetables. Take:

| | |
|---|---|
| 3 pints vinegar | 1 tablespoon each of white mustard, cloves, allspice, celery seed ground mustard |
| 1 pint or more sugar | |

Let vinegar and flavoring come to a boil, then add vegetables. Cook 10 minutes and put in glass jars.

### End of Season Relish—Mrs. O's Recipe

Cut corn from six ears, or use 1 pint of canned corn.
Put the following through the chopper:

| | |
|---|---|
| 1 quart ripe tomatoes | 1 pint onions |
| 1 pint cucumbers | 3 green sweet peppers |

Mix, add to corn. Then add to above mixture:

| | |
|---|---|
| 1 pint vinegar | ½ tablespoon celery seed |
| 1 pint sugar | ¼ cup salt |
| ½ tablespoon mustard seed | 1 teaspoon tumeric powder |

Cook about one hour. Seal while hot.

### Chili

| | |
|---|---|
| 1 peck ripe tomatoes | 1½ cups sugar |
| 10 large onions | 2 tablespoons ground cinnamon |
| 1 cup chopped green peppers | 2 tablespoons allspice |
| ½ cup prepared mustard | 1 tablespoon cloves |
| Salt and red pepper | 1 tablespoon nutmeg |
| 2 quarts vinegar | |

Scald tomatoes and remove skins, and mash or cut up. Chop onions fine and add. Add green chopped pepper; salt and red pepper to taste. Cook until soft or about half done. Then add other ingredients and cook slowly stirring frequently to prevent scorching. Boil until sauce is thick enough to pour. Bottle while hot and seal.

### Uncooked Chili Sauce

1 peck of ripe tomatoes
2 cups chopped onion
2 cups chopped celery
2 cups sugar
2 quarts vinegar
½ cup salt

½ lb. of white mustard seed
½ teaspoon cayenne pepper (more or less)
2 teaspoons cinnamon (ground)
½ teaspoon cloves (ground)

Peel and chop tomatoes very fine or put through the food chopper. Put in a bag and let drip over-night. Grind onions, chop celery very fine, mix all together well, put into jars and cover or seal.

### Tomato Chutney

12 red tomatoes
6 red peppers
4 green peppers
4 large onions
1 hot red pepper
½ lb. raisins

1 cup of vinegar
1 tablespoon sugar
1 teaspoon salt
2 teaspoons celery seed
6 medium apples

Dice all vegetables. Peel and dice tomatoes and apples. Mix all together, cook slowly until thick. Put up in jars while hot and seal.

### Tomato Catsup

1 gallon tomato pulp
4 tablespoons salt
4 tablespoons black pepper grains
2 tablespoons of ground mustard
4 tablespoons whole allspice
4 tablespoons cinnamon sticks

½ tablespoon whole cloves
2 hot peppers or cayenne to taste
1 pint vinegar
1 lb. of sugar, more or less to taste

Slice and cook tomatoes in their own juice, rub through a colander to remove seed and skin. Measure after straining.

Cook pulp until thick, about two hours. Add seasoning. Tie spices in cheesecloth and drop into mixture. Continue boiling until thick as desired. Bottle boiling hot, and cork. When cold, dip top in melted paraffin. Sometimes green bell peppers are added to the pulp—one dozen, boiled and mashed through colander. Remove seed before cooking. Onions may be added. Cook with tomatoes.

### Georgia Sweet Peach Pickle

1 peck ripe firm peaches
7 lbs. sugar
1 pint vinegar

1 quart water
2 doz. whole cloves
3 tablespoons broken stick cinnamon

Prepare peaches. (See recipe for Peeling.) Boil sugar, vinegar and water until a moderate thick syrup. Add spices tied in cheese cloth bag. Add peaches, boil until they can be stuck with straw to seed. Stir occasionally for even cooking. Fill jars with peaches. Continue boiling syrup until heavy, then add to peaches covering well. Seal.

### Mrs. S's Peach Pickles

| | |
|---|---|
| 1 peck firm peaches | 1 quart water |
| 7 lbs. sugar | 2 doz. whole cloves |
| 1 pint vinegar | Cinnamon to taste |

Boil sugar, vinegar and water until rather thick. Add peeled peaches and cloves and cinnamon. Boil until peaches can be stuck with straw. Fill jars with peaches. Boil syrup until thick again, then fill jars and seal.

See recipe for Peeling.

### To Peel Peaches for Pickles

| | |
|---|---|
| 2 tablespoons of red seal lye | 1 gallon boiling hot water |

Put lye into the water, keep at boiling point. Dip 5 or 6 peaches in at a time for a minute, more or less, remove, drop into a pan of cold water, rub off the skin or peeling with a coarse cloth. Change the cold water occasionally if many are fixed, and use fresh water. Also rinse the cloth as it takes a rough cloth to remove skins. A wire strainer makes a good receptacle with which to dip peaches.

### Pear Pickles

| | |
|---|---|
| 2 quarts prepared pears | 2 cups sugar |
| 1 quart vinegar | 1 teaspoon whole cloves |

To prepare the pears peel and core them and cut in quarters or halves.

Mix vinegar and sugar, add pears and cloves, boil until tender, put in jars, seal or not. Will keep without sealing.

### Pear Paste

Peel pears, and boil or steam whole until tender, but firm enough to grate. Cool and grate to fine pulp. Add sugar, one pound for each pound of grated fruit. Boil slowly, stirring often to prevent burning. Boil to a thick mixture much like apple butter. Spread on platters, pans or panes of glass to cool and set for 24 hours. Cut in bars or squares, roll in granulated sugar and pack in boxes with wax paper between layers. Serve as candy. This may be served same as guava paste if made in thicker blocks and cut in portions when ready to serve.

### Pear Relish

| | |
|---|---|
| 1 peck pears | 1 tablespoon salt |
| 5 medium size onions | 1 tablespoon mixed spices |
| 6 bell peppers (3 red and 3 green) | 1 tablespoon of tumeric (for color) |
| 2 lbs. sugar | 5 cups vinegar |

Run pears, onions and peppers through meat chopper; add other ingredients; cook 30 minutes after it begins to boil. Put in jars and seal.

## Spiced Pears

5 lbs. pears peeled, cored and quartered
3 lbs. sugar
1 pint vinegar or less

1 tablespoon allspice, whole
1 tablespoon cinnamon whole
1 teaspoon cloves

Boil pears until they can be pierced with a straw. Drain well. Put vinegar into sugar, bring to a boil; boil five minutes, add pears and cook until clear and red. Add spices the last half hour, put into jars, seal while hot. If pears are ground, cook all together until thick like jam or marmalade.

## Pear Mincemeat

7 lbs. ground pears
1 lb. raisins
3 lbs. sugar
1 cup vinegar
2 tablespoons cinnamon

2 tablespoons cloves
2 tablespoons nutmeg
2 tablespoons spice
2 teaspoons salt

Cook mixture until thick and pears appear transparent and done. This makes fine pies.

## Jernigan Sweet Pickled Peaches

Select ripe, firm fruit, peel and put into jar closely. Use a sweet spiced vinegar, tie whole spices in cheese cloth, bring vinegar to boil, pour over the peaches, repeat for 9 mornings. Keep fruit well under the vinegar. Cloves stuck into peaches (half dozen into each peach) make them look pretty. When this is done, do not add cloves to vinegar. Do not have to seal.

## Spiced Grapes

7 lbs. grapes
4 lbs. sugar
1 pint vinegar
2 tablespoons stick cinnamon broken
fine

2 tablespoons whole allspice
1 tablespoon mace
1 teaspoon whole cloves

Wash and remove stems. Pulp the fruit. Put skins to boil in a small quantity of water until tender. Cook pulps the same until they break, put into a coarse sieve and mash through to remove the seeds. Add the pulp and other ingredients to skins. Cook all together slowly, stirring to prevent scorching, until tender and thick as jam. This does not have to be sealed, but it is preferable to put into small jars and seal.

## Pickled Raisins

1 lb. cluster raisins
Water
Vinegar

2 inch stick cinnamon
1 dozen whole cloves

Soak the raisins in enough water to cover until fruit becomes plump and tender. Drain. Place in a crock and cover with a mixture of one-half vinegar and one-half syrup of the water in which they were soaked. Add cinnamon and cloves. Allow to stand for at least a week before using.

## Mrs. G's Crab Apple Pickles

| | |
|---|---|
| 1 gallon crab apples | 2 cups water |
| 3 lbs. sugar | 1 cup vinegar |

Peel crab apples and drop into cold water. Have sufficient water to float apples. Bring to boil and cook until they can be pierced with a straw. Stir often so all will cook. Remove from fire, and with an apple corer pinch out the core.

Fill jars and cover with a syrup made of the sugar, water and vinegar. Boil together for 5 minutes and pour boiling hot over the apples. Seal or close well.

The syrup may be colored yellow or green to color apples.

Do not cook apples too much or they will break. This makes a beautiful and delicious pickle. Spices may be used if desired.

## Watermelon Rind Pickles

| | |
|---|---|
| ½ gallon of cut watermelon rind | ½ ounce whole mace |
| 1 quart apple vinegar | 1 ounce white mustard seed |
| ½ ounce whole cloves | 2 lbs. sugar |

Cut the rind in small pieces, about two-inch cubes; pack in brine until ready to use. Put a layer of rind and a light layer of salt; let stand until ready to make up. Soak in water over-night or until they are fresh. Then boil in weak alum water until they are firm and brittle. Boil again in plain water to remove the alum, and the rinds clear.

Put sugar and spices into vinegar; boil together for five minutes. Add rind and boil gently for 10 minutes. Put rinds into a jar; pour the hot vinegar over, having the jar full; seal. They will be ready to use in a few days.

## Watermelon Sweet Pickle

Peel and cut in shapes seven pounds of rind. Soak 24 hours each in brine, clear water, alum water, and again in clear water. Boil in clear water until tender. Drop into one quart of vinegar with three and a half pounds of sugar, a small quantity of cinnamon, mace, cloves and allspice tied in muslin, and boil until the rind is clear.

## Watermelon Rind Sweet Pickles

### First Part

Cut green and pink from rind of a firm, medium-size melon, making about four quarts after cut in blocks or squares. Boil in clear water until it looks transparent. Pour in colander and drip over night.

### Second Part

| | |
|---|---|
| 1 quart best vinegar | ¼ pound broken stick cinnamon |
| 4 pounds sugar | 1 tablespoon whole cloves |

Bring vinegar and sugar to boil, skim well, tie spices in thin cloth, add and boil for ten minutes. Add cut rind and boil for about twenty minutes. Do not overboil, or the fruit will be mushy.

Put contents in stone jar or bowl and let stand one week. Pack fruit in glass jars (cold). Bring syrup to boiling point, pour over rind, brimming full, and seal. A little less sugar may be used if more acid pickle is wanted. The rind may be cut in cubes or squares. It will require about four quarts of rind for this vinegar. There must always be sufficient vinegar to cover the pickles well. These pickles will keep without sealing, but it is always safe to put into medium jars and seal.

### Cantaloupe Pickles

Select green, firm cantaloupes, peel and remove the seed. Cut into small pieces and make the same as watermelon pickles.

### Stuffed Cantaloupe

Select small, firm cantaloupes, remove one section and take out the seed, keeping the section with each melon from which it was cut in order to fit in again when filled with the following mixture:

| | |
|---|---|
| 1 gallon cabbage, cut as for slaw | 1 quart sliced green tomatoes |
| 1 quart of sliced onions | |

Cover with a generous sprinkle of salt and let stand four hours.

Drain off the water and put into a kettle, cover with cider vinegar and add:

| | |
|---|---|
| 2 cups sugar | 2 teaspoons ground mustard |
| 1 tablespoon whole black pepper or a few pods of the hot red pepper | 1 teaspoon of whole cloves |
| 4 tablespoons white mustard seed | 2 teaspoons whole allspice |
| 2 tablespoons black mustard seed | 2 teaspoons tumeric powder |

Mix mustard and tumeric with sugar and mix with vinegar. Boil all together for half hour. Fill cantaloupes while mixture is hot. Pack in a crock and cover with vinegar, having the vinegar cold. Sugar may be added to vinegar if a little sweet is desired. When cantaloupes are filled, fit the cut section back into place, sewing or tying it to keep it in.

### Cecilia's Stuffed Pepper Pickles

| | |
|---|---|
| 1 large cabbage. Grind and sprinkle with 1 tablespoon salt over night | 18 green bell peppers |

Cut stem end off peppers, remove seed and save each end. Soak over night in light, salt water. Next morning drain and dry peppers. Drain and squeeze the cabbage very dry. Add:

| | |
|---|---|
| White mustard seed (5c worth) | 1 dozen whole cloves |
| 1 teaspoon celery seed | 1 dozen whole spice |

Mix well and pack each pepper very tight with the cabbage. Replace ends and tie on, using a coarse spool thread. Pack peppers in crock. Boil together 2 quarts vinegar, and 2 lbs. brown sugar, and pour over peppers while hot.

Place crock in dish pan or deep vessel with water. Let water in outer pan boil until the vinegar in crock comes to a boil. Remove and tie up well.

## Louise's Relish

1 dozen bell peppers
1 dozen pimentoes (red peppers)
3 large apples
3 onions

1 pint of sweet spiced vinegar, left in keg from the pickles. (This vinegar may be purchased from any grocery store).

Grind vegetables and apples; drain very dry. Add vinegar and cook 15 minutes after it begins to boil. Put in small jars and seal.

## CANNING RECIPES

### Soup Mixture

One-half of mixture should be tomatoes (preferably tomato pulp); one-fourth corn, one-fourth okra. Lima beans may be used instead of corn or half of each to make the quantity needed.

Peel tomatoes and remove the cores or any hard part, boil in own juice until soft. Clean the corn and blanch in hot water for eight to ten minutes. Remove, cool and cut in thin slices from the cob; do not scrape, cut off the corn.

Shell butter beans, put into a bag, place in boiling water and cook for eight to ten minutes. This may be done with the corn. Use tender okra and slice in half-inch pieces or less.

Use 1 gallon of tomatoes, ½ gallon of corn or beans or both, ½ gallon of sliced okra, 1 medium onion sliced. Add 1 teaspoonful of salt-sugar mixture for each pint, put all together and cook for ten (10) minutes, stirring to prevent scorching. Pack in sterilized jars (use new rubbers), and process for two hours or intermittently in water bath one hour for three days. In pressure cooker, 35 minutes at 10 pounds.

Use 1 part salt, 2 parts sugar, for the salt mixture. Sweet bell pepper pulp may be used if desired. To make tomato pulp, prepare tomatoes, cook until tender, press through a colander or sieve which will remove skins and seed. Any other vegetable may be added to soup mixture.

### Canning Tomato Juice

Cut tomatoes, cook until very tender and put through a sieve. Reheat the juice at once after putting through sieve. If using glass containers, heat the juice to 190 degrees Fahrenheit (if no thermometer is available, heat just to boiling), pour into sterilized containers, and seal. No processing is necessary. If tin cans are used, heat the juice to 180 to 190 degrees Fahrenheit (or to simmering if no thermometer is available), pour into cans, seal and process for five minutes in boiling water. Begin to count time when the water actually boils. Do not leave headspace in either glass or tin containers. Cool glass containers in the air but out of draughts. Cool the tin cans in running water. If bottles are used, close with new corks, and when cold, cover top with paraffin. Exhaust means to set in hot water to drive out air. Salt-sugar mixture, one-third salt, two-thirds sugar. Use 1 to 2 teaspoons to every quart of juice.

## Canning Beans

7 quarts of beans after strung and          2 cups cider vinegar
    broken                                       1 cup sugar

Blanch beans by putting in a flour sack and pour over them boiling water and let stand five minutes; then plunge into cold water for three minutes. Place beans in boiler, add sugar, vinegar, cover with boiling water and boil for one hour. Put into sterilized jars, with new rubbers and seal.

Each jar should be full to the brim with the liquid. When ready to use, pour off the liquid, use fresh water and cook as fresh beans with a piece of seasoning meat.

## Canning Butter Beans

The beans should be gathered when in their prime, shelled and assorted carefully. Blanch for three to five minutes in a soda bath, using one teaspoon soda to one gallon of water. Plunge into cold salt bath, using one tablespoon salt to every quart of water. Drain and fill jars with beans. Fill jars with hot salt water, using two and one-half ounces salt to each gallon water.

Exhaust for five minutes. Place rubbers and tops and process (for quarts) one hour for three days in succession. Butter beans are canned exactly the same as string beans, except it is safer to do the processing for three days than all at one time, which some prefer to do. Butter beans, like corn, are harder to can than other vegetables.

## To Can Pimento Peppers

Pick and handle peppers carefully to prevent bruising. To peel, place peppers in pan and into a hot oven until the skin blisters, rub off skin. Cut stem around and remove seed. Flatten peppers and pack in jar. Place rubber and top, process (boil) for 30 minutes for pint, 40 minutes for quart. No liquid is used, peppers send out their own liquid. Another way is to make a light vinegar and sugar water, fill jars and process for 24 minutes. Seal while hot.

## To Can Peaches

Select ripe but firm peaches, peel carefully and cut into two pieces. Fill jars by packing the halves one on top of the other, the cut side down. Fill jars with syrup or water, paddle well to remove any air bubbles, put top on loose, process for twenty minutes for quart jars, forty for half-gallon. Remove, tighten tops and allow to cool. The peaches may be blanched if stiff and hard to pack. To blanch, having peeled and cut the peaches, tie them in a cloth and dip in hot water three to five minutes. Make the syrup as thick as desired. A good syrup is one cup of sugar and one cup of water, boil for three minutes, fill jar with this syrup. More or less sugar may be used according to taste.

## Canned Pears

Select ripe but firm pears, peel, cut in half, core or cut in rings. Drop into cold water until all are ready. Drain and pack rapidly in jars, have ready a syrup, fill jars, process quarts thirty minutes in hot water bath. The syrup may be light or thick to suit the taste as to sweetness. When hard pears such as Kiefer's and pineapple are canned, they must first be boiled in clear water until tender, then drained, packed in jars, the syrup poured over and processed.

## Canned Okra

Select young, tender pods, remove the stem end without cutting the seed pod, blanch in soda hot bath for three to five minutes, using one teaspoon of soda to a gallon of water; remove and drop into a cold salt water bath for half a minute. Drain and pack in jars, cover with hot brine and process two hours.

Use three tablespoons of salt to a gallon of water for packing. I prefer processing with the hot water instead of cold. It is quicker and surer. For the cold plunge after blanching use one tablespoon of salt to one quart of water. The soda bath and salt plunging assist in keeping the color.

# preserves, jams and jellies

# CHAPTER XIX

## Preserves, Jams and Jellies

### Pear Preserves

Peel, core and cut the pears into fourths. Then weigh the fruit and use 1 lb. of fruit with ¾ lb. of sugar.

Put pears into clear water and boil gently until they are tender and can be pierced with a fork. Take from the water and put into a bowl, put a layer of pears, then a layer of sugar and repeat until all are used. Let stand over night. Pour off the syrup, bring to a boil, add pears and cook until they are clear and the syrup is thick as preserve syrup. Cook slowly, stir often but gently so as not to break fruit. Remove any scum while cooking. Put into quart jars and seal.

### Georgia Peach Preserves

10 lbs. of peaches                    10 lbs. of sugar

Select firm clingstone peaches, peel and cut into two pieces from the stone, dropping into cold water while peeling. Drain well from the water and into a pan or kettle (aluminum or granite), put a layer of peaches and sprinkle well with sugar, using a pound of sugar for every pound of fruit. Let stand over night. Remove the peaches and bring the syrup to a boil and boil until it begins to thicken. Add peaches and cook slowly until they are tender, clear and rather transparent, and the syrup is thick.

When done skim out the peaches and fill jars good and full; boil the syrup longer, if not thick, and cover the peaches, filling the jar to the top with the syrup. This will keep without sealing. Some like the preserves very firm. This is achieved by removing the fruit and letting it stand in the sun for several hours; then cook again, repeating three or four times, then finish and put into jars.

### Peach Preserves

10 lbs. of peaches                    10 lbs. of sugar

Peel and cut from the seed good, firm peaches; cut into two pieces. When all are peeled and cut, put a layer of peaches and one of sugar until all is used; let stand over night. In the morning pour off the syrup which has formed into a kettle (aluminum or granite) and bring to a boil; add peaches and cook slowly, removing any foam or scum which will form on the top. Cook until the peaches are tender and a red color; skim out the peaches and spread on a dish where the sun or air can strike them. Continue to boil the syrup until it is thick; return the peaches to the kettle until hot; put into jars and seal or tie up with stiff paper. A handful of the peach stones gives a good flavor if put in and cooked with the peaches.

## Fig Preserves

5 lbs. figs                                3 lbs sugar

Put just enough water into sugar to wet. Put on fire and melt, boil until rather thick syrup. Put in half of the figs. Boil slowly until pink, and the syrup is thick; stir to prevent sticking. When figs look pink and clear, lift out on a platter and place in the sun or air. Put in the other half and cook the same way. When the second lot of figs is done, and the syrup thick, pack in jars and fill with the boiling syrup and seal.

Place the first lot cooked back into the boiling syrup, which is left, and bring to boil long enough to heat through. Fill jars and cover with syrup and seal. If lemon or ginger is liked, cook with the fruit. Add one lemon or more, cut in thin slices. For the ginger, four or five pieces about an inch long, cooked with the fruit.

When the figs are cooked in small lots, they float and are not so apt to burn, and are kept in better shape. The cooking must be slow; the stirring carefully done, so as not to break the fruit. Ripe, firm figs with the stems on are best. Use the soft and broken ones for jam. A recipe for peeling the fig is given.

## To Peel Figs

½ lb. sal soda                             3 pints of water

Keep boiling hot, drop eight or ten figs in, and keep hot until the skin cracks. This takes only a few seconds. The water is hot but not boiling. Remove and drop into cold water. Put in another lot. With a rough or coarse cloth rub the skins from those which have been scalded; drop into another pan of cold water. Continue until all are peeled. Drain, weigh and make preserves.

## Dried Figs

Select perfect but ripe figs. Let them stand in lime water for one hour using one ounce of calcium oxide to one gallon water. Drain and drop into fresh water for half an hour. Drain again. Make a syrup of one quart of sugar and one quart of water.

Boil together for ten minutes. Drop in figs and cook rapidly for forty to fifty minutes or until clear. Drain, place on platters or trays in the sun for several days, turning them every day. Spread in single layers on platter.

Bring indoors at night.

Each tray must be covered with net to protect from insects. If the weather should be damp, place in a warm oven until they can go again into the sunshine. Continue drying until you know they are not sticky.

## Strawberry Preserves No. 1

### (A Prize Recipe)

Wash, stem and drain well two quarts of berries. Place in preserving kettle over low fire and cook slowly until all juice appears to be extracted from the fruit. Skim out berries, which will appear pale, soft and collapsed. To one (1) cup of juice add three (3) cups sugar. Boil until the mixture is thick and jelly-like. Add the berries and boil three (3) minutes. Pour mixture in shallow pans and allow to become cold before putting in jars or glasses; seal or cover with paraffin. The berries will regain their original plumpness and color and will resemble sunshine preserves. They will keep indefinitely. Do not make more than two quarts in one batch.

### Strawberry Preserves No. 2

2 lbs. firm strawberries        ½ cup berry juice
1½ lbs. sugar

Wash and cap berries. Make a syrup of the juice and sugar; skim. Add the berries, bring to a boil slowly, then boil more rapidly until the berries look clear and syrup is thick. Let stand overnight in the syrup. Drain, bring syrup to boil and pour over berries. Let stand again overnight. Repeat for third night. Put berries in jar and pour hot syrup over them and seal.

### Strawberry Preserves—French Method
#### (A Prize Recipe)

Wash and cap large, firm, ripe berries, washing quickly so as not to have berries watersoaked. For every pound of berries allow three-fourths (¾) pound of sugar.

Sprinkle sugar over berries and let stand for several hours until a syrup is formed. Place on fire, bring to a boil, and let boil gently for one (1) minute. Remove from fire and set in cool place to stand overnight. The following day again bring to a boil and allow to boil two (2) minutes. Repeat first process, letting stand overnight. The third day repeat the boiling for three (3) minutes. Pour into sterilized jars and seal immediately.

### Perfect Strawberry Preserves

Carefully stem a quart of berries, wash and drain well. Place berries in a flat-bottomed saucepan, heat slowly and simmer in their own juice a few minutes, but do not cook.

Drain off the juice and add 3 cups of sugar to the berries, bring to a boil and boil rapidly four or five minutes. Seal when cold. This is delicious, and the berries stay whole and keep their color. The juice may be used for jelly. See jelly-making with commercial pectin. Follow directions on package or bottle.

### Quick Strawberry Preserves

Wash, stem and drain the berries well. Crush, using 6 cups of crushed berries and 6 cups sugar. Mix well and bring to a boil and boil ten (10) minutes after it begins to boil. Seal while hot. Never make more than six cups at one time.

## Strawberry Jelly—Using Commercial Pectin

4 cups (2 lbs.) berry juice  
2 tablespoons lemon juice  

8 cups (3½ lbs.) sugar  
1 bottle of fruit pectin

To prepare juice, crush thoroughly or grind about 3 quarts fully ripe berries. Place fruit in jelly cloth or bag and squeeze out juice. Squeeze and strain juice from 1 medium lemon.

Measure sugar and fruit juices into large saucepan and mix. Bring to boil over hottest fire and at once add bottled fruit pectin, stirring constantly. Then bring to a full rolling boil and boil hard ½ minute. Remove from fire, skim, pour quickly. Paraffin hot jelly at once. Makes about 12 glasses (6 fluid ounces each).

## Strawberry Jam—Using Commercial Pectin

4 cups (2 lbs.) prepared fruit  
7 cups (3 lbs.) sugar  

½ bottle fruit pectin

To prepare fruit, crush thoroughly or grind about 2 quarts fully ripe berries. Measure sugar and prepared strawberries into large kettle, mix well, and bring to a full rolling boil over hottest fire. Stir constantly before and while boiling. Boil hard 3 minutes. Remove from fire and stir in bottled fruit pectin. Then stir and skim by turns for just 5 minutes to cool slightly. Paraffin hot jam at once. Makes about 10 glasses (6 fluid ounces each).

### Watermelon Rind Preserves—Cousin Mattie's Recipe

After peeling and cutting rind, soak for 12 hours in lime water—3 cups of unslacked lime to 3 gallons of water. Remove from the lime water and soak for 4 hours in plain water, changing the water twice. Put into plain water and cook gently for 30 minutes. Dip from boiling water and plunge into ice water six times. To 1 lb. of rind use 1½ lbs. sugar. When taken from the hot water the last time sprinkle sugar over fruit with just enough water to melt sugar—let stand over night. Next morning boil until rind is clear and tender. If syrup becomes too thick before rind is clear add a little more water and continue to cook,

### Watermelon Rind Preserves—Mrs. J. A.'s Recipe

After the rind is prepared, weigh.

Put eight pounds of rind in rather salt water for a day and night; on the morrow put rind in fresh water to which add two tablespoons powdered alum, and let stand a day and night.

Next morning put rind in fresh water (cold) and boil until a straw will pierce through. Drain and add eight pounds of sugar in kettle, also a fresh sliced pineapple. Boil until clear. If rind begins to turn white, a little water must be added.

## Delicious Watermelon Rind Preserves

Use a thick brittle rind, peel all green from outside and all pink from inside. Cut in any desired shapes. Prepare rind in the afternoon, put in a vessel large enough so rinds can be covered with water. Sprinkle three-fourths of a cup of salt in water and soak overnight. Early next morning, pour off the salt water, rinse in clear water and cover again with water, adding a tablespoonful of pulverized alum and mix all through water. Let soak two hours. Rinse out again and fill with clear water. Dissolve one heaping tablespoonful of slacked lime in a pint of water, stir well and let settle. Pour the lime water, after it settles, over the rinds and soak two hours. Then rinse the rinds and put on stove with enough water to cover. Boil them until you can pierce them with a fork or straw. When tender, drain all the water off and weigh the rinds. Allow 1¼ pounds of sugar to 1 pound of rinds. Put them on the stove, add the sugar and enough water to cover. Use lemon or race ginger to flavor. Boil until rinds turn a creamy yellow and syrup is thick enough. Put in jars, cover with syrup, and seal.

When preserves turn to sugar after being made, it is because you did not put enough water in after putting in sugar. It takes longer boiling, but it pays. Boil two and one-half or three hours. You can eat your melon one afternoon and have your preserves in the jars in the next afternoon. These preserves are easily and quickly made and are most delicious. These may be crystallized (after standing awhile) and used in fruit cake.

And remember in selecting your rind be sure it is thick and brittle to start with. A thin, tough rind just doesn't make the best pickles or preserves.

## Cantaloupe Preserves

Take half ripe cantaloupe, peel and slice in rather thick slices. Sprinkle with salt. Put a piece of alum the size of a nutmeg to every gallon of fruit, cover with water and weight to keep down. Let stand about 2 days, then wash and let stand in cold water until all salt is extracted, perhaps changing the water several times.

Boil until tender enough to be pierced with a straw, drain and lay in colander to drain. Weigh and allow 1¼ lbs. sugar to each pound fruit. Make a syrup of the sugar and water enough to cover fruit well, add three lemons, sliced, to each gallon of fruit. Cook until clear, as you would watermelon rind.

## Pineapple Preserves

Peel, core and slice pineapple. For one pound of fruit use three-fourths pound of sugar.

Put layer of fruit and one of sugar, allow to stand over night. Drain off the syrup, boil for fifteen minutes, add fruit and continue boiling until fruit is transparent or clear. Skim while cooking.

Pack in jars, have syrup thick, seal while hot. Some prefer to partly cook in open pack and process for fifteen minutes. For jam, use the given amount, grind or cut fine, cook until thick and clear.

## Orange Marmalade

1 grapefruit          2 lemons
2 oranges

Select large perfect fruit, cut in slices, peel and remove seed. Put through food chopper, saving all juice. To each measured cup of fruit pulp add 3 cups of water. Let stand 24 hours then boil 10 minutes and let stand another 24 hours. To each cup of fruit mixture prepared as above, add one cup of sugar and boil until thick, clear and jelly like. Put in glasses or jars and cover with tops or paraffin.

## Pumpkin Chips

7 lbs. pumpkin        5 lbs. sugar
4 lemons

Peel and slice pumpkin in one inch squares one-fourth inch thick. Pack down in sugar, let stand over night. Drain off syrup, bring to boil, skim. Add chips and lemons sliced thin; cook until clear and transparent and syrup is thick.

## Pear Conserve

1 cup nut meats        ½ lb. raisins (seeded)
3 lbs. pears              1 orange
2 lbs. sugar              1 cup water

Peel, wash, and dry the pears and grind or chop them fine.

Make syrup of sugar and water, add pears and cook. When about half done, add raisins and the orange which has been sliced thin, quartered and seeded. Continue to cook until thick and transparent. Add nuts five minutes before taking up. Pack hot in sterilized jars and seal immediately.

Process pint jars for thirty minutes just below the boiling point.

Juice of a lemon is sometimes added. The orange may be used or not. The quantity of sugar must be governed by the fruit used, whether it is very sour, or sweet.

## Grape Conserve No. 1

3 lbs. grapes after seeding      1 lb. seeded raisins
1½ lbs. sugar                  1 cup shelled pecans
     Juice of 1 lemon         1 orange, sliced or ground

Pulp grapes and heat pulp to free from seed, pressing through colander or coarse strainer. Mix all together (except nut meats) and cook together until thick and transparent.

Add nuts, cook five minutes. Pack hot in jars and seal.

## Grape Conserve No. 2

3 lbs. sugar            1 lb. seeded raisins
5 lbs. grapes           1 cup nut meats

Wash and pulp grapes, cook pulp tender, run through a sieve to remove seeds. To the hulls add just enough water to cook; boil until tender.

Chop hulls or put through food cutter. Mix hulls and pulp. Weigh. Add sugar and raisins, cook until a real jam, thick and clear. When done, add nut meats and cook five minutes, pack hot and seal. Any fruit may be made into a conserve by adding raisins and nuts. Sometimes an orange or lemon pulp and rind is added. It must be ground fine and cooked with fruit.

### Damson Conserve

| | |
|---|---|
| 7 lbs. damsons | 1 lb. seeded raisins |
| 5 lbs. sugar | 2 oranges, juice pulp and rind |

Wash and pick over damsons, remove bad ones and stems. Add just enough water to sugar to make a syrup. Remove seed from oranges and grind the rind. Mix all together and cook slowly, stirring often to prevent scorching—cook until thick as jam (about one hour), put into fruit jars and seal.

### Pear Jam

| | |
|---|---|
| 8 cups of peeled and ground pears | 1 large can grated pineapple |
| 6 cups of sugar | |

Put all together and boil until thick and clear. Put into jars and seal, or put paraffin over top to seal.

### A New Jam

| | |
|---|---|
| 2 lbs. Concord grapes after being picked over | 2 cups water |
| 2 lbs. pears peeled and diced | 3 cups sugar |

Pulp grapes and add half of water to skins, half to pulps. Cook gently until tender, strain pulp to remove seed, put to the skins, add pears and sugar, cook until thick and clear.

### Muscadine Jam

| | |
|---|---|
| 5 lbs. fruit | 3 lbs. sugar |

Pulp grapes and put pulp to cook in small quantity of water; cook until broken. Put through coarse strainer to remove seed. To the hulls put sufficient water to boil until tender. Mix the two together, add sugar and cook slowly, stirring often to prevent scorching. Season with any spices liked.

### Spiced Muscadine

| | |
|---|---|
| 5 lbs. fruit | 1 tablespoon cinnamon |
| 3 lbs. sugar | 1 tablespoon allspice |
| 1 pint cider vinegar | 1 teaspoon cloves |

Proceed by pulping grapes and cooking as for the jam; add seasoning, and cook until thick.

### Blackberry Jam

Select good ripe berries; wash and remove any bad ones, and place over a gentle fire with one cup of water for about four quarts of berries. Cook until tender, stirring and mashing to make smooth. Weigh berries before cooking, using three-fourths of a pound of sugar for every pound of fruit. Cook until a thick jam. Put into jars and when cool cover top. This should keep without sealing. If you wish to seal as a precaution, close while hot.

Sometimes berries are put through food chopper. Weigh, chop, then cook.

### Rhubarb Jam

Wash, dry and cut; use equal weight of sugar. Mix and let stand over night. There will be sufficient juice to cook.

Bring to boil and cook half hour good boiling; stir as little as possible; simmer until clear and thick. Lemon or orange rind and juice may be added. Nuts added would make a conserve.

## JELLY HINTS

Do not use fruit that is very ripe.

Boil jelly rapidly, for long slow boiling injures the pectin.

Skim off the scum at the end of the cooking. This saves juice and labor.

Do not peel or core fruit; often the color comes from the peel.

Do not overcook the fruit to get the juice. Just a soft pulp will give better jelly.

If jelly fails to set it may be reboiled from five to seven minutes.

When using pectin, use one to four tablespoons to each cup of juice, according to strength of the pectin.

When using lemon juice, add one-half to one tablespoon to each cup of juice.

To add the lemon juice or pectin, bring juice and sugar to boiling point, add lemon juice and cook until it flakes.

Some commercial pectin recipes say: "Bring to boil, boil hard for one minute, remove from fire, add pectin, stir well, let stand one minute then pour into jelly glasses."

When covering jelly with paraffin put paraffin in a small tin coffee pot, melt and pour from spout. The covering is easy. Set glasses in pan of cold water so when filling, if any paraffin is spilled, it floats on the water and may be picked up and returned to coffee pot. No washing and scrubbing of pan or table will be necessary.

### Blackberry Jelly

Use berries which are not too ripe. Pour over them enough boiling water to cover well and cook until done. Pour into a thick cloth bag and let drip for several hours, until all of the juice has dripped. Put on stove and reduce to half the quantity. Then put one cup of sugar for one cup of juice. Heat the sugar before adding to hot juice; boil for about five minutes or until it jells, when tested with a spoon. The drops of juice will flake off, or try the juice in a saucer to see if it jells, letting it cool.

Remove any scum from the top while cooking. Have the glasses ready and hot to fill with the hot jelly. When cold and firm put melted paraffin over top, which seals if properly put on and not broken. The paraffin should cover jelly and extend up on sides of glass.

## Quince Honey

Six large quinces. Four pounds of sugar. About one quart of water. Pare and grate the quinces, cook the skins and cores in part of the water, and strain and add water to the grated pulp. Put the pulp and all the liquid on the stove and cook five minutes from time it reaches the boil. Add the sugar and cook down to jelly. Pour in jelly glasses.

## Apple Jelly

Use tart apples, those not too ripe. Wash, core and remove seeds and stems. Cover with cold water, bring to a boil and cook until tender. Drain in a thick jelly bag. Measure using a cup of juice to a cup of sugar. Bring juice to hard boil, add sugar and boil rapidly until it flakes. (To test, dip paddle or silver spoon in juice, hold up to cool and flake off; when two drops of juice flake off together the jelly is ready to pour. A wooden paddle or spoon is best to use). Pour in glasses and when cool cover top with paraffin.

Peelings and cores will make jelly. Use above method. Dried apples may also be used, but they must be soaked in cold water before cooking.

## Delicious Apple Jelly

1 peck apples                    ½ peck crab apples (just ripening)

Wash and cut the apples in quarters. Wash and cut in half the crab apples, removing stems. Cover with water and cook until tender. Drip over night through thick cloth bag. Measure, using 1 pint of juice and 1 pound of sugar. Put juice to boil for 15 or 20 minutes. While juice is boiling put sugar in large biscuit pan lined with brown paper and heat real hot, stir in sugar little at a time so as not to stop the boiling. The jelly will be ready to pour up almost immediately. Inexperienced people should not cook too much at a time. Small batches give better success.

## Crab Apple Jelly

Wash fruit, remove stems and all defective parts. Cover with boiling water and let stand until cold. Boil until fruit is tender. Pour into a jelly bag to drip without squeezing. When ready measure 1 cup juice to 1 cup sugar. Bring juice to boiling point, add sugar and boil rapidly until it flakes.

See Jelly Hints.

### Grape Jelly

Select grapes that are not too ripe, part green ones are preferable. Wash before pulling from stem. Place in porcelain kettle, just cover with water, boil until tender and broken which allows juices to flow. Drain juice and boil to reduce one-third or one-half. Measure, using 1 cup juice to 1 cup sugar. Bring juice to hard boil, add sugar and cook until it jellies or flakes. Pour into hot, sterilized glasses. When cool cover with paraffin.

If there are many green grapes, one-third reduction of juice will be sufficient.

### Cranberry Sauce

| | |
|---|---|
| 1 quart cranberries (1 lb.) | 2 cups sugar |
| 2 cups boiling water | |

Remove all faulty berries, wash and drain. Add water and sugar, cook gently for thirty minutes, simmering all the time, and they are ready to serve.

### My Favorite Cranberry Jelly

| | |
|---|---|
| 1 quart cranberries (1 lb.) | 1 cup boiling water |
| 1½ cups sugar | |

Wash and drain cranberries, removing any faulty ones. Put sugar, water and cranberries together and cook for ten minutes, stirring all the time. Pour into a coarse strainer to remove the skins; put into molds or dish to jell, first brushing mold or dish with salad oil before pouring in the hot jelly. Note: If gas heat is used it will require about 5 minutes for the mixture to come to boiling point, then continue cooking the remaining time, stirring constantly. If other heat is used, cook until a thick mixture which leaves a deep trace of the spoon. The mixture must be stirred constantly for it will scorch easily with such rapid cooking.

### Clear Cranberry Jelly

| | |
|---|---|
| 1 quart berries (1 lb.) | 1½ cups sugar |
| 1 pint water | |

Wash and drain cranberries, removing any faulty ones. Put water and berries together. Cook until done (about 15 or 20 minutes). Strain through cheesecloth. Add sugar, boil quickly until it flakes, the same as making any jelly. Put into molds or jelly glasses to get firm.

### The Best Cranberry Jelly

| | |
|---|---|
| 4 cups cranberries (1 lb.) | 1½ cups sugar |
| 1 cup water | |

Wash and drain berries. Add the water and cook until the berries pop open. Strain through a coarse sieve to remove skins. Return to the boiler, bring to a hard boil. Add sugar and boil hard for five minutes or until the mixture is very thick. Pour into a pan to get firm. Cut in cubes to serve.

When cooked sufficiently, this jelly is firm and will not leak or run. It may be molded in individual molds.

# invalid dishes

# CHAPTER XX

## Invalid Dishes

### A FEW DISHES FOR THE INVALID

#### Beef Juice

Heat well a piece of round steak, using a thick skillet. Have a hot cup ready. Squeeze the juice from the meat, season with salt and pepper, serve very hot. Sometimes the juice is put on toast. To squeeze, use a meat press, or put hot steak in piece of cheesecloth, twisting each end like wringing clothes, and the juice may be extracted readily.

#### Beef Broth

Select a piece of lean beef, round preferred. Trim off edge, and remove all fat, cut into cubes, cover with cold water. Let stand one hour. Bring gently to the boiling point and simmer until meat is tender and the soup the strength desired. Strain, season with salt and pepper. Serve hot. To one cup of meat cubes use three cups of cold water. Vegetables may be put to cook with meat, to flavor and give variety.

#### Scraped Steak Balls

Have a thick piece of round steak. With a heavy spoon scrape the meat, using just what comes off in the spoon. Make tiny pats, enough for one mouthful only, broil until as done as desired, turning from side to side. Have ready a piece of toast. On this, put the meat balls and sprinkle with salt and pepper.

Into the fry pan pour one tablespoon of water or just enough to get the meat juice which browned in the pan. Pour this juice, or gravy, over the balls and toast. Serve very hot. A little butter may be put on each ball if desired. Invalids and babies can take this if they can have any solid food at all.

#### Egg Delicious

A saucepan, boiling water and a tea cup will be needed.

Have the teacup in the hot water like a double boiler. Into the cup put a small portion of butter and break the egg into this. Leave the egg whole until the white begins to cook. With a spoon stir gently, not breaking the yolk at first, and having the water boil gently. When the white looks about half done, stir, breaking the yellow, until cooked as much as desired, season with salt and pepper and serve in the same cup or pour into a warm dish. If left in the cup, have very soft, for the hot cup will continue the cooking while the egg is being carried to the invalid. The cooking requires about two or three minutes.

## Poached Egg for the Invalid

Poach egg in milk instead of water, keeping the milk hot, but not boiling, until egg is sufficiently cooked. Serve on toast or in a warm fruit saucer.

## Orange Albumen

The juice of 1 orange           ½ glass crushed ice
White of 1 egg

Get the juice from the orange and remove the seed. Fill the glass half full of crushed ice which has been rinsed off before crushing. Add the orange juice, then the white of the egg and with a spoon mix the white in, stirring, not beating, as no froth is desired in this drink. This should fill an ordinary glass. A bit of sugar, ½ teaspoon more or less, may be added if too sour. Juice from ½ of a lemon may be added if more acid is liked. Use very fresh egg.

## Lemon Albumen

Make same as orange, except use lemon, adding enough sugar to sweeten.

## Lemonade

2 tablespoons sugar          Crushed ice and enough water to
                                      fill the glass

Use from one-half to a whole lemon for a glass.

Mix well, have very cold and serve. When making a large quantity dissolve the sugar in hot water, bring to the boiling point, let cool, using for every cup of sugar ½ cup of water. Use 1½ cups of sugar for every dozen lemons. Slice one lemon in thin slices and serve a slice in each glass.

## Toast

See toast in Bread Section.

# menus

# CHAPTER XXI

## Menus

### MAKING UP THE MENU

There are five groups of food necessary to nourish the body. Some food from each group should be chosen daily. There are quite a number in each group sufficient to vary meals. However, milk is the only food for which there is no substitute.

When food from all five groups is chosen you have a balanced menu, It is believed sufficient to have this balanced food every day, instead of every meal.

### The Five Groups of Food

1. Cereals, wheat flour, corn meal, rice, bread, and macaroni.
2. Milk, eggs, cheese, meat, fish, peas, beans, nuts and game.
3. Fats, butter, butter substitutes, drippings, cottonseed oil, olive oil, and bacon.
4. Sugar, syrups, honey, jelly, and preserves.
5. Vegetables and fruits.

### Breakfast Menus

Honey Dew Melon
Omelet                  Toast
Coffee

———

Cantaloupe
Poached Eggs        Cheese on Toast
Waffles                  Jam
Coffee

———

Orange Juice
Brains and Eggs     Hominy (grits)
Toast
Coffee

———

Fruit
Cream of Wheat
Sausage with Fried Sweet Potatoes
Popovers
Coffee

Grapefruit Cocktail
Mackerel                Hominy (grits)
Toast
Hot Cakes and Syrup
Coffee

———

Uncooked Cereal with Cream
Southern Hash          Hominy
Drop Biscuit    Preserves
Coffee

———

Grapefruit
Crisp Bacon                Eggs
Buttered Toast
Coffee

———

Baked Apple with Cream
Broiled Ham              Hominy
Hot Muffins
Coffee

339

Strawberries with Cream
Crisp Bacon          Baked Hominy
Toast
Coffee

Malaga Grapes
Oatmeal and Cream
Poached Eggs                    Toast
Coffee

———

Prunes
Toasted Cheese with Eggs dropped on
top
Old Fashioned Milk Toast
Coffee

Peaches and Cream
Crisp Bacon          Scrambled Eggs
Toast
Coffee

Tea, hot chocolate or cocoa may be served instead of coffee, if desired.

——— o ———

## Dinner Menus for Spring

Lamb Chops (Frenched)
Candied Yams
Tomato Aspic with Crackers
Ambrosia

Peppers Stuffed with Corn
Wheat Muffins

Cake

Coffee

——— o ———

Broiled Fish

Carrots
Bread Sticks

Mold of Spinach

Tartar Sauce

Mashed Potatoes
Cole-slaw

Lemon Pie
Coffee

——— o ———

Chicken Croquettes with Peas

Riced Potatoes

Squash Cups

Hot Biscuit
Lettuce with Roquefort Cheese Dressing and Crackers
Maple Parfait          Cake

Coffee

——— o ———

Leg of Lamb

Green Peas

New Irish Potatoes

Pineapple and Lettuce Salad
Mock Charlotte          Cake

Coffee

## Dinner Menus for Summer

Cantaloupe

Fried Chicken                                    Stewed Corn

Rice and Gravy                              String Beans

Hot Biscuit                    Sliced Tomatoes

Iced Tea

Peaches and Cream

——— o ———

Iced Watermelon

Barbecued Chicken                              Brunswick Stew

Baked Peaches                              Hot Egg Bread

Cucumber, Onion and Pepper Salad

Lemon Ice

Coffee

——— o ———

Sliced Peaches

Broiled Chicken                              Summer Squash

Corn Fritters                              Boiled Okra

Hot Biscuit                    Corn Sticks

Dressed Lettuce        Iced Coffee

Watermelon

——— o ———

Strawberry Appetizer

Barbecued Lamb                              Irish Potato Puff

Scalloped Tomatoes                              Squashes

Corn Meal Hoe Cake                    Hot Biscuit

Cole-slaw and Spring Onions

Iced Tea

Mint Ice

## Dinner Menus for Fall

Meat Loaf                    Potatoes au Gratin

Diced Turnips and Carrots with Butter Sauce

Cole-slaw             Hot Rolls

Butterscotch Pie

Coffee

———— o ————

Cream of Tomato Soup with Crackers

Celery         Pickles         Jelly

Brain Croquettes        Green Peas

Diced Carrots and Beets with Butter Sauce

Chicken Salad

Lemon Ice

Coffee

———— o ————

Fruit Cocktail

Cream of Asparagus Soup with Toast Fingers

Chicken         Rice and Gravy

String Beans        Carrots

Rolls

Tomato Salad        Crackers

Ginger Bread Pudding with Sauce

Coffee

———— o ————

Shrimp Cocktail

Smothered Steak and Onions

French Fried Potatoes

Creamed Cabbage        Hot Biscuit

Apple Pie

Coffee

## Dinner Menus for Winter

Prime Rib Roast                                    Stuffed Irish Potatoes

    Scalloped Tomatoes                         Buttered Beets

              Fruit Salad

    Charlotte                                   Cake

             Coffee

——— o ———

Pork Chops with Italian Spaghetti

Celery                                             Dill Pickles

          Bread and Butter

    Lettuce Heart with French Dressing

           Crackers

   Apple Dumplings                             Coffee

——— o ———

Vegetable Soup

Liver and Onions                           Creamed Irish Potatoes

     Field Peas                    Lettuce Salad

          Cornbread

   Lemon Pie                                   Coffee or Tea

——— o ———

Oyster Cocktail with Crackers

    Broiled Steak with Mushrooms

  Rice and Gravy                               Asparagus Mold

          Hot Rolls

   Fruit Salad                                 Crackers

         Coffee

## Thanksgiving and Christmas Menus

Oyster Cocktail

*Olives                         Salted Pecans*                       Celery*

Candied Grapefruit Peel*

Roast Turkey with Dressing

Rice and Gravy                             Cranberry Sauce

Hot Biscuit

Head Lettuce with French Dressing

Beaten Biscuit

Ambrosia                              Fruit Cake

Coffee

*To be placed on the table

——— o ———

Grapefruit

Olives*            Celery*             Nuts*             Fruits*

Turkey with Dressing

Scalloped Oysters                     Rice and Gravy

Sweet Potato Souffle           Cranberry Jelly

Hot Biscuit and Butter

Tomato Aspic with Lettuce and Mayonnaise

Beaten Biscuit

White Charlotte                        Caramel Cake

Coffee

*To be placed on the table

——— o ———

Tomato Bouillon

Roast Pork                                 Christmas Apples

Candied Yams                          String Beans

Chow Chow       Celery       Cole-Slaw

Hot Egg Bread

Mock Cherry Pie                      Coffee

## Thanksgiving and Christmas Menus—(Cont'd)

Roasted Pig with Dressing

Baked Apples                                                Candied Sweet Potatoes

Lye Hominy                                                        Spinach

Cole-Slaw                                                   Pickles
Hot Rolls

Pineapple and Cheese Salad with Crackers

Lemon Custard                                                          Coffee

———— o ————

Cream of Tomato Soup with Crackers

Baked Hen with Dressing                                         Scalloped Oysters

Cauliflower with White Sauce                    Green Peas

Celery                        Chow Chow                        Jelly

Hot Rolls                    Butter                    Coffee

Fruit Salad                Crackers

Boiled Custard                                        Cake

———— o ————

## A Typical Georgia Christmas Dinner

Half Grapefruit

Roast Turkey                                                Dry Stuffing

Dry Rice                                        Turkey Gravy

Candied Sweet Potatoes                Buttered Green Peas

Cranberries or Grape Jelly            Celery Hearts

Hot Biscuit                                        Sweet Butter

Ambrosia or Syllabub                        Cake

Coffee

———— o ————

## A Hunter's Dinner

Turnip Greens (with salt pork)                Green Tomato Chow Chow

Baked Sweet Potatoes                                Broiled Doves

Corn Bread                                        Buttermilk

Note: Cook greens with salt pork, enough to season but not to make greasy. Corn bread should be baked in plain corn pones. Doves may be broiled, fried or smothered. Any game may be substituted for doves.

## A Formal Dinner
### (Seven Courses)

Oyster Cocktail with Crackers

Olives*          Celery*          Radishes*          Salted Nuts*          Mints*

Consomme                              French Biscuit

Broiled Fish with Tartar Sauce

Parsley Potatoes                              Sliced Cucumbers

Bread Sticks

Broiled Chicken witth Mushroom Sauce Garnished with Broiled Pineapple Slices

Rice Croquettes                              Spinach

Dinner Rolls

Head Lettuce with Roquefort Cheese Dressing

Beaten Biscuit

Maple Mousse                              Angel Food Cake

Demi Tasse

*These should be on the table or passed at the proper time.

## Wedding Breakfasts

Creamed Chicken in Timbales

Fruit Aspic on Lettuce with Mayonnaise

Hot Buttered Rolls                                        Olives

Coffee

Crackers, Sandwiches or Beaten Biscuit may take the place of the rolls

——— o ———

Veal Croquettes                                        Green Peas

Tomato Aspic on Lettuce with Mayonnaise

Hot Rolls, Buttered                                        Coffee

——— o ———

Creamed Brains in Timbales

Stuffed Tomatoes on Lettuce with Mayonnaise

Olives                                        Cheese Balls

Hot Rolls or Beaten Biscuit

Lemon Ice

Coffee

Creamed Oysters in Timbales

A Whole Tomato on Lettuce with Mayonnaise

Hot Rolls                    Coffee

(Rolls to be passed or on the plate and coffee served from a table)

A dish of corn pudding and a platter of shaved ham may be added, if something more is wanted. This to be passed.

## Seated Wedding Breakfast No. 1

### First Course

A Fruit Cocktail

### Second Course

Half a Broiled Chicken on Toast

Rice Croquettes with Green Peas

**Broiled Pineapple**                    Hot Rolls

### Third Course

Tomato Stuffed with Cucumber and Celery on Lettuce with Mayonnaise

Beaten Biscuit or Crackers                    Olives

### Fourth Course

Cream or Charlotte                                                      **Cake**

### Fifth Course

Black Coffee                              Cheese Straws (passed)

This menu could have mushrooms, served with chicken. The pineapple is canned, each slice cut in half, dipped in dry flour and broiled in butter.

The tomatoes should be peeled, cut in sections and pulled partly open. The cucumbers and celery chopped, dropped in the opening of the tomato, with mayonnaise on top. Have all very cold.

The table may have olives, mints and nuts. The linen, china and silver should be perfect.

The fruit should be on the table when the guests are seated.

——— o ———

## Seated Wedding Breakfast No. 2

Cantaloupe

Broiled Chicken, with Mushroom Sauce on Toast, Garnished with Parsley

Buttered Hot Rolls

Tomato on Lettuce with Mayonnaise

Cheese Straws

Ice Cream in the shape of Waffles, with Chocolate Sauce

Black Coffee

The ice cream may be ordered in any fancy molds from the confectioners.

## A Seated Wedding Supper No. 1

Oyster Cocktail

Bouillon                                                    Crackers

Olives*                        Nuts*                    Bonbons*

Patties of Sweetbreads and Mushrooms

Individual Stuffed Squash                        Hot Rolls

Fruit Aspic                                Crackers

Individual Ice Cream                Wedding Cake

Black Coffee

*These should be on the table, with suitable decorations.

———— o ————

## Seated Wedding Supper No. 2

Fruit Cocktail

Cream of Corn Soup and Toasted Bread Sticks

Creamed Fish in Shells with Potato Roses and Radish Tulips

Bread and Butter Sandwiches

Broiled Chicken                    Rice Croquettes

Baked Peaches

Asparagus with Parsley Sauce                        Hot Rolls

Ginger Ale Aspic            Cheese Wafers

Individual Ice Cream                        Wedding Cake

Demi Tasse

———— o ————

## A Three Course Wedding Supper

Fruit Cocktail

Nuts and Bonbons*

Chicken Salad                                Tomato Aspic on Lettuce

Olives and Sandwiches

Ice Cream                        Cake

Black Coffee

*These should be on the table, with suitable decorations.

## Wedding Receptions

Chicken Salad on Lettuce
Vegetable Aspic, with Mayonnaise, in individual molds
Cheese Sandwiches                  Olives               Beaten Biscuit
Individual Ice Cream          Angel Food Cake
Fruit Punch, served from a nicely appointed table

——— o ———

Vegetable Aspic
Chipped Ham                         Chicken Sandwich
Beaten Biscuit                 Olives
Ice Cream         Individual Cakes
Fruit Punch, served from a nicely appointed table

——— o ———

Creamed Chicken in a Pattie
Olives                               Stuffed Celery
Fruit Aspic                   Beaten Biscuit
Strawberry Ice
(Served on one plate)

——— o ———

Creamed Brains and Mushrooms in Timbales
Cucumber Aspic                           Olives
Hot Rolls          Cheese Straws
Pineapple Ice
(Served on one plate.)
Fruit punch and coffee may be added to any of these menus, served as directed in other menus. All salads and aspics should be served on lettuce with mayonnaise.

——— o ———

## Buffet Supper No. 1

A platter of Shaved Ham
Aspic of Cucumber and Pineapple (large mold) on Lettuce with Mayonnaise
A Baking Dish of Chicken a la King (hot)
Rice Pilau in a Baking Dish (hot)
Hot Buttered Rolls                        Stuffed Celery
Ice Cream*                  Cake*
Coffee*
*Served from the pantry.

## Buffet Supper No. 2

A Platter of Chipped Ham                                    Potato Chips
         Pickles                                            Celery
              Chicken Croquettes with Green Peas
                    Hot Rolls or Biscuit
                          Coffee
    Boiled Custard                                          Cake
                            or
                  Charlotte or Ice Cream
    All of the above menu to be served on large platters.  Hot rolls passed and the
dessert served from the pantry.

## Buffet Luncheons

### First Course

          Fruit Salad on Lettuce, with Mayonnaise
          Peppers Stuffed with Creamed Meat
Cheese Straws                Hot Rolls                Olive Sandwiches
                          Iced Tea

### Second Course

    Ice Cream                                          Cake

——— o ———

### First Course

          Veal Croquettes in a Nest of Green Peas
    Fruit or Vegetable Aspic, on Lettuce with Mayonnaise
                  Cheese Sandwich
      Hot Rolls or Hot Biscuit, buttered and passed

### Second Course

Maple Mousse                                          Kisses or Cake

### Third Course
          Demi Tasse

——— o ———

## Morning Party

### First Course

          Creamed Chicken in Timbales or on Toast
Asparagus with Butter Sauce                          Olives or Pickles
    Tomato Stuffed with Cucumber and Celery on Lettuce Leaf with Mayonnaise
              Hot Rolls or Biscuit, Buttered
                          Iced Tea

### Second Course

    Ice Cream                                          Cake

## Afternoon Parties

### Receptions

Tomato filled with Chicken Salad on Lettuce with Mayonnaise
Nut Bread Sandwich
Olives          Beaten Biscuit          Pickles
Cup of Strawberry Ice, with Whipped Cream
(Serve all on one plate.)
Have tomatoes peeled and chilled. Cut half way in sections and pull open like
an orange. Fill with salad.

———— o ————

Frozen Fruit Salad on Lettuce with Mayonnaise
Two Dainty Sandwiches of Meat or Cheese, or One of Each
Iced Tea, with a sprig of Mint and Slice of Lemon
(Serve all on one plate.)

———— o ————

### Afternoon Tea

Chicken Sandwiches          Cheese and Nut Sandwiches
Fancy Cakes
Salted Nuts          Mints or Candy
Have nicely appointed table, with platters and dishes of the articles suggested and
see that they are kept filled as needed. A glass of tea on a small plate is served from
the pantry. Fruit punch may be served.

———— o ————

Frozen Fruit Salad with Crisp Crackers
Salted Nuts          Olives
Iced Tea
All on one plate, and each guest served a plate, from pantry.

———— o ————

A Vegetable Aspic on Lettuce with Mayonnaise
Chicken Salad Sandwich          Cheese Sandwich
Olives
Ice Cream          Cake
Fruit Punch*
*Fruit punch served from a nicely appointed table.

## Bridge Tea

Chicken Salad

Tomato Sandwich              Crackers                    Olives

Iced Tea

——— o ———

Frozen Fruit Salad

Nut Bread Sandwich                                       Cheese Straws

Coffee

——— o ———

Sandwich Loaf

Olives                                                   Coffee

——— o ———

## Family Dinners

Broiled Pork Chops                                       Turnip greens

Baked Sweet Potatoes

Green Tomato Pickle

Corn Bread

Apple Sauce with whipped cream                           Cookies

Coffee

——— o ———

Boiled Backbone                                          Sauerkraut

Baked Irish Potatoes

Stewed Tomatoes

Corn Sticks

Pound Cake                                               Coffee

——— o ———

Roasted Leg of Lamb

Minted Apples                                    Corn Pudding

Parsley Potatoes                              Hot Biscuit

Sliced Tomatoes on Lettuce          French Dressing

Beaten Biscuit or Crackers

Lemon Chiffon Pie

Coffee - Tea - Milk

The salad or dessert may be omitted.

——— o ———

## A Family Luncheon

Tomato Juice

Ring Mold of Spinach                        *Creamed Chicken in Center

Coffee - Tea - Milk

*Any meat may be substituted for chicken.

——— o ———

## A Fisherman's Dinner

Fried Fish                                               Hush Puppies

Canned Baked Beans        or                 Sauerkraut

Coffee - more Coffee

Doughnuts if desired

# table service

# CHAPTER XXII

## Table Service

It matters not how simple the meal or the table, if attractively arranged a pleasant atmosphere is created and the appetite is better.

### A Few Fundamental Rules

**1. Balance**

The dishes and silver placed in such a manner that no part of the table seems overcrowded.

**2. Lines**

These should be either lengthwise or across the table. To avoid the appearance of carelessness all silver, linen and dishes should be placed according to this rule. The threads of the linen should be parallel to the edge of the table.

**3. Convenience**

Dishes and silver must be placed on the table conveniently within reach of the guest.

**4. Cover**

Dishes, linen and silver are placed in position for one person at the beginning of the meal. A space twenty to twenty-four inches by fifteen inches will be required for each cover.

**5. Types of Service**

Russian—formal—servants serving the food.
English—informal—or family—all food served at table.
Mixed—using some Russian and some English.
Table is set according to the type of service used.

### Rules for Table Setting

**1. Linen**

Lunch cloth, runners or doilies may be used for breakfast, luncheon or supper, and for dinner a table cloth.

Under the latter place a silence cloth of cotton flannel or asbestos pad. Cloth should have only one fold, forming a line down the center of the table. It should hang at least nine inches below the edge of the table.

Luncheon cloth should come just to the edge of table or hang about seven inches below.

If mats are used one is placed under each dish.

Napkins are placed at left of fork and in such a way that the open corner is at the lower right hand corner.

**2. Decorations**

Flowers may be placed in a vase, flower holder or basket in the center of the table, but not high enough to prevent guests from seeing each other.

Candlesticks when used are placed opposite each other or in a definite balanced form.

## 3. Silver

Knives with cutting edge toward plate placed at right of plate in order of use—the one farthest from plate being used first—then soup spoon with bowl up, and oyster fork or fruit spoon next with tines or bowl up—unless first course is put in place before the meal is announced—then the oyster fork or fruit spoon is placed on plate with handle toward the guest.

Forks with tines up are placed at left in order of use, the one to be used first being on the outside. The dessert fork or spoon is served with the dessert and the coffee spoon served with the coffee.

All silver is placed from one half to one inch from the edge of the table.

Butter spreader when used is placed across upper side of bread and butter plate with handle toward right and cutting edge toward napkin and forks.

Salt spoon is placed across salt cellar or on cloth.

## 4. China and Glassware

Service plate is placed one inch from the edge of the table.

If individual nut dishes are used they are placed at head of the plate.

If bread and butter plates are used they are placed at the left of the service plate and above the forks.

Salt and pepper may be placed between two covers.

Bread and butter plate is placed a little to the left and above the service plate.

Cocktail glasses may be filled and placed on service plates before the meal is announced.

Dishes containing other foods are placed or passed—depending on the type of service used.

Glass for water is placed at tip of knife and other glasses for ginger ale, etc., are placed to the right and side of the water glass.

### General Rules for Serving

All dishes from which food is to be taken are passed to the left of those sitting at table.

Beverages and extra silver are placed at right, from right.

Before another course is served all dishes from the previous course must be removed.

Before serving the dessert all dishes are removed from the table, also salt and pepper, and the table is crumbed.

Dessert is placed in front of guest from right side and the necessary silver placed on right side of plate ready for use.

Coffee is placed at right of guest from right and then the cream and sugar passed from the left. Spoon for coffee is placed on right side of saucer and handle of cup is in position for immediate use.

The above shows how table should be laid for informal meal.

### Seating the Guest

The guest of honor, a lady, sits to the right of the host. The gentleman at the right of the hostess.

### Serving

Opinions differ as to who should be served first, the guest of honor or the hostess. I think the hostess should have the first service, then the guest of honor and on around the table. When two maids are used then begin with the hostess and guest of honor, provided the guest of honor is seated at the right of the host.

Dishes are passed first to the hostess then the guests. The hostess being familiar with the dishes sets the pace, causing the guest to feel perfectly at ease. If the guest of honor is an elderly person he or she may be served first.

## Good Kitchen Stunts

Use white sauce for making croquettes instead of eggs; this gives a soft, creamy croquette, while eggs make them firm and tough.

\*     \*     \*

When crumbing croquettes, roll them in crumbs first, then eggs, then crumbs again. Let them stand for half hour in the air, and they fry better.

\*     \*     \*

Add one tablespoon cold water to egg when dipping croquettes. Do not froth, only mix well.

\*     \*     \*

When frying in deep fat, do not have grease too hot. A piece of bread, browned in forty counts, is a good test.

\*     \*     \*

There are two ways of frying—shallow grease frying and deep grease frying. Some things are better fried in deep grease, some in shallow.

Fry only a few croquettes at a time, two or three. The work will be more quickly done. Too many put in at once chills the grease and leaves croquettes greasy.

\* \* \*

There are three heats needed for the everyday cooking—quick, medium, and slow. The first heat, if registered, would be 550 degrees F.; the second 350 to 400 degrees; the slow, 250 to 275. The greater part of cooking is done with the medium heat.

\* \* \*

In a gas range, thin things are placed in the top of oven down to the center or middle, with a quick heat; thick things in center of oven down towards the bottom, with less (medium) heat.

\* \* \*

The above rule has a few exceptions, and one is pie—custard and pastry shells. They should be baked near the bottom of oven to cook the bottom of the pie and not allow the top to scorch.

\* \* \*

All pastry should be firm and crusty, but a light brown.

\* \* \*

Cook corn pudding with a medium heat, and it will not whey.

\* \* \*

Cook cup custards in hot water placed on a trivet or many folds of paper, and they will be firm and smooth, and will not curdle or whey.

\* \* \*

If the cream is too thin to whip add 1 tablespoon of cocoa to each cup, mix and whip. Another help: add white of an egg to cream, let get very cold, and it will whip readily.

\* \* \*

Scissors will be found very useful for cutting many things in kitchen instead of knife.

\* \* \*

For cutting celery quickly, split the large stalks, place a dozen stalks together, hold tightly with left hand, place on cutting board and cut either large or small with knife. Take another hand full until all is cut. It is surprising how quickly a large quantity may be cut.

\* \* \*

When making sandwich paste and using celery, cut first, then grind and there will be no strings.

\* \* \*

Do not peel apples when making salad. The red adds to the salad.

\* \* \*

A brush that is better than one you can buy is made of flannel, folded several times and fitted into a clothes pin. Trim, allowing ½ inch on all sides.

\* \* \*

After washing lettuce, tie in napkin or cheesecloth and place on ice. It will drip and crisp. Lettuce tied in cloth and hung in draft will crisp as well as when placed on ice.

Place washed lettuce in tin bucket, close, place by ice. It not only will crisp but keeps well.

\* \* \*

Wash, shake free of water a bunch of parsley, drop in fruit jar, close top, place in refrigerator. It will crisp and keep well.

\* \* \*

To keep sandwiches moist cover with a damp cloth. Wring cloth as dry as possible.

\* \* \*

When bread or cake burns use a grater to remove burn.

\* \* \*

Use scissors instead of knife for cutting open fish and chicken.

\* \* \*

If apples are dipped in boiling water for a moment the skin will peel off like a tomato when scalded, leaving the apple smooth and red.

\* \* \*

When making apple salad add the mayonnaise to apples as they are diced and they will not turn dark. When ready to serve add celery and nuts, the mayonnaise is already there.

\* \* \*

To peel pecans easily, cover with boiling water for a few minutes, drain and crack on ends. The sides will break and the meats come out in halves.

\* \* \*

Camphorated oil will remove white marks made by hot dishes on a polished table. Rub until removed.

\* \* \*

To peel a cocoanut drain the milk out, place nut in a hot oven, allow to remain until the shell becomes quite hot to the hand. With a hammer tap over the shell well, especially at the ends where it sticks tightest. Give one hard knock, sufficient to crack shell. The shell can be lifted off, leaving the nut meat whole and free of shell. Peel off brown skin. Let get cold before grating or grinding.

\* \* \*

When there is no funnel to fill a bottle use half an egg shell with a hole in end; place on bottle and use as funnel.

### To Preserve Eggs With Water Glass

One quart water glass. Nine quarts water which has been boiled then allowed to get cold.

Mix the two together well. Use a large crock for keeping, which must be clean, scalded and dry. Place eggs to be preserved into the water day by day, or all at once. When filled, the solution must be two inches above the last layer of eggs. Place crock in cool dry place and cover top well to prevent evaporation. Should the top layer be too poorly covered (by evaporation) they would spoil, thus spoiling the entire lot. Eggs must be *fresh* and clean. Infertile eggs keep best.

This is sufficient solution for twelve dozen eggs.

# HOUSEHOLD HINTS

To remove ink spots:
1. Before washing rub with kerosene.
2. Cover spot with a paste of cooking soda and water. Let dry and rub off. Repeat if necessary.
3. Place spot in warm sweet milk and let stand until, when rubbed, ink will wash out. Repeat process if necessary.
4. Rub spot with damp match and the sulphur removes ink.

## A Splendid Finish for Pine Floors

Shave one-eighth of a pound of paraffin, and pour over it one quart of turpentine. In a few hours the paraffin will have dissolved; then add one pint of linseed oil. If the floors are dingy or badly spotted, add a very little oak stain, a drop at a time. Clean the floors thoroughly, and apply the finish with a paint brush. After 48 hours, wax with a good paste wax, and polish. This dressing will not scratch, crackle or water-spot.

## To Whiten Clothes

Add to a boiler of cold water 2 tablespoons of turpentine, 2 of kerosene, a bar of laundry soap shaved. Put in clothes, let come to a boil, but not boil. Rinse well and clothes are whiter than with the usual washing.

## Mildew

To remove mildew, soak in sour buttermilk, spread in sun.

## Iron Rust

Wet spot with lemon juice, sprinkle with salt, place where hot sunshine will strike it.

To remove coffee and tea spots from linen, rub spots with glycerine, let stand 30 minutes, then wash in the usual way.

## Beauty Hints

Clean finger tips, and nails by digging into a grape fruit hull left from the table. Lemon hull will answer the same purpose.

To clean stained finger nails, make a paste of oatmeal and water, place under nails, after five minutes wash out.

Powdered borax dampened and pressed under the finger nails, allowed to remain for a short time will bleach nails.

## To Clean Lace, Etc.

To clean lace use two parts corn starch, one part borax. Spread on lace, let stand about an hour and brush off. Put on second supply, fold up, let stand over night, brush well.

To clean white fur, use hot meal, rub into fur, brush well when finished. Repeat if necessary.

To clean a felt hat, use 4 cups of corn meal, 1 cup salt, 1 cup flour. Mix all together. rub on hat, let stand over night, brush well.

# INDEX